Creek Mvskoki Talwa Towns

~

Speck, Swanton, Hewitt, Opler, Howard

Jay Miller, PhD, editor

Mvdo to Blue Clark for a thorough proofing & Ted Isham for advice

Introduction

Native towns continue to be a vital aspect of Mvskoki Creek life and tradition. Originally these were social, political, and religious centers for their dispersed farming communities, often distinguished by high earthen mounds supporting temples containing sacred fires and curated chiefly bodies. Today, these towns exist as either square grounds celebrating the annual Busk harvest and world renewal rite or as Christian churches, Baptist and Methodist, of the same name as their ancestral town in Georgia as Lower Creeks or Alabama as Upper Creeks before the forced migrations to today's Oklahoma.

The ideal of scholarly research was that for the Southwest, where scholars went pueblo by pueblo to describe their common and idiosyncratic cultures, by language, location, and legendary origins. Euro-American impacts and traumas have made this difficult or impossible to do for the Northeast and much of the Southeast, except for the Mvskoki Creek Nation.

Creek Mvskoki Talwa Towns rescues and combines between these covers the classic works on *talwa* Creek native towns, beginning with the single town of Tuskigi, comparing and updating ceremonial towns, and then looking specifically at Arbeka, a mother town derived from Coosa, and New Tulsa.

For the 1900s, looking back or ahead, Muskoki Creek and Southeast research pivoted between the works of John Swanton, as if standing in the cemetery, and of Frank Speck, as if standing at the baptismal font. While Swanton relied on archives and documents supplemented by fieldwork, Speck was devoted to living traditions, much preferring interviews supplemented by archives. "In the same year that Swanton was concluding his Southeast work, Speck published two monographs and 10 articles reporting on Eastern Woodland communities."[1]

Allied work was contributed by procrastinating JNB Hewitt, himself a Tuscarora whose own nation was driven from the Carolinas to refuge near Buffalo, New York, among Iroquois Nations, Karl Schmitt, whose tragic death ended promising Oklahoma research, and James Howard, whose own Woodlands work also ended tragically in sudden death. Schmitt's Japanese wife Iva Osanai continued her own work among Navajo.

Editorial work has been kept to a minimum out of respect for these classic works. Internal comments/corrections and commentaries by editor J Miller appears between {curved brackets}. Schmitt's spelling of 'medecine' has been retained, though he did sometimes use the usual spelling. Swanton's frequent internal quotes from his own massive report on the Creeks in the 42nd Annual Report of the Bureau of American Ethnology are herein uniformly cited as BAE-AR 19th: followed by page numbers. Footnotes are numbered continuously, instead of originally beginning with #1 on each page. All native words are now in *italics*.

To help understand what a town name may mask of its own historical dynamics, we now consider what is known of Tuskigi itself, since a town of the same name was located among the Iroquoian-speaking Overhill Cherokees on the Tennessee River.[2] Robbie Ethridge[3] also noted its

---

[1] Raymond Fogelson *Southeast* Smithsonian Handbook 2004: 37. Swanton also benefited from Carnegie Institution's calendaring, translating, and copying French colonial documents.

[2] Gregory Waselkov and Kathryn Holland Brauns, eds, *William Bartam on the Southeastern Indians* 1995: 88.

[3] Robbie Ethridge, *Creek Country* 2003: 95. Her Figure 16 (p83) shows the anceatral town location and its surrounding vegetation at the confluence of Tallapoosa & Coosa Rivers.

foreign origins, but from another Muskogean Family branch: Benjamin "Hawkins adjudged the Tuskegees, who were originally in the Alabama province but who probably were descendants of the *Koasati* subset, to be more Creek than Alabama" and were now speaking only Creek, though they were less severe in punishing adultery and men helped their women in the fields, as Creek men did not. Nearby was the famous French army post of Fort Toulouse. Resettled in Oklahoma near Eufaula town, its *lusti* (Black) members later hived off to establish their own town square near Yuchi near the city of Tulsa.

Here is Swanton's[4] masterful summary:

THE TUSKEGEE

Many dialects were spoken anciently near the junction of the Coosa and Tallapoosa. Adair says:

> I am assured by a gentleman of character, who traded a long time near the late Alebahma garrison, that within six miles of it live the remains of seven Indian nations, who usually conversed with each other in their own different dialects, though they understood the Muskohge language; but being naturalized, they are bound to observe the laws and customs of the main original body.[5]

Some of these "nations" have already been considered. We now come to a people whose language has not been preserved to the present day, but they are known from statements made by Taitt and [208] Hawkins to have spoken a dialect distinct from Muskogee.[6] These were the Tuskegee,[7] called by Taitt northern Indians. On inquiring of some of the old Tuskegee Indians in Oklahoma regarding their ancient speech I found that they claimed to know of it, and obtained the following words, said to have been among those employed by the ancient people. Some of these are used at the present day, and the others may be nothing more than archaic Muskogee, but they perhaps have some value for future students.

> *lutcu'a*, a mug.
> *ki'las*, to break.
> *aia'lito*, I will be going; modern form, *aibastce'*.
> *tcibuksa'ktce'*, come on and go with us! (where one person comes to a crowd of people and asks them to go with him).
> *ili-hu'ko-lutci*, hen (-*utci*, little).
> *talu'eutci*, chicken.
> *ilisai'dja*, pot; modern form, *lihai'a la'ko*.
> *apa'la*, on the other side; modern form, *tapa'la*.
> *wilika'pka*, I am going on a visit; modern form, *tcukupileidja-lani*.

---

[4] John Swanton, *Early History of the Creek Indians*, BAE B 73 1922/1998: 207-211.

[5] Adair, *History of American Indians*, p. 267.

[6] Taitt in *Travels in American Colonies*, p. 541; Hawkins, see p. 210. Today some Indians repeat a tradition to the effect that the Tuskegee are a branch of the Tulsa, but this is evidently a late fabrication based on a friendship which in later years has subsisted between these two towns.

[7] This name perhaps contains the Alabama and Choctaw word for warrior, *taska*.

The town Tasqui encountered by De Soto between Tali and Coosa was perhaps occupied by Tuskegee. Ranjel is the only chronicle who mentions it, and it can not have impressed the Spaniards as a place of great importance.[8] In 1567 Vandera was informed by some Indians and a soldier that beyond Satapo, the farthest point reached by the Pardo expedition, two days' journey on the way Coosa, was a place called Tasqui, and a little beyond another known as Tasquiqui.[9] The second of these was certainly, the other probably, a Tuskegee town. It is possible that a fission was just taken place in this tribe.

Later in the seventeenth century, when English and French began to penetrate into the region, we find the Tuskegee divided into two or more bands, the northernmost on the Tennessee River. Coxe, who gives their name under the distorted form *Kakigue*, places these latter upon an island in the river.[10] While they are noticed in documents and on maps at rare intervals (I find the forms *Cacougai, Cattougui, Caskighi*), the clearest light upon their later history and ultimate fate is thrown by Mr. Mooney in his *"Myths of the Cherokee."*[11] He says:

> Another refugee tribe incorporated partly with the Cherokee and partly with the Creeks was that of the Taskigi, who at an early period had a large town of the same name on the south side of the Little Tennessee, just above the mouth of Tellico, [209] in Monroe County, Tennessee. Sequoya, the inventor of the Cherokee alphabet, lived here in his boyhood, about the time of the Revolution. The land was sold in 1819. There was another settlement of the name, and perhaps once occupied by the same people, on the north bank of Tennessee River, in a bend just below Chattanooga, Tennessee, on land sold also in 1819. Still another may have existed at one time on Tuskegee Creek, on the south bank of Little Tennessee River, north of Robbinsville, in Graham County, North Carolina, on land which was occupied until the removal in 1838. It is not a Cherokee word, and Cherokee informants state positively that the Tasligi were a foreign people, with distinct language and customs. They were not Creeks, Natchez, Uchee, or Shawano, with all of whom the Cherokee were well acquainted under other names. In the town house of their settlement at the mouth of Tellico they had an upright pole, from the top of which hung their protecting "medicine," the image of a human figure cut from a cedar log. For this reason the Cherokee in derision sometimes called the place Atsinak taun ("Hanging-cedar place"). Before the sale of the land in 1819 they were so nearly extinct that the Cherokee had moved in and occupied the ground.

While part of these people may have removed to the south to join their friends among the Creeks, the majority were probably absorbed in the surrounding Cherokee population.

A few maps, such as one of the early Homann maps and the Scale map of the early part of the eighteenth century, place Tuskegee near the headwaters of the Coosa. This may be intended to represent the Tennessee band of Tuskegee or it may show that the migration of the Alabama Tuskegee southward was a comparatively late movement, something which took place late in the seventeenth century or very early in the eighteenth.

The Tuskegee are placed on the Coosa north of the *Abihka* Indians on the Couvens and Mortier map of the early part of the eighteenth century. Perhaps these were the southern band

---

[8] Bourne, *Narrative of De Soto*, II, p. 111.
[9] Ruidiaz, La Florida, II, p. 485.
[10] French, Hist. Colls. La., 1850, p. 230.
[11] BAE-AR 19th: 388-389.

mentioned by Adair, in the badly misprinted form *Tae-keo-ge*, as one of those which the Muskogee had "artfully decoyed to incorporate with them."[12] He is confirmed in substance by Milfort, who states that they were a tribe who had suffered severely from their enemies and had in consequence sought refuge with the Creeks.[13] The town appears in the census estimates of 1750.[14] In the enumeration of 1761 we find "Tuskegee including Coosaw old Town" with 40 hunters.[15] The name does not occur in Bartram's list, but, as I have said elsewhere, it appears to be the town which he calls Alabama.[16] Hawkins (1799) has the following to say regarding it:

Tus-kee-gee: This little town is in the fork of the two rivers, Coo-sau and Tal-la-poo-sa, where formerly stood the French Fort Toulouse. The town is on a bluff on the Coo-sau, forty-six feet above low-water mark; the rivers here approach each other within a quarter of a mile, then curve out, making a flat of low land of three thousand acres, which has been rich canebrake; and one-third under cultivation in times past; the [210] center of this flat is rich oak and hickory, margined on both sides with rich cane swamp; the land back of the town, for a mile, is flat, a whitish clay; small pine, oak, and dwarf hickory, then high pine forest.

There are thirty buildings in the town, compactly situated, and from the bluff a fine view of the flat lands in the fork, and on the right bank of Coosau, which river is here two hundred yards wide. In the yard of the town house there are five cannon of iron, with the trunions broke off, and on the bluff some brickbats, the only remains of the French establishment here. There is one apple tree claimed by this town now in possession of one of the chiefs of *Book-choie-oo-che* [*Okchaiyutci*].[17]

The fields are the left side of *Tal-la-poo-sa*, and there are some small patches well formed in the fork of the rivers, on the flat rich land below the bluff.

The Coosau extending itself a great way into the Cherokee country and mountains, gives scope for a vast accumulation of waters, at times. The Indians remark that once in fifteen or sixteen years,[18] they have a flood, which overflows the banks, and spreads itself for five miles or more[19] in width, in many parts of *A-la-ba-ma*. The rise is sudden, and so rapid as to drive a current up the *Tal-la-poo-sa* for eight miles. In January, 1796,[20] the flood rose forty-seven feet, and spread itself for three miles on the left bank of the *A-la-ba-ma*. The ordinary width of that river, taken at the first bluff below the fork, is one hundred and fifty yards. The bluff is on the left side, and forty-five feet high. On this bluff are five conic mounds of earth, the largest thirty yards diameter at the base, and seventeen feet high; the others are smaller.

It has been for sometime a subject of enquiry, when, and for what purpose, these mounds were raised; here it explains itself as to the purpose; unquestionably they were intended as a place of safety to the people, in the time of these floods; and this is the

---

[12] Adair, Hist. Am. Indian, p. 257.
[13] Milfort, Memoire, p. 267.
[14] Ms., Ayer Coll.
[15] Ga. Col. Docs., VIII, p. 524.
[16] Bartram, *Travels*, p. 461; see also p. 197.
[17] The Lib. Cong. MS. has " Hook-choie."
[18] The Lib. Cong. MS. has "fifteen or twenty.
[19] The Lib. Cong. MS. has "five or six miles."
[20] The Lib. Cong. MS. has "1795" years.

tradition among the old people. As these Indians came from the other side of the Mississippi, and that river spreads out on that side for a great distance, it is probable, the erection of mounds originated there; or from the custom of the Indians heretofore, of settling on rich flats bordering on the rivers, and subject to be overflowed. The name is *E-cun-li-gee*, mounds of earth, or literally, earth placed. But why erect these mounds in high places, incontestably out of the reach of floods? From a superstitious veneration for ancient customs.

The Alabama overflows its flat swampy margins, annually; and generally, in the month of March, but seldom in the summer season.

The people of Tuskogee have some cattle, and a fine stock of hogs, more perhaps than any town of the nation. One man, Sam Macnack {Sam Moniack}, a half breed, has a fine stock of cattle. He had, in 1799, one hundred and eighty calves. They have lost their language, and speak Creek, and have adopted the customs and manners of the Creeks. They have thirty-five gun men.[21]

After their removal west the Tuskegee formed a town in the southeastern part of the nation. Later a portion, consisting largely of those who had negro blood {*lusti*}, moved northwest and settled west of Beggs, Okla., close to the Yuchi.

Although our early histories, books of travel, and documents are well-nigh silent on the subject, it is evident from maps of the southern regions that part of the Tuskegee got very much farther east at an early date. A town of Tuskegee, spelled most frequently "Jaskages," appears on Chattahoochee River below a town of the *Atasi* and above a town of the *Kasihta*. This appears on the maps of Popple [211] (1733), D'Anville (1746, 1755), Bellin (1750-55), John Rocque (1754-61), Bowen and Gibson (1755), S[r] Le Roque (1755), Mitchell (1755, 1777), Bowles (1763 ?), D'Anville altered by Bell (1768), D'Anville by Evans (1771), and Andrews (1777). Another appears on the Ocmulgee, oftenest on a small southern affluent of it, in the maps of Moll (1720), Popple (1733), Bellin (1750-55), and in Homann's Atlas (1759). This seems to mean that there was a Tuskegee village among the Lower Creeks, originally on Ocmulgee River, and after the Yamasee war on the Chattahoochee. The town is referred to in a letter of Matheos, the Apalachee lieutenant under the governor of Florida, written May 19, 1686.[22] Evidently it was then on or near the Ocmulgee. In a letter of September 20, 1717, Diego Pena in narrating his journey to the Lower Creeks says that he spent the night at "Tayquique," evidently intended for Tasquique, "within a short league" of Coweta. It must have been on the Chattahoochee, at a place given on none of the maps.[23]

During World War II, the original town site had become Tuskegee Army Air Field, Alabama, and served as the training base of the first African American military aviators in the U.S. Army Air Corps (AAC), a precursor of the U.S. Air Force. They formed the 332nd Fighter Group and the 477th Bombardment Group of the United States Army Air Forces, and flew more than 15,000 individual sorties in Europe and North Africa during World War II. Their impressive performance earned them more than 150 Distinguished Flying Crosses, and helped encourage the eventual integration of the U.S. armed forces. The name now applies to the navigators,

---

[21] Ga. Hist. Soc. Colls., III, pp. 37-39.

[22] Serrano y Sana, Doc. Hist., pp. 194-196.

[23] Ibid., p. 229. For a more particular account of the later condition and ethnology of these people see Speck, *The Creek Indians of Taskigi Town*, in Memoirs of American Anthropological Association, II, pt. 2.

bombardiers, mechanics, instructors, crew chiefs, nurses, cooks and other support personnel (https://en.wikipedia.org/wiki/Tuskegee_Airmen).

Today, in Oklahoma, Tuskegee is the name of a local Baptist church.

Abrams, Elliot, and AnnCorinne Freter, eds. 2005 *The Emergence of the Moundbuilders. The Archaeology of Tribal Societies in Southeastern Ohio.* Athens: Ohio University Press.

Bartram, John and William 1957 *Bartram's America.* Selections from the Writings of the Philadelphia Naturalists. Helen Gere Cruickshank, ed. New York: The Devin-Adair Company.

Bell, Amelia Rector
    1984 *Creek Ritual.* The Path to Peace. University of Chicago: PhD Anthropology.
    1990 *Separate People: Speaking of Creek Men and Women.* American Anthropologist 92: 332-342.

Berryhill, Alfred, ed. 2007 <u>Este Mvskukvlke Svkvsmkv En Yahiketv</u>. *Muscogee People's Praise and Worship Hymns.* Okmulgee, OK.

Bowne, Eric 2005 <u>The Westo Indians</u>. Slave Traders of the Early Colonial South. Tuscaloosa: University of Alabama Press.

Buffalohead, Eric 2004 Dhegihan History: A Personal Journey. *Plains Anthropologist* 49 (192): 327-343.

Bunny, George, Woodrow Haney, Rev. James Wesley, and Morina Wildcat 1998 *Nakcokv Esyvhiketv ~ Muckogee Hymns.* United Methodist Church, General Commission on Religion and Race, with the permission of Presbyterian Board of Christian Education, 1936.

Chappell, Sally A. Kitt 2002 *Cahokia – Mirror of the Cosmos.* Chicago: University of Chicago Press.

Chaudhuri, Jean Hill, and Joyotpaul Chaudhuri 2001 *A Sacred Path*, *The Way of the Muscogee Creeks.* Los Angeles: UCLA American Indian Studies Center.

Cloud, Henry Roe ~ Wa-na-xi-lay Hunkah 1929 Winnebago Cosmology. *The Ohio Archaeological and Historical Society Publications* 18. 4 May.

Ethridge, Robbie
    2001 Raiding the Remains: The Indian Slave Trade and the Collapse of the Mississippian Chiefdoms. Chattanooga, TN: Southeastern Archaeological Conference.
    2002 Shatter Zone: Early Colonial Slave Raiding and Its Consequences for the Natives of the Eastern Woodland. Riverside, CA: American Society for Ethnohistory, 7-12 November.
    2003 *Creek Country.* The Creek Indians and Their World. Chapel Hill: University of North Carolina Press.
    2010 *From Chicaza to Chicksaw. The European Invasion and the Transformation of the Mississippian World, 1540-1715.* Chapel Hill: University of North Carolina Press.

Ethridge, Robbie, and Sheri Shuck-Hall, eds. 2009 *Mapping the Mississippian Shatter Zone. The Colonial Indian Slave Trade and Regional Instability in the American South.* Lincoln: University Nebraska Press.

Ethridge, Robbie, and Charles Hudson 2002 *The Transformation of the Southeastern Indians, 1540-1760.* Jackson: University Press of Mississippi.

Fogelson, Raymond, ed. 2004 *Southeast.* Handbook of North American Indians #14. DC: Smithsonian Institution Press.

Gallay, Alan 2002 *The Indian Slave Trade*: *The Rise of the English Empire in the American*

South, 1670-1717. New Haven: Yale University Press.

Galloway, Patricia 2006 *Practicing Ethnohistory. Mining Archives, Hearing Testimony, Constructing Narrative*. Lincoln: University of Nebraska.

Gouge, Earnest 2004 *Totkv Mocvse ~ New Fire. Creek Folktales*. Jack Martin, Margaret McKane Mauldin, Juanita McGirt. Norman: University of Oklahoma Press.

Grantham, Bill 2002 *Creation Myths and Legends of the Creek Indians*. Gainesville: University of Florida Press.

Green, Michael
1979 *The Creeks*. A Critical Bibliography. Bloomington, Indiana University Press: Newberry Library Bibliography Series.
1982 *The Politics of Indian Removal*. Creek Government and Society in Crisis. Lincoln: University of Nebraska Press.

Hahn, Steven 2004 *The Invention of the Creek Nation, 1670-1763*. Lincoln: University of Nebraska Press.

Hawkins, Benjamin
1848 *A Sketch of the Creek Country in 1798 and 1799*. Collections of the Georgia Historical Society, Volume III, Part I, 1-88. [1971, Kraus Reprint]
1916 *Letters of Benjamin Hawkins, 1796-1806*. Savannah: Collections of the Georgia Historical Society IX.

Hewitt, John Napoleon Brinton 1939 *Notes on the Creek Indians*. John Swanton, ed. Bureau of American Ethnology, Bulletin 123, Anthropological Papers #10.

Hill, James H.
Ms-a. Description of Hilabi Round House. Creek Texts by Mary R Haas and James H Hill. APS. www.wm.edu/linguistics/creek/hass-hill/texts.php.
Ms-b. Origin of the Spokokaki. Creek Texts by Mary R. Haas and James H. Hill. APS. www.wm.edu/linguistics/creek/hass-hill/texts.php.

Howard, James Henri 1968 *The Southeast Ceremonial Complex and Its Interpretation*, Missouri Archaeological Society, Memoir 6.

Hudson, Charles
1976 *The Southeastern Indians*. Knoxville: University of Tennessee Press.
1975 Vomiting for Purity: Ritual Emesis in the Aboriginal Southeastern United States. *Symbols and Society. Essays on Belief Systems in Action*. Carole Hill, ed. Southern Anthropological Society, Proceedings 9: 93-102.
1990 Conversations with the High Priest of Coosa. *Lamar Archaeology*, Mississippian Chiefdoms in the Deep South: 214-230. Mark Williams and Gary Shapiro, eds.
1997 *Knights of Spain, Warriors of the Sun*. Hernando de Soto and the South's Ancient Chiefdoms. Athens: University of Georgia Press.
2003 *Conversations with the High Priest of Coosa*. Chapel Hill: University of North Carolina Press.

Hudson, Charles, ed. 1979 *Black Drink. A Native American Tea*. Athens: The University of Georgia Press. [2004 Reprint]

Innes, Pamela, Linda Alexander, and Bertha Tilkens 2004 *Beginning Creek ~ Mvskoke Emponvkv*. Norman: University of Oklahoma Press.

Jackson, Jason 2003 *Yuchi Ceremonial Life. Performance, Meaning, and Tradition in a Contemporary American Indian Community*. Studies in the Anthropology of North American Indians. Lincoln: University of Nebraska Press.

Jenkins, Ned 2009 Tracing the Origins of the Early Creeks, 1050-1700 CE. Ethridge and Shuck-Hall, *Mapping the Mississippian Shatter Zone*, Chapter 8: 188-249.

Lankford, George, ed. 1987 *Native American Legends. Southeastern Legends: Tales from the Natchez, Caddo, Biloxi, Chickasaw, and Other Nations.* Little Rock: August House.

Lankford, George

    2007a The Great Serpent in Eastern North America, Chapter 5: 107-135. *Ancient Objects and Sacred Realms: Interpretations of Mississippian Iconography.* Kent Reilly and James Garber, eds. Austin: University of Texas Press.

    2007b The "Path of Souls": Some Death Imagery in the Southeastern Ceremonial Complex, Chapter 8, 174-212. *Ancient Objects and Sacred Realms: Interpretations of Mississippian Iconography.* Kent Reilly and James Garber, eds. Austin: University of Texas Press.

Lewis, David, Jr., and Ann Jordan 2002 *Creek Indian Medicine Ways. The Enduring Power of Mvskoke Religion.* Albuquerque: University of New Mexico Press.

Long, Fred, and George Scott 1998 *Nakcokv Esyvhiketv ~ Muskogee Hymns.* General Commission on Religion and Race, the United Methodist Church. [1936 by Presbyterians]

Loughridge, Rev. R.M., and David Hodge 1890 *English and Muskokee Dictionary.* [1964, Okmulgee Baptist Home Mission Board].

Martin, Jack, and Margaret McKane Mauldin 2000 *A Dictionary of Creek/Muskogee*, with notes on the Florida and Oklahoma Seminole dialects of Creek. Lincoln: University of Nebraska Press.

Morgan, William 1999 *Precolumbian Architecture in Eastern North America.* Gainesville: University Press of Florida.

Nairne, Thomas 1988 *Muskhogean Journals ~ The 1708 Expedition to the Mississippi River.* Alexander Moore, ed. Jackson: University Press of Mississippi.

Piker, Joshua 2004 *Okfuskee. A Creek Indian Town in Colonial America.* Cambridge: Harvard University Press.

Reilly III, F. Kent, and James F. Garber, eds. 2007 *Ancient Objects and Sacred Realms. Interpretations of Mississippian Iconography.* Austin: University of Texas Press.

Richards, John D., and Melvin L. Fowler, eds. 2003 *A Deep-Time Perspective: Studies in Symbols, Meaning and the Archeological Record.* Papers in Honor of Robert L Hall. The Wisconsin Archeologist 84 (1 & 2).

Robbins, Lester 1976 *The Persistence of Traditional Religious Practices among Creek Indians.* Dallas: Southern Methodist University, PhD Dissertation.

Roe, Peter 1982 *The Cosmic Zygote.* Cosmology in the Amazon Basin. New Brunswick: Rutgers University Press.

Schmitt, Karl, and Iva Osanai Schmitt 1940s-50s Notes on Arbeka and New Tulsa.

Schultz, Jack 1999 *The Seminole Baptist Churches of Oklahoma. Maintaining a Traditional Community.* Norman: University of Oklahoma Press.

Speck, Frank G. 1907 *The Creek Indians of Taskigi Town.* American Anthropological Association, Memoir 2 (2): 100-164.

Squier, Ephraim G. 1851 *The Serpent Symbol and the Worship of Reciprocal Principles of Nature in America.* New York: George F Putnam. [1975, Kraus Reprint]

Squier, Ephraim G., and Edwin Davis 1848 *Ancient Monuments of the Mississippi Valley.* Smithsonian Contributions to Knowledge 1. [1998, Smithsonian Classics of Anthropology]

Sturtevant, William 1987 *A Creek Source Book.* NY: Garland.

1987 *A Seminole Source Book.* NY: Garland.

Swan, Caleb 1855 Topical History: *Position and State of Manners and Arts in the Creek, or Muscogee Nation in 1791. Information Respecting the History, Condition and Prospects of the Indian Tribes of the United States.* Henry Schoolcraft, ed. Volume 5: 251-83 [Busk 267-68]. Philadelphia: J.B. Lippincott and Company.

Swanton, John

1911 *Indian Tribes of the Lower Mississippi Valley and Adjacent Coast of the Gulf of Mexico.* Bureau of American Ethnology, Bulletin 43.

1912 *A Dictionary of the Biloxi and Ofo Languages.* Bureau of American Ethnology, Bulletin 47.

1922 Tokuli of Tulsa. *American Indian Life*, by Several of Its Students. Elsie Clews Parsons, ed. New York: B.W. Huebsch, Inc.

1922 Early History of the Creek Indians and Their Neighbors. *Bureau of American Ethnology Bulletin* 73. Washington, DC.

1928a *Social Organization and Social Usages of the Indians of the Creek Confederacy.* Bureau of American Ethnology, Annual Report 42 for 1924-25: 23-472.

1928b *Religious Beliefs and Medical Practices of the Creek Indians.* Bureau of American Ethnology, Annual Report 42 for 1924-25: 473-672.

1928c *Aboriginal Culture of the Southeast.* Bureau of American Ethnology, Annual Report 42: 673-726.

1928d *Chickasaw.* Bureau of American Ethnology, Annual Report 44: 169-273.

1928e *The Interpretation of Aboriginal Mounds by Means of Creek Indian Customs.* Smithsonian Institution Annual Report 1927: 495-506, 7 plates.

1929 *Myths and Tales of the Southeastern Indians.* Bureau of American Ethnology, Bulletin 88.

1931 *Source Material for the Social and Ceremonial Life of the Choctaw Indians.* Bureau of American Ethnology, Bulletin 103.

1931 Modern Square Grounds of the Creek Indians. *Smithsonian Miscellaneous Collections* 85 (8): 1-46. Washington, DC.

1932 *Green Corn Dance.* Chronicles of Oklahoma X (11): 170-195.

1998 *Early History of the Creek Indians and Their Neighbors.* Gainesville: University Press of Florida. [Bureau of American Ethnology, Bulletin 73, 1922]

Taborn, Karen 2004 *Momis Komet* ("We Will Endure"). The Indigenization of Christian Hymn Singing by Creek and Seminole Indians. City University of New York, Hunter College MA.

Vega, Garcilasco de la 1980 *The Florida of the Inca.* John and Jeannette Varner, trans. Austin: University of Texas Press.

Wright, James Leitch

1981 *The Only Land They Knew.* The Tragic Story of the American Indians in the Old South. NY: The Free Press.

1986 *Creeks and Seminoles.* The Destruction and Regeneration of the Muscogulge People. Lincoln: University of Nebraska Press.

Zellar, Gary 2007 *African Creeks.* Estelvste and the Creek Nation. Norman: University of Oklahoma Press.

Frank Speck (1881 - 1950)

Frank Gouldsmith Speck (November 8, 1881 – February 6, 1950) was an early Boasian Americanist. Raised in Brooklyn, New York and Hackensack, New Jersey, with summers in rural Connecticut, he had a sister, Gladys H. (8 years younger), and brother Reinhard S. (9 years younger). The family's live-in servants included a German woman, Anna Muller, and a mixed Native American/African American woman, Gussie Giles from South Carolina.

Entering Columbia University in 1899, he worked closely with Algonkianist John Dyneley Prince, who introduced him to Franz Boas. During a 1900 summer camping trip to Fort Shantok, Connecticut, Speck met Mohegans of his own age (Burrill Fielding, Jerome Roscoe Skeesucks, Edwin Fowler) who welcomed him into the community, especially to Fidelia Fielding, a widow and diarist fluent in Mohegan Pequot. Much of her writings were lost when Prince's home burned, but Speck published through the BAE a surviving diary.

Speck earned his BA from Columbia in 1904, made a comparative study of Southeastern literature for his M.A. in 1905, and studied among Oklahoma Yuchi for his 1908 PhD conferred by the University of Pennsylvania, where he spent his career, because they had a policy of hiring their own and he had held a one-year George Lieb Harrison Fellowship at the University Museum (now the University of Pennsylvania Museum of Archaeology and Anthropology). In 1908 the Harrison was held by Edward Sapir, who lived with Speck, along with his orthodox cantor father Jacob, who kept kosher.

During his Yuchi research, Speck collected from Laslie *kabicimała* Cloud (? - 1905) specifics about Taskigi, his Creek talwa town which closely interacted with Yuchi, who had been adopted into the Creek Nation centuries before. Such comparative ethnography was vital to all of Speck's work.

Assistant Curator of Archaeology and Ethnology George Byron Gordon arranged for Speck to receive a dual appointment, as both Assistant in Ethnology at the University Museum, and Instructor of Anthropology for the University. Constant friction with Gordon (See Swanton's autobiography below) eventually led to a separate 1913 Anthropology department with Speck as full professor and chair for four decades until his health failed in 1949. Yet every free moment was spent in the field devoted to his so-called "salvage operations" in New England, and further north in Labrador and Ontario in Canada.

In the 1920s through 1940s, Speck studied with Cherokees in the Carolinas and Oklahoma, especially with Will West Long of Big Cove, who is listed on the title page as co-author with Speck and Leonard Bloom of their 1951 *Cherokee Dance and Drama*.

Among his outstanding students are A. Irving Hallowell, Anthony F.C. Wallace, and Loren Eiseley, and he encouraged efforts by Clinton A. Weslager, Bill Fenton, and Edmund Carpenter, as well as native scholars. He was named *Gahehdagowa* ('Great Porcupine') when adopted into the Turtle clan of the Seneca.

His professional ties included American Philosophical Society, American Association for the Advancement of Science, American Anthropological Association, American Ethnological Society, Geographical Society of Philadelphia, Archaeological Society of North Carolina American Museum of Natural History in New York, and the Smithsonian Institution in Washington, DC.

His thousands of Native American objects – along with many reels of audio recordings, reams of transcriptions, and photographs – are now in multiple museums, most notably the

Museum of the American Indian in New York (now National Museum of the American Indian in DC), Canadian Museum of Civilization, and Peabody Essex Museum. Speck's papers are archived by the American Philosophical Society, Canadian Museum of Civilizations in Gatineau, Quebec and at the Phillips Library of the Peabody Essex Museum in Salem, Massachusetts. Speck published prolifically, often in obscure regional journals that once took considerable time to ferret out, but now can easily be found on the internet.

A much more personal portrait of Speck is provided by Clinton Alfred Weslager (1909 - 1994), a former student with a life long interest in mid Atlantic natives despite a long career as a DuPont executive.

Speck's Office

"Speck's office at the University was unlike any business office I had ever visited. One climbed the splintered steps to the top floor of College Hall, which was on the third or fourth level of the building, and then ascended a rickety staircase hugging the wall which seemed to lead to the kind of garret where Bluebeard murdered his seven wives. At the top of the steps there was a worn door stippled with thumbtack holes. The door itself had a sort of mysterious solidity and one wondered what lay hidden behind it.

"Within was a long, narrow room with a high ceiling, a threadbare rug, and three murky windows whose weather-beaten frames allowed cold air to whistle through in winter weather. Actually the room was a combination office-library-museum, much in need of a thorough housecleaning. At the far end of the room was Speck's disorderly desk, and near the door was a second desk used by one of his colleagues. In the center of the room was a battered table used for seminars, and it too needed a scouring with soap and water and a new coat of varnish. Shelves along the walls overflowed with anthropological books and journals, and Indian baskets gathering dust were piled on top of the shelves.

"A bison skull, a half dozen or more painted wooden Indian masks peered down from the walls. Colored prints of the portraits of Indian chiefs, interspersed with crossbows, snowshoes, gourds, turtle shells, deerskin shields, feather bonnets, a spear, and a variety of other artifacts hung from the walls as though clinging by some magnetic force. A hand-lettered cardboard sign reading "Dr. Speck is Busy. Do not Disturb" was on the table, waiting to be tacked on the door when he convened a seminar or was in conversation with an Indian visitor. One of the sections of the bookshelves against the wall was covered with a dusty, frayed cloth drape. Behind the drape were extra copies of the books and numerous articles Speck had written. This literature was available to his students for reference, but some of them took advantage [58] of his generosity and didn't return books they borrowed, which irritated him. He told me he was going to prohibit students removing literature from the office.

"Speck had been chairman of the Department of Anthropology for many years, but he tired of the responsibility, and there was a time when he was able to persuade both Hallowell and Davidson to take the post. When Hallowell resigned to go to Northwestern and Davidson went to Oregon, the job fell on Speck again. He complained to me about the paperwork he had to handle. He said he was not "overworked" but "overscheduled." I teased him and said that all the paperwork he was compelled to handle in a week as the department head could be processed by any efficient corporation executive in a couple of hours.

"He smoked little cigars called "Between the Acts," about the diameter of a pencil. In my youth we called them "Recruits." He was a chain smoker, lighting a fresh cigar by holding it against the lighted end of the one he was ready to discard, invariably spilling ashes on his coat and vest. Once, on a trip to Sussex County, Delaware, in the fall when the chilly air forced me to close the windows of my car (and this was after several trips with him when I was nauseated by the smoke), I quietly said to him, "Frank, don't you think that by now you have thoroughly fumigated my car and killed all the infectious germs?" Without changing the expression on his face, he stomped out the cigar. From that day on he never smoked in my car, but he would often ask me to stop on the pretense of looking at a wild bird, a dead animal on the road, or some other reason, which permitted him to light up a little cigar, and then crush it under his heel before he got back in the car. He carried a small box of the cigars in the pocket of his vest, which he always wore, and there was an ample reserve in the brown bag.

"On one of my visits to his office I noticed a pair of new shoes under his desk, although he was wearing the old, unpolished ones that I had seen him wear so often. He told me he was wearing the new shoes to please Mrs. Speck and his daughters, but after arriving at his office changed to the old ones for comfort. I had the impression that like many of his informants Speck usually sought to avoid confrontations.

"Once when I arrived unannounced at his office he was getting ready to deliver a lecture to a class of undergraduates. I was amazed to see him display a vanity I never suspected he possessed. He took a hairbrush from a desk drawer full of pencils, old string, paper clips, arrowheads, a broken pair of scissors, and other odds and ends, and carefully brushed his thinning hair. Then he used the same brush on [59] his coat and trousers. I asked him if I could attend the lecture. He didn't want to give me a flat negative answer, but he said, "Maybe it would be best if you wait here until I come back." I persisted, and said, "Maybe I'll learn something if I attend." He answered, "No, I don't think you will." Knowing how much he disliked argument, I was aware that for some reason he preferred that I not attend, but didn't want to say so. I waited in his office as he suggested.

"Several times he invited me to participate in seminars in his office when the students gathered around the table. The participants were all graduate students, and the discussions mature and stimulating. He encouraged the students to do most of the talking. Speck smoked his little cigars with an impassive expression on his face as he listened. Several times he asked for my comments. Now and then he would interrupt the discussion with a provocative question.

"Speck was not susceptible to moving suddenly from one subject to another. His method was to concentrate on one topic and exhaust it before going to another. A thought advanced by one of the participants on a particular issue would lead him to make a relevant comment which often was the preface to a lengthy discussion. More than once I have seen a bland expression come over his face when a questioner tried to make a sudden transition from one subject to another during a moment of reflection when Speck was organizing his thoughts prior to exposing another side of the question under discussion. One question could trip the trigger for a long monologue, each thought adding a different aspect to the subject. He was like a terrier with a rat in his teeth — he shook it, threw it up in the air, picked it up, shook it again, and wouldn't give up until there was no life left. But his actions and reactions were never hasty or impulsive. His manner was slow and deliberative, and in this trait of character he was more Indian-like than his best Indian informant.

"What irritated Speck most (although his facial expression never revealed it) was to be interrogated in a rapid-fire manner by newspaper or magazine interviewers. If the questions came too fast he suddenly became silent, as though he didn't know the answers. He was especially irritated by newspaper reporters who stomped into his office, opened their notebooks, and began to question him about subjects having to do with Indians or a recent trip he had made.

Often he pretended he didn't know the answers to the questions, although those of us who knew him well were aware that behind his feigned ignorance was a keen mind. One time a writer of fiction about Indians visited his office for a hurried interview. Her questions came rapidly, and she asked a [60] second one before he had time to answer the first in his characteristic detail. He didn't change the expression on his face, but merely clammed up and acted as though he was stumped by her questions.

"On the other hand, he was always willing to assist a worthy student or a visiting colleague by sharing the vast amount of knowledge he had accumulated. The thought of commercializing the information he possessed never entered his head. One day after I had participated in a seminar he conducted at the table in his office, we made arrangements for a trip to visit the Nanticokes in Indian River Hundred the following weekend. One of the graduate students who had lingered behind overheard our conversation. He interrupted and asked Speck if he could accompany us. I thought this interruption was rude, and the request presumptuous. I fully expected Speck to reprimand him, as I would have done if he were one of my subordinates. Instead Speck surprised me by saying, "By all means come along. You are cordially invited. This isn't my trip, but ours. You have as much right to participate as I have."

"On one of my visits to the University he showed me a large elm growing on the campus — it may still be there. He told me that it had been raised from a shoot cut from an old elm at Shackamaxon, under which William Penn is supposed to have held his first treaty with the Delaware Indians in 1682 or 1683. Many people would have done nothing about it. But the unforgettable Speck, who recognized the significance of the tree to Delaware Indian descendants living in distant Oklahoma and in Ontario, Canada, took the time to clip shoots and mail them to Delaware informants. This enabled them to perpetuate the tradition of the treaty elm which was highly regarded by their ancestors. He did this at his own expense, and he also absorbed many other expenses relating to his Indian studies and publications, which far exceeded the moderate grams he received from the University and other institutions."

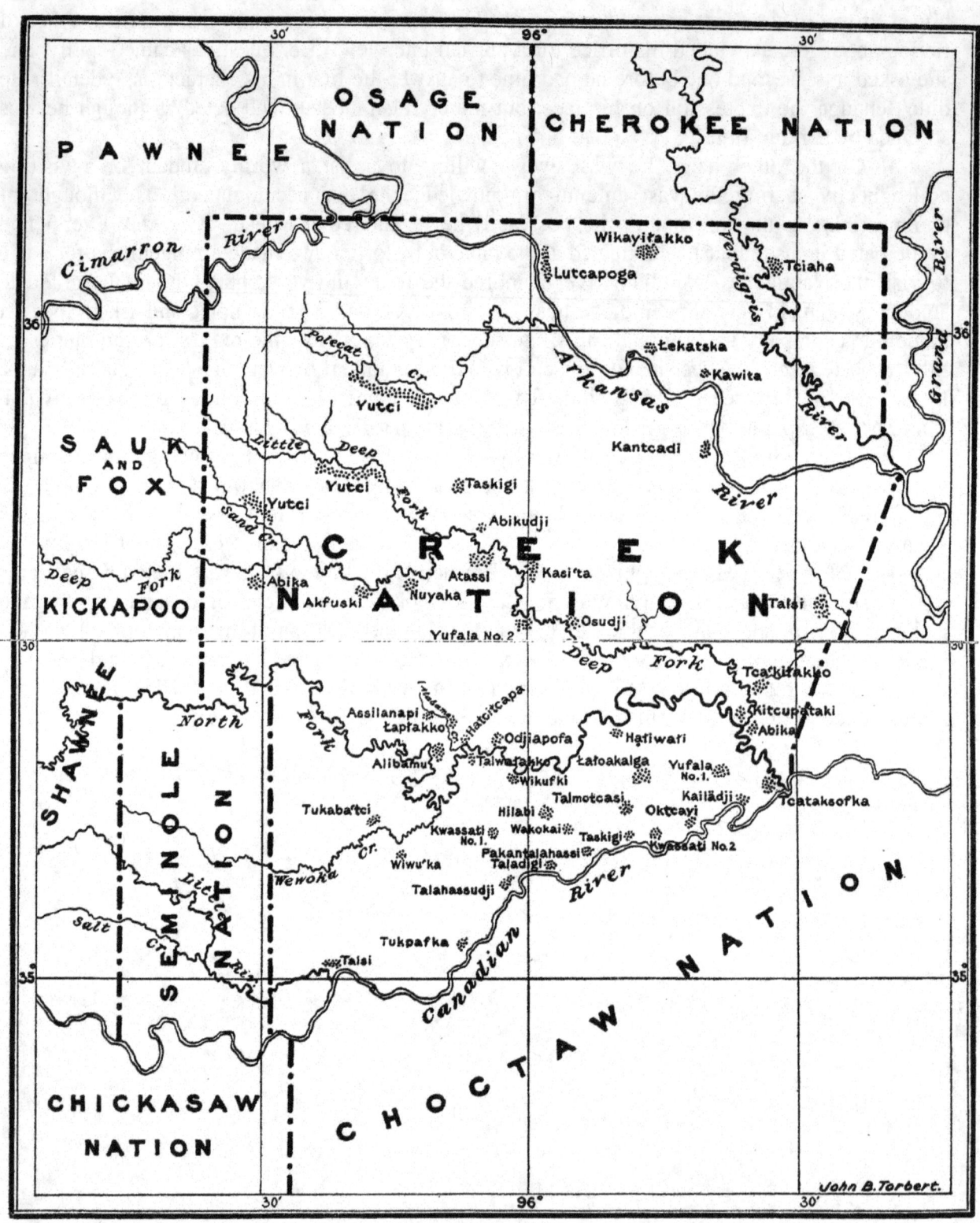

MAP SHOWING APPROXIMATE LOCATION OF CREEK TOWNS AND NEIGHBORING TRIBES

(COMPILED CHIEFLY FROM GATSCHET'S LIST)

5

THE CREEK INDIANS OF TASKIGI TOWN[24]
By FRANK G. SPECK

CONTENTS

---

[24] Published with the permission of the Bureau of American Ethnology, Washington, D.C., and the American Museum of Natural History, New York, which, on the recommendation of Dr Franz Boas, furnished funds for the study of the Yuchi Indians in 1904 and 1905, during which time this material was incidentally obtained.

THE CREEK NATION

As the Taskigi formed one of the towns constituting the Creek Nation, a short account of this group of tribes may present more clearly the political background in which we find them living.

The old Creek Nation was a loose confederacy, as it might be called, of a number of Maskogian-speaking towns and sub-tribes, avowedly for the purposes of keeping peace and of offering a front of strength against hostile and alien neighbors. Many of these towns were tribal units sometimes themselves separated from each other by far-reaching differences in dialect and customs. Even alien linguistic stocks were admitted into the Nation, as we find the Yuchi, Shawnee, and, until lately, the Natchez, represented in the Creek assemblages as prominently as the Maskogi tribes proper. On the whole, however, the differences in material culture and customs that separated these independent towns from one another were not so great as it may be thought, as a certain amount of uniformity pervaded the whole Southeastern region. The fact that none of these towns has been specifically studied as yet in completeness, makes it' impossible to say just how far suspected differences extended. From what we do possess of special treatment, however, it seems evident that in ceremonial and religious matters divergences in detail existed. If the following description of the square-ground and ceremonies of Taskigi town be [104] compared with that of *Kasi'ta* and *Tukaba'tci* given by Gatschet, of *Odshi-apofa* by Swan, and of *Atasi* by Bartram, this will be seen more readily. In mythology, too, there is probably some variation from one town to the other. [104 AMERICAN ANTHROPOLOGICAL ASSOCIATION [MEMOIRS 2 Speck]

At the present day (1905) the following towns[25] are recognized by the Creek national government, in various stages of disintegration and intermixture. They give a total of about 10,000 souls for the Creeks.

Abika	*Kwassati*	*Talmotcasa*
Alabama	*Lutcapoga*	*Talwałakko*
Atasi	*Łałakalga*	*Taisi*
Greenleaf	*Łapłakko*	*Taskigi*
Hatcitcapa	*Łekatska*	*Tciaha*
Hickory Ground	*Łewałi*	*Topofka*
Hilabi	*Okfaski*	*Tukaba'tci*
Hitciti	*Oktcayi*	*Wiłtakko*
Kantcati	*Osotci*	*Wiwo'ka*
Kasi'ta	*Pokontalahassi*	*Wiyogafki*
Kawita	*Taladiga*	*Yufala*
Kayaligi	*Talahassudji*	*Yutci*

---

[25] Gatschet, in his *Migration Legend of the Creek Indians*, has given a similar list and offered translations for many of the names of towns extant in 1884.

Of these, Abika, Yufala, Okfaski, Kwassati, and Taisi have split apart into smaller settlements bearing the name of the parent town, usually with some local modification. But these offshoots mostly celebrated their religious rites with the home town, as they had no square-ground of their own. Gatschet mentions another settlement belonging to Taskigi. The negro freedmen of the Creeks were also represented politically by three or four town names, and their settlements were admitted into the Nation on an equal basis with the Indian towns after the Civil War.

The accompanying map attempts to show approximately where the survivors of the old town divisions are situated, with some tendency toward centralization and maintenance of their former relations amid new surroundings, since the removal to Indian Territory in 1836-40. But it must be understood that by situation is meant only the densest settlement of those [105] belonging together under the one town name. Some of the old towns have become extinct and other new ones have been formed by negro freedmen and emigrants.

THE TASKIGI

INTRODUCTION

Benjamin Hawkins was one of the first writers to mention the Taskigi.[26] In his time they formed one of the towns of the Upper Creeks, occupying the fork of Coosa and Tallapoosa rivers in Alabama, where formerly stood Fort Toulouse of the French. They numbered then, 1798-99, thirty five gun-men. Hawkins states that five conical mounds of earth were situated near the village, which were explained by the Indians as places of safety in times when the river overflowed its banks. He also says that the Taskigi came from across the Mississippi; that they have lost their language and speak Creek, and have adopted the customs and manners of the Creeks. Gatschet[27] gives a review of the information on Taskigi town and suggests that, in consideration of its supposedly foreign name, the word Taskigi might be related to a Cherokee town name on Great Tennessee river. Mooney[28] gives a short historical review of the Taskigi and the situation of the three Cherokee towns bearing the name. The largest settlement of those incorporated with the Cherokee was on the south side of Little Tennessee river, just above the mouth of Tellico, in what is now Monroe county, Tennessee. Here was born Sequoya, the inventor of the Cherokee syllabary. Another so-called Taskigi town Mooney gives as being on the north bank of Tennessee river, just below Chattanooga, Tennessee. And the third settlement was on the south bank of Little Tennessee river, north of where Robbinsville, Graham county, North Carolina, now is. Mooney states that the Taskigi were classed as a foreign people [106] by the Cherokee, and thinks that they were probably of Maskogian affinity.

Adair[29] and Milfort assert that the Taskigi were one of the weaker tribes of the Southeast which were broken up by the more numerous Creeks and Cherokee in their advances, and subsequently incorporated by them, along with other tribes in a similar condition, like the Natchez in later years and the Yuchi who joined the Creeks.

---

[26] Sketch of the Creek Country, *Georgia Hist. Soc. Coll.*, III, pt. I, pp. 37-39, ... 1848.

[27] *Migration Legend of the Creek Indians*, I, pp. 143-146, 1884.

[28] *Myths of the Cherokee*, Nineteenth Report Bureau of American Ethnology, part 1, pp. 388-389, 534.

[29] *History of the American Indians*, 1775, p. 257.

Leaving these theories without discussion, it appears that the present name Taskigi does not yield to definite analysis. The Taskigi themselves say that it is an old word, and suggest a relation to *taskáya*[30] warrior, and *tastanági*, warrior.

The language of the Taskigi is normal *Maskogi* and they call themselves *Maskogalgi* (-a*lgi* = collective plural). In another article[31] I have attempted to give an outline of the *Maskogi* language, and the Creek material used in it was obtained mostly from Taskigi town. Their present location is approximately between Polecat creek and Canadian Deep Fork, in the northwestern part of the Creek Nation, Oklahoma. Here the accompanying notes were made in spare time during the course of linguistic studies among the Yuchi who are now the nearest neighbors of the Taskigi on the north. The culture of this tribe is practically the same as that of the other forty-two Indian towns of the Creek Nation, the only points of difference being in details of ceremony and town life. The Taskigi were represented in the Creek Confederacy council after the Civil War by a chief, in the [107] House of Kings, and two delegates in the House

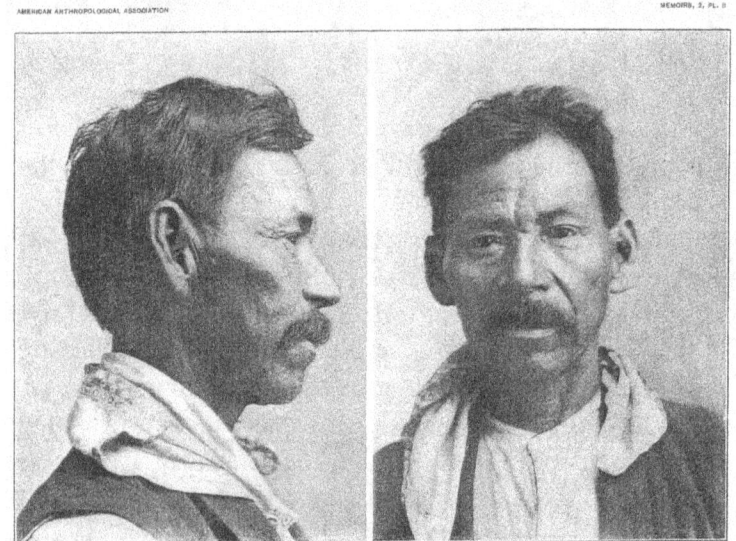

of Warriors until 1906. The cultural condition of this town has undergone many radical changes in the last ten years. The annual ceremony of the corn harvest has been discontinued and the old people are the only ones who retain any knowledge of their ethnology. Most of the material here given was obtained from Laslie Cloud, *Kabitcimała*, of the Raccoon clan, a former dance leader and ceremonial official, and until his death in 1905 a practising shaman of the town. The matter deals exclusively with Taskigi town. No attempt has been made to correlate it with that of other towns, as it may become possible at a later time to procure material from some of them for maturer comparison.

Nowadays it is very hard to say how many Creeks class themselves as Taskigi; but there are probably not many more than 150, and of these it is highly improbable that any are of pure Indian blood. The admixture of white and negro blood has proceeded so far since the close of

---

[30] PHONETIC NOTE: Surd *tc* and sonant *dj*, lingual alveolars, *dj* represents a sound about midway in position between *dz* and *dj* ; *b* is indeterminate between surd *p* and sonant *b* ; *d* is also of the same indefinite nature and produced as an alveolar dental ; *ł* is a soft palatalized spirant surd ; *g*, a palatal sonant ; *q* a velar surd ; *g* the sonant of the same series ; *f* a normal labial dental surd ; *c* like English "sh" ; *l, m, n, s, k*, are like the English. Semivowels are *h, w, y*. Prolonged consonants are written doubled: *kk, tt*. Vowels *ā, ē, ī, ō, ū* are long ; *a, e, i, o, u* short; a̱ open and obscure like " u" in English " but" ; â like "a" in English "all" ; *ä* long and open like "a" in English " fare " without the "r" tinge ; [n] nazalized ; *ai* diphthong. Accent is denoted by `ˋ` and `ˊ`; ' indicates aspiration ; [ε] a glottal catch.

[31] *American Anthropologist*, N. s., IX, no. 3 1907.

9

the eighteenth century that the number of unquestionably pure Indians in the Creek Nation is very small indeed. The younger generations are much more visibly of mixed race than their elders. Yet despite this, and the general decay of their material and ceremonial culture, the language is rigidly but unconsciously preserved by the natives almost without exception. It is true that many of those whose features are characteristically negroid are proficient only in the Creek tongue and genuinely exhibit in sentiment all the peculiarities of Indians.

MATERIAL CULTURE

ECONOMICS. — In their original habitat in Alabama and Georgia the Taskigi enjoyed extremely warm summers, especially along the river bottoms where they had permanent villages, and very moderate winters. A great variety of animal and vegetable products surrounded them in all seasons. Like the rest of the Creek tribes, the Taskigi were much concerned with agriculture. Corn was, and is to-day, their chief vegetable product. They spent much time, however, in hunting deer, [108] turkeys, and bison, in which they were aided by dogs. They utilized the non-edible parts of these animals in various domestic ways. Songs were believed to charm the game so that it could be approached and shot. They still practise the old method of shooting fish with a straight simple bow made of the osage orange (*bois d' arc* of the French), and long arrows tipped with a piece of rolled sheet-metal. The fish arrows often lack feathering. They poison the streams to secure the fish by pounding up quantities of horse-chestnuts and throwing them into pools which they have dammed up at different points. Then the men go into the water to mix up the poison, beating around with their arms and stirring up the water so that the fish cannot escape by staying near the bottom. The fish are then stabbed with arrows and thrown out to the women on shore who stow them away in large splint baskets. Large quantities of catfish were procured in this way.

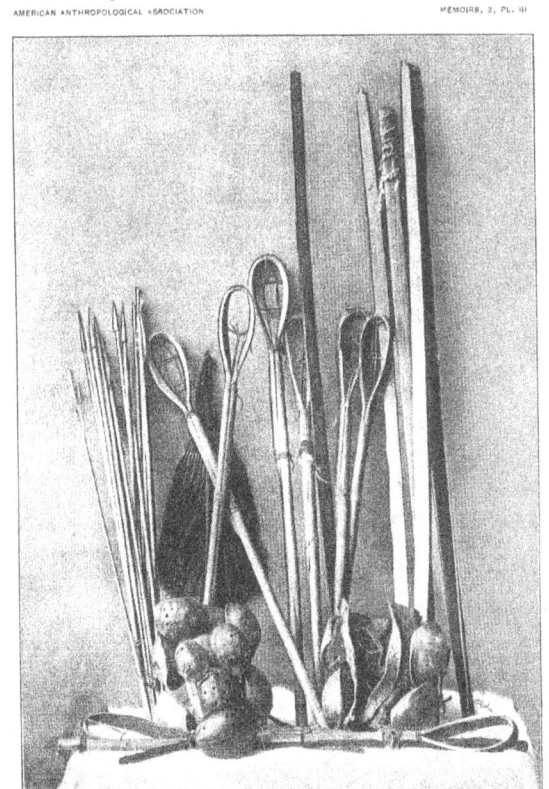

AMERICAN ANTHROPOLOGICAL ASSOCIATION   MEMOIRS, 2, PL. III

CREEK BOWS AND ARROWS BALL STICKS TURTLE-SHELL RATTLES, FEATHER FAN, ETC.
(From Report of the Indian Inspector for Indian Territory, 1901)

The only form of house remembered by the present inhabitants of Taskigi town is the log house, *djógo*. This they use to-day with the addition, in front of the door, of a square shade arbor of leafy branches supported by four or six crotched posts. Much time is spent beneath this shelter, and in warm weather the family prefer to sleep there. According to Bartram, the typical house of the Creeks consisted of four upright corner posts, arranged to inclose a rectangular space of about four or five hundred square feet, with smaller posts ranging between. The roof and sides were covered with slabs of bark. These structures numbered from one to four to each household, according to the town or tribe, and were often so set up as to inclose a square yard. Notched-log structures were also observed at an early date among the Creeks and the Cherokee, and it may be that the present-day log-house is a descendant of an older type. The modern example is seldom larger than the ordinary

10

settler's cabin, containing one or two rooms formed by a partition. Home-made shingles cover the pitched roof, and a clean-swept area or yard lies before the door. Corn, melon, or potato patches are nearby.

The sweat-house, so far as is now remembered, was a temporary [109] structure of poles covered with skins, and was erected near a stream. To this the men resorted before going to war or before other important undertakings. Steam was produced by throwing water on heated stones passed inside by attendants. The men remained in this inclosure until they perspired profusely, then jumped into the stream.

UTENSILS. — Pots were manufactured, even up to a short time ago, of clean red clay coiled upon a disk-like base. To fire these they were covered with dried grass and the mass was ignited. When the combustible covering had burned off the pot was black, and so hard that it could withstand the effects of daily contact with fire. Pipes of unbaked clay are still made in some of the remote parts of the Taskigi district.

AMERICAN ANTHROPOLOGICAL ASSOCIATION

MEMOIRS, 2, PI. IV

BASKETRY OF THE CREEKS
(From Report of the Indian Inspector for Indian Territory, 1901)

Baskets of various shapes were made of cane and hickory splints for household use. The favorite technique in basketry was the twilled. The weaving showed some diversity in details, produced by allowing the woof strands to pass over one, two, three, and frequently four warp strands at a time. Decoration on baskets, so they say, was rare, but when desired was obtained by manipulating varicolored splints in the woof {weave}. The splints were shaved from the rind of the cane. This gave a smooth glossy surface on one side which was turned outward in weaving. The commonest basket shape had the bottom quite flat and wide with the wall tapering slightly inward toward the top. Sieves of open twilled work were made for sifting pounded corn. Twilled mats of cane were formerly made, but are not now to be seen.

The corn mortar which stands to-day as a permanent fixture in nearly every house-yard is made of a plain log hollowed out, and the heavy-topped wooden pestle is usually five or six feet in length. A very common article of diet, called *sófki*, is made of pounded and sifted corn boiled in water. Sometimes wood-ashes, pounded hickory-nuts, or bone marrow are mixed with it *sófki* tastes quite bitter, but it is very nutritious. A bowl of it stands, with a wooden spoon in it, at the door of nearly every house, from which the stranger is invited to help himself. Woodenware was not very extensive, nor did it bear elaborate [110] decoration. Pot stirrers were paddle-shaped, with a disk at the handle end. Spoons and ladles were common, with rather deep bowls tapering almost to a point at the front. For navigation upon the sluggish rivers of their old home large trunks of cypress yielded them excellent canoe material. It is claimed that these dugouts were slightly elevated and pointed at both ends.

CREEK POTTERY AND WOODEN SPOONS
(From Report of the Indian Inspector for Indian Territory, 1901)

The bows used in hunting and warfare were staves about four feet in length, made of hickory or osage orange. Arrowshafts were made of cane or arrow-wood and were feathered by binding trimmed quills on three sides near the nock. Turkey feathers were much in use for this purpose. Another implement of the chase that was common to the Southeast was the blow-gun, *wókko*. It was made of a cane stalk about as long as a man is tall. To remove the pith, it was sometimes necessary to section the cane, then bind it together again. The darts were made of sharpened stems wound about one end with some soft material, such as cotton, which acted as a piston. The blow-gun was used chiefly for killing small game.

CLOTHING. — Men's clothing consisted of deerskin leggings, shirts, blanket-like robes, and moccasins with the seam running up on the instep from the toes to the ankle. During much of the year, however, no covering was needed for the feet and they went barefoot. After the advent of the whites at least they wore woven sashes of wool with tassels hanging down on the sides. Bands of woven woolen stuff were used as garters below the knees. Both of these articles were ornamented with beads sewed on in geometrical designs the significance of which has now been forgotten. The breech-cloth, which passed between the legs, either ended at the belt or had flaps that could also be decorated. The man's daily outfit was made complete by a pouch, slung over the shoulder on a broad beaded band, to hold tobacco and pipe. They wrapped bands of skin or obtainable cloth stuffs about their heads after the fashion of a turban, according to surviving tradition. Under this the hair was trimmed about the ears and banged across the forehead. Sheets of hammered-out metal shaped like crescents were much in vogue as [111] dependants upon the chests of distinguished men. Earrings and brooches of German silver were manufactured in quantity during early colonial times and used as ornaments by both sexes. Women wore deerskin skirts hanging to the knees, with a cape-like covering thrown over the shoulders and upper arms and fastened at the throat. The borders of these garments were ornamented with beads and metal brooches. Their hair was tied in a club behind, while a metal comb-like band surmounted the crown from which hung highly-colored streamers.

SOCIAL ORGANIZATION

THE TOWN. — The present settlements of these Indians are scattered along the creeks and rivers, in no respect forming a compact town. But in their ancient territory in the Southeast they were more centralized, and had many regulations governing the cultivation of land and its apportionment. The name for town is *talwa* and is used also to denote tribal affiliation; a mere settlement not having the town organization and ceremonies is *talófa*. As all of the former cultural conditions have changed so much, the town is now a very loose institution. Gatschet says that Taskigi was one of the White or Peace towns of the Nation, wherein no blood could be shed and which was governed by civil instead of military officials.[32]

The town, however, is still the political unit, and like the other Creek towns the Taskigi had a public square-ground or yard to a certain extent of a sacred character.[33] In former times the square was situated in the heart of the town itself, but later it came to be established where most convenient for the scattered families. On the four sides of this square, which faced the points of the compass, lodges or cabins with brush-covered roofs and open sides were erected. Rows of logs raised above the ground formed seats inside. The earth floor of the square was kept hard and smooth, and no vegetation was allowed to encroach upon its limits. At one corner was [112] the council house. The whole square, house and all, was called *djogo łakko*, 'big house.' All meetings, ceremonial and civil, formal and informal, took place in the square when the weather was pleasant, or in the council house when it was inclement. Nearly all the inhabitants of the town were accustomed to gather here for social purposes or dances in the evenings. In the center of the square lay the bed of ashes where the fire, *tutka*, was kept burning at all gatherings (see diagram, fig. I).

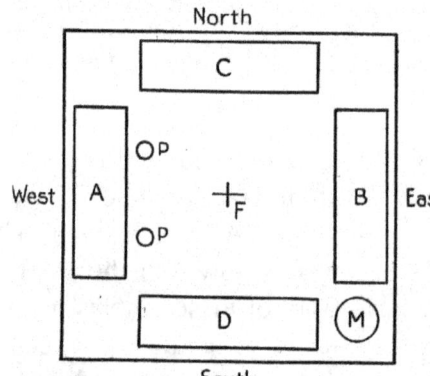

FIG. 1. — Diagram of Taskigi Town Square. [*A*, Lodge for town chief, chiefs, and *hiniha łakko*; *B*, *C*, Lodge for warriors and *tastanagi łakko*; *D*, Lodge for women, children, and strangers ; *F*, Fire ; *P*, Pots of medicine ; M, Mound of earth. *F*, *P*, and *M* are employed during the celebration of the annual ceremony.)

Here the new fire was kindled, at the annual ceremony, for distribution to the various households. Near by, in a cleared space, ball-games and other athletic contests were held with other towns, or with tribes as it often happened. [113]

TOWN OFFICIALS. — As has been said, the town, composed of the various clan groups, was the political unit with its own officials and its open religious ceremonies where the clans took part subordinately. The highest in rank of these officials was the *miko,* town chief. He was chosen from a certain clan in the town and his tenure was for life. In Taskigi the *miko* was chosen from the Bear or the Wind clan. The function of this dignitary, as the civil head of the town, was to receive all embassies from other tribes, to direct the decisions of the town council according to his judgment, and finally to stand as the representative of the town in foreign negotiations. If the

---

[32] Migration Legend, op. cit, I, 122.

[33] The last town square of this sort was situated on the Little Deep Fork of the Canadian river, near Tuskegee, in the present Oklahoma.

miko could not leave his town he appointed a delegate who bore his title to attend the councils of other towns or those of the Confederacy. The town chief had also to appoint the time for the annual harvest ceremony. He had personal charge of the town square and the lodges about it, and it was his duty to distribute the broken sticks to the heads of families by which they were to number the days to elapse before the ceremony. The Taskigi have been known to depose their town chief on the ground of inefficiency and to elect another from his clan instead. The title *imko* was used after the full name, as *Nokusi hadjo miko,* 'Bear Crazy Chief,' the last town chief of the Taskigi. The head of the Creek Confederacy council was called *miko* as well, and the title was even applied in a loose way to the high officials of a town when spoken of by outsiders.

Next in rank to the *miko* were three men chosen from any clans called *tastạnagi,* 'warriors,' who formed the chief's council which decided matters of public importance. One of these men was their nominal head and bore the title *tastạnagi łakko,* 'big warrior.' These councilors were the actual potentates of the town in affairs of war or in its relations with other tribes. In later times, when a form of legislation was introduced in imitation of the whites, a sort of court developed out of the public gatherings in the town square. A judge, *futdjidja,* and pleaders, *ahágamanédja,* appeared who imposed penalties of fines and whippings for cases of theft and rape, and death for murder. The *tastạnagi* as police executed the sentences. The title was also used as a term of address and as part of the personal name. [114]

Besides these civil officials there were a few others having special functions in the harvest ceremony. There were always two men of recognized ability in dancing, having also a knowledge of the rites, who were known as *hiniha,* or *hiniha łakko.* Their occupation was chiefly to procure leaders for the various dances or to lead themselves, and to encourage the participants when they became fatigued. War parties leaving the town were always headed by a man of proved physical prowess and cunning, and his title as leader was *pakadja łakko.* Another individual, called *hobáya,* 'prophet,' accompanied such forays. He was versed in songs and rituals with which he could weaken the enemy and blind the eyes of their warriors. He could also foretell events and determine whether raids or hunting excursions would be successful or not. A man who amassed property or raised himself in public esteem by other means was called *isti adjaqa* 'man beloved.' No civil office, however, was indicated by this title, but those bearing it occupied a certain place in the lodges about the square. In a general way 'beloved men ' also means those who have observed all the dietary taboos of the ceremonies, and even, in its broadest sense, those who have undergone the purging and taken their part in the religious performances.

The above names and titles are those used in Taskigi town, but in some of the other Creek towns they were used in different ways and the persons bearing them had different functions.

Facial painting was employed to indicate rank in the town. Persons bearing the title of *miko* or *hiniha* wore black paint on one side of the face and red on the other, coloring either the whole face or only the space around the eyes. The second pattern belonged to ordinary initiated men having the title *taskáya,* and consisted of four stripes, from the cheek-bone to the angle of the jaw, alternating in red and yellow.

The general arrangement for the seating of persons bearing the above titles in the lodges of the town square is given in the accompanying diagram.

THE CLAN. — The Taskigi social unit was, and is, the clan, *matē'kida.* There are at present fifteen of these remembered, [115] as follows, the first four in their order of precedence: Bear

14

(*Nokusalgi*),[34] Panther (*Katcalgi*), Wind (*Hodalgalgi*), Deer (*Idjowalgi*), Bird (*Fuswalgi*), Fox (*Djulalgi*), Raccoon (*Wotkalgi*), Beaver (*Itcaswalgi*), Alligator (*Halpadalgi*), Mud-potato (*Ahalaqalgi*), Mink or Otter (*Okdjatkalgi*), Snake (*Tcitalgi*), Buzzard (*Sulalgi*), Skunk (*Kitnipalgi*), Rabbit (*Tcofalgi*). In former times, no doubt, others existed, but they are now extinct and forgotten. The clans are believed by the Taskigi to have been created in the beginning by the Master of Breath, deriving their animal characteristics from certain traits displayed by beings as they passed in review before him. He enjoined them not to marry their own kind lest they die out, and since that time they have observed the exogamous principle. Clan descent is reckoned through the mother. All the males of one clan call each other "brothers," the females call each other "sisters." One of the names by which a man addresses his clan sister is *anhombida haya*, 'my food maker,' or cook. Property is not, however, generally inherited from the mother, but passes from father to son. The leading clans among the Taskigi are the Bear and the Wind. The town chief was chosen from one of these two. As descent is traced back to the totem animal itself, it is considered wrong for a man to kill or eat an animal having the form of his totem, as it would be the same as eating his own human relations. Such offenders are nowadays punished by fines which have to be paid to those of his clan who catch him in the act. Furthermore, should one person ridicule or belittle another's totem, he is likely to be taken and fined for wrong-doing by the offended clan. The fine is believed to appease the totem. No legislation was carried on by the clan itself, nor was there any clan chief. Murder of a clansman was avenged by concerted action on the part of his kinsmen. But should the murderer escape them and hide until the next harvest ceremony he was received by the community without further molestation. There was no special arrangement for the clans in assembly; they occupied quarters [116] in the town where they chose, having their assigned planting grounds at a convenient distance. The rules of land and harvest tenure have been completely forgotten in Taskigi, owing to their changed conditions of life since their removal westward in 1836.

CUSTOMS

BIRTH. — During menses the woman remained in seclusion and did not come into contact with anything belonging to her household. At the approach of childbirth she also retired to the seclusion lodge and neither she nor the father resided in the usual house for the period of a month. The mother was allowed to partake of food from the time the child was born, but the father fasted for four days thereafter. For a month after the event, the mother was not allowed to prepare her husband's meals nor to eat or sleep with him, and he on his part was not allowed to touch her.

NAMING. — A male child was given no name until he had been initiated, but was known by the name of his totem, *Fuswa* 'bird,' *Tcitto* 'snake,' or perhaps some other epithet derived from a personal peculiarity. Girls were not called by the totem name however, but were generally addressed by the kinship term or named after some natural occurrence or object connected with their birth. This name they retained without change through life. Examples of female names are now very rare.

INITIATION. — When the boy had reached the age of puberty he was prepared for his initiation into the rank of manhood in his town. This conveyed to him the privilege of marrying, taking up land, occupying a man's place in the lodges about the public square, and taking an active part in

---

[34] -*algi* denotes collective plural.

civil and military matters. The initiation of such boys and their acquisition of names took place at the annual harvest ceremony in the following manner: The boy who had been known from infancy as *Fuswa* 'bird,' *Wotko* 'raccoon,' or some other clan name, had to undergo the scratching operation and take the emetic with the men of his town. At a certain time during the procedure of the harvest ceremony, the *tasianagi łakko,* 'big warrior,' arose from his place and called one of the candidates forward. He then presented him with a [117] piece of tobacco and pronounced aloud one of four titles, which henceforth belonged to the candidate as an addition to his clan name. There were four of these 'titles, all of equal rank:

Hadjo 'crazy' 'droll,' *Fiksigo* 'heartless,' *Imáła* 'leader,' and *Yaholo* 'one who makes a loud cry or whoop.' The Big Warrior chose one of these names for each of the boys at his own option. After this simple ceremony the boy was considered a man and entered into a class of *taskaya,* 'warrior' in his town. A rather detailed course of preparation was necessary to the boy before his public receipt of the title, but none of these rites are remembered very well. Examples of men's names in Taskigi are *Nokusi hádjo* 'Bear crazy,' *Kátca fiksigo* 'Panther heartless,' *Wasinda hádjo* 'Washington crazy,' *Tcáswa fiksigo* 'Beaver heartless,' *Idjo yahblo* 'Deer cry.'

MARRIAGE. — When a young man desires a young woman for a wife nowadays there is very little in the way of ceremony to be performed. Desired sexual relations are had at will among most of them, personal attachment being the chief consideration between the parties. The usual method adopted by the young man is to ask the girl's parents for her, and with their consent to take her to a cabin already prepared for them or to reside with the parents until one can be made ready. If the man marries into another town he becomes a member of that town, the children all belonging to it as well. The husband, however, still retains allegiance to his own town and must not play ball at any time against it. Should he do so he is likely to be maltreated by his townsmen in the game, and the name 'traitor' *okáisa,* is given him. A man could have more than one wife, if he chose. Divorce was always possible by mutual consent, but the man was apt to become unpopular. Persons separated in this way never again held any manner of intercourse. The wife sometimes accompanies her husband to his town and resides there; the children in that case belonging to that town.

WARFARE. — As to war, little first-hand information is obtainable. However, on frequent occasions during colonial times the whole town went on the warpath; that is, all the able-bodied men as representatives of their town joined 'their brother towns of the Confederacy in the battlefield. [118]

Small parties of adventurous youths, or raiders, were frequently made up under some proven leader to go out on minor expeditions. It is said that they carried a bundle of magic herbs and fetishes which was in charge of the leader, *imissi* or of the shaman and prophet, *hobaya.* One of the medicines in this bundle was believed to be parts of the horns of a certain mythical snake that was captured and killed by the people after it had destroyed many of them for generations. These horns were believed to render the warriors immune to wounds. Another object remembered as part of the bundle's contents was cedar leaves, *atcina.* When a warrior became wounded he called for the *hobáya* to come to him and give him an emetic of the *atcina* which was thought to insure recovery. A wounded man had little hope for recovery if this could not be done. The *hobáya* was a busy man in battle, for, besides carrying the fetishes and administering the emetic, he had to sing and shout certain songs and formulas which would frighten and confuse the enemy. When such a party returned with scalps they were welcomed in the town-square and often publicly raised to a higher rank in the town and given a new title, such

16

as *tastanagi,* if they were of age, or a title denoting the full rank of manhood if they were boys. Many rites of preparation before taking the warpath were observed in the past, but these are now forgotten with the exception of the practices of taking the emetic made of red root, *miko huyandīdja,* chief physic, and the sweat-bath under the supervision of a shaman.

As already intimated, scalps were taken from enemies. The act was accompanied with a whoop terminating in several tremulous throat tones in imitation of a turkey's gobble. This was given to announce success to the band. Prisoners belonged to the captor, and could be killed by him for their scalps or taken back to the town to be tortured in the town square, or held for ransom.

MORTUARY. — The body, as soon as the soul, residing m the heart, has left it, is treated as follows: The male members of the family take their guns and go outside of the house and here fire them off to make known the death to the rest of the village. [119]

The friends and relatives then assemble at the house and spend some time in mourning and expressing grief. No one, however, cares to touch the corpse in fear of evil consequences. It is said that during an epidemic some time ago there was such difficulty in getting persons to dispose of the dead that the bodies lay around the village unburied until the people had to leave. Only persons who have been properly fortified by magic rituals dare handle the body.

The corpse is then carried to the burying ground, where a grave has been dug, and lowered in. Some relative then discharges a rifle toward the four cardinal points. Slabs of elm-bark are put over the body, and as soon as the earth is thrown in they clap their hands and shout and laugh. Coffee is put in a cup over the left shoulder and clothes are laid along the side of the body. The fresh earth dug from the grave is believed to produce sickness in the form of rheumatism in the person who steps on it. A small house, either of logs or of boards, is then constructed over the grave. A fire is kindled at the head of the grave and tended for four days by the relatives until the soul is believed to have reached the passage to the sky. As soon as they reach home after the interment the members of the family put some powdered ginseng, or white root, into a cup and blow it around the house and yard to keep the spirit of the dead from returning. Formerly horses were killed at the grave in order that their spirits might carry the soul toward the spirit land.

The fire, which was always burning in the house, was allowed to go out when a death occurred, so when the mortuary rites were concluded a new fire was kindled with a ceremony and song called *tu'tkamodjasa ingasúpid,* 'fire new its cooling.'

TEMPERAMENTAL CHARACTERISTICS. — A few remarks on the temperamental characteristics of the Creeks are of incidental interest although not offering much that is unusual to other Indians. The men do not appear to be very desirous of giving the impression of dignity; they mingle freely with others and exhibit a certain loose-mannered joviality. They seem to relish jokes on each other, and a little obscenity adds to the flavor of a story of gossip. Nicknames and comic epithets, [120] such as *Halpạda* ' alligator,' *Istidjulī* ' old man,' *Halpạdadjū'li* 'old alligator,' and others of like nature are frequently given to persons of droll appearance.

In their quarrels, too, a great deal of abandon is shown, and if nothing interferes to stop them, fighters are soon carried away by their fury. Butting the opponent in the abdomen with one's head is a common method of attack. Another procedure, known as "pitching," is employed to obtain mild revenge. The vindicator and several friends waylay the offender, seize him by the legs and shoulders, and drop him upon the ground. They pick him up and drop him in the horizontal position over and over again until he is sufficiently bruised or injured to suit their taste. Fighting of any sort is greatly to the liking of the Creeks.

There is a certain exuberance of spirits among the men which at times finds its expression in bursts of song. When riding along the trail in lonely places, or at night when everything is quiet, in fact whenever the feeling seizes them, they break out into these plaintive strains to drive away spirits which make them feel sad or lonesome, as they say. Of these snatches, or burdens we might call them, there are several which seem to be used indiscriminately when the mind is weighted with emotions of amorousness, loneliness, sorrow, joy, or other excitement. Drunken men may be frequently heard singing in this way. Some of the Indians call the songs "drinking songs" on this account. The syllables are without meaning, and the theme is repeated with some variation in the syllables and in the stress and tones according largely to individual fancy. The key, too, seems to vary in accordance with the singer's range. The best known burden among the Creeks of this and neighboring districts is —

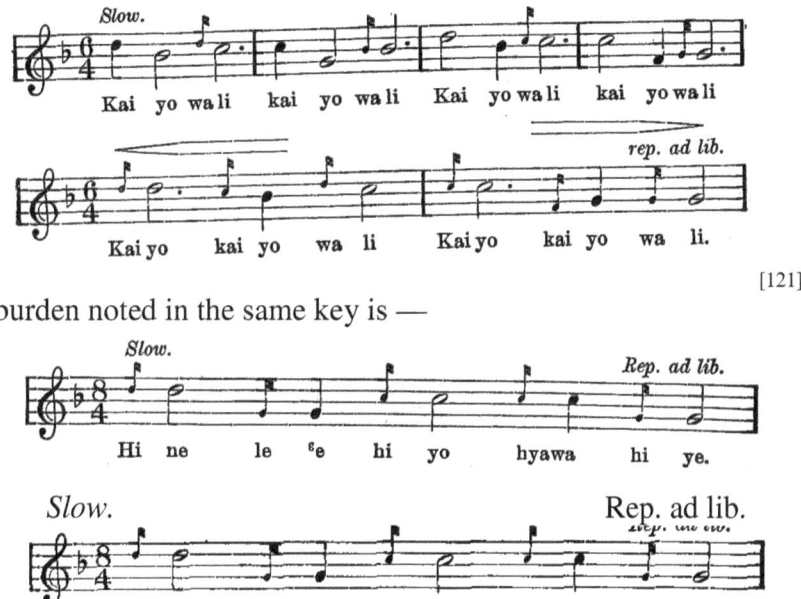

[121]

Another burden noted in the same key is —

SHAMANISM

All bodily affliction is believed to come from the presence of some foreign and harmful matter in the system, placed there by either some animal spirit or a conjurer. So long as this substance remains in the body it can not be cured, and it is likely to come from so many sources that the Creek finds it necessary for his health to be constantly on guard against the operation of malevolent spirits and conjurers by observing the proper taboos.

To have the noxious substance removed, the services of a shaman, *owala,* are required. He must first discover what animal or malevolent spirit is causing the trouble. This is done by secret methods upon which the skill and reputation of a medicine-man usually rest. Some of them can tell a patient's ailment by examining his shirt, for which a charge of twenty-five cents or its equivalent in tobacco is made.

Certain roots and medicines are necessary to the shaman to drive out the trouble, and formulas and songs for various complaints mention the medicines needed. When these have been procured and steeped in a pot, the shaman produces a tube through which he blows into the mixture between the stanzas of certain songs which go with the herbs constituting the formulas. The blowing strengthens the medicine until it is stronger than the causative agency. The

18

medicine is taken by the patient internally and externally after it has been properly exorcised. The purpose of the shaman is to throw the disease into an animal, but not the one that causes it. A medicine-man may also be hired to cause disease in others, but it is dangerous for him to act thus as he might be detected and punished by death. The shaman had a sort of ceremonial rank, too. His position [122] was that of a highly important public practitioner. He even furnished charms for young men to use in influencing the affections of girls, in the nature of songs called *póyagwitska yahaigi*, 'lonesomeness song.'

The origin of the formulae referred to is attributed to the animals themselves. According to the belief that in the beginning the animals made the diseases, so we find that they made the remedies for them. The myth telling of the origin of disease mentions the following animal causes: panther, bear, snake, hog, bird, cat, horse, beaver, dog, lynx, otter, fish, game animals, water creatures, seashore creatures, marine creatures, snakes collectively, fish collectively, small water animals, raccoon, opossum, sky-hog (a sidereal being), rainbow, spirits, earth of various colors and sorts, old fire, buzzard, living people, turkey, water wolf, seashore wolf, deer, rattlesnake, owl, and what-is-inside-of-me. Incidentally some idea of Maskogian concepts of the animal world is reflected in the list. The medicinal herbs and objects mentioned in the formulae as physical aids are, in part, cedar, bird's nest, wild-cherry bark, broken twigs and leaves, corn-cob, sassafras, ginseng, button-snake root, and other plants with the following names, translated from Creek: hog-ear, hog-medicine, deer potato, yellow-in-the-water, in-the-water-white, looks-toward-the-sun (sun-flower), and panther-medicine. A characteristic of these medicinal antidotes is that they are chosen in the belief that "like cures like." For instance, the medicine that goes with the formula for headache caused by the sun is sun-flower, 'it-looks-toward-the-sun'; for the complaint caused by deer, it is deer-potato; for that induced by the hog, hog-ear, and so on. The belief in sympathetic healing and the significance given to cardinal points and colors are also characteristic of the medicine practices of the Cherokee.[35]

The texts of the formulae and songs are invocatory to the various animal causes. They often describe the peculiarities of the deer, snake, bird, or whatever it might be, as though the shaman were following its course of movement in his imagination. [123]

Frequent mention is made of the cardinal points, and a color symbolism is assigned to them — north, *kasapófa*, 'where it is cold,' is black; south, *nigatofa*, is red; east, *hasosa*, 'sunrise,' is white; and west, *hasakalatka*, 'sun-sinks-into-the-water,' is yellow. Even the color idea is extended to the animals, and when one is addressed in a song or formula he is named with first one color then another until the four are completed. The sacred number of the whole Maskogian group is predominantly four. The music of the songs is chiefly a repetition of certain themes with now and then a variation in some notes. At the end of the song the cry of the animal mentioned in it is imitated in many cases.

The plant spirits play an important part in the relief of the sick person. In some such way as the animal invoked in the formula is believed to withdraw his cause, so the spirit of the plants used are invoked to aid in driving the trouble out. The medicines are taken internally and also applied externally. To use a concrete case the deer are believed to cause such and such a sickness. When the words of the formula or song exorcise the deer to relieve the patient, the actual plant matter, which bears some analogy according to the native philosophy to the animal itself and therefore belongs in the same class, is used as the tangible aid in the operation. Hence it happens that a plant called "deer potato" is steeped in water and this is drunk as medicine.

---

[35] Mooney in BAE-AR 7th: 329 et seq.

A few additional folkloristic facts belong here; for instance, gentian is commonly used to put on cuts to draw out inflammation; a terrapin shell charred and pounded to powder is mixed with opossum oil and used as a salve for cuts, burns, or bruises. Rattles from the rattlesnake are believed to be direct causes of sick feelings if they are looked upon. Deer antlers are held in same light, and the Taskigi refuse to touch them on this account. When deer were killed the horns were burnt up lest they cause sickness in someone. A great horned snake is remembered by the Taskigi, the horns of which were used as a powerful medicinal agent.

FORMULISTIC SONGS[36]

The following shamanistic songs and formula were sung by *Kabitcimała* (Laslie Cloud) in 1905 and recorded on the phonograph.[37] Many of the words of the texts are obsolete. This fact, coupled with that of the apparent syncopation and apocopation of many of the verb forms and derivatives, makes the exact analysts of the words very often difficult. Hence the translations, which were offered by the informant, are only approximate ones in many places and some forms expressed in the texts are omitted from them owing to uncertainty.

1. HEADACHE SONG (*Iganuki yahaigida*). — The deer are believed to cause headache. *Mikoamdja*, 'chief physic' (*Salix* species ?), is the root used as a brew. The sufferer drinks a quantity of it and has some blown over his head by the shaman. The formula is sung four times; after each several vigorous blowings are given to the concoction.

Formula: *Hyawahie* (repeated a number of times).
scatter
ahólodjē láni   des   awáhin
cloud   yellow these scatter
hólodēi djádi des   awáhin
cloud   red   these scatter
hólodjē lásti des   awáhin
cloud   black these scatter
hólodjē hátki des   awáhin
cloud   white these scatter

---

[36] The usual accent of words is found to be frequently changed in the song and formula texts to meet the requirements of rhetorical and musical accent. In such cases the sounds and accents are given, as nearly as possible, as they were heard. But where there is uncertainty regarding the accent it is left out, being reserved for treatment when the musical records have been transcribed. The rhythm of the songs and formulas is usually pronounced and regular, but often it shows irregularities which may be attributed in part to the physical infirmities under which the informant, was laboring. The texts, as here given, lay no claim to philological accuracy.

[37] The records are now in the storerooms of the American Museum of Natural History, New York, under the labels P.R. 1048, 1037, 1053, 1068, 1042, 1035, 1036, 1040, 1013, 1034, 1016, 1046. [PR generally stands for 'poison room' because they were filled with cyanide gas to keep out parasites and other harmful critters.]

2. SUN THE CAUSH (*Hassi aledja*). — This is also a headache formula where the cause is believed to be the sun. Sunflower [125] (*Helianthus annuus* ?) blossoms, *hassi yahagi*, 'looks toward the sun,' are used as ingredients of the medicine. The formula is sung four times, with blowing in the intervals.

Formula: *Sīwā* (sung a number of times)
            scatter
            nitta hássi
            day sun
            niłi hássi
            night sun
            kolaslobótski
            small stars
            sīwā
            scatter

3. DEER THE CAUSE (*I'djo alēdja*). — Swelling boils on the body and limbs are caused by the deer. The brew for this complaint is composed of *atcina*, cedar leaves (*Chamaecyparis thyoides*), and *idjo maha*, 'deer potato' (*Licinaria scariosa*). The root of the latter is a bulb, and both this and the leaves are used. The song consists of five parts, the first word, with an invocatory significance, being varied in each. The intervals between the parts are employed in blowing into the medicine.

Formula: *Hafinonogī'ī hidjinomī'ī* (repeated a number of times).
            He patters his feet. We see him.
            djo miko lánudji
            Little yellow deer chief.
            hidōodjides   yawákladi
            we see him   here he was lying
            hī'ya ásasálgosan
            here we run him
            yahwī'łidałin omasdjē'
            here he stood and wandered about

The other four verses of this song are the same as the foregoing, but the first line in each is different. Where *djo miko lánudji* 'little yellow deer chief,' stands in the first verse, the second has *ī'djo adjūli* 'old male deer,' the third *īdjo djofágana* 'yearling deer in his virile period,' the fourth *ī'djo koláswa* 'mother deer,'[38] and the fifth has *īdjudji* 'little deer.'

4. WATER WOIJF THE CAUSE (*Wiyogof yaha alēdja*). The [126] water wolf causes nausea and gripes accompanied with dysentery. The root of sassafras (*Sassafras sassafras*), *wisu*, is the medicine used for this. The formula is sung as follows:

---

[38] The modern colloquial word for 'mother' is *itski*.

Dandayī' (repeated a number of times)
(?)
wīyogofa̠
in the water
yahaláni
yellow wolf
łagwīlagāgadi
they are two big ones (?)
łii̯ᵋ ilabátkin
(?) on the shore
łii̯ᵋ isohōsey
coming from ashes (?)
yosfa hī'ladi
in ashes he died
ī'ladi wo'wo' ohō
he died (wailing)
dándayi (repeated a number of times)
(?)

SNAKE THE CAUSE *(Tcítto alēdja).* — Swelling cheeks, aching teeth and gums are caused by the water-moccasin (*Ancistrodon piscivorus*), *ahálasakáda.* About a handful of rotten wood, *ído ligwi* 'tree twigs,' and dried leaves, *idiwisī* 'tree hair,' are placed in the pot of water and receive the blowing before and after the verses of the following song:

ninoxkulúlwa di[39]
 in the path he was coiled up
dómahasokūlulut dī.
on a long stick he was coiled up (?)
wiyófobákolulut dī
on the edge of the water he was coiled (?)
dīháksamóxkululut ogadī
around a tree branch he was coiled, it was said
dīkaugisókolūlut dī
on a hollow tree he was coiled up
sifsifkit os
he hisses
yilaga hágadī
lying he made a noise
djadáphades
stone is in the grass [127]
hīyoxpidadä'git
(?)
yilaga hágadī
lying he made a noise
dómahásin

---

[39] The *x* occurring in these song texts is a soft palatal spirant.

22

on a long stick (?)
īyoxpidadä'git
(?)
yilaga hagadī
lying he made a noise
nénahasin
in the sunny path
īyoxpidadägade
(?)
īyoxkololágade
(?)
yilaga hágad'ī
lying he made a noise
sifsk
hiss
(Prolonged hissing concludes the song)

6. YOUNG DEER THE CAUSE (I'*djo lowagi*). — Swelling of the joints and stiffness of the muscles are caused by the young deer, born in the same season, or yearling deer, *i'dudji*. Cedar leaves, *atcina,* are steeped in water and blown into four times between the verses of the following song:

īdjodjiyä
little deer
(call repeated four times)
īnádades
the game animals
lowágofan
when they are tender
tcafiknosīd
being healthy
alī'bofan
when they wander about

There are five more verses of this song which in their last three lines are the same as the last three of the preceding verse. Accordingly only the parts that are different will be given.

īdjódjides
the little deer [128]
īláksides
his hoofs
(Repeat last three lines of preceding verse)
īdjódjīdes
he little deer
īsúksodes
his loins
(Repeat as above)
īdjódjides
the little deer

iłáfani
his back bone
(Repeat as above)
īdjódjides
the little deer
īnádjides
his vital parts
(Repeat as above)
īdjódjides
the little deer
ī'gades
his head (Repeat as above)
dogō !!! dogō !!!
(exclamation)
īdjódjiya. !!
little deer
i^{n}wā^n
(imitating cry of fawn)

7. WILDCAT THE CAUSE *(Katcalē'dja)*. — The different members of the cat family, *posi* 'cat,' *kátca* 'wild cat,' or *koakūdji* 'panther', cause nausea and gripes. The medicine used with the formula is made up of a large number of plants and called *koákudjilíswa*, 'panther medicine.' This formula is repeated by the shaman with marked rhythm quite rapidly.

katcalē'dja dī
wild cat was the cause
ī'ga łakko dī
head big
yū'bo łakko dī
nose big
ído łakko dī
face big ' [129]
tółwa łakko d'ī
eye big
hátsko łakko dī
ear big
nógwa łakko dī
neck big
łatsi łakko dī
throat big
ifulwa łakko 'dī
shoulder big
sakpa łakko dī
arm big
łatsi łakko dī
throat big
īi'dabiksī łakko dī

24

(?)
nádji łakko dī
teeth big
hokpi łakko dī
breast big
łafani łakko dī
backbone big
inátki łakko dī
his belly big
isúksī łakko dī
his buttocks (?) big
ihafī łakko dī
his thigh big
īnadjala hid'ī
(?)
sákpadj'alá hidi
arm (?)
hádjidjalá, hid'ī
tail (?)
hadjífana łidjadī
under the tail bone

There are two more verses of this formula which are different from the above only in the first word. The second verse begins, instead of with *katcale'djadi* 'wild cat the cause,' with *koakudji łakko* 'panther big,' and the third has *posi łakko* 'cat big.'

8. SPIRIT THE CAUSE (*Poyafikdja aledja*). — The spirits of the dead, who have not reached the home of the spirits but who wander about the earth, cause fever in its various forms. [130]

The medicines steeped by the shaman for this trouble are given as *kafatska* and *ahalbakstce*, and were unable to be identified. The medicine is given a blowing between the eight verses which are sung. The first words of address are different m each verse, but the rest of each is the same:

djidjiwehegī (repeated a number of times)
(?)
djitskī   *īladī*
your mother   is dead

The other verses have the following words after the repetition of the meaningless introduction.

djiyóban
 (?)
djiłkī
your father (clan brother)
djiłáha
your elder blood brother

25

djīdjō'si
your younger clan brother
djidjítwa,
your clan sister
djitskúdji
your little mother
djibáwa
your mother's brother
djībó'si
your grandmother
djibō'dja
your grandfather

The song ends with the following:

taóokilíns
(?)
djiłā'fani
your backbone
wogódj'weīdjayándom'ī
(?)
djīgāfani
your skull

9 BEAVER THE CAUSE (*Itcaswaledja*). — Constipation and soreness in the abdomen are caused by the beaver. *Akhatka* in water white," probably black willow (*Prunus nigra*), and *adjilalaska* [131] probably a tulip variety, are the roots used in the preparation of the medicine. Four songs of the formula were recorded, each addressed to a different animal believed to be, in the native classification, related to the beaver; namely, the otter, a species of weasel, and a small weasel, probably the ermine.

lä'gadihī'   *ónabaha*
he was sitting (?)   (?)
wahála ᵋahā
south
djā'di ᵋahā
red
ītcáswa ᵋahā
beaver
ili'dja ᵋahā
he kills
iliá ᵋaha
he dies

There are four verses of each song having the only difference in the first two words which indicate the cardinal points and their color symbolism.

hasakalátka	$^\varepsilon ah\bar{a}$	łāni	$^\varepsilon ah\bar{a}$
west	$^\varepsilon ah\bar{a}$	yellow	
honīła	$^\varepsilon ah\bar{a}$	lasti	$^\varepsilon ah\bar{a}$
north	$^\varepsilon ah\bar{a}$	black	
hasosa	$^\varepsilon ah\bar{a}$	hatki	$^\varepsilon ah\bar{a}$
east	$^\varepsilon ah\bar{a}$	white	

The second, third, and fourth songs are the same as the first except that they substitute for the word ītcáswa 'beaver/ osā'nna 'otter,' hoksútko 'weasel (species),' and sagitpa 'ermine,' 'stoat,' respectively.

10. BIRD THE CAUSE *(Fúwalē'dja)*. — Birds cause nausea, gripes, and diarrhea. A bird's nest of any kind, *fus imbognaga*, is steeped in the water as a medicine which receives the blowing before and after the song. It is sung four times.

> hágidosī' (repeated a number of times)
> they chatter
> hágidałitbgi hagī'
> they chatter and flitter about
> hágidosī' (repeated a number of times)
> they chatter
> idạ́lwa lä'git áyamó
> their settlement is here
> fulótkit   ałdogī
> gathering together   they make a fluttering noise
> djil djil
> martin
> tins ti^{n}s (in imitation of the cry made by *tasi*, bluejay)

The following diseases and antidotes are given without the song and formula texts as they have not been completely translated and recorded:

11. FISH THE CAUSE *(Łáło alēdja)*. — Insomnia is caused by the various kinds of fish, and the plant used in the cure is *hilis hatki* 'medicine white,' ginseng root *(Panax quinquefolium)*.

12. SNAKE HUNTING MEDICINE *(Tcitio hiliswạ isfága)*. — Swellings on the face and limbs are caused by snakes. The herb used in curing them is cedar leaves, *atcina*.

13. TURTLE HUNT *(Hilúdja fága)*. — A cold in the lungs, with coughing and sores on the limbs and neck, is caused by turtles. A handful of wild-cherry bark *(Prunus ?)*, *tofạmbī*, is boiled and sweetened to be drunk.

14. BEAR THE CAUSE *(Nokusi alēdja)*. — Bears cause nausea and diarrhea. The whole plant wilana, 'in the water yellow' *(Chenopodium anthelminticum)*, is soaked in water and given to the patient.

15. HORSE THE CAUSE *(Łakko alēdja')*. — Swelling of the abdomen and numbness are caused by horses. A drink is made of four corn-cobs, *talabi*, about four inches long, soaked in water.

16. ALL THE SNAKES *(Tcítto súlga}*. — Swellings on the legs, possibly rheumatism, producing

serious lameness, are caused by a large mythical snake about twenty feet in length with horns on its head. The medicines used in treating this disorder are the roots of *akhátka* 'in water white,' *akdjilaláska, akwa'na* (?), and *ido ligwī* 'tree stems.'

17. RACCOON THE CAUSE *(Wotko alēdja)*.— Insomnia and melancholy are caused by the raccoon. The plant used by the shaman is *tohiligo*.

18. HOG THE CAUSE *(Súkha alēdja)*. — Indigestion is caused by the hog. The whole plant of *sukha hatsko* 'hog ear' *(Hierocicum scouleri)* is used by the shaman to cure it.

SHAMANISTIC CONTESTS. — It was not uncommon formerly for shamans to hold contests to determine their superiority. Trials of this sort were also the occasion oftentimes of meetings with other tribes from which disputes arose. One of these, a translation of which is given, is still remembered by the Taskigi. In the old days the Creeks and the Osage used to have many contests between their shamans, endeavoring to outdo each other in magic tricks. So one time a meeting was arranged between the two people for the purpose of conducting one of these trials on a stretch of prairie a little north of Tulsa, Indian Territory. It was near Bird creek. The Creek shaman of the day was *Pofkadjuli*, a Creek mulatto. The Osage had a great man, and each tribe was expecting that its shaman would surpass his rival.

In the morning they began. The Osage shaman did a trick. He danced and mumbled and performed a wonderful exploit. But when *Pofkadjuli* got up on the space where the contest was taking place, he did one just as good as the Osage's. Then the Osage did another. *Pofkadjuli* equaled him. The Osage did another, but *Pofkadjuli* equaled him again. And so it continued. Now, the Osage kept performing better ones all the time, and the Creeks began to think that *Pofkadjuli* was going to lose after all. At last the Osage made medicine and performed a feat that could not be excelled. Then it was *Pofkadjuli*'s turn. He went out to the plot in the center and began dancing all around the Osage, singing and enchanting, and all the time closing in on the Osage shaman. Suddenly, just as he was in front of the latter, he jerked up his blanket from behind and swung his back around toward the Osage. Immediately a swarm of bumblebees poured from beneath the blanket and crowded about the Osage's head, driving him headlong from the field. [134]

RELIGIOUS BELIEFS AND CEREMONIES

The principal religious ceremonials of the Taskigi, as well as of nearly all the Creek tribes so far as is known, center about the celebration of the corn harvest. As the cultivation of corn is one of their chief occupations, their religious activities are highly concerned with this important product. When the crop has about reached maturity a time is decided upon by the town chief for the celebration. Before this no one uses any of the grain for food, because it is thought necessary for the presiding supernatural being to be properly propitiated beforehand. The origin of the ceremony, or ceremonies, in which this is accomplished is ascribed to the being called *Hisakidamissi*, freely rendered, 'Master of Breath' *(hisdkida* 'act of breathing,' *imissi* 'its controller'). In how far this concept has been influenced by Christian ideas in former times it is now impossible to say. As no other culture-hero, in the broadest sense of the term, is remembered at the present day by the Taskigi, all creations, when thought about at all, and nearly all reasons for the existence of things, are simply attributed to Master of Breath. It is significant in this connection, however, that Hawkins says of the Creeks, referring particularly to Kawita and Kasi'ta towns, that they derived their ceremonies, and fire also, from four deities,

28

Hiyouyulgee (H*ayayalgi* ' light people,' or *Hayalgi* ' teachers'), who appeared from the sky and after instructing the people in the rites and the plants to be used in them, returned to the upper regions in a cloud. The Taskigi, on their part, claim that Master of Life enjoined upon them the necessity of following the harvest ceremony to insure the continuance of the crops and their existence upon the earth as a people. They attribute their present decline naturally to their failure in maintaining the ceremony.

The annual ceremony of the corn harvest is called *Paskida* 'act of fasting' (mentioned by early writers under the form *Busk),* from the fact that no corn is eaten until it is over and that going without certain foods is a part of it. Upon the same occasion the clan totems and other animal spirits are worshiped and propitiated by numerous dances each with its own song and [135] gestures. These address prayer and express gratitude to the propitious ones and correspondingly placation to those that are believed to be nocuous. To take an example, the *stikini,* 'little screech owl' is an unfavorable spirit of the dead, causing death or announcing death to the one who hears it. So the *Siikino banga,* 'Little-screech-owl dance,' is functionally a prayer to the screech owl for immunity from its visits. These dances are performed publicly on the square ground and all spectators may take part freely. In other cases dances are directed, as acts of worship by emulation, to the spirits of animals whose flesh is eaten so that they will not become averse to being killed for food. The emulation is believed to affect the spirits of the dead animals in their reincarnation upon the earth. So with the Fish dance, Buffalo dance, and others.

As many of these game animals are also clan totems it is to be expected that the members of the Fish clan, for instance, when the Fish dance is being performed, are the most concerned, since they are the descendants and kinsmen of the fish. Whether participation in such a dance was formerly restricted to the members of that clan alone, the Taskigi cannot say. The extension of the animistic concept over acculturated objects, such as the chicken, horse, mule, and gun, which contribute to daily existence in the same way as other animals and objects, has stimulated the invention of the Chicken dance, the Mule dance, the Horse dance, and the Gun dance, since the advent of the whites.

A list of the dances performed at the last ceremony a number of years ago is as follows:

Skunk dance, *Kunobanga.*
Gun dance, *Tabótskobanga.*
Mule dance, *Bai'kobanga.*
Alligator dance, *Halpádabanga.*
Duck dance, *Futcobanga,*
Buzzard dance, *Sūlibanga.*
Horse dance, *Tciłákkobanga.*
Rabbit dance, *Tcófibanga.*
Fish dance, *Łáłobanga.*
Drunken dance, *Hāskobanga.*
Leaf dance, *Tiwisībanga.*
Skeleton dance, *Istīfánibanga.*
Crazy dance, *Hádjobanga.*
Buffalo dance, *Yánasobanga.*
Chicken dance, *Tolósobanga.*
Screech-owl dance, *Siikinobanga.*
Long-eared owl dance, *Obobanga.* [136]

Besides these were the Ball-game dance, *Pokidjida obạnga,* to invoke supernatural aid for the players in the ball game, and the Steal-each-other dance, *Dihothbpkobạnga,* where men and women ranged in opposite lines on the square ground and the men tried to snatch the women from the opposite line. This latter is regarded as a pleasure dance. Much licentiousness followed it. Another, known as the Crazy dance, was the provocation of unusual intimacy between the sexes, in which the men made obscene motions and came into bodily contact with the women in circling about the fire. During this dance, and for a short time following, sexual intercourse was promiscuously indulged in, without reprehension, by the spectators and the dancers. Nothing was carried on, however, by force intentionally.

A collection of Taskigi dance songs was made on the phonograph as sung by *Kabitcimała* (Laslie Cloud), but as they have not yet been analyzed little can be said of them. They exhibit some variety in melody, while the rhythm is mostly in twos, in accordance with the drumming which follows or determines the regular stamping step of the dancers, with the weight on the first beat. The songs are divided into stanzas, at the end of which the dancers whoop or imitate the cry of the animal invoked by the dance. To a certain extent the dances are imitative in posture, gesture, and step. The last, however, is about the same in all the dances, being a shuffling advance with first one foot then the other only slightly raised from the ground, then brought down with vigor. A leader, or sometimes two leaders, heads every dance and sings the first period consisting of a few words. Then the followers repeat after him a stanza of equal length or a few syllables only, as the case may be, thus producing a rather harmonious alternation. The majority of the dances take place around the fire in the center of the town square, and the direction of movement is from right to left. In the latter days dance regalia has been abandoned, but probably was used earlier. A stuffed buffalo's head used in the Buffalo dance was the last mask to survive.

Musical accompaniment to the dances is produced by a hand-rattle [137] rattle in the hand of the dance leader, and in many of the dances four women were brought in with dried terrapin shells, having pebbles in them, strapped to each leg below the knee, which produced another heavy rattling sound. The place of these women was just behind the leader or leaders. The drum was also indispensable in most of the dances. This was a hollow vessel partly filled with water and stood near one of the lodges on the square-ground where it was beaten by a specially detailed person.

The foregoing remarks are true in regard to the majority of special dances, but there are other elements of the annual ceremony which can better be described in their order of occurrence.

ANNUAL HARVEST CEREMONY (*Pạskida,* 'Act of Fasting'). — The ritualistic events which marked the annual ceremony occurred in a regular order on certain days. When the town chief considered the corn crop to be about ready for harvesting, he appointed a day for the town to assemble. On this day they performed a few dances for pleasure and cleared off the top layer of soil from the square ground, heaping it in a pile near the southeast corner. This heap of sacred soil symbolized the earth. The lodges about the square were put in good order and their roofs repaired with a new covering of branches. And finally each family departed home with a bundle of small shaved sticks — one for each day before the ceremony. These were distributed as a tally by the town chief.

The *first day* found the families of the town encamped about the town square. The town chief occupied his seat, consisting of a hollowed-out trough-like log filled with leaves and covered with a robe, in the west lodge. With him in this lodge was seated the *hiniha łákko*. The northern and eastern lodges were occupied by the warriors and with them the *tastanagi łákko*. The southern lodge was for women and children, and spectators from other towns (see diagram, page 112).

On this day the use of salt in food was under a strict taboo until the ceremony was completely over. In the morning two men, who had their faces colored black with soot, visited a place the woods where they had previously dug some red root [138] (*Salix* species ?), *miko huyanidja* 'chief physic.' Two others were appointed to secure the button snake root (*Eryngium yuccaefolium*), *pása*. These two roots were sacred plants given to the Taskigi by the Master of Breath as purifiers and insurers of good health in being free from possession by harmful spirits. When these men returned with the plants they announced it by singing and whooping. The rest of this day was spent in dancing the various dances before described. In these dances a peculiar arrangement was made whereby someone besides the actual leader was enabled to learn the songs. A man was invited to dance at the leader's side and repeat the song with him, in that way gradually committing it to memory. The line of dancers was then double, men and women often being side by side. The Crazy dance and the Drunken dance were much favored at this time.

CRAZY DANCE (*Obanga hadjo*). — This is a favorite dance, wherein the leader often improvises witticisms. Amusement is its chief purpose.

LEADER	CHORUS
tciłakko baíixka[40]	*ámo'padédjes*
my mule	saddle him for me
háyapołakko	*djólädjiófan*
big prairie	when we get there
yánasatcifakna	*īlīdja ófan*
young bull elephant	when I kill him
tcáhaiwa itskī	*tēnhombīofan*
my wife's mother .	when we eat together with her
tcáhaniófa	*wásasī míkko*
when she will scold me	Osage chief.
ínhadixsinófa	*wā'sasosalgi*
when I become his son-in-law	many little Osages (children)
ódjutskaiófan	
*w*hen I make them	
háyadidjałákka.	
great morning star	*hā'djahalwadjófa*
pítnadjadjahóga	when it is rising
old turkey gobbler	*djā'hoginpóxhät*
amīdjalíska	when I hear him gobbling
my old gun	*ángałonáyid*
	I start with it on my shoulder [139]
ayíxint	*ī'łołaiófa*
I'll go along	when I get there
ítoładjiłakko	*híxdjät*

---

[40] The x occurring in these songs is a soft palatal spirant.

on limb of big tree	I'll see him
ídohwī'łan	*icixjät*
on tree standing there	I'll see him
hásmīlä'yät	*idjä'hät*
I'll point my gun at him	I'll shoot him

łahä't	*ilidjätłółut*	*tcā'haiwa, ítskī'*
when I shoot him	I kill him, returning	my wife's mother

łáidjogódjät	*łi'sala.gaófa*
I'll take it on my back	when I get there
tcáhadjaw̱algi	*pinhokpīabíswa*
my sisters-in-law	turkey breast meat
dinhombiófa	*sídihanīof̱an*
when we eat it	when they begin quarreling
sidibóhin	*isnafä'kät*
when they get fighting	when I knock them about
ándalogī'bit	
I'll eat it all myself	

DRUNKEN DANCE (*Hā'skoḇanga*). — Men and women dance. The men jostle and grab the women in an obscene manner. This dance is followed also by wantonness. It is a great favorite. The leader sings the song, followed by several women with turtle-shell rattles fastened below their knees. The replies he makes are supposed to be given by a woman, but she does not speak. The leader can vary the words to suit his fancy. It is rather a difficult matter to describe the religious function of the Drunken dance and the Crazy dance. They are explained nowadays as being chiefly for pleasure; but there is some connection in the minds of the Indians with procreation and the supernatural beings who control childbirth.

(A)

yowáhiyi yä
hólena we'
hégaya kai yó wali (repeated a number of times)

giłago	*djahádji*
I don't know anything	I am drunk
nák homi	*temiski*
something strong	we drink with each other
ístama	*he dohaks*
something wonderful	is it not ?

(B)

wehéyona	*hahwēage*	*djakédjiba*
	let us go	they say to me

djahésigo
I have no husband (supposed women speaking)
djíndaba łamónäyas
tell me where your bed is
djiháde nene łamónäyas
tell me where is the road to your home
nohē'yale (repeated a number of times)

(C)

djī'hi waka	*súmhogi ałis*
my husband lies down	(I will) run away from him and wander about
djéhe läga	*sumhogi ała*
my husband stays home	(I will) run away and wander about
djáhe läga	*sumhogi ałis*
my wife stays home	(I will) run away from him and wander

(D)

hoyawē' (repeated a number of times)
yoligō' yanohē' (repeated a number of times)

łisa lä'gosin	*tcinhasin*
when the moon rises	I'll cohabit with you

(E)

yá	*nade gán*		
here	the entire abdomen		
náłkaba degosin	*tcinhasin*		
in the center of the body	I'll cohabit with you		
nódja łis	*niłi*	*hámgosäs*	
I'll sleep with you	night	just one	
nini	*dimbosäs*		
road	close to		
niłi	*óstosäs*		
night	just four		
djógo lískosa	*niłi*	*palosäs*	*łis nodjäs*
that old house	night	just ten	I'll sleep with you

holinā'weᵋ'eye yohalē weᵋehe (repeated number of times)

éhe déb kadjoks	*djíkai hodji kai hosa*
husband will whip her	they say of you, they say of you
éhe náfkadjoge	*djigē' hodjigēe' esa*
husband will strike you	they say of you, they say of you
díinhokoígesa	*djigē' hodjigēe' esa*
he will call you	they say of you, they say of you
hēehenoē'gesa	*djigēe' hodjigē' esa*
when you are called	they say of you, they say of you

The second day was the most important one. The medicine plants were now steeped each in its own pot, by the two attendants who obtained them, as the first step in the approaching ceremony. Then the principal shaman of the town blew through [141] a hollow cane into the medicine, repeating at intervals a formal ritual. This procedure was kept up until nearly noon. On this day nothing could be eaten by the men. When the medicine had become properly conjured the town chief and the other occupants of his lodge advanced to the pots, where they stood before the lodge, and drank about a quart of the decoction each. Then the occupants of the western lodge took their drink, then those in the northern lodge, and lastly the women and children in the southern one had their turn, but they washed only their hands and heads in it. After this the women engaged in dancing, generally performing dances similar to those performed by the men.

On the afternoon of this day the drinking was continued, the intervals between drinks alternating with the *Tafosobanga,* 'Feather dance.' For this important dance, wands about six feet long were brought out from the chief's lodge, each of which had a number of white heron feathers attached to it. These feathers were obtained and the wands made with a certain ritual. A shaman had to make them, as he was the only one who could handle the feathers with impunity. From the time when he commenced making the wands until they were finished he had to fast. The dancers who used them usually paid him something for the wands and the receipt was shared with the town chief. Only the feathers of *wagohatki,* white egret, snowy heron, or wood ibis could be used, and the Taskigi never molested or handled this bird for any other purpose. The dance is said to be in honor of the feather, an important white fetish which shields the people from the attacks of human or spiritual enemies. White is symbolic of peace.

At the end of the second stanza of the Feather-dance song the men, who held the feather wands, whooped and rushed in a body first to the western lodge where the town chief was. They stopped suddenly before this lodge, raised their wands high, then stuck them in the ground. This took place successively in front of each lodge on the square ground at the end of each new song, and before the occupants of that lodge took their drink. [142] After the drinking it did not take long for the medicine to act. The men vomited profusely upon the earth floor of the lodge where they sat. One informant stated incidentally that on certain occasions four women were allowed to take the emetic.[41] The emetic was taken as a propitiatory purification to the Corn deity, and was, with the rest of the rites, instituted by Master-of-Breath.

After the ceremony of the emetic was finished the town chief swept away the pile of ashes from the previous fires in the center of the square ground and fresh wood was brought up. He then kindled a new fire with fresh material and sparks from it were carried by the women to their various domestic hearths from which the old fire had previously been brushed away. This new fire event instituted a new period of time in their religious reckoning, corresponding in a sense to a new year. After this all personal differences, previously standing unsettled and liable to provoke disputes, were effaced and everyone began a new season of peace and friendship. The participants, and in fact all the townsfolk, wore their best new clothing, and all old and damaged property was put out of the way. Some time during this day a formal speech of encouragement to the participants was made in public by the town chief.

From this time on the afternoon was spent in dancing as described before, and the same method for a novice to learn the songs by dancing beside the leader was employed. The dances were then open to all who desired to participate therein for the sake of securing the benefits derived from pleasing the supernatural beings, or for the purpose of obtaining supernatural favor for the town. Strangers from other towns, and even tribes, were invited to participate.

Some time before sunset, however, the racket ball game was [143] played. The game is still played by the Taskigi, but it has been stripped of its ritual and is done nowadays solely for amusement and betting. Only a very brief description of this wide-spread game, *pokidjida,* will

---

[41] It was learned that the Creeks of Hickory Ground town near Henryetta, Oklahoma, allow the women to take the emetic. The first day of the ceremony here is given over to dancing, the second to the taking of the emetic, and the following night and the third day to dancing incessantly without partaking of food until that afternoon, according to one account. For the various elements in the harvest ceremony of three or four other towns, see Bartram, Hawkins, Swan (in Schoolcraft), and Gatschet, above cited. [143]

be attempted. The players each have two sticks with a netted scoop at the end with which to catch the ball. The ball is made of deerskin stuffed with deer-hair, and in its center is a fetish. The goals are horizontal sticks supported on poles about 12 feet high, set 150 yards apart. An equal number of players is on each side, divided into three groups to the side. One group guards its goal, the other holds the center of the ground, while the third is halfway between them. The ball is thrown up in the center and the players then strive to throw it with their sticks through the opposite goal. It is then called "killed." Foul play by touching the ball with the hands necessitates throwing it up again. Twenty goals scored on either side wins the game. Each side used to conjure the opponents' goal with the help of a shaman. If they could get a pregnant woman to pass around the goal sticks it was considered a great piece of luck as it would impair their enemy's running powers. It is likely that most of the rites connected with this game in the neighboring tribes were formerly shared by the Taskigi.[42] Sometimes the men played against the women and then all used their bare hands.

Serious injuries often resulted to the players after these games, and bad feeling between towns engaged in a game frequently resulted from misunderstandings or foul play. On the other hand the ball game is the occasion for squaring accounts between individuals and towns, and even takes the place of minor warfare, as related in the following:

> "*Kasi'ta* town and *Kawita* town are always at odds, especially in the ball games. There is an oldi story to account for this. Once when the *Kasi'ta* men were away hunting, the *Kawita* men went over there and raped all the *Kasi'ta* women. So thereafter the *Kawitas* call the *Kasi'ta* women their wives, and the *Kasi'ta* men are angry." [144]

After the ball game, the men of the town proceeded to the nearest water where they plunged in and washed off all their paint. Before sunset the people all indulged in a feast of corn and other vegetables, and those who had not eaten since the beginning of the ceremony broke their fast as well. The taboo of salt also ceased forthwith.

The ensuing night was spent in dancing as before, amid great relaxation from the strain of the occasion. Ribaldry and licentiousness made this an uproarious night — so much so that it was expected for those of the women who were not wantonly inclined to remain away from the square-ground.

By sunrise on the *third day* the families who had come from a distance began to return to their homes, and the others rested to recover from their fatigue and excesses.

After a lapse of four days, that is, on the *seventh day* from the commencement, it was customary for the town to reassemble at the square-ground for another medicine drinking. This occasion was more informal than the first, and on it the red-root was taken "cold," as they say, meaning without the formal ritualistic accompaniments.

At other times of the year, when desired, the various dances of the annual ceremony were irregularly performed in the evenings when the villagers were gathered in the square-ground. But this was possible only in the old Creek country where the town was more compact. The regular attendance at these dances of all the families for the good of the town was thought necessary only at the harvest time and the new-fire rites.

As a final word in regard to the rites of the Taskigi town and the beliefs connected with

---

[42] For a description of the Cherokee game, see Mooney in American Anthropologist, III, 1890, p. 105, also Culin in *Twenty-fourth Rep. Bur. Am. Ethnology.*

them, it may be expected that there has been some interchange of ideas with the Yuchi Indians, in close proximity to whom the Taskigi have lived since their removal from the East.

Only a few mythical texts[43] and translations were obtained from the Taskigi. From these and other prevalent beliefs which [145] are current among the people but not preserved in any connected form, a partial view of early Creek concepts can be derived. The whole myth fabric of the tribes of the Southeastern group seems to be made up of elements showing close similarity. So the tales and myths from Taskigi town have many cognates in the myths of the other Creek tribes, as well as of the Yuchi, Cherokee, and Choctaw.

In brief, there are several classes of myths among the Creeks. In a rather loose way the first origin of the earth is ascribed to the animal spirits of the sky-world independent of any other agencies. Another class deals with the period when Master-of-Breath effected his innovations on the then existing creatures and made things on earth as they are now. The Creeks assert that they were made from the red earth of the old Creek nation. The whites were made from the foam of the sea. That is why they think the Indian is firm, and the white man is restless and fickle.

But the majority of tales refer to animal trickster events in which Rabbit is the chief actor. These include many of the elements which are found widely distributed over the eastern and central portions of the continent. Among the tales of what are called "the old times" there area number in which the stupidity of their human ancestors is shown in a ludicrous sense, and these are great favorites, being called *hoboŧinigōd*, 'senseless.' Many of the other tales seem fragmentary and aimless. The ones given are all from Taskigi town, but they offer, on their part, nothing particularly characteristic or new. The collection is so fragmentary, however, and belongs so intimately to a complete whole to be found throughout: the Creek Nation, that the discussion of Creek mythology should be deferred 'until a general and more comprehensive collection from its various branches has been made.

Origin of the Earth

The time was, in the beginning, when the earth was overflowed with water. There was no earth, no beast of the earth, no human being. They held a council to know which would be best, to be some land or to have all water. When the council had [146] met, some said, "Let us have land, so that we can get food," because they would starve to death. But others said, "Let us have all water," because they wanted it that way.

So they appointed Eagle as chief. He was told to decide one way or another. Then he decided. He decided for land. So they looked around for some one whom they could send out to get land. The first one to propose himself was Dove, who thought that he could do it. Accordingly they sent him. He was given four days in which to perform his task. Now, when Dove came back on the fourth day, he said that he could find no land. They concluded to try another plan. Then they obtained the services of Crawfish (*sakaju*). He went down through the water into the ground beneath, and he too was gone four days. On the fourth morning he arose and appeared on the surface of the waters. In his claws they saw that he held some dirt. He had at last secured the land. Then they took the earth from his claws and made a ball of it. When this

---

[43] The texts are reserved for future presentation, before which time, it is hoped, a larger number can be procured.

was completed they handed it over to the chief, Eagle, who took it and went out from their presence with it. When he came back to the council, he told them that there was land, an island. So all the beasts went in the direction pointed out, and found that there was land there as Eagle had said. But what they found was very small. They lived there until the water receded from this earth. Then the land all joined into one.

The Origin of Clans

The old-time beings were gathered together. They began acting in different ways and showing different qualities. Master-of-Breath observed them. Some began jumping upon trees and running about. Someone asked, "What sort of beings are those?" "They are like panthers," someone answered. "Henceforth they shall go about as panthers," said Master-of-Breath. Then again, some began leaping and running. "What are they like?" some one asked. "Like deer," was said. "Henceforth they shall go about as deer," said Master-of-Breath. Then again, some went hopping high among the leaves of trees and alighted on the branches. "What are they like?" asked [147] somebody. "Like birds," someone answered. "They shall be birds," said Master-of-Breath. Then again, some were very fat and when they walked they made a great noise on the ground. "What are they like?" asked someone. "Like bears," was the answer. "They shall be bears, then," said Master-of-Breath. Then again, one started off to run but could not go fast. When he came back he had black stripes near his eyes. "What will that be?" was asked. "It is like a raccoon," said one. "That kind shall be raccoons," said Master-of-Breath. Then one was so fat and round-bodied that when he started off he could hardly walk. "What is that kind?" was asked. "It is like a beaver," someone answered. "They shall be the beavers," said Master-of-Breath. Then again, one kind was fat and could not run very fast. When this one had gone off to a distance and returned, someone asked, "What is that like?" "Like a mink." "They shall go about as minks," said Master-of-Breath. Then again, one was very swift when he started to run. He darted back and forth very quickly. "What is he like?" was the question. "Like a fox," came the answer. That kind shall be foxes," said Master-of-Breath. Then again, one was very strong and could pull up saplings by the roots. He went off to a distance and returned. Then some asked, "What is he like?" "Like the wind," was the answer. "That kind shall be wind," said Master-of-Breath. Then again, one started off into the mud. When he had come back out of it, someone asked, "What is he like?" "Like a mud-potato," was answered. "Such shall be mud-potatoes," Master-of-Breath. Then again, one of them had short legs, his back was covered with ridges. When he started out returned, someone asked, "What is he like?" "Like an alligator," was the answer. "That kind shall be alligators," said Master-of-Breath. Then again, one with stripes on his back went running off, and when he came back, someone asked, "What is he like?" "Like a skunk," was the answer. "That one shall be skunks," said Master-of-Breath. Then again, one went away jumping, and when he came back to the starting place, someone asked, "What is he like?" "Like a rabbit," [148] was the answer. "That kind shall be rabbits," said Master-of-Breath. Then again, one went off squirming along on the ground. When he returned, someone asked, "What is he like?" Like a snake," was the answer. "That kind shall be snakes," said Master-of-Breath.

Master-of-Breath, after he had given them their forms on the earth, told them not to marry their own kind, but to marry people of other clans. All the red people know what clans they belong to and do not marry in their own clan. If they did they would not increase.

Origin of Diseases and Medicines

The old people, our Maskogi ancestors, were gathered together in the olden times. The deer said that he was the cause of a sickness. So he made the medicine for its cure. The panther said that he was the cause of one. It was he, then, who made the medicine for that trouble. Then again, the bear was the cause of one. He said that he made the medicine for that. Then the snake caused one, and made its medicine. Then again, the hog said he was the cause of one, and he made the medicine for it. The bird was the cause of one, and he made the medicine for it. Then again, the wildcat was the cause of one, and he made the medicine for it. Then again, the horse said that he was the cause of one, and he made the medicine for it. Then the beaver said he was the cause of one, and made the medicine for it. Then again, the dog said he was the cause of one, and made the medicine for it. Then again, the otter said he was the cause of one, and made the medicine for it. Then again, the fish said it was the cause of one, and made the medicine for it. Then again, the game animals said they were the cause of one, and made the medicine for it. Then again, the water animals said they were the cause of one, and made the medicine for it. Then again, the animals of the sea-shore said they were the cause of one, and made the medicine for it. Then again, the animals in the sea said they were the cause of one, and made the medicine for it. Then the snake tribe said they were causes and made medicines for [149] them. Then again, the animals-moving-about-in-the-water said they were causes and made medicines for them. Then the small-living-things-in-the-water said they were causes and made medicines for them. Then again, the raccoon said he was the cause of one and made the medicine for it. Then the white-hog (opossum) said he was the cause of one and made the medicine for it. Then again, the sky-hog said he was the cause of one and made the medicine for it. Then again, the rainbow said he was the cause of one and made the medicine for it. Then again, the spirits of the dead said they were causes and made medicines for them. Then again, the different kinds of dirt said they were causes and made medicines for them. Then again, new-fire-when-it-is-cold said it was the cause of one and made the medicine for it. Then again, the buzzard said he was the cause of one and made the medicine for it. Then again, living-people said they were causes and made medicines for them. Then again, the turkey said he was the cause of one and made the medicine for it. Then again, the wolf-in-the-water said he was the cause of one and made the medicine for it. Then again, the land-wolf said he was the cause of one and made the medicine for it. Then again, the deer said he was the cause of one and made the medicine for it. Then again, the rattlesnake said he was the cause of one and made the medicine for it. Then again, the owl said he was the cause of one and made the medicine for it. Then again, what-is-inside-of-me said he was the cause of one and made the medicine for it.

Rabbit and Tar-baby

Rabbit and Wolf were friends, they say. Rabbit used to drink out of a well, but he would stir up the water till it was muddy. Then they wanted to kill him for it. To catch him they made a man's image out of pitch and set it where he came along. The rabbit saw the image of the man. He came up close, and said, "Get out of my way!" It did not move. "Out of my way, I told you; I'll kick you!" he said. But it did not move. He went up and kicked it. Then his foot got stuck, "Let go of me!" he said. "I'll kick you with my [150] other foot!" He kicked again with the other foot. It got stuck, too. "Turn me loose, or I'll hit you with my hand!" said he. He hit him, and his hand got stuck. "Turn me loose, or I'll hit you with my other hand!" he said. He hit him with that, and it stuck. Then he said, "I'll butt you again with my head, that is left me, if you don't

38

turn me loose!" The image of the man did not loose him. He struck him with his head, and that got stuck. Then he was caught.

Rabbit Outwits Wolf

Now we'll start with this. Rabbit had played so many tricks on everybody that they wanted to kill him. They set out to get him, and at last caught him with the image of a man made of pitch and tied him up in a bag. Then they held a council to decide what they should do with him to be rid of his mischief forever. At first they said, "Shall we throw him in the river or shall we burn him in the fire?" But Rabbit called out from the bag, "O, don't put me in the fire, but throw me in the river! The fire is terrible; it will burn me to ashes; O, throw me in the river!" He did not want them to throw him in the river because he knew he would be lost. But he thought that if they threw him in the fire the bag might burn so quickly that he could jump out and run away. So he howled that way. Well, they did not know just what to do. Some of them put stones into the bag to make it heavy before they threw it into the river. But they did not decide yet. As it was getting dark they thought it would be better to wait until morning and dispose of him then. So they left him in the bag by the shore and went home. Rabbit did not know what to do.

In a short time Wolf came along that way and Rabbit called to him, "Aha, brother Wolf!"

"Aha!" answered Wolf, "what are you doing in that bag?" Wolf and Rabbit were friends in those days.

"Oh!" said Rabbit, "They caught me and told me that I must eat up four little boys. But I can't do it, and so they are going to throw me into the river tomorrow. Oh, what shall I do! I can't eat up boys!" [151]

"Why, that's easy. I like to eat them up. It makes me hungry even now, said Wolf."

"What shall I do!" cried Rabbit from the bag.

"You let me get in that bag," said Wolf; "I'll show them how to eat up boys!"

Well, Rabbit was willing, so he told Wolf to undo the fastenings. Then they changed places. Rabbit got out and Wolf got into the bag, and Rabbit tied up the bag again. Then he ran away as fast as he could.

The next morning they came to the place to kill Rabbit in the bag. They noticed that it was a little larger than it was the night before, but someone said, "Never mind that!" Then they decided to throw him into the fire. Wolf did not like that, but he said nothing. They put a lot of wood on the fire, and when it burned high they threw the bag on it. It was very hot and Wolf got burned all over, but he managed to jump through the bag where it burned away. Everybody was so surprised at seeing Wolf that they could do nothing, and he dashed away into the woods. He immediately set out to find Rabbit who had thus fooled him. He was going to kill him. Wolf was very badly burned and very angry, and soon he found Rabbit's trail and started in pursuit.

Now, after Rabbit had gone some distance, he looked back. He knew that Wolf would be on his trail. Before long he did see Wolf coming along on his trail and catching up with him, too. So Rabbit crept into a hollow log and lay still.

Pretty soon Wolf came to the place where the log was, and as he was very tired and worried by his burns, he sat down right over where Rabbit was concealed. Then he began to complain about his bad luck: "Everything is against me. All my friends are trying to injure me, and I am deceived and my life is threatened. Ah, if I only could find that Rabbit, I would make him pay for this!" He was whining and complaining. The part of the log where he sat was just over a hole that reached down into it, and from where Rabbit lay he could see up to the buttocks of Wolf. Then he reached up with his claw and tickled Wolf's testicles a little, "Worse and worse!" said [152] Wolf, "Everything is against me. Even the ants have to torment me. How they scratch! And I am all burned too! If I could only find that Rabbit!" So Wolf moved a little to avoid what he thought was the scratching of the ants. But he was over the hole in the log yet, and soon Rabbit could do nothing but tickle him again in the same place. "Will those ants ever let me alone!" cried miserable Wolf. Then he got up and looked into the hole to see where they were, and he was able to see just a little of Rabbit inside the log. Now I've got you, you trickster! And it was you who would still torment me I'll soon fix you! Come out of that log!" cried Wolf. But he could not get Rabbit out. So he said, "I'll go and get an axe," and went to a house near at hand, but they would not lend him an axe. Now, while he was gone Rabbit came out of the log and ran on, in another direction. When Wolf returned to the place, he found that Rabbit had escaped. So he set out on the trail as fast as he could, vowing that he would not let the rascal escape again. At last Rabbit found out that Wolf was gaining on him, so this time he crawled into a hollow tree and got up a little way from the ground.

Pretty soon Wolf came along and tracked him to the tree. "Now I've caught you again, you trickster, but this time you shall not escape! I will surely kill you now!" said Wolf. While he was thinking what to do next, Heron came along. Then Wolf told him that he had Rabbit secure in the hollow tree and he got Heron to agree to help him. They thought that they would surely kill the mischievous Rabbit this time. "Now," said Wolf to his new friend and helper, "I will go and get an axe. I know where I can get an axe. I know where I can get one this time. Rabbit will not get away from me again!" The thought of all the things that Rabbit had made him suffer, made him very angry, and he hurried away to the place where he could get an axe.

Now as soon as Wolf had got out of sight, Rabbit, from the inside of the tree, said to Heron, "Well, do you think that you are going to kill me now?"

"Yes," said Heron," "you will not escape me. I know how to keep watch!" [153]

"Well, you had better keep close watch on me. I am very tricky. Why, I may be somewhere else at this moment. You know you are not sure that I am talking to you from this tree now. You had better look in here and see if I am really here." By this, Heron thought he might not be in the tree, so he bent his head down and stuck it up into the hollow of the tree, trying to get sight of Rabbit. Now, Rabbit had some tobacco and was chewing it. Just then he spit some of the juice into Heron's eyes. Heron pulled his head out, screaming and shouting with pain. He defecated all over the ground near the tree. He was blinded for a long time by the smarting and burning of the tobacco juice. But meanwhile Rabbit came down from where he was and ran away as fast as he could. Heron was still screaming and defecating all around.

Pretty soon Wolf returned with the axe. Heron had partly recovered from his trouble, so that when Wolf came up he was sitting near the opening as though nothing had happened.

"Well, now we shall have him," said Wolf, as he made ready to cut at the tree with the axe. "Yes, yes," answered Heron.

"But whose excrement is this all around here?" asked Wolf.

"Oh," said Heron, "Rabbit tried to get out while you were gone, and when he came down I punished him so severely that he defecated all about. I had a very hard time in subduing him, but he is safe in the tree now!"

Now, Wolf went over to one of the places where the excrement lay, and looked at it. "Is this Rabbit's?" he asked.

"No, that's mine," answered Heron indifferently.

Then going to another, he asked, "Is this Rabbit's?"

"No, that's mine," said Heron. And so on until he had gone all around, each time, Heron answering that it was not Rabbit's but his own. Then Wolf went over to the tree and cautiously looked up into the hollow. He soon saw that there was no Rabbit there. Then he became very angry at being fooled again. He raised his axe and made for Heron to kill him. But Heron saw him coming and with a great cry of "*qank*" flew out of reach just in time to escape. And that is [154] why Herons, when they become frightened, always fly away with a great cry that sounds like "*qank*." So now Rabbit had escaped from his enemies again.

Rabbit Outwits Panther

Rabbit and Panther were friends. They were traveling together. After a while they came to a place where there was a creek with a bad name. It was "*Dofogaga hatchi.*" Now, Rabbit wanted to go on and said that, as the creek had a bad name, it would not be good to camp there for the night. He said, "This creek has a bad name."
"Why is that?" asked Panther.
"Because everybody who camps here at night gets burned up." That is what Rabbit told him.
"Well, I think it will be all right." remarked Panther, "We will camp here anyway."
But Rabbit did not want to, so he said. But at last they made ready their camp for the night, as Panther would go no farther.
So when it got late they prepared to sleep. They had talked all the evening about the place and other things. Now Rabbit asked Panther, "What kind of a noise do you make when you are asleep?" He meant how did he snore.
"Why, I say '*nutslagum! nutslagum! nutslagum!*'" said Panther. Then he asked Rabbit what kind of a noise he made when he slept.
"I say, '*nuts! Nuts! Nuts!*'" replied Rabbit.
Now, they went to bed and in a short time Rabbit pretended that he was asleep. He began to snore, saying "*nuts! nuts! nuts!* And Panther thought that he was surely asleep, so he went to sleep himself, snoring "*nutslagum!*" Now, when Panther was sound asleep Rabbit got up and got a piece of bark and shoveled a lot of coals from the fire on it. Then he threw the coals on Panther, and fell down quickly, lying as though he had been asleep all the time. Panther jumped up, howling with pain, and woke Rabbit. He told him that he was right, that he had been nearly burned to death. Rabbit would only say, [155] "I told you so. I told you so." Pretty soon they settled down to sleep again. As soon as Rabbit heard Panther snoring he thought that he was asleep and got up and played the same trick on him again. But this time Panther was only pretending to be asleep, and he caught Rabbit in the act and jumped up to kill him. Rabbit barely escaped his claws and ran as fast as he could. Then Panther gave chase. Several times he nearly caught him, but Rabbit managed to keep ahead. But soon he began to lose strength. Then to save himself, he made an ocean spring up between himself and the angry Panther. Panther could not get across that. And that is why there is an ocean.

Rabbit and Turtle Race

Turtle had heard that Rabbit was the swiftest runner. So one day he went to Rabbit, and said, "I understand that you are the fastest runner. I want to run a race with you."
Rabbit said, "What! You run a race with me? Why, look at your legs. You can't run at all!"
But Turtle said that he could, and he would not be satisfied until Rabbit agreed to have a race with him. The Turtle set the day for the race, and set the fourth day from that time. He said,

"When you see me with a white feather on my head, you will know that it is I and not some other turtle." Then the Turtle went and got three more of his friends and put a white feather on the head of each. Now, the course over which they were to race was chosen by Rabbit. It was where there were four hollows and four hills. They were going to start on top of the first hill and race for the top of the last. Now, when the fourth day came around, Turtle placed one of his friends in each of the hollows. When, all was ready Rabbit whooped to start, and they started. When Rabbit got to the top of the first hill he saw a turtle with a white feather going up the other hill ahead of him. And when he got to the top of that one he saw a turtle with a white feather going up the next. And so on till the last ridge. When he reached the goal, there was Turtle ahead of him. [156]

"Well!" said Rabbit, "You are a great runner! Who would think that you could run with such short legs!"

Rabbit Fooled by Opossum

Rabbit and Opossum were friends. One day Opossum was sitting under a persimmon tree eating persimmons. Rabbit came along and saw him. He thought that he would like some persimmons. He asked Opossum how he got the persimmons. Then Opossum said, "Look yonder on that ridge. Now run from that ridge and butt the tree with your head and they will fall down." So Rabbit, who had already eaten some of Opossum's persimmons, said that he would get some too, so as to pay up. So he started out for the ridge, and when he got there turned and ran and butted the persimmon tree. But he only squealed *"Twii!"* and fell over dead. "Why," said Opossum, "you were a fool. I climb up for them."

Rabbit Outwits Tie-snake

One day Rabbit and Tie-snake met. Rabbit had heard that Tie-snake was the strongest beast there was, so he made up his mind that he could fool him. He went to where Tie-snake had his den and told him that lie had heard that he was the strongest puller in the world, but that he wanted to challenge him to a contest. "Why, nothing in the world will compare with me in pulling," said Tie-snake. But Rabbit was determined to hold a contest with him. Well, after a while Tie-snake agreed. Rabbit then gave him four days to prepare, and appointed the day.

Then Rabbit went to where another Tie-snake had his den, and told him that he had heard it said that he was the strongest puller in the world, and challenged him to a contest. "Why, you are too small, You can't pull much," said this Tie-snake. But Rabbit urged and urged, and at last this Tie-snake agreed to have a contest with him. So he appointed four days later for the trial, and left him.

Now, Rabbit went to the river where the contest was to be held and fixed a big grapevine across it with an end resting on [157] each bank. This was the way they had of doing the pulling, one on each side of the river trying to pull the other into the water.

On the fourth morning Rabbit took his place in the brush along the river bank, and soon saw the Tie-snakes come to the place agreed upon, and they took hold of the ends of the grapevine and were ready to commence. Rabbit gave a whoop, which was the signal to begin, and the Tie-snakes began pulling. Each one thought that Rabbit was on the other end, but he was pitting them against each other. Now, they kept on pulling nearly all day, and at night they gave it up and went home. The next day Rabbit went to see the first Tie-snake, and the snake said, "Well, I am surprised! Who would ever think that such a little animal could pull like that! I never pulled so hard in my life! Well, you certainly are stout!" Then he went to see the other

Tie-snake, and he told Rabbit that he was very strong, but that nobody would ever suspect it by looking at him.

Now, by winning this contest with the Tie-snakes, Rabbit won also the privilege of going to the river to get his water, instead of having to go to wells for it.

Punishing a Shaman

They had a village far away from the town. They killed a great many deer, where they stayed on a hill. They applied medicine given them by a shaman and were successful. They stayed four days, then returned. When they got to the town they found that their game had vanished. So they gave the shaman a deer in payment. When he ate it, it killed him. That is all.

The Panther and the Deer

There was a panther who went down to the creek to drink. He stopped at the edge of the water and saw a shadow reflected there. It was the shadow of a deer standing on the opposite bank. The panther poised himself and sprang into the water. He crawled out, and when the water settled he sprang in again. He did this a number of times. At last he crept away because this time when the water settled the shadow was gone. The deer on the opposite bank had gone.

Half an hour later the panther was seen to enter his den with a doe thrown over his back.

The Stupid Woman

The people wore deerskin clothes. There was a hunter who went out hunting. He shot a deer and brought it home. He hung it up. The next day he wanted to go out again, and he said to his wife, "You must take the back-bone and throw it in the water." He meant that he wanted her to cook it in the water with the *sófki*. But she threw it in the creek. When the old man got back he asked her if she did it. She said, "Yes." He said, "When the back-bone is cooked in the water it is very nice these hot days. Fix me a plate and I will eat some of it." Then she told him that the back-bone was in the creek and she could not get it. He said to her, "I did not mean that way. I meant to cook it."

Now, in those days they used to have hickory *sófki* too. They pounded hickory-nuts and put them in the water with the *sófki*, and it was very good when cold. The next time the old man went hunting, he told her to put hickory in the *sófki* for him when he got back. So she put a hickory-nut in it. When he got home the old man asked for his hickory *sófki*. She poured it out for him, but he said that he did not taste the hickory in it. He asked her if she put it in. She said, "Yes." Then she stirred around in it with a spoon and at last brought up a hickory-nut, and said, "There it is." He was angry, and said, "I meant to have it pounded up and to have a whole lot put in."

The Foolish Hunters

A long time ago people were very stupid. There were two hunters who started out for turkeys. They had never seen a turkey or a deer, but they had been told about them. As they went along a grasshopper flew up between them when they [159] were about a hundred yards apart. Neither of the men knew what a turkey looked like. The grasshopper new a little way, then alighted on one of the foolish hunters. It alighted on his breast. Now, the man whistled to his companion, and then called to him. He pointed to the grasshopper on his breast. Now, the other man saw the grasshopper on his friend's breast and thought it was a turkey. So he shot at it

43

and killed it. He killed the man too.

The Foolish Cook

They say that the old people were gathered together. A house they made, of bark. When it was raised they settled there and fasted for four days. They had something to hunt the deer with, so they went hunting. They were boasting of deer killing to one another. Now, they had a woman for a cook, who stayed in camp. The fasting hunters went out, but they found nothing, and returned. When they reached camp they wanted food, but there was none. Then the woman cook took a breech-cloth and cooked it and set it in front of them. They ate it. Then they told stories and tried to outdo each other in bragging about killing deer. That's what they used to say about the olden time people.

The Hunters and the Alligator

In the old times there were four hunters who started out to hunt. They made their hunting camp in the woods and had been out some time. But one day one of them disappeared and they did not know what had become of him. The next morning another disappeared. This man had set out to find the first one. And on the next morning the third went to search for the first two, and he also disappeared. Now the fourth hunter took his dog and found their trail. The dog tracked them by a trail of blood to a hollow tree. The hunter found that an alligator had eaten them. Then he had a great deal of trouble. The alligator came out and attacked him. The dog helped the man. A long time they fought and soon the alligator got hold of the dog. And the man struck the alligator on the head and [160] then on the back and killed him. Now, he dragged the alligator home to his people. He told them all about how it had eaten his friends. They all set out for the tree where the alligator lived, and found that the first two were entirely eaten up, but the last one was not all gone. They took the bones of the third man and went home. Then they held a great feast and carried him to the grave. On the next night they had a war dance for farewell. That was the end of him. After the fourth day they called all the people together and all went to the place where he was buried, and camped. Then they held a farewell feast there. That is the story they tell.

The Talking Dogs

There was a young man who loved a young girl. Soon he married her, and in a short time started on a hunting trip. He took his dogs and set out. But his luck was no good. Sometimes he would strike a bear's trail and after a while would get a shot at the bear, but he could not hit him with his arrows. This kind of thing went on for some time. Then he gave it up and went into the woods and lay down to sleep. He lay beside his dogs.

Soon he heard a strange noise out on the prairie, and when he got up and looked he felt very uneasy about it. The oldest dog became restless too, and soon left the camp. He did not return. So the man decided to follow him. He followed for some time and soon emerged from the timber out on the prairie. It was bright moonlight. There in the light the hunter saw his dog talking with some other animal. It was a wolf. When the dog saw his master, he turned and said to him —

"We are having poor luck in hunting!"

The man was too surprised to answer, as the dog was speaking to him in his own language, and he never knew that dogs did that. The dog then said the same thing twice again.

Then the hunter said —

"Yes, we are. But who were you talking to?"

"I was talking to a wolf," he said. "The reason for our bad luck in hunting is that the woman you married is unfaithful. [161] She has another man, and your guiding spirit has left you. You are disgraced, and that is why. You must kill that man."

After he had heard this speech from the dog, he thought about it. But he did not want to kill the man.

Then the dog spoke again and said, "We will do it for you. You wait here."

So the wolf got his kinsfolk, and together with the dog they started out for the town where the hunter had left his unfaithful wife. They reached this place at night and found the man in bed with the hunter's wife, and killed them. Then they returned to the hunter's camp and found him. By this time he had a great deal of meat all dressed. They all joined together and had a great feast. From that time the hunter had good luck. Now, he broke camp and went home to his town. He went to the house of his mother. When he saw her, she said, "You have had bad luck. Your wife is dead. But it is not so bad because she thought that you would never come back. So she went and got another husband. And one night the wolves came and killed them both."

But the man knew it before she told him.

The Hunter and the Talking Dogs

One man went out hunting in the old days. He had five dogs with him. He pitched his camp in a certain place. Now, all these five dogs knew how to talk; and more than that, they knew beforehand what was going to happen. Then they would tell their master. After their master had gone to sleep they would turn themselves into deer and go off amongst the deer. But the hunter could not seem to kill any deer.

These five dogs loved their master. Soon there was a great starving time because he could kill no deer. Their master was now nearly dead from hunger, so in order to save his life they made themselves into animals. Therefore they turned to deer. He was asleep. They went out as deer and returned with five deer in their company. When they arrived with the deer, he was asleep yet. They said, " Master, get up; it is daylight! We have been starving a great deal, but now we are to have a [162] happy time! Now, get your gun!" They had the five deer with them. Then they said, "Master, you must kill the smallest deer first. When you have killed the smallest, then kill the other ones. If you kill them all, you can lie down and we'll do the packing and carrying. You mark out the hides across the belly, and we'll do the skinning, too." The hunter stayed at the camp, the dogs brought them in and he did as they said. Then he took his knife and cut the hides and they did the stripping. They told him to cut the meat so that they could manage it and pack it up. "And when we have packed it up, we'll eat the smallest deer for a love feast. We'll eat all together." Then the smallest dog said, "Eat the smallest and first deer, and it will be great enjoyment. Roast the smallest deer first, it will roast more quickly. Put on a pot of *sófki*, and we'll build a fire around it when it is ready. When all is cooked we will eat together."

They built a fire, and the meat and the *sófki* were cooked. The little dog spoke again, and said, "This is the first time that we have feasted together for love. When we eat together we shall know what is going to happen next."

The oldest dog said, "We have been starving, but now we have plenty. You have great influence and plenty to eat; now, who is to be the first in starting to eat? It is the young meat, and the youngest dog ought to start. But whatever you say must be done. I was young when you began to teach me to talk; now I am old. The younger ones you taught to talk. That's why we are all out today. Do you love all of us?"

"Yes," said the man, "I love you all, the five of you."

Then the largest dog spoke again. "I asked you who should start to eat the meat. The deer was young. So we leave you to decide, now."

The little dog then said, "Master, you begin. The master always eats first and feeds us afterward. So keep it up. You fix it and we'll eat it. We haven't eaten for ten days."

The old dog said, "Let's eat clean food, to make love between us all."

Then the master told them to go and get some leaves to [163] spread on the ground to eat on. They did it. The man was weak and could hardly walk. The meat lay close to him, so he spread it out before them. When all was ready, he said, "Now if we are ready, let us eat." The master took a bite.

The small dog said, "Take five bites of meat. Take only five drinks of *sófki*. If you take more than that, things will not go right with us. You must think about this, and not miss what I tell you."

This worried the man. Then he thought and remembered that when a man is very hungry and eats too much, he will die. That's why the little dog spoke to him so.

"Did you see what I told you might happen?" asked the little dog.

"Yes," said his master.

"If you eat too much, you will get so weak that we can not get you home." They all agreed.

On the first evening they ate only a little. The large dog said, "We'll eat a little bite all around. On the next morning we'll eat more and then we will defecate more. I couldn't defecate well because I was eating grasshoppers. But now I'm all right, I'll defecate meat. We'll keep busy eating, but when we get home they'll be nearly dead."

So in the evening they prepared to go home. There were five deer, and each was packed, and they started off. Their journey was one and a half days. The man found his wife and children nearly dead when he arrived home. Then the small dog said —

"Let's eat a love feast with your family as we did in camp. Cut off the meat well, and we will hand it to them. In the evening, cut off two chunks for each. This will be because we have escaped starvation. After giving it to us this way, tomorrow we will all eat together." Then they ate a love feast, and all got well.

"If it is going to be the last, let us all eat together again," said the big dog. "Take the deer bones and make soup in the trough. You have been eating with us, now go back to the old way, and eat as you used to, without us. We don't know [164] when we'll have another love feast. This is my last day. We have gotten home safely now, but in ten days I'm going to leave you. I'm going to die."

In ten days all the dogs died. "I never can get such dogs again," said the master. He and his family grieved, and decided to raise no more dogs.

On the seventh day, before the ten were passed, the master wanted to die too. But he lived to see all his dogs die. After they were all dead, he did not want any more dogs. They were prophets while they lived. "It troubles my mind to know what things are going to happen beforehand," said he. He lived till he died without owning any more dogs.

UNIVERSITY OF PENNSYLVANIA,

PHILADELPHIA.

John Reed Swanton (1873 - 1958)

As Julian Steward[44] wrote for the National Academy of Sciences, John Swanton was born after his father died and John and his two brothers were raised frugally by his mother, grandmother, and great-aunt. "This matriarchy, whose ancestors included several clergymen, stressed moral and religious values more than an intellectual life, although his mother managed to provide for his education through college" as well commitment to Swedenborgians. He married Alice M. Barnard on December 16, 1903, and their three children were Mary Alice Swanton, John Reed Swanton, Jr., and Henry Allen Swanton. He died in Newton, Massachusetts on May 2, 1958, at the age of 85.

"His adherence to the Swedenborgian religion, or the New Church or Church of the New Jerusalem ... He found this faith congenial in contrast to some of the sterner orthodoxies of New England; for it taught "the continued existence of man after death in a life of active service," liberated him from the "abhorrent view" that after death man lay "prone in the ground waiting for a final 'judgment,' " and freed him from the belief in an "illogical and inconceivable tri-personal Deity." [Swanton was one of the founding members of the Swedenborg Scientific Association in 1898.]

"But there was a more specific feature of Swedenborgian teachings which had central importance to Swanton. Emanuel Swedenborg believed that he had had direct and free communication with the inhabitants of the spirit world. Owing to the rigors of his scientific training and his respect for empirical research, however, Swanton had rejected the claims of psychical research that mental telepathy, spirit communication, and the like were possible. This created a serious dilemma and inner conflict, and it caused Swanton to keep his opinions on religion to himself. He expressly attributed his lifelong digestive troubles to the partial "mental withdrawal" this entailed. The conflict was resolved by the researches of Dr. J.B. Rhine and other parapsychologists, which he considered to constitute such proof of extrasensory perceptions as to substantiate his religious convictions and to warrant his finally speaking out on the matter. After his retirement, his friends were a little astonished to receive a number [337] of mimeographed memorandums which did not proselytize but urgently admonished that they keep an open mind on the question of extrasensory perceptions."

"The Bureau [BAE] was made to order for a man of Swanton's temperament. Extraordinarily shy and prone to digestive ailments, which he recognized as largely of nervous origin, he found the Bureau a retreat and refuge from the demands of a more public life. He did no teaching, and only rarely lectured. When bestowal of kudos forced [332] him to appear in public, as when the fruition of his historical research brought national honors in connection with the celebration of the four hundredth anniversary of the De Soto expedition, the occasions were truly terrifying ordeals. Even the gathering of a small group of his Smithsonian colleagues upon his retirement to express their personal affection and scientific esteem and to present him with an armchair and reading lamp was as embarrassing to him as it was heart-warming.

"Despite his extreme shyness, Swanton helped the growth of his profession in many practical ways. He was a founder of the American Anthropological Association, which he

---

[44] John Reed Swanton (1873 – 1958). A Biographical Memoir by Julian H. Steward, National Academy of Sciences, Washington, D.C., Any opinions expressed in this memoir are those of the author(s) and do not necessarily reflect the views of the National Academy of Sciences 1960: 329, 335, 336. http://www.nasonline.org/publications/biographical-memoirs/memoir-pdfs/swanton-john.pdf

served as president for one year and as editor for many years [1911, 1921 – 1923 as a compromise with Boasians]. He was president of the Anthropological Society of Washington and the American Folklore Society, and vice-president of Section H of the A.A.A.S. He served on the Social Science Research Council and the National Research Council. He was elected to the Washington Academy of Sciences and the National Academy of Sciences (1932), was made Corresponding Member of the *Societe d'Anthropologie de Paris*, and was appointed a member of the *Cuban Orden Nacional de Merito de Manuel de Cespedes* with the rank of "Official."

Swanton hugely benefited from the Carnegie Institution's funding of Nancy Miller Surrey to calendar French colonial documents and then to provide copies to US repositories.[45] He culled these sources as they arrived "so thoroughly that the job is virtually done for all time; for ordinary purposes, one consults Swanton rather than the primary sources."

As his DC Smithsonian colleague Neil Judd reminisced:

"John R. Swanton, who joined the Bureau staff in 1900, was an even more tireless and proficient writer ... Prior to his retirement in 1944, he wrote twenty essays, five for the old, royal-octavo *Annual Reports* and fifteen for the *Bulletins*. In four of the *Bulletins* Swanton generously credited others for aid although he plainly did all the work. His first Bureau of American Ethnology assignment was with the Haida as part of a three-way [43] plan arranged between Franz Boas and WJ McGee for researches among the Northwest Coast Indians. As potboiler jobs, Swanton reported upon the Chinooks, the Dakotas, and the Sioux. Later he turned his thoughts from the Northwest to southeastern United States and became our foremost authority on the aboriginal peoples of that area.

"Swanton's informative essays on the Creek Indians (*Bulletin* #73), the Choctaws (*Bulletin* #103), and the Caddoes (*Bulletin* #132)* were only preliminary to his unparalleled *Indians of the Southeastern United States* (*Bulletin* #137) and his *Indian Tribes of North America* (*Bulletin* #145) — anthropological histories that were recognized, in part, by his election to the National Academy of Sciences in 1953 and by his designation as recipient of the Viking Medal and Award for 1948.

"Swanton's scholarship and his knowledge of southeastern Indians and their background led also to his appointment as chairman of the De Soto Commission, of whose official report he was the unnamed and unheralded author. This report, no less than the bulletins noted above, is still in demand. Together they comprise a lasting contribution to American history.

"Quiet and self-effacing, even among his colleagues, Swanton was by no means a recluse. Tall and thin, he looked perpetually undernourished; as a follower of Swedenborgian philosophy, he was overly sensitive to human weaknesses. He measured the foibles of his neighbors but remained silent. As a gentleman and a scholar he had no peer.

"Franz Boas, professor of anthropology in Columbia University, had been interested in Arctic peoples and their languages since 1883. He wrote a lengthy article on the Central Eskimos for the *Sixth Annual Report* (1884-85) and may have received a small sum in return. He was employed three months in 1888 preparing Salish vocabularies (10th *Annual Report, xxiii*). In 1894 his *Chinook Texts* was published as *Bulletin #20,* to be followed shortly by *Kathlamet Texts* (*Bulletin #26)* and *Tsimshian Texts* (*Bulletin #27*). To judge from [44] the record, few Institutions at that time accepted linguistic material for publication; therefore, having opened the door, Boas speedily attached himself to the B.A.E. and

---

[45] As noted in #1, Patricia Galloway, *Practicing Ethnohistory* 2006: 3.

considered himself a member of the family [Judd, a suspicious WASP, had Boas censured].

"On January 1, 1897, [Boas] wrote WJ McGee, acting director, "as one of the most sincere friends" of the Bureau, to relate gossip he had heard "of personal squabbles and enmities" within the walls and to complain of "Major Powell's deliberate slowness in publishing ... accumulated material" (B.A.E. File 4372). On October 9, 1899, he asked $350 each for three manuscripts. Apparently it was a custom of the times to pay not only expenses for assigned work but sometimes a fee in addition. Nevertheless, Boas complained of the secretarial assistance made available to him, the delays in typing, and the inadequacy of the Bureau's symbols for linguistic recording.

"In 1901, Boas moved from Columbia University to the American Museum of Natural History as head of its department of anthropology, and shortly thereafter he and WJ McGee agreed to a plan for Northwest Coast researches toward which the Bureau would supply a scientist and his salary, the American Museum would provide field expenses, and Boas himself would supervise the researches and their results.

"In consequence of this arrangement John R. Swanton, who had joined the B.A.E. staff on September 1, 1900, was chosen for studies among the Haidas and Tlingits. Following his return, Swanton's first Bureau paper was a ninety-four-page article, "The Tlingit Indians," in the *Twenty-sixth Annual Report* (1904-1905) and then a second, *Haida Texts and Myths,* in *Bulletin* #29.

Immediately following is the much more fascinating 1950 account of his own life and his supportive role in major projects, expeditions, and excavations in pioneer Americanist research.

Notes Regarding my Adventures in Anthropology and with Anthropologists
[John R Swanton]

When I was still in my teens in Gardiner, Maine, where I was born, I instituted a system of self-elevation consisting of a course in the reading of miscellaneous volumes on human history. I had an American history of course, and I had a history of Greece, and a universal history. I saved up my various earnings and donations for a three volume work entitled "The Seven Great Monarchies of the Ancient Eastern World" by George Rawlinson, brother I believe of the celebrated Henry who opened up Assyrian archeology. [I still have it.] Later I possessed myself of a copy of Labberton's "Historical Atlas," and at a much later period was reminded of this by being presented with another copy by my associate in the Bureau of American ethnology, Mr. J.N.B. Hewitt. This being the age of simplicity and naive credulity, I accepted everything I read as gospel truth. The serpent of adverse criticism had not yet entered into my peaceful Garden of Eden. Besides the books I owned I drew rather heavily on the small but excellent library of my native city, and among its volumes fate led me to Prescott's "Conquest of Mexico," the reading of which marks a definite turning point in my career. I may be more specific and say that the turning point came when I read those passages of Prescott's magical prose in which he describes the pyramids of Teotihuacán and speculates upon their origin. That directed my interests from history in general to ancient history in particular and still more to the ancient history of our own continent. Full of that enthusiasm I followed Prescott's Mexico up with his "Conquest of Peru," and then went on to H.H. Bancroft's monumental work, confining myself to the first three volumes it is true, and I also added "Footprints of Vanished Races," and several others dealing with the "mysterious Mound Builders, " among which I remember a most unsound, but therefore highly interesting, volume entitled "Ancient America" by one Baldwin who I believe was a former congressman. Perhaps that accounts for his ability to make myths attractive.

In the fall of 1890 I accompanied my chum Alexander Forsyth and his [2] family to Chelsea, Massachusetts, where Alex and I entered the high school to prepare for Harvard. Our reason for selecting Chelsea as a spring-board undeterred by the current by-word "as dead as Chelsea" was the fact that my chum had relatives there. At the end of that year we took our entrance examinations, and Alex and his family moved to a house in Somerville just over the Cambridge line so that he could attend college. In the meantime, however, I had decided that, as I should be obliged to enter with conditions, it would be best to take one more year at Chelsea, and this time my family took a house in that city, one on the slope of Bellingham Hill and just around the corner from the school. My brothers were then at the M.I.T.

Our family was increased, nevertheless, by a cousin from Bath, Maine, with the same first and last names as myself. He entered the same school to prepare for "Tech," where his brother Fred had been a senior, in the class of 1890. Fred and John were almost diametrically opposites, different in character, Fred being studious and aloof, while John C. was athletically in inclined and a social favorite with both boys and girls. John C. played first base on the Chelsea team that year and his home run brought in the winning runs in the game against Lynn. We drilled together in what was called the Second Massachusetts School regiment and were in the competing company in the annual field day at Brookline where our school landed about in the middle. Next year we all moved over to Somerville to live with Alex's family, and I entered Harvard in the class of 1896 while John C. entered "Tech." After a time, however, my brothers found the distance from the Institute too great and left us.

My decision to take a second year at Chelsea was vigorously opposed by my chum but proved, unknown to either, of us, to mark another turning point in my career, for it was in the Harvard catalogue published ... that instruction was indicated for the first time in "American Archaeology and Ethnology," though only to "properly equipped graduates." When I saw [3] that I remembered Teotihuacán and decided that American archeology and ethnology was what I was going to study. In order to prepare for the "graduate work" offered, I called at the home of Prof. Frederick W. Putnam who had succeeded Jeffries Wyman[46] in charge of the Museum of Archaeology and Ethnology and asked him to suggest suitable preparatory courses. His suggestions were decidedly variegated and may be set down for the edification of present day Americanists. Besides the three, or rather one and two half, prescribed courses in English, I added an advanced course in English composition under Professor Barrett Wendell which proved of utility later as I knew little about English in spite of having spoken what went by that name in New England, and having written a history of the world on a series of composition books. In this connection I may add as one of my youthful enterprises that I set down long lists of monarchs, presidents, and other heads of states, even including, I believe, the monarchs of Ashantee or Dahomey, I forget which. A contemporary interest in geography was evinced by another set of blank books in which I set down the names of every town and city in the six New England states together with the latitude and longitude of each – somewhat liberally construed. Prof. Barrett Wendell had a red beard and a pronounced English accent but professed to be something of an anglophobe on account of some Dutch ancestry. We had to present daily compositions in his course and these were afterwards exchanged and we were asked to correct one another's. I remember to have handled most severely the three best compositions handed to me because I could not seem to find anything the matter with them and thought it was my duty to confirm. One of these compositions was by a youth who afterwards became well known. I was rather good in expositions, not so good in forensics, and distressingly medium in imaginative work though one of my compositions was spoken well of and another was rather good except a bit too moral. I believe I shocked Prof. Wendell when the question of seventh-commandment stories came up by saying that, as to that commandment, all I wanted of my heroines was to keep it. Such a sentiment was not so heretical then as it is today. [4]

There was one course prescribed for freshmen besides English, Chemistry A, which consisted in one lecture a week in chemistry for the first half year. This was in part to acquaint budding intellects with a fundamental subject which they might have escaped in their preparatory schools, and in great part it would seem to give a somewhat mellow professor something to do instead of retiring him. He died a year later, I believe, but I do not know whether my class was to blame or not. Our mental labors were shortened in this course from the very beginning since we were told that everything that was to be on the examination paper would be told us at the last lecture. This has a kind comic opera suggestion, but Prof. Josiah Cook was no comic opera performer. He had been one of the great chemists of his time and he made one remark which has been with me through the years and that is more than many of my other teachers can say. This was at his very first lecture when he said something like this, "During my life I have had to learn two different systems of chemistry, and, I do not believe that the one I am about to explain to you is final, but it has been found extremely useful." It is only this small man who gives you to understand that he has the last word on any subject.

---

[46] {Jeffries Wyman inaugurated archaeological study of sites, especially mounds, in both Maine and Florida.}

The remainder of my courses as they were suggested by Prof. Putnam, are as follows: One course in general history, two courses in Fine Arts, including Prof. Horton's famous Fine Arts 3, Davis's courses in Meteorology and Physical Geography, Shaler's introductory course, Geology 4, and his advanced course in Palaeontology, Introductory courses in Zoology and Botany, one and a half courses in French, three in Spanish, and Philosophy 1. In this last we had three of the great men of our time as lecturers, Palmer in Logic, James in Psychology, and Santayana in Philosophy proper. Palmer had to me the atmosphere of a literary surgeon. If I had been brought into direct personal contact with him, I should have expected to be laid wide open by one stroke of his incisive intellect. James would probably have been just as capable of doing so but he seemed to be far too kind-hearted to do it without the most liberal use of anaesthetics. It was perhaps a slight foreign accent that made me think Santana [5] a bit affected. I should have feared to approach him, just as I should have affeared to approach Professor Charles Eliot Norton, for fear of shocking his aesthetic feelings. Only James carried about him the atmosphere of "a classless society," but I never had any intimate dealings with him.

William Morris Davis and Nathaniel Southgate Shaler I would link up as in some measure parallel to Palmer and James, Davis being the surgeon and Shaler the human being. Nevertheless, I derived enormous advantage from Davis. He was rigidly scientific and taught one to weigh the last grain of evidence before announcing that a fact was indeed a fact. On one occasion, I thought I would interest him by telling of an old sea beach I had discovered near the Kennebec River. "Not a sea beach," he said, "not a sea beach. It may be a sea beach, but that is to be demonstrated." Such a reply was a bit shooting but good for early training in scientific method and good also for the soul. However, I never had a feeling of affection for him as I did for Shaler. To be sure I was a member of a class which the latter declared had treated him with the most contumely he had every experienced, but in his advanced course I learned more of the Doctrine of Evolution than from the volumes I subsequently read. He was a pronounced Lamarckian and enjoyed nothing so much as to point to certain organs or certain characteristics of an animal and say, "that would be useless until fully developed, and how could it have come into existence through the selection of slight variations?" Or, he would say. "That is a very, beautiful feature, but it happens to be hidden entirely out of sight, and how could it have played any part in sexual selection?" On one occasion I asked him "What do you mean by accidental variations?" "By an accidental variation," he said, "we connote – and denote – our ignorance. We do not know what causes them." And as he said so he smiled all over. While Lamarckianism is, I believe, out of fashion in biological circles, but the points Shaler raised still fit illy into the selectionist pattern.

Prof. Mark's lectures in Zoology demanded an attention conducive of headaches since he rarely repeated himself, unless one bought a set of notes, and [6] I seemed to be one of the few who didn't. It was in Zoology 2, I think, that my afterward famous classmate Walter Cannon acted as a laboratory assistant. One course in Zoology recommended by Prof. Putnam I fell down on. Many in my family are susceptible to the sight of blood and even cannot bear to hear stories of accidents. In spite of that I valiantly dissected everything presented to us in the laboratory up to and including a dogfish, but when we began Zoology 3 and were presented with a cat to pull apart, I nearly passed out and dropped the course. That ended my career in the Zoological department except for a half course in Osteology which I took as follows. The course was then under an old gentleman named Slade whose health was fragile. His instruction, which had once been somewhat formal, was now reduced, or it was reduced in any case at least, I being incidentally his only student, to perusing a textbook on osteology by a scientist named Flower, and going over trays containing the bones of various animals. This examination took place in Dr. Slade's office in the Agassiz Museum. Midway of the year, however, Dr. Slade fell sick and was confined to his home. When he left, he made arrangements with the janitor to let me into his office and continue osteologizing all by myself. For a few days that worked very well, but presently, while I was busy with my (or rather the) bones, a sharp-featured gentleman let himself through the office, eyed me suspiciously, and then passed on without saying anything. However, the next time I repaired to the Yorick chamber, I found the door locked. I hunted up the janitor, but he said that a day or two before Agassiz (Alexander of course) had come through and found someone whom he thought had no business to be there. Hence the lockout, the "someone" being of course me. That was the first time. Many years afterward I was suspected by the good people of South Carolina of being a German spy, and on another occasion in Texas I was taken for a man advertised in the local paper who had fled from his family. All of which goes to support Mr. J.N.B. Hewitt's aphorism regarding "anthropologists and other suspicious characters." The dangerous nature of my profession seems, indeed, to have been of long-standing, [7] since I am told that gendarmes were present at all the early meetings of the Anthropological Society of Paris.

I presume the incident above narrated shows the difference between Alexander and his father, but I entertained no ill-will towards the former who was presumably acting in what he conceived to be the best interests of his Museum, though I am somewhat puzzled to know just what damage my examination of bones was supposed to produce. The rest of my course of study in osteology consisted in studying the skeletons in the exhibition halls, and perusing Flower. All of this yielded me a C which was, indeed, all that could reasonably be granted though I was hardly to blame for the chaotic nature of my introduction to the study of bones. Poor Dr. Slade died, I think, the following year.

This C [grade] was one of four others. It was the best I could get in English C though I might put up a claim that the gentleman who rated me was over influenced by the title of the course. I got a B, in fact, in English B, but here the hypothesis seems to break down for I did not get A in English A.

The C's which I particularly regretted were two in Spanish 1 and Spanish 2 which were in charge of a very precise and aesthetically sensitive professor named Nash. Professor Nash (I would not dare call him Prof. even now) was very particular regarding the exact wording of one's translation. I have seen him begin to wriggle in agony when some student not similarly endowed emitted a rendering which, although it might convey the sense of the original, was in English of questionable validity from the point of view of construction. Although I sometimes produced this reaction in our instructor, I did not commit the sin of translating *malos fisicos*, "bad physics" like one of the sports. That I was not a complete dunce in my knowledge of Spanish was proven when Nash was retired and his courses given to an Assistant Professor whose name, Marsh, rhymed with that of his predecessor, but whose method of rating students was preferable. From him I got an A– during the first half year, but for reasons in no way connected with the instruction [8] decided to drop it then. Perhaps I delude myself, but I have always believed that the two C's I got in Spanish were mainly responsible for knocking me out of a Phi Beta Kappa. As it was I graduated magna cum laude.

Nothing more is to be said regarding the general courses I took preparatory to plunging into anthropology except that I believe Prof. Putnam made a serious blunder in advising me to drop German. At that time he was mainly interested in archeology, and in that of the New World, and since Germany played no part in settling it and had never any American colonies, the professor thought I should confined my linguistic studies to the nations that had played a part there. Hence the advice to keep on only with French and Spanish. But as my interest expanded into ethnology, I found myself cut off from a great deal of valuable literature and always regretted it though I had had two years of German in the high school and entered Harvard on Advanced German. The rest of my courses I feel were of utility both on the ground of general culture and in forming a background to my special work. I would, however, except Fine Arts 1 which, while interesting and important to men who intended to devote their future career to fine arts in general, was of very little service in my case.

By the time I reached my senior year The Archaeological and Ethnological department had descended out of graduate work and offered Anthropology L, a general introductory course on the subject. I believe I took this course the second year it was offered though it may have been the first. It was in immediate charge of George A. Dorsey[47] who had assisted Prof. Putnam in preparing the anthropological exhibit for the World's Columbian Fair at Chicago in 1893. He received, I think, the first doctorate in Anthropology given by Harvard. Owens, who conducted the first Peabody Museum expedition to Copan, Honduras, might have been the first, and he was spoken highly of by all who knew him, but the poor fellow died of a fever in Honduras, and his work was carried on by George Byron Gordon[48] who had been in charge of the engineering end of the problem. During my two years, 1896-98, which I spent at Harvard as a graduate student, Gordon devoted all [9] his time to the copying of materials collected on the Copan expedition for future publication and he did so I believe until he was called to be Director of the University Museum in Philadelphia, his qualifications for that job having been confined apparently to the above work. As I recall he drifted into the Peabody Museum late, and worked entirely apart from everyone else.

In my senior year, if I remember rightly, I took the new general course in anthropology under Dr. Dorsey. Shortly after the completion of this course, Dr. Dorsey became Director of the Anthropological Department of the Field Museum of Natural History, then known as the Field-Columbian Museum, and I think he did no more teaching. Indeed, his strength did not lie in that direction. His nature was too restless and he was at his best when on the move as a collector and promoter. His lectures were little more than a replica of the text book which he recommended to us, "*Precis d'Anthropologie generale,*" by Hovelacque and Herve. Although the course was supposed to be conducted by Professor Putnam as well as by Dr. Dorsey, Putnam's work was confined to two weeks devoted mainly to the story of how he found a fiber moccasin in the Great Cave of Kentucky and one or two other similar enterprizes. He was, it must be confessed, no more a natural teacher than was Dorsey, and his field work was limited in character, his principal contribution to American archeology being in advertising the subject and building up the

---

[47] {George Amos Dorsey (February 6, 1868 – March 29, 1931) famously wrote a best seller titled *Why We Behave Like Human Beings*, as well as a novel *Young Low*. He became a popular lecturer after he left the Field Museum, and had a reputation as a womanizer, traveling around the world with his "secretary".}

[48] {George Byron Gordon (1870 – 1927) took over after the sudden death of John Owens (27 September 1865 – 18 February 1893) at Copan. At Penn Gordon famously hired the Tlingit noble George Shotridge to bolster their Northwest Collection at the University Museum. Many of these crest and clan artifacts have since been rematriated to Tlingits, Tsmshians, Haidas. Gordon also locked horns with Frank Speck, who was able to leave this conflict at the museum and assume the chair of the new Anthropology department.}

Peabody Museum. Dr. Frank Russell[49] who succeeded Dorsey in the conduct of Anthropology 1, was the first real teacher of the subject at Harvard. He came from the University of Iowa, had travelled to the Arctic Ocean down Mackenzie River, was western in mentality, as forthright as his name, thorough in his work, and honest to the core. Unfortunately, his work at Harvard was cut off by the incidence of tuberculosis, a result I imagine from the hardships of his Arctic expedition. In hopes that this disease might be stayed, an assignment to visit the Pima [*Tohono O'otam*] Indians of Arizona under the Bureau of American Ethnology[50] was secured for him. Unfortunately for him, he [10] carried this on with his usually industry exposed much of the time to the inhalation of alkali dust, and although he returned to the east and prepared his report on the Indians, he passed away shortly afterwards.

In organizing the collections of the Peabody Museum Prof. Putnam had another outstanding assistant in Charles C. Willoughby,[51] a man without college training but with natural artistic ability and an enthusiasm for order very much needed in the Museum at that time. Under him the labelling of the collections probably became better than in any other similar museum in the country.

It so happened that my first contact with real anthropological work, in this case archeological, was under Willoughby during the summer of 1894 when I accompanied him to Maine whither he went in continuance of his work on the mysterious Red Paint[52] people whose remains he had located at Bucksport and Orland the year before. Another site was located on this trip on the banks of a tidal river south of Ellsworth. We roomed in an Ellsworth hotel and drove down to the site every day. One day, as I was sitting on the hotel porch, a young man drove past at high speed in a light rig, whereupon a gentleman on the porch near me said, "That is Senator Hale's son. He kills horses." This "son" was a member of my class at Harvard and afterwards became in succession representative from the First District of Maine and U.S. senator. He was one of those who, in political ideology, "advance rapidly toward the rear."

Our Red Paint site showed on the surface as three depressions, and on digging into these we found a layer of red paint at the bottom of each overlain with beds of ashes which showed that great fires had been built there. This was apparently to consume, or at least pulverize, bodies of the dead, traces of which we found. The only actual bone, however, was the fragment of a skull on the edge of one of the pits, near the surface, and associated with some copper beads. This Mr. Willoughby considered an intrusive burial by more modern Indians. The important finds were in the layers of red ochre and consisted of stone plummets, beautiful long spears of

---

[49] {In 1997, John B. Zoe, Elizabeth Mackenzie, Mary Siemens, and Tom Andrews accepted from University of Iowa on behalf of the Northwest Territories, the Dogrib caribou skin lodge collected in Rae by Frank Russell in 1894 and now in Yellowknife.}

[50] {Neil Judd *The Bureau of American Ethnology ~ A Partial History*. Norman: University of Oklahoma Press 1967.}

[51] {Charles C Willoughby *The Turner Group of Earthworks, Hamilton County, Ohio*. Papers of the Peabody Museum of American Archaeology and Ethnology, Harvard University VIII (3): 1-132 1922. Willoughby succeeded Frederick Ward Putnam at Harvard and continued its Ohio excavations, including the spectacularly detailed human clay figures at Turner.}

[52] {Bruce J Bourque, With contributions by Steven L Cox and Ruth H Whitehead *Twelve Thousand Years ~ American Indians in Maine*. Lincoln: Bison Books 2001: 51-66. Now known as Moorehead Phase (5000-4500 BP) of Late Archaic, it relied on swordfish and cod along the coast, and made red ocher offerings in huge cemeteries.}

slate, and other stone objects. [11] But the find Willoughby prized most highly was what seemed to be the handle of a stone knife at the bottom of the largest and deepest pit. On this were rude scratchings which Mr. Willoughby believed intended to represent a settlement of very obtusely roofed houses located at the falls of a stream.

These notes are drawn merely from my memory and may not altogether agree with his published account. Later we went to Damiscotta and visited what Mr. Willoughby believed had been another site of the same people, but he concluded that all that was worth finding had been dug out by collectors. Here Gordon joined us and he and I waited at the hotel while Willoughby went scouting. Later we all went to Augusta, the State Capital, and, while Mr. Willoughby proceeded on to Riverside where a possible site had been reported, Gordon and I put up at the Coney House. For one night only, as it proved, for we then discovered our beds were populated and we forthwith shifted to the Augusta House near the capitol building. The wilds of Honduras apparently had not hardened Gordon against discomforts, but he conceded that the Augusta House was "passable." He arrived in Damariscotta with some Honduras cigars but they gave out early and he afterwards found it difficult to get anything decent to smoke, except the highest grade of fifteen-cent-ers in Augusta, presumably those used by the state solons.

A few days later Mr. Willoughby returned and took us to Riverside from which little village we were driven several miles into the country and lodged in a farm house. Here we were royally entertained although the only item of fare that has impressed itself upon my memory was raised biscuit soaked in rich, fresh cream. One day I remember that Gordon fell to descanting upon the difficulties he had experienced in finding anything decent to eat upon this trip, whereupon our hostess said, "If what we have doesn't suit you, we shall have to ask you to leave." This solar pluxus [plexus] brought forth an instant's avowal from Gordon that everything there was very nice indeed which was the highest compliment he paid to anything during the trips though with a little of the air of approval of one accustomed to dine with royalty. Poor Gordon, I fear his fondness for the trencher was largely responsible for the sudden attack of [12] apoplexy which finally, carried him off. Willoughby and Gordon were about as ill-assorted a couple as could have been found, but they maintained what is called "a correct attitude" toward each other during the expedition. Our new site was on a long knoll where there had seemingly been a number of pit burials, but these had been lined with bark instead of ochre and Willoughby thought they belonged to another people. Although the pits were thought to represent so many burials, we failed to locate anything but the bark, soon gave up work, and all returned to Cambridge.

During my next summer vacation, that of 1895, Prof. Putnam sent me to join Mr. Volk at Trenton, N.J.[53] Mr. Volk was an old German from the Black Forest region who, however, had been in America a long time. Every morning he would set out with a good sized basket under his arm in which were brought home the findings of the day. He had only one or two men under him, and I used the pick and shovel myself to the extent I was able, long enough to enjoy the sound of noon whistles and appreciate the taste of cold spring water. Volk's scene of action was along the edge of the bluff overlooking the bottom lands of the Delaware River on a property owned by two old ladies named Laylor. The estate was an old one and there were said to be in possession of this family letters by some of the great men of Revolutionary times, but I saw none of these. Our interests lay farther back still. The populated part of Trenton was growing in this

---

[53] {Ernest Volk *The Archaeology of the Delaware Valley*. Papers of the Peabody Museum of American Archaeology and Ethnology, Harvard University V: 1-258, CXXV plates 1911.}

direction, and a less desirable part indeed occupied by Slavic immigrants of miscellaneous types who were wont to appropriate outlying parts of the Laylor crops and other possessions. The finds here were of two kinds. In the black soil at the top were flint articles in whole or in part and pot sherds. In red or yellowish soil beneath we came upon a sparing number of pieces of argillite some of which seemed to have been worked – at least Mr. Volk thought they had – while others seemed to have been mere products of nature. We used the usual Putnam method of procedure, laying out the ground in squares, establishing a vertical front and, gradually undermining it, generally with [13] the trowel, in order not to injure possible specimens. Put after one had proceeded in this manner for some time without results, it was a temptation, and indeed allowable, to bring down a large amount of material by one or two blows with the pickax. On one such attempt, however, the virtue of the trowel method came out clearly, I used my pick twice on this occasion, the first time with the small end. At the second blow the earth came down as desired, but on going over it with the trowel I discovered an earthenware pipe which had been broken into three pieces by my first attempt with the pick. To hit such a small object as this with a so much smaller point by intention would have demanded extreme skill, yet the miracle, and a very much undesired one, had taken place by accident. This is an episode of the expedition that I presume Volk left unpublished but there was little germane to science that escaped him. Indeed, I rather suspect that he overdid his record after the German type of error. Two years later, when I was working in Ohio, we had an old German working for us who was sometimes left to make records of his findings, and it was said of him that he recorded the width of opening of the mouths of skeletons although the lower jaw was disarticulated and half a foot away. However, this is a kind of error of which field investigators have less to complain ordinarily than of another type.

I have to confess that the scientific finds which turned up in our excavations do not stand out more clearly in my mind than the thought of a luscious watermelon which a neighboring farmer brought down one morning and placed in a neighboring spring so that it would be cold by lunch time. Lunches then had an aura about them which they have since lost. I also remember with unarcheological, but possibly highly anthropological, intensity, my visits to the home of a college friend at Penn Valley a few miles to the westward. This was a man named Buckman who used to describe himself as substitute pitcher on the worst baseball nine Harvard ever had. The record in that direction may have been broken since. He was a splendid fellow belonging to an old Quaker family and was not the only child belonging to it. Along with J.C.L. Clark '97, [14] and David Gibbs '98 we had a little literary circle which met once a week, one contributing a short story, another part of a continued story, a third play perhaps, and myself a poem. No, indeed, none of these were original. Later Buckman became a highly successful business man, I have been told and opened an office in New York, but suffered deterioration in his fortunes, perhaps at the time of time Great Depression, and the last heard of him he had gone to Alaska.

But to return to the subject, one week, I think it was when our expedition was near an end, Buckman and I paid a visit to Washington, and that was my first view of the nation's capital. As I remember, we went down the Delaware to Philadelphia by steamer and the rest of the way by rail, but I may have confused the first part with an earlier venture of mine to Philadelphia alone. In Washington we put up at the old Willard Hotel before it was rebuilt. The front of this building then set back farther from the street line of Pennsylvania Ave, and had four huge round columns. We took most of our meals at a little lunch room opposite the Treasury building. Our week included Labor Day of '95, and I remember watching the procession from our hotel. The great avenue itself reminded one still of the main street of a city of the third class, and, as I remember, the Willard was not the only building which did not extend to the sidewalk. On the train back we bought fried oysters put up in little card board boxes.

I received my A.M. in June of '97, and that summer was sent along with Rowland Dixon '97 {Roland Burrage Dixon November 6, 1875 – December 19, 1934} and Ingersoll Bowditch by means of a fund contributed by Bowditch's father, to assist Dr. Metz in the exploration of a village site at Madisonville, Ohio.[54] It was here that the meticulous German was employed, and the man in charge of the whole operation, in theory, that is, Dr. Metz, was also a German. He was a local physician and of excellent ability, one who had previously assisted Prof. Putnam, but unfortunately addicted to the liquid that, like woman, "seduces all mankind," and the result was that he was seldom in condition to supervise adequately the work of three [15] green undergraduates. His supervision consisted in little more than an evening visit to see what we had found during the day. He would stand on the pile of earth thrown from a trench in a very warbly manner and gaze abstractedly at anything to which we called his attention.

Dixon had preceded me by about a week, and when he left turned over to me the camera he had used, one of his own, with careful directions as to its use. I feel that a great part of the worthwhile results of this expedition were due to him. This was the richest archeological site I had worked in up to that time, and it is unfortunate that a first-class expert was not in immediate charge. However, the excavated area was carefully laid out into sections, the stakes properly set, and we took pictures of practically every skeleton after it had been exposed and cleaned by means of trowel and brush. In only one case did I slip up I believe, when we cleared a skeleton late one afternoon intending to photograph it next morning, but removed it then under the impression we had done so. The great damage done here lay in the fact that we were exploring in very hard soil and skeletons were broken-up in bringing them out through our crude methods which modern techniques would undoubtedly have saved. Besides the skeletons there was another type of find, "ash pits," deep circular holes which usually contained a miscellaneous assortment of bones among which those of deer predominated. One or two were filled with carbonized corn, and it is provident that some of them were originally storage pits, but almost all had ultimately been used for the disposition of garbage. The Madisonville site has been reported upon and I need not detail our findings. We made some discoveries, however, innocently enough, which have deeply annoyed later archeologists. These were evidences of contact with Europeans in the shape of a fragment or two of iron and a number of blue glass beads. Most of the latter were in the neighborhood of a child's wrists and had seemingly been bracelets, but they were also found in three or four ash pits.

After my return to Cambridge I was set at the job of working up the results of our exploration for future publication and that consisted largely in [16] washing bones, a technique of which Prof. Putnam was very fond but which destroyed the interest of some of his students. It was not really attractive to me but I worked manfully at it all winter, and was still doing so in April or early May when Prof. Putnam descended to the vault where I was engaged and asked me if I would like to go to the Pueblo country with Mr. Pepper. To a young man with my limited travel experience this was like striking the pot of gold at the rainbow's end and it did not take me long to accept the proposition, leaving the results of the Madisonville expedition to gather dust

---

[54] {Penelope Ballard Drooker *The View from Madisonville*. Ann Arbor: University of Michigan: Memoirs of the Museum of Anthropology #31 1997. This huge site, now encroached on by Cincinnati, marks the departure of peoples from the Ohio to the Missouri to take advantage of Plains bison herds.}

until a very much later period. In due course I joined Pepper in New York and traveled with him to the Chaco Canyon in New Mexico where the American Museum of Natural History was exploring the great ruins of Pueblo Bonito.[55] We had passes signed by George Gould over the Wabash and Missouri Pacific Railroads, changed at Pueblo to the Denver and Rio Grande, and went south from Mancos on horseback. The term "on horseback" applies to myself, however, only in part. By the end of the second day I had slidden forward and back on the saddle of my pacer so many times that I was about worn to the bone. Very fortunately for me we there caught up with the wagon that was bringing along our equipment and the goods for the store we were to open, so I shifted to a seat beside the driver and continued for the rest of the way in a less heroic but more comfortable fashion. It is a strange fact that, although I was on horseback only once between this time and my departure about six weeks later, when I returned I rode all the way without the least inconvenience, and on one day we covered fifty miles.

Mr. Pepper was an agreeable young gentleman to work with. He had come to the attention of Prof. Putnam through the discovery of an Indian site on Staten Island and without a college education. He was short and dark and through and through a product of Manhattan, the dialect of which was as natural to him as cockney to a Londonese. When he first went west his ideas of western life were of the Kit Carson pattern as understood by writers of the Harry Castleman school, and he accoutered himself accordingly, in particular allowing [17] his raven locks to grow down over the back of his neck much to the admiration I gathered of a circle of admiring damsels to whom he recounted his adventures in the "wild and wooly west" after his return. When I went west with him, however, much of this naivety had worn away and his locks had been sheared. I cannot say that he was devoted to the monotonous work of sitting upon the edges of Pueblo rooms in the alkali dust to see what turned up and prevent the wily Navaho working man from concealing turquoise beads in his headband. Some of that work fell to me but I was run down nervously at that time and quite unable to keep from falling asleep at intervals so that the Navaho nation was no doubt rich in turquoise in consequence. The tall beau and comedian of the Navaho, *Tomasito* (pronounced *Tomasitah*) aroused considerable mirth by imitating my intermittent noddings and sudden recovery. They called me by several names of which the only one I remember was *Hastin Hazho*, *Hastin* being some sort of equivalent for our Mr. and *Hazho* signifying something like "Look out!" because I was always using it when I thought an excavator was careless. The Indians were summoned to work morning and noon by a yell at which Mr. Pepper was very good, but my voice was apt to crack in the middle. Therefore, when it was possible, I shoved that duty off on Pepper or Richard Wetherell who was in charge of the outfitting and with his wife attended to the store. At noon I was so tired that I took a sheepskin up to a crack in the overhanging cliff and lay down there until work recommenced. The Indians timed themselves by the sun, and I was put to shame on one occasion when I attempted to work them overtime because of the failure of my Waterbury {watch}. Work was terminated by a general strike. We were in some danger from the collapse of walls while we were clearing a room, and if I were disposed to excite the gallery, I might enlarge upon the occasion when a wall fell in and half refilled a narrow room that an old Navaho and I had been at work upon. Had we been at work, we might have been incommoded by a half ton of rock but the catastrophe occurred during the lunch hour and a shovel or two were the only casualties. Our store was housed in a [18] oblong building made of stone set in adobe. It had a flat roof with a

---

[55] {George Pepper *Pueblo Bonito*. Anthropological Papers of the American Museum of Natural History XXVII: 1-398 1920 Reprinted UNM Press 1996.}

stone parapet all the way round and I slept on top under Navaho blankets along with a cousin of Mr. Hyde, sponsor of the expedition, a young fellow with whom I associate the name Lawrence though I won't answer for its accuracy. Those were really grand nights under the gorgeous starry skies, made doubly so by the clear dry air of New Mexico. It was equally grand when the moon was near the full. When we went to bed it was so warn that we hardly needed covers at all, but presently the regular down-canyon wind set in and before morning we were glad to pull all the blankets back. "Lawrence" was a splendid companion and I wish that my acquaintance with him might have been prolonged. Mr. Pepper had a tent by himself in which some of the better finds were preserved. As I have said, he was not fond of routine, but he would work indefatigably on any sticking job that took his fancy.

The year before he had nearly made himself sick digging out an underground room in the alkali dust. He began the year on which I accompanied him by polishing up his turquoise rings, of Navaho make. Later, however, we came upon an apartment in which the women of the Pueblo had evidently been grinding corn while they exchanged gossip, for there was a row of metates down the center. Pepper took a fancy to prepare for an accurate reproduction of this room, using a rough-and-ready type of papier-mache of his own devising with which to model the metates. What ultimately became of this I do not know. After his return to New York he devoted himself to the preparation of a case containing choice specimens of turquoise. I do not wish to seem too critical of Mr. Pepper. We all have our separate abilities and his was an interest in special exhibits involving an aesthetic sense far above mine, while I am rather a plugger who attends to the run-of-mine material. Mr. Pepper was easy to work with, perhaps too easy. I returned to Boston with "Lawrence" and the journey was pleasant.

Shortly after I reported to Prof. Putnam, he said to me that he gathered from what I told him that I did not care so much for archeology. "I guess [19] you always did hate a bone," he said, although I do not think I had expressed a very strong antipathy. Anyhow, he concluded that I had better go to New York and study under Dr. Boas who then had a position under him at the American Museum of Natural History. In the fall of 1898, therefore, I ended my eight years of life in and around Boston including six at Harvard and went on to New York where I engaged a hall bedroom on West 85th St. within easy walking distance of the Museum and only two or three streets up town from the one on which Dr. Boas and his family were then living.

Shortly before Dr. Boas had returned from a visit to the Columbia River region and had obtained there a quantity of texts and supplementary material in the nearly extinct language of the Lower Chinook Indians. The work on which he set me was the extraction of material from his notebook in order to determine the grammar of the language. This proved to be as interesting as, and rather more important than, a crossword puzzle, and after I grasped the proposition I got along very well, so that the results of my work were accepted as a thesis for the degree of Ph.D. at Harvard which was entitled "The Morphology of the Chinook Verb."

The circumstances connected with my first linguistic discovery, or rather supposed discovery, are important on account of the light they throw on the character of my teacher and the strong hold he had on the affections of his pupils. He had noticed that certain sounds in Chinook tended to change in consonance with changes in the sounds preceding, and he suggested that I make lists of the words in which such changes were exhibited. One morning, after I had been engaged in this work for a while, Dr. Boas looked over my material and told me that it indicated a certain law to exist. At that moment his secretary happened to come in and Dr. Boas said to her, "Miss Andrews, Mr. Swanton has just discovered an interesting law." The discovery was his but the credit was given to me. Dr. Boas did not even say "we have discovered?" He was too much interested in the discovery to care who made it. Later I made sufficient finds in my own right I am sure, but this one particularly impressed itself upon me and stamped upon my mind an assurance of the high-mindedness [20] and disinterested devotion to truth of the man under whom I was working. Later I could recognize that he had his weaknesses like the rest of us, but the incident above related has had an enduring effect upon me. At that time I was in a highly nervous condition so that isolation in a hall bedroom which is no doubt a horror to many new arrivals in the metropolis was just what I needed and my health improved.

In the summer of 1899 I was sent to South Dakota with some of the texts which George Bushotter had written out for J.O. Dorsey some years before. These I was to go over with Dakota informants to see what I could make out of them and correct the phonetics if such corrections were found necessary. My first objective was the agency of the Rosebud Dakota reserve, but, not knowing how to get there, I arrived at Pierre, S.D., and found that I was on the wrong side of the reservation. A few days later, however, I learned that the postmaster of a place on the northern edge of the reservation was about to return and would take me with him. This was by horse and buggy, of course, or rather horses and buggy for spans were the rule throughout the western country. On the far side of the Missouri we seemed to pass into the kingdom of Beelzebub, since his name signifies, I believe, "the god of flies." These were the common type which do not sting, but their persistence when we stopped for a noon siesta drove one nearly wild. The first night we camped on the open prairie but my sleep was abbreviated by a thunder storm on the wake of which mosquitoes presented themselves out of nowhere. So I climbed up on the buggy wet and cold and fought mosquitoes until morning. The postmaster was a Jew who refused to take anything, kept me over night, and next morning found an Indian bound for the agency who carried me there in safety.

During this trip and subsequent residence on the reservation I saw more of rattlesnakes than anywhere before or since except in the snake pit at Crystal Lake, Florida. The first rattler I ever saw was a baby specimen that we nearly ran over during my wagon trip into Chaco Canyon in 1898. There were plenty of them not far from our camp but I did not happen to "meet up with" any others [21] until I went to South Dakota. During our first day out from Pierre the smoothness of our trip across the prairie was suddenly broken by the horses who stood suddenly up on their hind legs, jumped to one side of the road and then lit out across country. My companion said that this was due to a snake lying coiled on the side of the road but I didn't happen to catch sight of him. My second experience on this trip was in the company of the Indian just mentioned. This time the man caught sight of the reptile first, said "snake", and pulled his horses to one side of the road, and took the really profound risk of entrusting me with the reins while he got out and broke the back of his snakeship with one or two well directed blows of his buggy whip. The reptile was a big fellow just crossing the road in front of us and it was as well that the horses did not catch sight of him. The episode also shows that my Indian was not an old timer for in that case he would as soon thought of demolishing his grandmother.

At the Rosebud Agency where I was put up in the home of the Agent himself and very kindly treated, my stay was enjoyable but unproductive until I learned of a Yankton Dakota Indian named Joseph who conducted a school in the eastern part of the reservation and would put me up and help me with the language, his school not then being in session. During the few weeks I spent with him, I covered considerable ground and was able to introduce some necessary changes into the first hundred of the Bushotter texts though it was by no means a complete job. The winter of 1899-1900 I continued work under Dr. Boas, this time in connection with the Bushotter texts. As in the year preceding I was also entered at Columbia University where I took linguistic courses under Dr. Boas, and in 1898-99 had a general course in anthropology under Dr. Livingston Farrand later head of the Red Cross and still later President of Cornell.

In June of 1900 I went to Cambridge to take my final examination for the doctorate in anthropology. My examiners consisted of the Prof. Putnam, Dr. Boas, Dr. Russell, and Mr. Bowditch, and the examination was a curious affair but as good as could be offered in anthropology probably in 1900. [22] Putnam began by asking a few questions in general anthropology but more particularly in archeology which I was able to answer, in part no doubt because I happened to know his particular prejudices. Dr. Boas, the only one present who knew anything about the special subject which I had worked up for my thesis and understood my qualifications already, asked a few things about the Chinook verb. Mr. Bowditch, as I remember, rather asked advice of me than made an examination, not I am sure because he expected to learn any more than he knew already but because he was feeling his way toward further work in the Mayan field which he had already promoted. When the examination was turned over to Russell something unique happened. He spoke something like this, "It is foolish to hold an examination of this character and we shall not give anthropology a respectable status until we specify a major and minors as in other departments." I may add that he was kind enough to say that he did not intend this as an adverse criticism of the candidate, because, he said, "I admire the man" (though I confess I am not sure that he knew me well enough to admire me which was perhaps why he could say it), finally, he said, "No, I have no questions to ask."

Rowland Dixon got his degree the same year although, having taken his A.B. one year later than myself, he had gained a year on me. During our undergraduate course we were members of a small folklore society which he organized and of which he was the moving spirit. He developed into an outstanding anthropologist and was always a good friend to me. His comparatively early death was a great loss to the science, and to all who knew him.

My Dakota work had behind it the purpose of fitting me to take up the work and editing the manuscripts of James Owen Dorsey {October 31, 1848 – February 4, 1895} who had collected a vast amount of material from the Siouan group of languages. Dr. Dorsey and Dr. A.S. Gatschet shared between them the greater part of the linguistic work in the early days of the Bureau. Except when forced to undertake an expedition to Oregon – to his utter disgust as H.W. Henshaw told me, Henshaw being the man to do the ordering – Dorsey confined his work in the manner [23] just indicated. His records were made with meticulous care and have been highly commended by all later students who have handled his material. He began work with the Omaha among whom he had been a missionary and extended it to Osage, Iowa, Oto, Winnebago, Quapaw, Kansa, and finally to the Biloxi after Gatschet discovered that language. For Dakota, however, he depended on the records of the missionary Riggs, and for Hidatsa on those of Matthews. His principal omissions were Crow and Catawba, and the last-mentioned occupies such a peculiar position that it is unfortunate he did not take it up when more speakers of that language were available. The records of Dakota and Hidatsa would also have been more satisfactory had he done the work upon them himself.

Dr. Gatschet was a Swiss and the only university man in the original Bureau group. Like Dorsey he spread his attention over numbers of very distinct languages. In spite of his educational advantage, he was very far below Dorsey in his recordings and his ear was by no means as keen. But what was lost in one way was compensated in another since through his willingness to spread his activities we are indebted to the rescue of material from some languages now extinct. In spite of the time he spent among Indians, Gatschet never really understood the mentality of his subjects. He was no ethnologist, but a linguist pure and simple, and singularly lacking in logical faculty when confronted with the problem of interpreting place or personal names. Thus he derived Tulane from the Choctaw word for a certain bird, and that of the Biloxi Indians from a creek in Oklahoma with which they could not have been acquainted for a hundred and fifty years after their name first appears in history. Gatschet's head was of a peculiar shape and to this we may charitably attribute some of his eccentricities, especially a salacious slant of his mind. Two men could hardly have been more unlike than the two linguists of the early Bureau.

In furtherance of the plan to have me take up Dorsey's work, Dorsey having passed away in his prime in 1896, I was given a civil service examination [24] in the summer of 1900. I spent several weeks in Washington at this time and was introduced to the extent to which Washington climate can go in making one uncomfortable in summer. My previous experience had been at a later time in the year and under more favorable climatic conditions, I had a small second-floor hall bedroom in a block of stone houses which still exists I believe, on the south side of L St. between 15th and 14th. It was a front room but that made conditions all the worse, because almost every afternoon there was a thunder shower so close to the termination of office hours that it was called "the clerks' storm" I believe. Anyhow, instead of cooling the air, these storms would drop just enough rain to turn to steam which rose into my windows, or rather window, and changed the baking process we had suffered all day into a steaming one. I came to know two other young fellows rooming in the same house, and almost every evening the three of us would walk round to a drug store on the corner of 14th and K Sts, to imbibe cool drinks or ice cream. Sometimes we would go up 14th to a little out-of-doors ice cream parlor – now long ago abandoned and the property probably built over. On one occasion a larger crowd, including the three of us, went to a beer garden on the other side of 14th street, east that is, somewhat higher up. Here I was introduced to the vicious treating system then in vogue, since each of the six or seven people felt it incumbent upon him to supply drinks all around. To be sure soft drinks were served as well as beer but no one, not even in a Washington midsummer, needs six bottles of cold liquid. However, some went the limit, and very probably out of courtesy to each other, and when the six were not soft drinks the effect was likely to be still less salutary. In particular there was one alcoholic in the party who did not require any extra stimulation to his besetting sin. Even soft drinks are not good for my own digestion, and the only beer I ever took was on a doctor's prescription with the idea of building up my waist girth. But my waist refused to respond and I was changed over to prunes. Of my two summer companions, one dropped out of my [25] life completely, a tall and rather elegant youth. After I returned to Washington to live permanently, the other, a short and dark man from up New York State named Seaman was still there and I kept in touch with him for a few years, until a tragic event befell him. One day, in trying to board a street car, he was thrown back and fell on his head on the pavement. He recovered from the accident after a time and went back to the boarding house where I had met him, but presently he began showing signs of a mania of persecution, believed that a young lady in the same house intended to kill him, presently talked of arming himself, and was sent to St. Elizabeth's for examination, he had hoped that he would get over this delusion but it stuck to him and he remained there till his death.

I do not think that I shone particularly in my examination and I am under the impression that, if my rendering of the Ten Commandments into Sioux had been followed, that tribe would have become extinct. However, I gave an account of myself sufficiently good to be passed and given an appointment to the Bureau taking effect September 1, 1900 upon which I got out of Washington and returned to my mother's home in Boston with the utmost speed.

Shortly before this, Morris K. Jesup, Director of the American Museum of Natural History had made a very large grant of money for anthropological work on and near the North Pacific coast and Dr. Boas had been placed in charge of this. Anthropologists being scarce in that epoch, Dr. Boas made an arrangement with the Bureau of American ethnology by which I was to conduct an investigation among the Haida Indian's during the winter of 1900-1901, the American Museum paying my field expenses and the Bureau my salary. My salary being fifty dollars a month, that made no great drain on the latter. In September 1900, I reached Skidegate via an old side-wheel steamer named, if I recollect correctly, The Princess Louise. Actually she should not have been allowed out of sight of land, but the sea happened to be smooth. At that time there were but two permanent settlements on the Queen Charlotte [26] Islands, Skidegate which was connected with the outside world by one steamer a month out of Victoria, and Masset on the north coast of Graham Island, which enjoyed one steamer annually bringing supplies for the Hudson Bay Post. There were but two white families at Skidegate at the time of my visit, that of the Methodist missionary in the Indian village, and that of Mr. Robert Tennant a mile higher up the inlet. Mr. Tennant was an old miner formerly in the Cassiar country on the mainland, and his wife an Indian from the Fraser River region. The latter had been brought up by an English woman and was white in everything but birth and color. She was a meticulous housekeeper and I was very comfortable there during my stay.

To one used to the Atlantic seaboard, the North Pacific coast surprises one by being so much warmer in winter and so much colder in summer than he expected. This climatic difference is, however, confined to a comparatively narrow strip of land between the coast and the mountains. The clouds lie low, and in the fall, winter, and spring there is a rainfall about every day. One takes one's slicker and hip boots – if one is to travel inland that is – as a matter of course, wherever one goes. Hip boots are needed, because just back from the high tide mark there begins a jungle of bushes and behind it a dank and lofty forest and underneath the latter a mattress often of fallen monarchs of the forest, so that one may sometimes climb many feet off of the ground in trying to cross such an obstruction.

During spare moments, when I was not working with informants [speakers], I used to climb to a high rock not far from the house, sit down there, and watch the changes of weather on the ocean and the movements of bird life. Although it rains so much, it is usually in showers with intervals of sunshine between. One can see a storm some little distance at sea and watch the changes it undergoes. Flocks of sea fowl float about or take off in long lines, flap, flap, flap along the surface of the water and then gradually into the air like so many aeroplanes. There was scarcely a sign of civilization anywhere. Mr. Tennant's home was on the site of an old story town, [27] and my mind was full of the stories, so that I almost expected to see a killer whale come to shore and dissolve itself into a manlike supernatural being or be a witness to some similar prodigy. It was to me a weird and beautiful country and remains so in recollection.

In the spring I hired an Indian to take me to Masset in his canoe, but like most of the commercial minded Indians of this region, he allowed me to outfit with provisions for several days and set me ashore on the near side of Rose Spit from which I had to walk into Massett. I don't altogether wonder that he did not want to round that long and shallow spit in a heavy sea, and I have fully forgiven him for the deception, because I thoroughly enjoyed my walk. The north shore of this, Graham Island, is one long beach at low or half tide and not very difficult to negotiate except when the tide comes way in. That happened after I had walked some hours and drove me up into the bushes. At one point, in order to make a short cut to *Hi-ellen* (or rather, *Thlielung*) River, I turned inland and was forced to climb over a natural fortification made by

64

huge trees fallen and lying in all directions. Every time I jumped from one trunk to another, the pack I carried on my back came thump against me and nearly knocked me from my perch. In due course, however, I reached the river, worked my way up it till I found a tree I could cross upon and a few minutes later found an Indian shack where I prepared to spend the night. A short time later two or three Indians presented themselves there and built a fire in the middle. I disposed myself for slumber as well as I could but it was a cold night, and the airs of heaven came in *ad libitum* through the door and the smoke-hole so that I got little sleep. In the morning, however, we got something to eat, and I started out with revived courage, I do not remember just when I reached Massett but it happened. There I found it necessary to choose between staying with the white man who had charge of the Hudson Bay Post or going to the home of an Indian, Henry Edenshaw. I made the mistake of choosing the white man until Monday; It was Saturday when I arrived. This white man had roughed it on the coast [28] for many years and gotten roughed in the process. The Massett Post did practically no business and this gentleman was left in charge of the property awaiting its final disposition. He treated my coming considerately but not cordially, and it soon appeared that his consideration for visitors meant just that. His cooking was one of the greatest hazards I had to face during my visit to the islands. Ultimately this gentleman was taken from the island insane and no wonder.

It was interesting to compare the Christian missionaries at Skidegate and Masset. The former was a Methodist whose other name was "Thorough." If his flock did not take to religion, he took them to it in the spirit of the church militant. Religion to him appeared to consist in the number of religious services that one attends whether voluntarily or by compulsion, and he used every means to herd the sinners and the saved into church. His one great regret was that he was not clothed with the civil as well as the religious authority, and bitterly resented the invasion of his bailiwick by the Salvation Army. He also maintained a feud with Mr. Tennant, and had set up a dogfish oil factory in competition with the latter and for the supposed benefit of the Indians. This would have in itself been an admirable institution if he had had the genius of Dr. Duncan of Metlakatla but that is doubtful. I was not on the islands long enough to know how the business turned out.

The missionary at Massett was of a different stripe altogether. His mission was supported by the Church of England. He was the son of a missionary among the Tsimshian Indians of Nass River where he had grown up, and he spoke the Tsimshian dialect fluently. He apparently maintained the rites of his church with due order, and forestalled competition from the Salvation Army by organizing a Church Army along similar lines. Whether from native disposition or early association with Indians, he was tolerant to the point of indifference and during the two months or more that I lived in Massett I saw him but twice in any of the Indian houses. While Skidegate was seething with religion and scandal, Masset seethed not at all, although [29] no doubt indulging in the gossip of an isolated and self-supporting community with few outside contacts. The principal outside contacts were in summer when both Skidegate and Masset were practically abandoned, the inhabitants of both settlements betaking themselves family by family to their Columbia River {Chinookan style} boats and crossing to the mainland to work in the canneries and incidentally exchange news with the mainland Indians. No compensation could induce any of them to remain at home, and, no wonder, considering the isolation of their lives during such a large part of the year.

During most of my stay at Massett I lived with Henry Edenshaw who was a splendid cook and kept a neat house. I had a large front room with a wooden bedstead with high head and footboards. One morning as I lay awake in this just beginning to open my eyes, the bedstead was shaken violently as if some giant had seized the headboard and pulled it back and forth. I realized almost instantly that it was an earthquake and bounced out of bed in hopes that I might escape through the window if the house came down about my ears. Needless to say, it did not.

Later in the spring, Henry took me across to the Haida (*Kaigani*) towns in Alaska, all of which except Kasaan I visited. Dixon Entrance is sometimes turbulent, but we made the passage successfully, and when nearing Howkan, the first objective, Henry shot a deer which was trying to swim across the channel. After our return to Masset, we voyaged back to Skidegate, and at this time the summer was so far advanced that it was light all night. While the sun passed below the horizon, its course was marked by a great yellow patch of light on the southern horizon. I returned to the east as I had come except that on recrossing the Rocky Mountains, I made the mistake of side-routing through the Kootenay country instead of remaining on the main line and enjoying again the gorgeous scenery of the Kicking Horse Pass. I also shifted off at Lake Superior and went down by steamer through that great sea of clear blue water into Huron and to Port Huron. I reached Toronto at night, but at my hotel the accommodations had been so far absorbed through the attractions [30] of the nearby Buffalo fair that I had to sleep on a billiard table. That was almost my sole contact with the game.

Before reporting at the Bureau I spent some time with my mother in Roxbury, Boston, and made my final transfer to Washington in September about the time when our country was shocked and saddened by the assassination of President McKinley.

My only contacts with members of the Bureau of Ethnology before I took my examinations were during some meetings of Section K of the A.A.A.S. In particular, I remember a meeting at Columbia attended by William H. Holmes and WJ McGee {October 31, 1848 – February 4, 1895, married to anthropologist Anita Newcomb McGee in 1888, three children, died of cancer}. At that time there was a somewhat furious feud between those Washington gentlemen on one side and Prof. Putnam, and Prof. Wright of Oberlin on the other. Putnam and Wright believed that the occupancy of America by human beings went back to a remote period, and accepted the antiquity of flint objects found at Trenton and the Calaveras skull, while McGee and Holmes were in pronounced opposition. As in the case of the famous six men of Hindustan and their elephant, each party proved to be "partially in the right and partly in the wrong" [JRS: correction needed]. Putnam and Wright as to Trenton and Holmes and McGee as to the Calaveras skull {human, found 25 February 1866 by miners 130 feet (40 m) deep, confirmed by Josiah Whitney, California State Geologist and Harvard Professor, later by Putnam.}. I remember that Hrdlička testified that a thigh bone found in the Trenton gravels was human, though I do not know whether he, at that time, sided with Putnam and Wright or not. At the Columbia meeting Dr. Wright showed a small stone object with the figure of a mastodon (or elephant) scratched upon it {Davenport stone tablets hoax}.

The demeanor of Holmes and McGee at these meetings was quite different. Holmes was, as usual, quiet and reserved, but McGee asserted his beliefs in the hammer and tongs fashion with which his earlier occupation as blacksmith had made him familiar. At an earlier period his hair is said to have been jet black but when I first met him it was threaded with patches of gray. However, he still shook his "mane" violently in argument, and made up in aggressiveness what Holmes lacked. The argument on the other side was maintained with no such vim. [31]

Of course I saw little of the Bureau of Ethnology until I returned from the Queen Charlotte Islands in September of 1901. The Bureau was then housed in the Adams Building on the north side of F St, N.W., opposite the building in which the ideological Survey was then located. The main offices were on the top floor and the Bureau library two flights below. Dr.

Hodge had been the librarian but was at that time in the Smithsonian Building assisting Dr. Langley. The librarian at that time and for many years afterward was Miss Leary who was assisted by a girl, part Negro I think and part Indian, named Ella. For a time the library force was augmented by the youngest daughter of Dr. Cyrus Thomas, a splendid girl who lost her life shortly afterwards by drowning during a skating party.

Upstairs at the front was the office of Major Powell, and between it and the head of the stairs where was also the head of the elevator, was the office of Mr. McGee and the head clerk. The rear of this floor had originally been a single room but was cut up by temporary partitions, which did not reach the ceiling, into several "cubby-holes" where most of the scientific staff did their work. I believe that the illustrator had an office at one end but have almost forgotten. Between this "cubby-hole" section and Major Powell's office there was a passageway which led through a small room where the members of the staff often took their lunches together. This was a very pleasant feature of Bureau life at that time.

Major Powell lived only a year after my return to Washington, and I had but one interview with him, all business being then conducted through Mr. McGee. Seeing that a new man had arrived, he asked me one day to come into his office. He began, as I remember, by saying that he wanted to tell me something of what they "were trying to do," but his intention was perhaps rather to draw me out, although his increasing infirmity might explain why he appeared to wander from the subject. At any rate, he seemed, to me to be buried in thought most of the time, and I do not know but he might have forgotten my presence. A few months later he passed away. [32]

McGee had been Powell's right-hand man during the last years of his life and fully expected to succeed him, but in some way or other he had gotten into the bad graces of Dr. Langley, then Secretary ~~head~~ of the Smithsonian Institution, and Langley appointed Holmes instead. Holmes and McGee had before this time been on the most intimate terms, and there was some surprise that the former should accept the headship of the Bureau. Holmes, however, though an excellent archeologist and a consummate artist, his specialty being water colors, was highly sensitive and very timid. A row of any kind would occasion in him a nervous upset, and those who knew this weakness could impose upon him very readily. It also happened that Holmes was the only man whom Langley could place in charge of the Bureau with any justification, and, although I am sure that the whole thing was distasteful to Holmes, he yielded to the compulsion. Indeed, it was reported that he and McGee went out to dinner together and after a discussion of the whole problem agreed that it was best for Holmes to take the position. While such a meeting may have adjusted matters as between McGee and Holmes, it did not alter the feelings of the former regarding the action taken. Along with several other members of the staff - all those then in Washington - I was present when Langley brought Holmes over and introduced him to us as our new chief. In the course of his remarks Langley spoke of his high esteem and great love for Major Powell, and upon this McGee was moved to remark that he was glad to hear of Langley's appreciation of the Major "in view of the reproach which is now being cast upon his memory." I think that these were the exact words.

Then the position was offered to Holmes. Dr. Langley put it up to him as to what title he would choose and, not feeling himself endowed with Powell's executive gifts, he chose that of "Chief" instead of "Director." For some time longer McGee continued in his position as assistant chief but presently resigned under the following circumstances. I am under the impression that McGee talked of taking some legal steps to secure the position he coveted, but whether that was actually the case or whether Langley felt that he must holster up his own case, an investigation of the affairs of the Bureau was instituted. [33] I feel quite sure that nothing like a misappropriation of funds, certainly not an intentional misappropriation, had taken place under McGee but he was careless in the conduct of his affairs and it was probably not difficult to point to irregularities. There was the greatest difference between the appearance of Prof. Holmes's desk – we always called him "Professor Homes" – and that of McGee. The former was in scrupulous order, nothing upon it not in current use, and everything else in meticulously exact files. McGee's desk on the contrary was covered with a miscellaneous assortment of books, papers, separates, and so on to a depth of several inches and many of those on the edges were falling off on the floor.

One of the questions at issue, as it happened, was the status of the funds under which I had been working before entering the Bureau. There was a provision at that time under which the Bureau was empowered to buy certain completed manuscripts and I think it still exists. I had been working on Chinook and Dakota with the understanding that my manuscript would be paid for at the end of the year and that was done, although Professor Boas advanced the money out of his own pocket from time to time before being reimbursed. There were other angles to the question, as to whether the payments had not been excessive, and so on. A similar question was raised regarding the purchase of certain photographs from Prof. Frederick Starr {first anthropologist at University of Chicago, famous for serving ice cream in the colors of the marjor races at his final exam}. I was called down to the Smithsonian to testify along with others, and from a transcript of my testimony which came up later I judge that my replies were not in Addisonian[56] English. I really do not know what the final report was, or even whether one was made, but it is probable that irregularities of one sort or another could be made out. At any rate, McGee gave up the struggle and resigned. Afterwards, I believe, he did work under the Geological Survey with which he had had earlier experience, and not many years later he died {and won a bet with Major JW Powell as to which had the bigger brain}. He did not impress me as a profound thinker but as intensely desirous to win scientific consideration and while aping originality desperately rather by means of unusual verbiage than new ideas feared to depart from the scientific "party line" of his day. Knowing [34] about his previous work in geology, I once asked a very able geologist I happened to know about McGee's work in that field, and he said that he thought there was little of value except for one short article which he highly praised. I think he was earnest in his desire to be a true scientist and was warm hearted in his relations with others. He always treated me with the utmost consideration and only differed from me when I expressed my belief that the matrilineal system of the Northwest coast Indians was not primitive. At that time [Lewis Henry] Morgan was the presiding genius of Bureau thought in sociological lines. The significant dissenter in the older group was Mooney who declared that the Kiowa Indians had not matrilineally organized clans and he could find no evidence that they ever did have any.

Since Boas had dealt through McGee and the transactions between them were in part the occasion for the investigation just mentioned, Prof. Holmes was not prepossessed in my favor, but he always treated me courteously. I happened to share with him a sensitive make up but that was our only point of resemblance. I am not artistic in any sense of the word; my sensitiveness is crudely physical and not connected with any appreciation of color, form, or tone. As a "Boas man" I shared {in} the opposition to Boas entertained by many, if not most, of the Washington anthropologists at that time. More than in his later life, Boas was inclined to lay about him with

---

56 {Joseph Addison (1672-1719) and Richard Steele (1672-1729) published early London newspapers, *Tatler* and *Spectator*.}

his rapier intellect, and while he was more often right than not, only the very great or the very unselfish can accept a rebuke to their self-esteem without entertaining a dislike of the source from which it comes. And while in my experience of Boas I have always found him eager to accept truth whether or not it supported a private theory, he was not always right nor always just in his estimate of men. The affection which most of his students had for him was based on their admiration of his ability and respect for his scientific honesty as illustrated in my own case as given above. He had not that sympathy for the man underlying the error he entertained which drew everyone to Lincoln. But how many scientists have? [35]

When I entered the Bureau I was the only member of it who had even that purported to be an anthropological education and goodness knows that was thin enough. Powell, as I have said, was soon to pass off the scene. In spite of his paper on Wyandot social organization in the very first volume of the Bureau reports, and some notes on the Ute Indians, he contributed comparatively little to anthropological research,[57] but through his ability in handling successive generations of congressmen he performed a major service to all anthropologists in securing the foundation of the Bureau of Ethnology, just as his work in the establishment of the Geological survey has placed all in geology in his debt. As I have intimated, Holmes was of an altogether different type. By himself he would have been utterly incompetent to secure the foundation of the Bureau, and he lacked entirely that mixture of tolerance and firmness demanded of an executive. To be sure he had tolerance enough. That was his bane. Firmness was the element wanting. This was due evidently to his highly sensitive artistic nature. He could not bear rows, and was I know injected into that at the very beginning of his service as Chief wholly against his will. He could be imposed upon easily by anyone who understood his weakness, and I have seen him tremble all over at the mere suggestion of any serious difference either within or without the Bureau. He usually gave in at once if any of his staff chose a different line of action from the one he apparently thought should have been taken. I have known him to take an apparently firm stand in favor of a certain measure, and give in completely when the issue actually came to a head. He was thoroughly unhappy as an executive, but thoroughly contented and entirely competent when left to himself. His papers on archeological subjects were composed with meticulous care and thoroughly illustrated. Nevertheless, it was the general feeling among his associates that he was rather an artist than a scientist and they believed it would have been better for him to have devoted himself entirely to his art in which there is no question as to his transcendent ability. He was, I believe, regarded as the greatest water colorist of his time, and the sketches with which he accompanied [36] some of his scientific papers, notably one on the ruins of Maya cities, are inimitable. His sketch of the Grand Canyon of the Colorado, made to illustrate a geological paper before he came into the Bureau, has been copied over and over, and I well remember the enthusiastic praise bestowed upon it by as exacting a scientist as William Morris Davis. Holmes's sensitivity led him to lean upon others and during the latter part of his life, both before and after his resignation from the headship of the Bureau the particular "other" was Aleš Hrdlička who had been appointed Curator of the new department of Physical Anthropology in the National Museum. Dr. Hrdlička was the outstanding physical anthropologist of his time and not only built up the collections in his department to become one of the greatest in the world but founded the central organ of the science, the *Journal of Physical Anthropology*. There is no doubt as to his ability, his energy and his devotion to his subject, and also as to his honesty, though it must be added that he honestly believed that he had all of the

---

[57] compiles his massive notes from the Great Basin.

answers. His prejudices were so much a part of him that he did not realize he had any. Whether he possessed any sense of humor may be questioned. Anyhow, I do not think that he considered that there could be any joke connected with science or that a scientific man could be the victim of one. And as to a joke on himself, one might as well make merry with the Ten Commandments.

I do not know what Hrdlička's private opinion was as to the antiquity of man in America before he came to Washington although he did on one occasion back up a contention of Prof. Putnam's regarding the human character of a thigh bone unearthed at Trenton. This did not, however, involve anything conclusive in the matter of age, and from what I knew of Hrdlička later, I do not feel that he lacked honesty in the expression of any opinion. After he came to Washington, however, he sided immediately with the Holmes-McGee view in denying any great antiquity to man in America. This was, as I think I have said, a very useful corrective to such an extreme view as that involved in the assumption that the Calaveras skull belonged to the stratum in which it was found, but Hrdlička carried his opposition to such extremes that he was wholly in error regarding finds of real [37] antiquity in Florida, and certain parts of the west. In his picture of Hrdlička like a modern Horatio, defending the continental bridge from too early intrusion, Hooton has beautifully characterized the situation. In defending almost alone the claims of Neanderthal man to a place in the ancestry of Homo sapiens Hrdlička was somewhat more fortunate as later discoveries indicate. Right or wrong, he did not have a character likely to make him widely popular. It is said that an Indian in the Southwest once shot at him, but fortunately missed. Except for Holmes, Hough, and one or two more of such an easy and genial make up as to have gotten along with the devil, most of Hrdlička's confreres were alternately moved to wring his neck or shout with laughter at the Hrdličkaresqueness of him. Fortunately American scientists generally have a saving sense of humor. Had Hrdlička flourished in pre-war Europe, I fear he would have been involved in more than one duel. From this point of view one can understand how Hooton got along with Hrdlička so well. The one could indulge his sense of humor, and the other would never take it home to himself.

One of the happiest days of Holmes's life, it seemed to me, was in 1910 when he retired from the headship of the Bureau and returned to head the Division of Anthropology in the National Museum and become Curator of the American Gallery of Art. The staff of the former was small and its appropriations taken care of along with those of the Museum as a whole, and the latter was in Holmes's own special line in which he had no peer. Still later he confined himself to the latter entirely and his Head Curatorship of Anthropology was given to Dr. Walter Hough, a long standing friend. As I have already intimated, Hough came to understudy him as a companion of Hrdlička. Hough was a very genial, lovable person, and I shall always remember with gratitude the kind things he said to me from time to time when I was the kid member of the Bureau and none too sure of myself. It was his misfortune to share some of Holmes's weakness as an executive. But I have more than a little sympathy with that sort of defect, and my consciousness of the lack was partly responsible for my decision to decline the headship of the Bureau at a [38] later date. The proper association of strength and sweetness and of executive with intellectual ability seems relatively uncommon.

One of the oldest members of the Bureau of Ethnology in years when I entered was Professor Cyrus Thomas. Previous to his appointment here he had been engaged in work in Entomology. He came from that part of southern Illinois locally know as Egypt, presumably on account of the name of its chief city Cairo. Although from a section in which there had been much sympathy with the Southern cause during the Civil War, he was strongly Unionist in his beliefs and related to the Logans. On coming to the Bureau he had been a pronounced strong believer in the existence of race of Mound Builders distinct from the American Indians, and Major Powell gave him the commission to put this theory to the test. Offhand one might suppose that the investigation would have been prejudiced in advance but evidently the Major knew his man, for, while Thomas certainly was "sot" in his opinions, his other name was honesty and, when he came back with his opinion on this matter entirely altered, the case for the negative acquired additional strength. Whether he would have changed all of his opinions as readily I do not know, but he did abandon another view, an attempt to relate the Polynesian tongues to some American languages. His natural conservatism came out, however, when I mentioned simplified spelling then being pushed by Andrew Carnegie and some other reformers. Like the old "party line" linguists he thought that if we dropped _ugh_ from _through_ and _although_ and spelt _trough_ thru we would destroy the etymology of our speech, and he also animadverted against such an attempt by "an unauthorized committee," though what he would have considered authorized I do not know. Whether the Thomases were in the majority at this time I do not know but the attempt at reform failed although it almost succeeded in dropping the E out of whiskey. On examining the advertisements of those distilleries which seem to be the main support of our periodic literature, I find that one out of seven drops the E. It is too bad that the elimination stops there and that so many people choose to drug their way [39] through life. However, the history of condiments and of spelling alike show the strength of habits, particularly bad ones. The fact is that an intrenched defect is the very devil to get rid of – and no doubt for that reason. We are thus condemned to the indefinite typing of "_GH's_" because it takes too much mental effort to eliminate them. In the same way, I suppose our standard typewriter key board does not have the best possible arrangement of letters as one is aware every time he has to use "also" or try to work in both hands on words ending in "-_erty_." But it is standardized and that settles it, I rather admire the old days when editors were non-existent and spelling eclectic. After all, you generally know what Shakespeare meant. The only way to reform anything that has become "standardized" seems to be to revolutionize the whole thing. I mean to cut under the entire process that has been frozen in this way. Thus, if we could talk our letters and our books into something that would talk back to us, the use of letters might be abolished and the supernumerary letters along with them. I do not know just how that is to be done but I hope it will be by some system unlike the present radio which can't keep anything to itself but must spill it over the entire neighborhood.

While Dr. Thomas's ideas were to some extent standardized, he compromised not at all with the truth. He was not case hardened. You knew where he stood at any moment but you might not find him there when you came back. In that last particular he differed from Hrdlička. When you came back to Hrdlička he was always there, just where the Lord created him, on the rock of ultimate Hrdličkian knowledge.

Another of the older men with pronounced opinions, and who, though not a member of our staff, spent most of his time with us, was Dr. J.D. McGuire. He was a man of means who had owned a large farm in Howard county and been much involved in Maryland politics but had sold his property there and moved into the District. He was thick set, unlike Dr. Thomas, and with a florid face which turned purple in some of the heated arguments he had [40] with the latter. He had two anthropological interests which amounted to obsessions. One of these was tobacco on which he had written an excellent report, and he was pursuing this subject during the last years of his work among one us. This consisted in setting down the words for tobacco and pipe in all of the Indian languages in which he could find the terms, and his material was afterwards profitably consulted by Dixon. His other obsession was the recent and Old World origin of

Indian arts and industries. On certain smoothed objects he thought he could distinguish parallel marks that must of necessity have been made by an iron, and therefore European, file. American work in copper was also supposed to be, if not European in origin, at least European in motivation. In this he represented an extreme reaction from the old Mound Builder theory, and it was in line with the sentiments of Holmes and McGee. One day he came to me with a book on the antiquities of Scotland, and pointed triumphantly to some illustrations of copper circlets resembling in a measure the copper collars made on the North Pacific Coast. He thought that the latter had undoubtedly been copied from the old Scottish specimens, until I called his attention to the fact that the Old World specimens antedated Christianity while those of the Northwest Indians could have come into existence only during the last few centuries, and that Scotland and Alaska are not very close neighbors. "Evidently very late" was his comment when almost any artifact of relatively high quality was under discussion. On these matters he and Dr. Thomas frequently locked horns, especially in their discussion of copper. At times Thomas would contradict him flatly, and to contradict a southern gentleman of north of Ireland ancestry is not to be lightly undertaken. As the two gentlemen often occupied one of our cubicles together, they suggested somewhat the saw-pits in which the famous Kilkenny cats settled their differences, and the heat of the discussions made us wonder whether the end of the encounter might not be the same. Mr. Hewitt used to tell with his rare gusto how McGuire on one occasion came out to the elevator purple with rage and said "I could kill [41] that man." The next day they were probably at it again with no blood shed. In fact, I am sure that they had a real regard for each other, but they were at odds so much that it was considered a triumph when I obtained a snap shot of the two sitting side by side and smiling. Both passed away in the early days of my association with the Bureau, Dr. McGuire was stricken with some nervous affection which began to show itself in his left arm, causing it to shake continually, finally he got so feeble that he had to remain at home and I called upon him once finding him sitting at the top of the front steps of his house on Sixteenth Street. Not long afterward he passed away. However, some time elapsed after Thomas left us before Dr. McGuire was forced to remain at home, and during that period the latter was, in constant association with Dr. {Jesse Walter} Fewkes, later Chief of the Bureau. After that there were no more Donneybrook Fairs, Fewkes being more of the type of Holmes and Hough.

Mooney and Mrs. Stevenson were in the field when I settled down in Washington permanently after returning from the Queen Charlotte Islands. "Tilly" (Matilda Coxe) Stevenson was the widow of James Stevenson, an intimate friend of Major Powell and his right hand man in securing appropriations for the Bureau. He died before my time, but was said on all hands to have been possessed of a delightful personality which assured him a wide circle of friends. His wife was of another order. She obtained her effects by going after what she wanted and taking it. She shared so little in the esteem her husband had enjoyed with Powell that he wished to drop her from the staff of his organization after having appointed her to it. However, during her husband's lifetime she had secured a rather large circle of friends in the political world, and he found it advisable to reinstate her. It is quite likely that most of these gentlemen knew her husband rather than herself. All this was under the bridge in my time, and she was generally in the Southwest making that study of the Zuni Indians afterward published by the Bureau. I was appraised of her first return to Washington by the irruption of the [42] chief clerk, Mr. Clayton, into my room and. appropriation by him of my favorite chair which, as it seemed, Mrs. Stevenson had used before she went west and which she regarded as personal property. In 1910, when we moved down to the Smithsonian building, she was assigned a room in the north tower on the second floor which it was thought would be more convenient for her than one higher up. She was then in the field, and on her return demurred somewhat at the assignment and fell in with the plan only after the room had been thoroughly clean and reconditions while she stood on a chair in the middle of the floor superintending the operation. She was motivated largely, it seemed, by the fact that that room had been occupied by the fish specialist of the Institution for I do not know how many years without the admission of a renovator. She worked away from the office, however, a great deal of the time, and ultimately formed a partnership with another lady and together they bought a ranch in New Mexico. Probably the ladies were too much alike for they presently fell out and the other being younger outlasted and outlived the subject of this sketch, who, I think, died in that country. Mrs. Stevenson was related to the famous "Fighting Bob" Evans of Spanish War fame, and claimed that her devotion to cleanliness as exemplified in the above instance was due to her experience with "Cousin Bob's ship," though it was rumored that her affection for "Cousin Bob" was not mutual. Well! as Miss Clark, secretary to our Chief at the time, remarked, "Something was always doing" when Mrs. Stevenson was about. She was able to appropriate to herself more personal service than the rest of the Bureau combined.

Mooney did not return from the field much before our removal to the Smithsonian building, but after that I saw more of him than of any other of the staff until his untimely death, except possibly for Dr. Fewkes. Like some of the other members Mooney was "set" in his opinions, and he had the courage of them. The peyote question came to the fore about this time. Some wished to prohibit its use altogether asserting that the Indians were being demoralized by it, but Mooney held that the use of it, like that of wine in the Christian communion, was an essential element of a native cult, and that [43] those who used it uniformly gave up the much more damaging use of alcoholic spirits. In this he was supported by the Omaha Indian, Francis LaFlesche, who had been added to the Bureau's force in 1910. I attended a congressional committee investigation on this matter at which Mooney testified strongly in favor of peyote and in opposition to his co-religionist, Father {William} Ketcham.[58] Mooney, like most members of south Ireland families, had been brought up in the Roman Catholic faith, one of his sisters was a mother superior, and practically all of his connections had strong Catholic affiliations. He told me that he believed Catholicism was best suited to the Irish temperament and that he should always be of that faith. In this particular, however, the very strong political views he held clashed rather sharply with strict Catholic doctrine. For Irish Nationalism was, it seemed, even dearer to his heart than religion. It came near being his religion. Naturally, he entertained a distinct dislike of England and this made his position a difficult one during the first World War. But his nationalistic faith involved an even more pronounced antipathy to the higher clergy in his own denomination which he accused of being responsible for smothering every effort of the Irish to obtain their independence. He claimed, and quoted expressions to prove it, that the higher clergy was willing to sacrifice Ireland in the interests of the Church in the British Empire as a whole and that they were afraid that much of that stream of young men which had been pouring into the Catholic priesthood would be deflected into purely political life if Ireland had her own government. He commended the French clergy because the Catholic priesthood in other lands accused them of being "too French," and expressed the opinion that the Church in each country should be autonomous. I imagine this view could hardly have received the approbation of many of Mooney's Catholic friends if he ever expressed it to them as he was quite capable of doing. His study of the Irish situation made him liberal and favorable to reform in other lines as well, even to socialism though that was anathema in Catholic circles. As I was myself interested in the

---

[58] {Bureau of Catholic Indian Missions, DC. When its records were set to be discarded, they were rescued by Marquette in Milwaukee, Wisconsin.}

subject at the time, we found ground of common interest [44] in this as well as in many other matters.

Some time after Fewkes became chief of the Bureau, Mooney had a falling out with him due in considerable measure to a clash of temperaments. Mooney, when this break took place, was in the Kiowa country, I think, at least in the far west studying certain Plains Indian ceremonies, and complaint was sent to the Office of Indian Affairs by some field agent that Mooney was encouraging practices inimical to the best interests of the Indians and which the Office was trying to stamp out. On receiving this complaint, Fewkes ordered Mooney to come home and report. If I have gotten the story straight, I believe this to have been a mistake. The head of an office should be prepared to back up his men until an accusation levelled against any of them is substantiated, or at least until he has had a chance to reply. But Dr. Fewkes resembled Holmes to some extent in hating a row and being too sensitive to hostile criticism. Therefore, he reacted immediately by calling Mooney home to report and thereby interrupting his work, instead of presenting the complaint to him in a written form to be answered by mail. That is in accordance with my understanding of what took place, but I have not, and never had, access to the details.

This accusation, that the Bureau was encouraging the perpetuation of "heathenish ceremonies," was not a new one. At a much earlier period when Mooney and George A. Dorsey, then of the Field Museum, were studying the Cheyenne, it was claimed by the agent of the latter, a man who indeed had an excellent record in dealing with the Indians, that Dorsey and Mooney had paid the Indians to stage a Sun Dance. So far as Mooney was concerned there was nothing whatever in this nor do I think Dorsey would have needed to be at any expense to secure such a ceremony which was given from time to time until a much later date. Agent Sage's attitude reflected probably the missionary influence of the time which was directed to the total suppression of native Indian ceremonies, since then the churches have learned something of that toleration inculcated by the founder of Christianity and missionaries take courses in anthropology before entering upon their work, but it was not so when I first entered the Bureau. [45] The shift from hostility to tolerance and later to appreciation, study, record and even preservation of ceremonies has been rapid since then, reaching its apex with the Collier administration.

Mooney's health had suffered greatly from the privations necessitated by his many years of fieldwork, and it was not long after the difference of which I have spoken that he was taken sick and died. We all felt his loss keenly and perhaps no one more than myself.

Once I met Washington Matthews in Mooney's office. That was before 1910 when we were still on F St. and my memory of the event is rather dim, but the impression left on my mind is of a vigorous, large-framed man with a very active mind and it seems to me that he had lost an arm or at least was one sided.

John Napoleon Bonaparte Hewitt {See p114} was a kind of Bureau institution. He was appointed back in the 1880's I think and died in office in his 80's. He had been brought in in 1886 to complete the work of Mrs. Erminnie Smith on a dictionary and grammar of the Tuscarora language in which he had been acting as her assistant.

Those acquainted with Mr. Hewitt will be somewhat amused to read in the report announcing his appointment that the works in question were "soon to appear." Hewitt was descended, as he told me, from the Bear clan of the Tuscarora and that was founded by a captive white woman. He had lived away from his people for some time before his appointment and was obliged to learn Tuscarora anew. He was, he has told me, a conductor on a street railway system in northern New Jersey. The wages were low but in spite of that and a long day's work, each conductor had to clean out his own car or pay a small sum to an assistant to do so. Generally they were so tired as to choose the latter alternative, and as illustrating the corporation morality of the period he told me that his own superintendent was surprised to learn that, instead of embezzling this money out of the day's take in, the men paid it out of their own pockets. The super's comment was "They're fools if they do." If that was typical of the principles [46] prevalent among the officials, one wonders how much money ever got through to the stockholders. We all liked Hewitt, and his conversation, which generally turned upon Indian ceremonies, was always interesting, but he was not the type to be hurried. He had to do things in his own way, and his own way consisted largely of detours. Set upon any job, there was always some good and sufficient reason why it could not be completed immediately. Equally plausible was the excuse brought forward next day, next week, or next year. This was perhaps a holdover from his Indian ancestry. At any rate, he would procrastinate, even if it was against his own interest. For instance, he was promised a substantial rise in salary if he would catalogue the manuscripts in the vault of which he had been given charge. In vain was the completion of that work urged upon him and urged repeatedly. He never got round to doing it, and in despair it was turned over to the then chief clerk. The result was, not unnaturally, defective in many ways and there were not a few errors which Hewitt enjoyed calling one's attention to. He did not develop a profound dislike of the individual in question, however, as might have been expected. He criticized us all more or less, but I think his peculiarities arose from a realization of his inferiority in education to most of his associates and his inability to concentrate on a problem and see it through to its completion. It was a kind of defense mechanism. If, however, anyone attempted to discuss things Iroquois Hewitt's defense went over into the offensive with great promptitude. His adversary might well complain that he had had to do the best he could because of Hewitt[1]'s only failure to give what might well have been the orthodox version. On such an occasion Hewitt might be stimulated to promise that his conclusions on this phase of Iroquois life were "soon to appear" after which he continued on as before. The volcano relapsed into slumber. Hewitt did indeed publish some Iroquois myths and edited at the same time some others by Curtin but not until the manuscript was fairly torn from him. Part of his procrastination was indeed a commendable desire for accuracy, but perhaps still more a fear of inaccuracy and consequent criticism. The less one publishes, the less one has to fear hostile, or any other, criticism of what he does. He has taken to heart the well known old exclamation "Oh!, that mine enemy would write a book!" There is, however, one way to get material from the confirmed introvert, or shall we say "introscript" and that is by printing something adverse to his prejudices or indeed downright wrong. In an old Haida legend the trickster and clown Raven obtains a much-desired diet of sea urchins which the ducks were gathering by standing on the shore where they were fishing and insulting them. The result was, of course, that they could not resist the temptation to bombard their assailant with sea urchins and he profited accordingly. Some of Hewitt's smaller contributions were teased out of him in a similar manner. His criticisms of an opponent were most peculiar. He would never call anyone a liar or a fool in good old United States, but approached the subject through a most delightful and characteristic maze of verbiage. "Mr. Jones had unfortunately exhibited inhibiting tendencies toward the facts in the case which should have been evident even to highly abbreviated intelligencies." If in conversation or in any other way you trenched upon his areas of belief, he might not dissent immediately, and the first intimation of your trespass might come through some remote member of the staff to whom Hewitt had communicated his grievances. He was given a great deal of work within the office answering queries, and to one of these he might devote a month or more, branching off during his quest into no end of country lanes, so that he acquired in that way a great fund of information. How to bait your hook so as to get it out of him was the problem.

Hewitt came to the Bureau when Powell was constructing an anthropological philosophy and this included the then ruling cult of Morganism with proper regard to the Frazer, Lubbock, and McLennan theory of an original matriarchate and systematic change to our patriarchal society. Hewitt had absorbed this view and the McGee terminology which went with it as part of the necessary equipment of every Bureau member, and I got in bad with him [47] in consequence. Nevertheless, my relations with Hewitt were quite uniformly cordial, and what I am saying now about him is not in an unfriendly spirit. It is characterization, not criticism. I am sure we all came to be very fond of the old fellow and his failings rather amused than irritated us. If he did not publish much, he left Iroquois manuscript material of value to future workers.

When the Bureau was established an impression existed in Congress that its work would be temporary, and we had to answer the question to every new session of the national legislature when we would be through. It also wanted to see results, and fortunately it did in the very solid series of volumes which constituted the annual reports and the bulletins. However, in my time it was thought that something more appealing to the untechnical minds of legislators ought to be provided, and we resumed with vigor an undertaking started some years before independently by Prof. Otis T. Mason of the National Museum and Mooney under the name "Synonymy of the Indian Tribes." To take over all editorship of this work, the name of which was changed to "Handbook of the American Indians," Mr. Frederick W. Hodge was recalled to the Bureau where he had formerly served as librarian. The editorship could not have fallen into more competent hands as I am sure everyone who has had occasion to use that extensive publication will agree. The work of preparing special articles was assigned to the several members of the Bureau staff, to those anthropologists connected with the National Museum and to others both in and out of Washington. We also held meetings to discuss the assignation of articles and matters of general policy and these were very interesting to me. Whatever contributions any of us made, however, are incidental to a work which remains a great monument to the industry and intelligent handling of its editor.

A few other men were brought into our circle to work at that time. One of these was a physician named McCormick, a friend of Powell and McGee, I believe, who was a very enthusiastic Mason and when he left us took up work for his order in Mobile. Another was Frank Huntington who occupied the same cubicle as myself. These were retained to do editorial work. Huntington was, I regret to say, somewhat addicted to the flowing – or rather the overflowing – bowl, and that may be why, when I returned from one field trip, I discovered that he had been using my office coat as a penwiper.

Mention of the flowing bowl reminds one not unnaturally of the then head of the illustration department, Delancey Gill, about whose artistic abilities and convivial propensities there could be no doubt. He was very friendly with everyone, not merely between times, and I must add that I never saw him deflected from the straight line of march or of thought in consequence of his habits. He had been with the Bureau from very early times and remained with it until a few years before his death.

John R Swanton

MODERN SQUARE GROUNDS OF THE CREEK INDIANS
By JOHN REED SWANTON,
ETHNOLOGIST, BUREAU OF AMERICAN ETHNOLOGY
1931 (WITH FIVE PLATES)

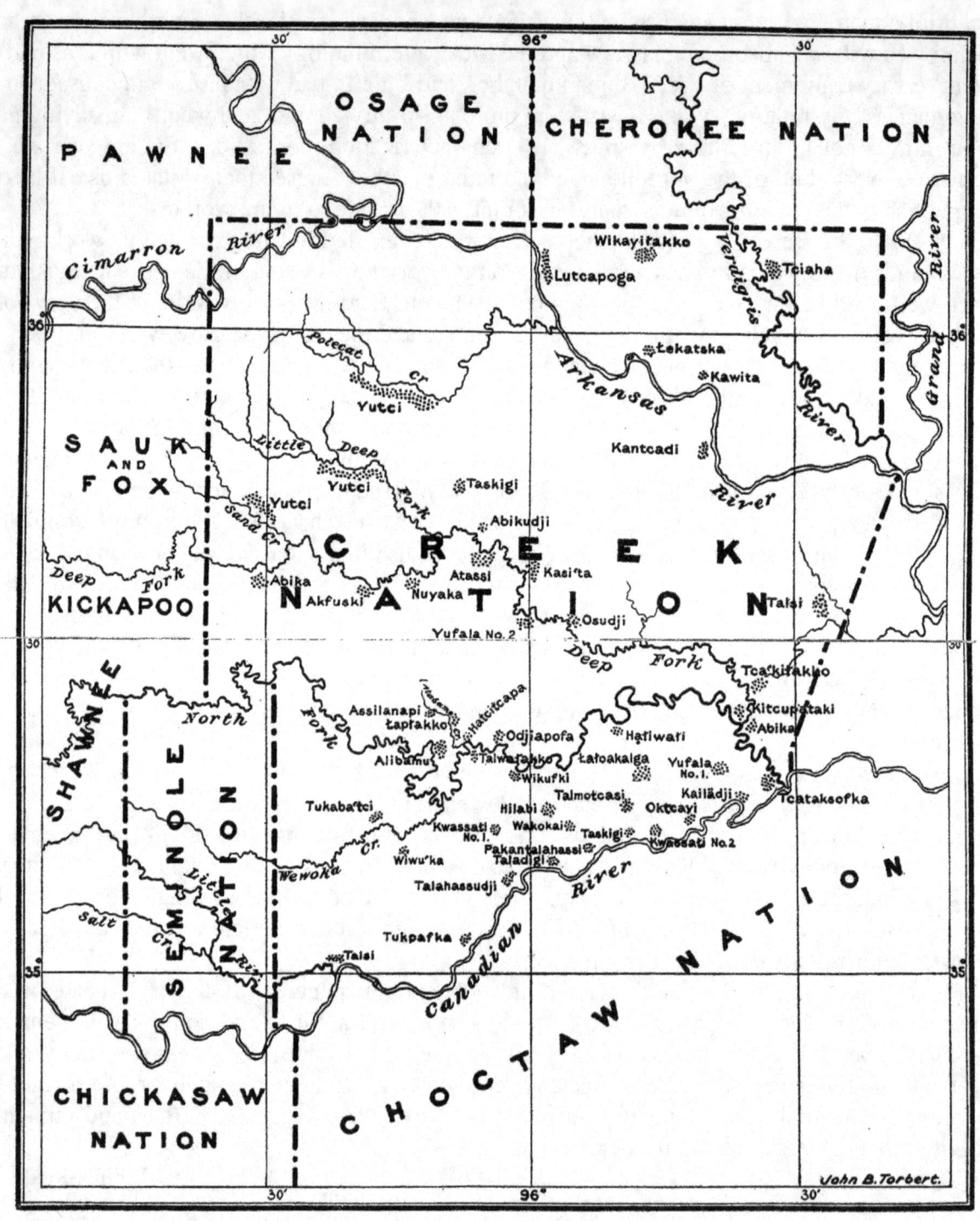

MAP SHOWING APPROXIMATE LOCATION OF CREEK TOWNS AND NEIGHBORING TRIBES

(COMPILED CHIEFLY FROM GATSCHET'S LIST)

The writer has already published descriptions of many of the square grounds of the Creek Indians, the sacred areas where their husks and other annual ceremonies took place.[59] In collecting this material, however, my endeavor was to learn the most ancient arrangement of the several grounds and the arrangement of those grounds no longer in use. During the summer of 1929 I visited the Creek country again to secure information regarding the organization of the extant grounds. This work duplicates and supplements the earlier to a considerable extent, but the main purpose was somewhat different.

Besides the three Yuchi grounds, now in the vicinity of Kellyville, Bixby, and Depew, respectively, with which I did not concern myself, there are or were in 1929 17 square grounds, as follows: *Ahibka* and *Otciapofa* near Henryetta ; *Nuyaka* north of Okemah ; *Lałogalga*[60] or Fish Pond and *Asilanabi* west of Okemah: two *Tulsa* grounds near Holdenville; *Tukabahchee* at Yeager; *Lapłako* near Wetumka; *Alabama* east of Alabama Station on the Frisco Railroad; *Eufaula* west of Eufaula; *Kasihta* east of Okmulgee: and *Hilibi, Kealedji, Okchai, Pakan Tallahassee,* and *Wiogufki* about Hanna. *Abihka, Otciapofa, Nuyaka, Lałogalga, Kasihta, Hilibi, Pakan Tallahassee,* and *Wiogufki* were visited, and new information obtained regarding all of the others except *Eufaula*, of which I secured very good descriptions 17 years before. The *Eufaula* ground, that of *Asilanabi*, one of the *Tulsa* grounds, *Tukabahchee, Alabama,* and *Okchai* were visited in the winter of 1911-1912. *Kasihta* is the only square ground representing the Lower Creeks now maintained. It was not in existence during my earlier work in the Creek Nation, nor were *Lapłako* or *Kealedji*.[61] These two last and the Yuchi grounds are the only ones that I have not seen. I was present at part of the busks at *Otciapofa, Nuyaka,* and *Pakan Tallahassee.* Not much attention was devoted [SMITHSONIAN MISCELLANEOUS COLLECTIONS, VOL. 85, No. 8] [2] to the Seminole grounds, but information was obtained regarding one of these, *Ochesee* Seminole, which had been discontinued in 1912, when I visited the Seminole squares, but was afterwards revived.

In order to make the material obtained in 1929 intelligible, it will be necessary to give a brief outline of the Creek political, social, and ceremonial organization.

The name Creek is a shortened form of *Ochesee Creek* Indians, a name which English traders from South Carolina came to apply to that part of the Indians of the Creek Confederation who were living upon Ocmulgee River in the closing decades of the seventeenth century and the opening years of the eighteenth. The word *Ochesee* signifies "people of a different speech" in the language of the Hilchiti, one of the minor constituents of the Creek Confederacy, being equivalent to the word *Tcitoki* in the Creek or Muskogee language. It was applied to the Creeks proper or Muskogee by the *Hitchiti* along with many other tribes, but came in some way to be particularly associated with the Muskogee and the river upon which they were then living.

Anciently there seems not to have been a single term applicable to all of the Muskogee, the latter name having been unknown to the Spaniards who first entered this section. It does not make its appearance until the English had settled in the Carolinas. The origin of the word is uncertain, but there are indications that it was derived from Shawnee, since a band of Shawnee lived for a time near what is now Augusta, Ga., and from a very early period occupied an intermediate position between South Carolina and Georgia on the one hand and the Creek Nation

---

[59] BAE-AR 42nd, 1924-23: pp. 204-296, 1928.

[60] In the present paper, å indicates the obscure 'a' in such a word as ability, and ł or Ł is a surd l approximating lth in English.

[61] But see p. 35 [p100 herein] regarding the former.

on the other. It is probable that there were originally several tribes speaking the same language but having separate names and that the necessity for a distinguishing term for all did not present itself until the number of non-Muskogee tribes in the Confederation came to be considerable. As to the names of these Muskogee tribes, we seem to have indications of the following:

Abihka, Coosa, Okchai, Pakana, Tukabahchee, Hilibi, Eufaula, Kasihta and *Coweti* (or perhaps an original tribe of which the *Kasihia* and *Coweta* {*Kawita*} were sections). There were some other groups on the lower course of Talapoosa River, such as the *Atasi, Kealedji,* and *Kolomi,* which cannot be definitely placed and may have been independent of these or early subdivisions of them. Of course some may represent people of wholly different connections who had become assimilated to the Muskogee and had lost their own language and customs. This is rendered probable from the fact that we have [3] several actual cases of such assimilation in later times. However, so far as the tribes enumerated are concerned, this must always remain in doubt.

When the tribes of the Confederation first became known to white people, they were distributed geographically into two main sections to which the names Upper Creeks and Lower Creeks have become attached. The former were on the Coosa and Tallapoosa rivers and the upper course of Alabama River in the present state of Alabama, the latter on the lower and middle courses of the Chattahoochee, which now forms part of the boundary between Alabama and Georgia. It was this latter division principally which lived upon Ocmulgee River for a time and thus gave rise accidentally to the popular English name for the entire people. A minor division also existed between those Creeks living on the middle course of Coosa River and those centering about the lower Tallapoosa, the two being sometimes designated as Upper and Middle Creeks, respectively. In the distribution of the original Muskogee tribes, the *Abihka* and *Coosa* constituted the greater part of the Upper Creeks, while the *Kasihta* and *Coweta* were the dominating element among the Lower Creeks. The *Okchai, Pakana, Tukabahchee, Atasi, Kealedji, Łiwahali, Łapłako, Kolomi,* and a number of towns descended from the *Coosa,* including *Otciapofa,* the *Tulsa* towns, and the *Okfuskee* towns, besides several minor groups, formed the bulk of the Middle Creeks. The Eufaula had the distinction of being connected with all three. Their oldest seat seems to have been in the Upper Creek country; later they established themselves among the Middle Creeks and about the period of first white contact they formed a colony well down Chattahoochee River, among the Lower Creeks. To complete the story of their migrant habits, we may add that they seem to have furnished the first true Muskogee contingent to the Forida Seminole in the Red House or *Tcuko Tcati* Indians north of Tampa Bay.

Tradition seems to be borne out by circumstantial evidence in pointing to the Lower Creek country as that region in which the tribes in question began their federation. According to the story this had to do on the one hand with the division of the Muskogee into the *Kasihta* and *Coweta,* and on the other with the relations between them and the non-Muskogee elements, particularly the Apalachicola. The relations of the *Kasihta* and Coweta to each other are somewhat uncertain for while it is at times implied that they resulted from the fission of a single body of people, the most popular traditions speak of them as having come from the west [4] as two distinct tribes and it is possible that the one-tribe idea may be the result of later rationalizing. The story goes that, having defeated all of their enemies, the *Kasihta* and Coweta instituted periodical ball games as a kind of "moral equivalent for war," and afterwards, when either of them established relations of friendship with other Indians, whether Muskogee or not, these Indians entered on the same side as their friends so that this dual system soon became general.

One of these sides, that of *Kasihta,* came to be known as the "White or Peace side, though it did not receive that specific name; while the side of *Coweta* was the Red or War side.

At the same early period the Muskogee entered into intimate relations with the *Apalachicola* Indians, who spoke a dialect related to *Hitchiti*. This was the outgrowth of a treaty of peace following upon hostilities, or to avert threatened hostilities. The Apalachicola were then taken into the Confederation on the same side as *Kasihta*. In some particulars, however, they are held to have been more representative of the White towns than *Kasihta* and for that reason their settlement came to he called *Talwa Łako*, "Big Town." Indeed, the migration legend related to Oglethorpe by Tchikilli {brother of Brim} implies that *Kasihta* was at least partly Red, their hearts being "red on one side and white on the other." However, in all later times *Kasihta* assumes the leadership of the White towns among the Lower Creeks, as does Coweta the leadership of the "Red towns. Four having been the sacred number — the sacred formulae being gone through four times, four arbors or beds constituting the ceremonial buildings in the square ground and four sticks the number employed in the ceremonial fires — it is not surprising that the Creeks should select two towns from the Upper Creeks, taken collectively, to add to these two leading Lower Creek towns. The While towns of the Upper Creeks were represented by Abihka, the "Red towns by Tukabahchee, the second being from that group I have called Middle Creeks, the other from the northernmost bounds of the Nation. These four towns were the "bark sticks" of the Confederation, and each had a special ceremonial name, viz., *Kasihta Łako* ("Big Kasihta"), *Coweta Mahmayi* ("Tall Coweta"), *Tukabahchee Ispokogi*, and *Abibka Nagi*. Ispokogi was the name of the culture heroes of the *Tukabachchee* and it may he a Shawnee term. It bears a suspicions resemblance to that of the *Kispokotha* band of Shawnee. I do not know the meaning of <u>Nagi</u>. The Abihka were also called specifically "the door shutters" because they protected the northern frontier of the Confederation. [5]

In course of time the non-Muskogee element represented by the Apalachicola Indians was increased, first by other groups related to the last mentioned — such as the *Hitchiti, Okmulgee, Sawokli,* and *Tamałi* — who spoke closely related languages and called themselves *Atcikhata*, a term said to have some reference to the ashes of the ceremonial fire in the square grounds. These Indians formed the greater part of the first Creek invaders of Florida who presently constituted the Seminole nation. The leading town in this southward movement was *Oconee*, almost certainly affiliated with the *Atcikhata*, and the titular leadership among the Seminole remained with them until after the Seminole War. However, the complexion of the Seminole as a whole was changed from *Atcikhala* or *Hitchiti*, to Muskogee by the multitudes of refugees which fled to Florida after the Creek War of 1813-14. The later removal to Oklahoma seems to have reversed the situation since more than two-thirds of the Indians now in Florida speak a language of the *Hitchiti* group.

There is strong evidence that the *Chiaha* Indians originally spoke *Hitchiti* and that the *Mikasuki* of Florida branched off from them, but some early event in their history separated them from the other *Atcikhata* and made them allies of the *Coweta*. This friendship they shared with the *Osotci* who seem originally to have belonged to the Timucua linguistic group of Florida. To the Upper Creeks were added the distinct but dialectically related Alabama, *Koasati*, and *Tuskegee*, while bands of *Yamasi* and *Apalachee* were temporarily connected with both Upper and Lower Creeks. The Alabama town of *Tawasa*, seems to have had an origin similar to that of the *Osotci*. At a very late date the wholly alien Yuchi population was admitted into the Confederation, most of them making their home among the Lower Creeks though there was a small body also among the Upper Creeks. And more divergent still were the Shawnee, from among whom two towns made their homes in Creek territory for several decades during the eighteenth century. One of these probably continued on into the early years of the nineteenth century.

It may be added that towns are known to have changed from one side to the other. Alabama was once a White town closely associated with the *Okchai*, but later they were affiated with the Tukabahchee and came to be reckoned as Red. Wiogufki, *Hilibi*, and *Wiwohka* are also said to have shifted from one side to the other. In the case of the two last this may be partially explained by the fact that, if we may trust native tradition, they were built up of refugees from other settlements. [6]

In former times a certain aloofness was maintained by the towns of one moiety toward those of the other. They did not encourage intermarriage and did not attend each other's annual ceremonies. This latter inhibition is now breaking down and it is claimed that men of all towns attend the busk of *Otciapofa* {Hickory}. *Otciapofa*, however, has long occupied an exceptional position. A chief belonging to the Bird clan of this town always delivered the principal speech when a new chief of the Confederation was installed. This town was also the residence of the Creek dictator Alexander McGillivray, and was here that Crazy Snake, leader of the Creek conservatives, called his important councils. Evidently the functions of the White and Red sides in maintaining peace or bringing on hostilities were formerly of great importance and some White towns, certainly Apalachicola and Coosa, were places of refuge for murderers. The "regular" ball games, as distinguished from practice games, always took place between towns of different sides and the supporters of each town marched to the encounter in much the same spirit as if they were going to war.

The principal White towns were: *Kasihta, Apalachicola, Hitchiti, Okmulgee, Sawokli, Yuchi, Abilika, Coosa, Otciapofa, Tulsa, Okfuskee, Okchai* (including *Lałogalga* and *Asilanabi*), *Pakana, Koasati, Tuskegee,* and *Wiogufki*.

The principal Red towns were: *Coweta* (including *Likatcka*), *Eufaula, Chiaha, Osochi, Tukabahchee, Liwahali, Lapłako, Atasi, Kealedji,* and *Hilibi*. *Alabama* changed from White to Red in the manner described.

The people of each town were subdivided into clans which were usually named after animals and were invariably perpetuated in the female line. The only clan of importance not named for an animal was the Wind clan and with this the Skunk was closely associated, the Skunk clan having always been linked with it. I obtained the names of over 50 clans but some of these were known to only one or two informants {speakers}, and a number of others were small and bound into phratral associations with clans of greater prominence. Some clans were considered as equivalents throughout the entire nation. The Skunk, Fish, Rabbit, Otter, and Turtle seem always to have been united in one phratry with the Wind; the Wolf and Salt with the Bear; the Pahosa with the Deer; the Wildcat with the Panther; and the Turkey and *Tami* with the Alligator. In the same way the Snake, *Kapitca*, and *Woksi* were almost invariably counted in with the *Aktayatci* {fierce water snake ~ tiger}, the Mole, Toad, and *Tcikote* always went together and were generally allied with the Deer and *Pahosa*; and the [7] *Lidjami*, Eagle, Hickory nut, Fox, Cane, and Muskrat[62] were usually placed with the Raccoon.

Some phratral associations, however, were confined to one or a few towns and did not extend throughout the nation. Thus the Potato was commonly placed in one phratry with the Raccoon but in *Tukabahchee* it was separated. The Beaver was usually placed with the Bird, but in Alabama it was quite distinct. On the other hand it was sometimes classed with the Alligator. Occasionally the *Aktayatci* formed one phralry with the Raccoon, and much more rarely the Deer

---

[62] In BAE-AR 42nd (p. 116) I [JRS] erroneously called this the Mink.

and Panther were found together. Differences of this kind were due in some measure to the council system. Every important clan in a given town, or every group of related clans, held meetings during the annual ceremony known as the busk and each listened to an address by its oldest capable male member or "uncle." If an individual came to live in a town in which his own clan or his phratral group was not represented, he would elect to affiliate with one of those already in existence. It was usual for all of the children of each group of this kind to consider themselves brothers and sisters between whom marriage was ordinarily prohibited. However, the information received shows plainly that sexual intimacy between individuals of linked clans was not considered as serious as between members of the same clan. It is specifically stated regarding some of these clans that "they were kin" up to noon, or up to midnight, and separate the rest of the time, i.e a limited taboo was maintained against them. It is also said that a man would sometimes pretend that a woman whom he wished to marry was of a certain clan for which he would manufacture a name, although she was in fact of his own, and that if he were a man of influence, he often "put over" this new creation of his. On the other hand, I have been told that, even though children of certain of the primary clans were brought up together, they would never be regarded as brothers and sisters. It is quite plain that all sorts of variations had grown up in response to unpredictable situations.

When one eliminates the obscure and the constantly linked clans, about nine are left of something like major importance. These are: Wind, Bear, Bird, Beaver, Alligator, Raccoon, *Aktayatci*, Deer, and Panther. We should perhaps add the Potato. The Beaver, however, has importance mainly in one group of towns, and the *Aktayatci* appear to have been rather closely associated with the *Hitchiti* and the Seminole, but also with *Hilibi*, *Wiogufki*, and *Eufaula*. [8]

The question naturally arises whether some of these clans may not have been brought in with formerly independent tribes. All we can say is that certain clans are more prominent in some of these tribes than among the true Muskogee but whether they were brought in by them we do not know. Thus, as just mentioned, the *Aktayatci* was particularly prominent among the *Hitchiti*, as were the Snake, *Kapitca* and *Woksi*, and in a more pronounced manner the Toad, Mole, and Tcikote. The Daddy-long-legs and Salt were similarly associated with the Alabama, the former, indeed, being hardly known outside of that tribe.

Besides this division into phratral groups all of the clans were ranged in two moieties called respectively, *Hathagalgi*, "White People," and *Tcilokogagi*, "People of a different speech."[63] The Wind and Bear with their phratral associates were almost invariably White, and the Raccoon and *Aktayatci* and their allies almost invariably *Tciloki*. The Bird is usually White but among the Alabama and *Koasati* it is *Tciloki*. The Beaver is also White usually, but when it is associated with the Alligator and when the Alligalor is not a White clan, the Beaver often becomes *Tciloki*. The Alligator is most often *Tciloki* but in a number of towns it is White. The Deer is usually *Tciloki* but it is White in a few towns. Today the Panther is almost always *Tciloki* but some of the oldest myths and some of my best informants {teachers} assert that it was anciently White.

When I first went among the Creeks, I was told that in one or two towns the clan moieties were exogamous, but the greater number of my informants held the contrary opinion. I was much surprised, therefore, during my last visit to have most of my informants maintain that they were exogamous. This much is certain, that there were striking exceptions to this law in comparatively early times, for instance, in the case of the famous Creek speaker *Hobołē Yahola*.

---

[63] < *hatha•ka* = white / *čilo•kki* = red (Fogelson 2004 *Southeast Handbook* #14: 39) >

Probably it will never be possible to say whether this phratral exogamy was breaking down or growing in times known to us. In recent years the principal function performed by these moieties has been to determine the line-up of the players in practice games within the town. The important bearing the mere character of a name may have in social evolution is shown by the fact that, on account of the name, persons of European blood were usually reckoned as "friends" of the *Hathagas*, and in consequence the latter acquired a reputation as "progressives," while the *Tcilokis* were considered, and acted like, "conservatives."

Besides the clans, phratries, and moieties there were certain groups in each town which had official functions. Some of these were [9] determined by the individual ability — usually military — of those who belonged to them. Thus a man might start his public career as a common warrior or *tasikaia*, a word now often translated "citizen," be promoted to the position of an *imała łabotski*, or "Little *imała*," then to that of an *imała łako*, or "Big Imała," and finally become a *tastanagi*, or "war leader." If sufficiently prominent he might be made a *tastanagi łako* or *hołibonaia*, "war speaker," though of these there was never more than one in a town at any one time. There were "beds" or seats in the square grounds for each of these classes, but not all were promoted into them. Men who belonged to the clan of the chief (*miko*) would be given seats in his section and form the *mikalgi*, "chiefs," who acted as a kind of special executive council. If they belonged to a certain clan known as *henīgalgi*, they would be given seats in another place. The functions of the *henīgalgi* are somewhat uncertain but they were concerned largely with the maintenance of peace and charged themselves with the internal prosperity of the tribe. The *henīgalgi* were almost always formed of the Wind clan, and if, for any reason, the Wind clan could not be used, the Bird or Beaver, or at least some clan considered White, would take their place. There was also a class of men called *istatcagagi*, the old, experienced men from all tribes, retired from active service but keepers of the tribal lore. It seems fairly evident that a correlation existed anciently between White towns, White clans, and the *henīgalgi*, and that the *miko* of a White town was generally chosen from a White clan. It is even possible that the *miko* of a Red town was formerly chosen from a White clan. Certainly there is a marked tendency to choose chiefs from the Bear clan, even in Red towns, though many of them are also from the Raccoon and the *Aktayatci*.

A word must now be said regarding the ceremonial grounds. Originally every Creek town had such a ground which at a still earlier period was probably the ceremonial ground of a small tribe. As a tribe increased in numbers, however, the ground often became too small to accommodate all of its members comfortably and so it split into two or more. Undoubtedly, before the organization of the Creek Confederation, there was great diversity among these grounds and a certain element of diversity has persisted until the present day, but on the other hand considerable standardization has undoubtedly taken place. Creek legend asserts that the first ceremonial ground was given to the *Coweta*, the *Kasihta*, or the *Tukabahchee* by the Breath Controller or by other supernatural beings, and copied by the remaining towns from them. While this represents a modern [10] rationalization, there can be no doubt that the earlier ceremonial grounds of the constituent members were altered in many particulars in conformity with the prevailing pattern.

All the grounds known to us originally consisted of three elements, a *tcokofa* or community hot house used in bad weather or for secret ceremonies, a "square ground," and a "chunkey yard," or ball ground. The name "chunkey yard" is derived from an old pastime {spread from the mound city of Cahokia} which consisted in rolling a stone disk along a level plot of land and throwing certain long poles after it, the game turning on the relative nearness of the poles to the roller after all had come to rest. There was a single pole in the middle of this yard surmounted by a cow or horse skull or by a wooden figure, and about this men and women played against each other in a kind of ball game. This game was mainly confined to people of the town and was social in character while the great ball game, similar to our game of lacrosse, was played by men only and was highly ceremonial. The fact that the "chunkey yard" was a part of the ceremonial ground may indicate that the single pole game formerly had more religious significance than was the case in later times.

The *tcokofa* has long been out of use, though at Tukabahchee fire was until recently lighted in the middle of a circular offset of the ceremonial ground where this structure would stand if it were still in existence, and one such building was put up at Pakan Tallahassee after the Civil War.

The most important part of the ceremonial area today is the "square ground," so called because in the largest towns there were on it four long cabins {beds} or arbors, in native parlance "beds," forming four sides of a square. Partly from tribal idiosyncrasy and still more on account of failing numbers, several of these grounds now lack one cabin, and the Alabama ground lacks two.[64] Today the cabins consist merely of two or three rows of split logs to serve as seats and an arbor of {willow} boughs to shield their occupants from the direct rays of the sun, but anciently the seats consisted of mats woven out of cane raised upon short posts and the cabins were provided with a back and roof of wattle or split shingles plastered with clay. The arbors in the largest modern towns are supported on eight posts, four in front and four behind, but some have only six, and most of the Seminole towns only four. On the other hand, a sketch of one of these cabins made by a Frenchman early in the eighteenth century shows ten posts, five in front and five at the back. Today, however, the eight post arrangement seems to be considered orthodox, and the three sections marked off by these [11] posts are used for the seating of as many clans, groups of clans or related officials.

Considerable variation in the ancient and intended plan has been brought about by the attrition which the tribe and its several divisions have undergone, loss of the keepers of the sacred lore, and other factors, but it is plain that normally one of the four cabins was mainly devoted to the *miko* and his clan. Hence it was called *mikalgi* (or *mikagi*) *intupa*, the "Chiefs' bed." Another was devoted mainly to the *henīhalgi* and was named from them. Another to the higher class of warriors, the *tastanagalgi*, and so received their name, and still another to the novitiate warriors or youths from whom it was called *tasikaialgi intupa* or *tcibanagalgi intupa*. The positions of these in the square ground varies considerably. It should be stated, in the first place that the cabins are placed normally toward the four points of the compass, but that for some unexplained reason in the square of *Tukabahchee* the entrances are toward the cardinal points. In the old *Kasihta* square, which seems to have set the fashion for many other towns, the *mikos'* cabin lay west, the *henīhas'* south, the *tastanagis'* north, and the *tasiktaias'* east. In the Okfuskee towns, of which Nuyaka is an example, the *mikos'* cabin lay north, the *henīhas'* east, the *tastanagis'* west, and the tasikaias' south. In *Pakan Tallahassee* the *mikos'* cabin is north, the henihas' south, the *tasiktaias'* west, and there is no east cabin. In *Eufaula*, the *mikos'* cabin is north, the *henīhas'* east and the *tastanagis'* south, the west cabin being missing. In Alabama, where there are but two cabins, the *mikos'* cabin is east.

The other variations in the arrangement of the squares will come out in the subjoined

---

[64]   <Mvskoki *intupa* = *em-* + *topv* 'their + bed' (Martin & Mauldin 2000: 122, 198); See Swanton p87 herein >

material, but before presenting it something must be said regarding town officials.

The *miko*, as already stated, was chief of the town, its head presiding officer and responsible executive. Like many of the other officers he had a special companion or *henīha* taken from the Wind clan or whatever clan occupied the position of *henīhalgi*. This *henīha* is sometimes called *miko apokta*,[65] "second chief," but the latter name is also given to still another functionary who shares the burdens of state with his superior. The chief had one or more *yatikas* or interpreters who also bore the name *asimbonaia*, "speakers." Unless wanted to make an announcement or to send upon an errand, they sat with their clan or other group to which they normally belonged. The *tastanagalgi łako* and *hołibonaia* have been mentioned. The position of *hołibonaia*, "war speaker " was the most exalted military position, and it is possible that there was only one such official at a time in [12] the entire Creek Nation. It was the position occupied by *Hobołi Yahola*, famous leader of the Creeks during their removal west and of their subsequent troubled history until the Civil War. He is not a *miko* even of one town, but his influence was actually greater than that of any *miko*, or any number of them. There were two *ta'pala*, {*takpa:lv*} whose chief function was to act as messengers before and during the women's dance, and there were two singers for the women (*inyahaikalgi*, "singers for them"), who sat at the end of one of the cabins just in front of the spot where the women began dancing. They were usually selected for their knowledge of songs rather than on account of their clan affiliations. The *hilis haya* was the head priestly functionary. He supervised the preparation of the medicines and gave them their final potency and he ordered *everything* in any way touching upon the supernatural. He was assisted by one or more men called *hilis tcalaba* or "medicine mixers," whose functions are defined by the name, and by two or more young men called *hilia hoboia*, "medicine gatherers," who collected the red root, *pasa*, and other plants that went into the sacred medicine. Some towns seem to have had a separate official called *tutka dīdja*, "fire builder," to start the fire, but in others the *hilis haya* did that, and there was instead a *tutka oktidīdja*, "gatherer of wood" for the fire. A number of boys known as *oidjawalgi* brought water for the medicines. In one town we learn of *ahaga haiyalgi*, "law makers," who are said to carry out the instructions of the *tastanagi*s and may be identical with the *imałas* elsewhere mentioned. There were also officers called *simiabaia*, or "leaders." The *hioktagi immiko*, "chief of the women," and his *henīha*, may have been identical with the *ta'palas*. Anciently the *tastanagi*s and their assistants acted as town police, but nowadays three or four light horsemen are selected at random to police the square ground during ceremonies, and there are boys called "dog whippers" with long whips stationed at each opening into the square during the women's dance to drive away dogs. Many of these officers were chosen for four years only. If one died before the expiration of his term, a substitute was selected from the same clan, which seems to indicate that the position was something of a clan prerogative.

Of the ceremonies which took place on these grounds, only two have survived. One, called by the popular local name of "stomp dance," was confined to the people of the town and was simple in character, the *miko hoyanīdja* (red willow) being ordinarily the only medicine used during it. There were no dances other than the common and relatively secular ones, no ceremonial lighting of the fires, no [13] ceremonial complications of any sort. It seems to have been usual to hold three of these dances in the spring and early summer, a month apart, the series paving the way for, and leading up to, the second ceremonial, the "busk," which was the great annual ritual. This last is usually considered as lasting four days, though in that four are included

---

[65] < literally, 'chief twin' *vpoktv ~ apo:kta* (Martin & Mauldin 2000: 141, 339)>

the days of assembling and departure. The principal event on the second day is the women's dance. On the third day the men fast, take medicine four times, and near its close march down to the creek and bathe. After they return, they are dismissed to their camps and break their fast. Later they are summoned to the square again where they dance four times, and then the dance becomes "common," visitors from friendly towns being admitted to it. A fire is kept up all night in the center of the square and dancing continues about it until it is nearly day. In former times many, perhaps all, of the towns extended their busks over eight days, but from what can be learned of these longer ceremonials they seem to have been in the main a simple doubling of the shorter ceremony, except for a few features like the kindling of the new fire which took place but once annually.

Let us now turn to the new material regarding the square grounds and the ceremonies conducted there. Under each heading I give the notes obtained from native informants {sources} belonging to the square or town in question.

ABIHKA

Figure I gives the general arrangement of the square of Abihka, or Talladega, and Plate 1, Figure 1, gives a view of the ground itself near Henryetta, Okla., as it appeared in 1912. The exposure was made from the southwest.

The medicines were taken first by those in the Bears' bed, then in succession by those in the beds of the Raccoon on the west side, the Raccoon on the east side, the Deer, and those in the south bed. The *asimbonaia* in the northern section of the east cabin acted more particularly as the chief's messenger: the one in the western compartment of the south cabin called first the women and then the children to come to take their medicine from the vessel at the north end of the east cabin. The *ta'palas* were changed every four years. The women gathered preparatory to their dance at a tree on the edge of the *tadjo* (the ridge of sweepings that makes the edge of the ceremonial ground) and entered the section about the fire at its northwestern corner. Five pots of medicine were prepared at the north end of the west cabin (fig. 1, 11). Afterward one pot [14] was placed a little farther north and west for the boys (12) and another was carried around to the north end of the east cabin for the women and children (13). The ingredients of this medicine

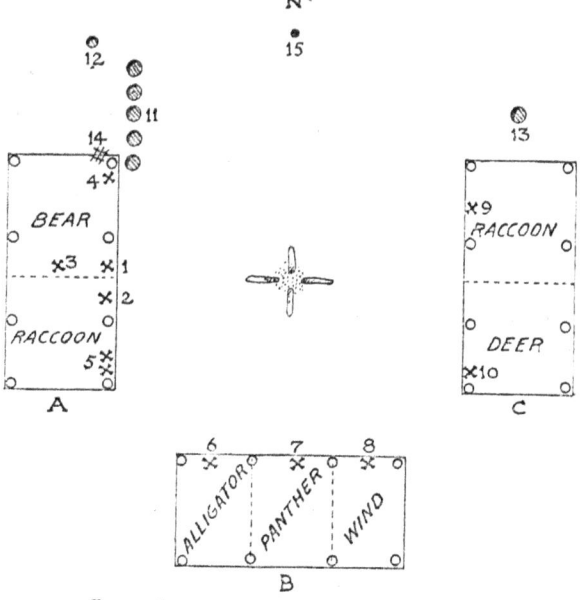

FIG. I. — General arrangement of the square of Abihka.

A. Chiefs' Bed (*mikalgi* or *makagi intupa*); 1, *miko* (Bear); 2, *heniha* (Raccoon);
     3, *hilis haya* (Raccoon); 4, *hilis tcalaba*; 5, *yahaikas* (any clan).

B. Heniha' Bed (*heniha intupa*): 6, *asimbonaia* (Alligator); 7, *ta'pala* (Panther);
     8, *ta'pala* (Wind).

C. Warriors Bed (*tastanagalgi intupa*): 9, *asimbonaia* (Raccoon); 10, *tutka* didja (Deer).

11. medicine pots (1st position); 12, medicine pot for boys (2nd position); 13, medicine pot for women (2nd position); 14, place where medicines were piled immediately after they were in; 15, ball post (*pokabi*).

It is to be noted that, in all of these diagrams, the ball post was actually much farther from the center of the square than is indicated.

were *miko hoyanidja* ("red root"), *pasa* ("buttonsnake-root "), *wilana* ("wormseed "), and *hobaga* ("maypop"); *tcato hatki* ("white stones ") were added. After the ceremony was about over and the fasters were ready to go down to bathe in the creek, what was left [15] of the medicine was poured on the fire. It is said that one gallon of spring water was brought for all five pots. This must mean a gallon for each. Following are the busk names of the present officers:

miko	*Tcuktcat Heniha*
heniha	*Itchas Hadjo*
hilis tcalaha	*Konip Yahola*
ta'pala	*Katca Tastanagi*
"	*Kona Yahola*
tutka didja	*Tastanakutci*
asimbonaia	*Wotko Fiksiko*
"	*Kapitca Hadjo*

The *Hathagalgi* of this town are Wind and Bear; the *Tcilokogalgi* are Panther, Raccoon, Deer, Beaver, Alligator, and Bird.

My information regarding this ground was obtained mainly from Jim Star who described the *Talladega* ground to me in 1912, the plan of which is in the Forty-second Annual Report of the Bureau of American Ethnology, page 205. The different aspect of the east cabin is mainly due to the fact that the earlier account gives a more ancient arrangement, when the warriors were graded into *tastanagi*s, and big and little *imałas*. The position assigned to the *hilis haya* in the earlier plan is probably erroneous. The other differences are due mainly to the more extensive information obtained on my last trip. My new information disagrees with the older, however, in assigning the Bird, Beaver, and Alligator clans to the *Tciloki* side as was said to be the case at *Abibka*-in-the-West instead of to the White side as was given me for *Talladega* and the old *Ahibka* town near *Eufaula*. It is probable that the new information is correct since the last mentioned square was given up when the man from whom I obtained data regarding it was a boy. However, it must be remembered that these allocations are not invariable and probably changed at times even within the same town.

OTCIAPOFA ~ HICKORY GROUND

Figure 2 shows the square ground of *Otciapofa*, popularly known as Hickory Ground.

The *hilis tcalaba* was changed every four years and was not taken invariably from the same clan.

At the southernmost front post of the east cabin were fastened two poles with black feathers tied to the ends and at every other front post were three similar poles but with white feathers. These were carried by the men in the "feather dance." [16]

In women's dance there is but one leader who carries a notched stick called *atasa*, the old name for the war club, from the middle of which depends an eagle feather.

Besides the invariable *miko hoyanidja* or "red root," the busk medicine contained *tutka hiliswa* ("fire medicine"), *wilana* (" wormseed "), *tutka-tcok-hissi* (a place on the ground where wood has been burned and moss has sprung up), and *hobaga* (" maypop ").

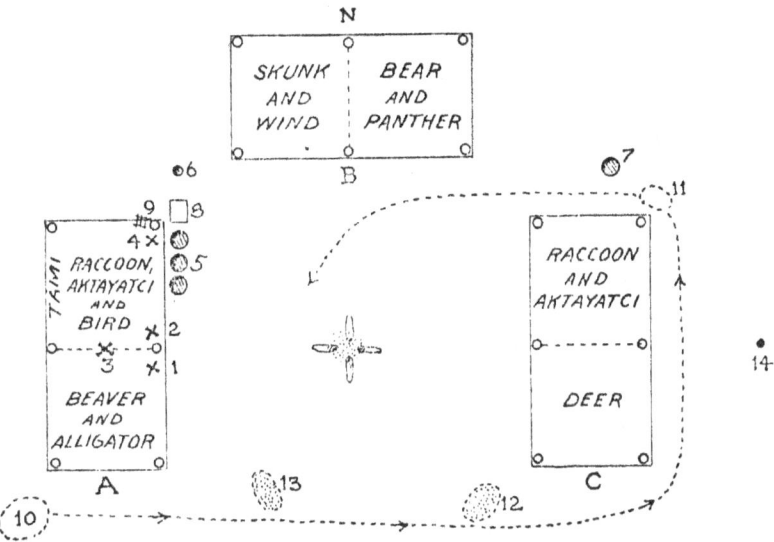

FIG. 2. — The square ground of Otciapofa, or Hickory Ground.

A. Chiefs' Bed: l, *miko* (Beaver); 2, *miko apokta* (Beaver); 3, *hilis hiya* (any clan; at present Wind; 4, *hilis tcalaba* (changed every 4 years; now Beaver).

B. *Henihas'* Bed.

C. Warriors' Bed.

5, medicine pots (1st position): 6, medicine pot for boys (2nd position); 7, medicine pot for women (2nd position); 8, log on which medicines were laid and macerated with a small wooden pounder; 9, place where medicines were kept; 10, point where women gathered preparatory to their dance; 11, point where women made a final stop before entering to dance; 12, where the ashes from the central fire were deposited every year; 13, sweepings from the square ground (*tadjo*); 14, ball post.

As usual, the doctor perfected this medicine by blowing into it through a hollow reed. Two men took medicine at the same time, using gourd dippers. After all were through a dipperful was poured on the fire.

For a drum they use a stout jar [crock] and there are two coconut-shell rattles.

There is a line of *tadjo* (sweepings) around the four cabins but it does not include the ball post. In playing the single pole game a [17] hit on the skull at the top counts five and a hit on the pole above a certain mark counts two when it is struck twice in succession.

The *Hathagas* consisted of the Beaver, Alligator, Bird, Bear, Skunk, Wind, and Rabbit; the *Tciloki*s of the Raccoon, Deer, Panther, and *Aktayatci*. The Rabbit, Wind, and Skunk formed one phratry.

The information regarding this ground which I obtained in 1912 was particularly incomplete. It is therefore gratifying to add that there are no serious discrepancies between the plan based on that (BAE-AR 42nd: 211) and the present information. Some clans are given in one and omitted from the other, but where the same ones appear in both they have practically the same positions except for the Bear, which, according to the earlier description, sat in the west cabin and according to the later at the east end of the north cabin; and the *Tami*, which the former places at the west end of the north cabin and the latter at the back of the northern section of the west cabin. The location of the *miko*, *miko apokta* or *heniha*, and *hilis haya* is probably more exact in the later plan which also adds many more details. The informants differed somewhat regarding the *Hathagas* and *Tcilokis*, the earlier authority placing the Beaver among the *Tciloki* and the Panther among the Whites, allocations exactly reversed by my later informant.

LITTLE TULSA

Next we come to one of the two divisions into which the Tulsa have recently split, this being known as Little Tulsa (fig. 3). Plate 1, Figure 2, shows the old Tulsa ground in 1911 from the southeast before the fission had occurred.

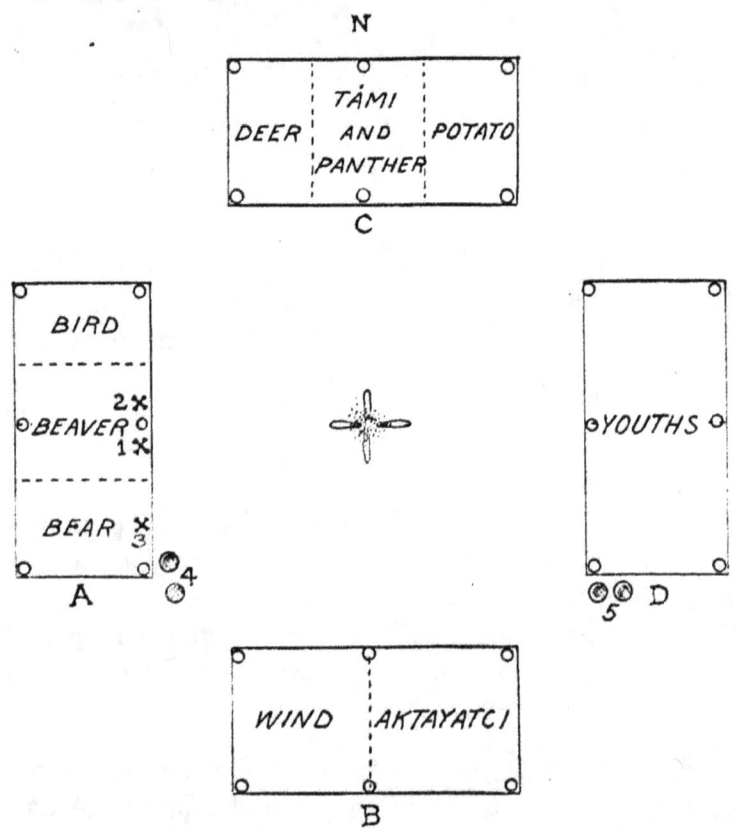

FIG. 3. — Little Tulsa square ground.

A. Chiefs' Bed: 1, miko; 2, *heniha*; 3, *simiabaia*
B. *Henihas'* Bed.
C. Warriors' Bed.
D. Youth's Bed
    4, old location of medicine pots; 5, modern location of medicine pots.

It is said that all of the offices are filled from particular clans. The following is a list of the present officers; exclusive of the *miko* and his *heniha*: [18]

tastanagi łako	*Ispani Tastanagi*
tastanagi	*Kapitci Tastanagi*
"	*Lata Miko* (controls the two above)
ahaga haiyalgi ("law makers")	*Kapica Tastanagi* (*Aktayatci*), and
(messangers for the *tastanagi* ...	*Tami Tastanagi*
simiabaia	*Kantcati Miko* (busk name) or
	Nukos Hadjo (common name)
hilis haya	*Miko Tcapko* (Beaver)
hilis tcalaba	*Tami Yahola* (*Tami*)
tutka oktididja	*Tamałakutci* (*Tami*) [19]
ta'pala	*Nokos Fiksiko* (Bear)
"	*Tami Hatkutci* (*Tami*)
yahaikas	*Kapitca Fiksiku* (*Aktayatci*)
....	*Pin Hadjo* (*Tami*)
Captain of the Light Horsemen ...	*Yahola Tcapko* (*Tami*)
Light Horsemen	*Oktan Hadjo* (Bear)
	Fus Yaholutc (Beaver)
	Kapitcutci (*Aktayatci*)

The *ta'palas* functioned at the women's dance, the *yahaikas* sang at the women's dance and at the feather dance.

My original Tulsa data, published in (BAE-AR 42: 213), was obtained from an old man and was intended to reflect the most ancient arrangement he could remember. Since that time the Tulsa Indians who used to meet at the Little River ground have divided and maintain two distinct squares. The general agreement between the older and the later plan is therefore surprisingly close. The principal difference seems to be in the position given the *Aktayatci* who appear in the north bed in the earlier plan and in the south bed in the later one. The earlier plan may also be in error in the position given the medicine pots but this was subject to change from town to town and during the ceremony itself. The Eagle clan, which appears on the older plan, died out so long ago that it can barely be remembered by any living Creeks.

NUYAKA

The plan of this ground is given in Figure 4 and a view of it as it appeared some years ago in Plate 2, Figure 1. The positions of *hilis haya*, *hilis tcalaba*, and *tutka didja* were held for four years when the man and clan were changed so as to teach others the duties of these offices. The *tastaanagi*s and *imałas* had become confined to one or two clans. The *hoktagi immiko* and his *heniha* controlled the women's dance and were called *istatcagas*. The term *hola'ta* was applied to a certain class at the square ground in some towns, sometimes to the *Tcilokis*, but its application here is not explained. The first *ta'pala* acted under the women's chief. He was taken from the Bear clan, or, failing that, from the following it order of preference: Wind, Raccoon, Tami.

In taking the medicines they drank of the *miko hoyanidja* first and *pasa* second.

A rock was placed under the *miko*'s seat "to make the seat heavy." Anciently there was a *tcokofa* northeast of the square. Nowadays the ground is hoed off only once a year. [20]

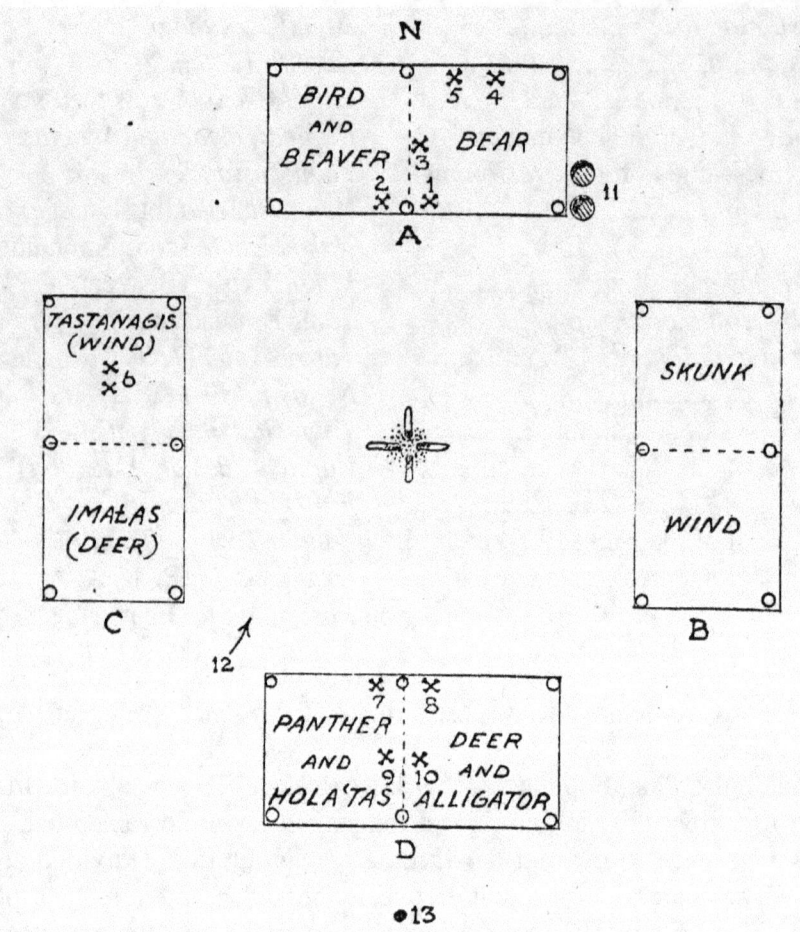

FIG. 4. — Nuyaka Square ground.

A. Chiefs' Bed: 1, *miko* (Bear); 2, *heniha* (usually Wind; Deer in 1929); 3, *hilis haya* (changed every 4years; Turkey in 1929); 4, *hilis tcalaba* (Alligator); 5, *tutka didja* (Raccoon).

B. *Henihas'* Bed.

C. Warriors' Bed; 6, two *tustanagis* (or law makers).

D. *Tcilokis'* Bed (*Tcilokogalgi intupa*), or Taskiaias' Bed (*Taskiaias' intupa*); 7, *hoktagi immiko* (*Aktayatci*); 8, *heniha* for *hoktagi immiko* (Alligator); 9, 1st *ta'pala* (Bear preferentially); 10, 2nd *ta'pala* (Alligator). 11, medicine pots; 12, point where women enter; 13, ball post. [21]

In this town the Turkey and Alligator clans belong in one phratry and so do the Wind and Skunk. The present officers are as follows:

miko	*Nokos Miko*
heniha	*Miko Tcapko*
hilis haya	*Tastanakutci*
tutka oktididja	*Hotalgi Hajudji*
hilis tcalaba	*Lodja Yahola*
hoktagi immiko	*Wotko Yahola*

When the present Nuyaka data are compared with that which I obtained in 1912 for *Nuyaka* and the related towns *Okfuskee, Abihkutci, Talmutcasi,* and *Tcatoksofa,* the agreement is found to be close except in the cases of the two last where the square grounds had long been given up and were described by individuals from memories of their early years. The main correction is in locating the *miko*, *heniha*, and *hilis haya* and the difference here is not great.

PAKAN TALLAHASSEE

Figure 5 gives the plan and Plate 2, Figure 2, and Plate 3, Figure 1, views of the ground, one showing the three cabins, or arbors, and the other the chunkey yard and ball post.

The *tutka oktididja*, *hilis tcalaba*, *hilis haya*, and *oidjawas*, were appointed every four years from any clan. The *ta'palas* and *hilis hoboia* were appointed every four years from the same clan. The *miko* and *asimbonaias* held their positions for life.

Here we seem to meet some strange innovations. The Bears' section of the south cabin receives one name connected with war, *tasikaialgi intupa*, and the section of the Birds, Beavers, and Alligators another, *tastanagalgi intupa*, while, at the same time, they are White or Hathaga clans and their cabin is called *hathagalgi intupa*. Yet one section of the west cabin is called *tastanagalgi intupa* also, and the whole cabin receives the unusual name of *laksafaskalgi intupa*, "bed of the Blacks," the Blacks being evidently the clans elsewhere called *tcilokogalgi*.

The *tcukofa* was to the northwest and this was the last town to put up such a structure.

The Birds' section was called *istatcagaga intupa*. The Deer and *Pahosalgi* were formerly called the *imatagalgi*.

Three poles with white feathers attached were fastened to each of the front posts for use in the feather dance.

Back of the *tastanagis'* section of the west cabin was a little structure in which to inclose the medicine pots when they were not in use. [22]

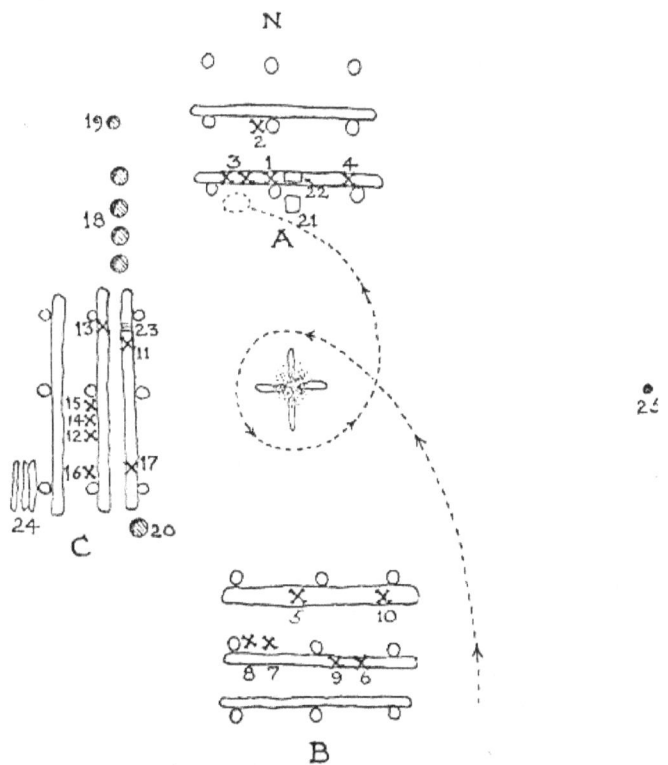

FIG. 5. — Square ground of Pakan Tallahassee.
A. Chiefs' Bed (*mikalgi intupa*): 1, *miko* (Bear); 2, *hilis haya* (Panther in 1929); 3, *yahaikas* (singers for women); 4, dog whipper; *hilis hoboia* (Panther); 5, a (instead of *heniha*) (Raccoon).

B. Whites' Bed (*hathagalgi intupa*): 5, *asimbonaia* (Bird); *ta'pala* (Bear); 7, *hilis hoboia* (Bird); 8, *oidjawa* (Bear); 9, *oidjawa* (Bird); 10, dog whipper.

C. Blacks' Bed (*laksafaskalgi intupa*): 11, *asimbonaia* (Deer); 12, *ta'pala* (Bird, father Raccoon); 13, *hilis tcalaba* (Deer in 1929); 14, *tutka oktididja* (Raccoon in 1929); 15, *hilis hoboia* (Raccoon in 1929); 16, *oidjawa* (Panther in 1929); 17, dog whipper; 18, medicine pots (1st position); 19, medicine pot for boys (2nd position); 20, medicine pot for women (2nd position); 21, drum; 22, box of tobacco; 23, place where medicine is laid before being used; 24, woodpile; 25, ball pole.

The dotted line marks the course pursued by the women when they entered to dance. [23]

In this town the *Hathagas* were the Bird, Alligator, Heaver, Bear, *Tami*, and Wind. The *Tciloki*s were the Deer, Raccoon, Panther, and perhaps *Aktayatci*. The two moieties were anciently exogamous.

The particular opponents of this town in regular ball games were the people of *Atasi* but they also played against *Eufaula Hopai, Alabama, Hilibi*, and Upper *Eufaula*. The *Koasati* Indiana are said to have divided up in the ball games, some playing on each side.

The names of the present officers are:

miko	*Nokos Miko* ("Bear Miko") (Bird)
asimbonaia	*Tastanak Imała* (Deer)
"	*Tastanak Hadjo* (Bird)
hilis haya	*Katcutci* ("Litlle Panther") (Panther)
hilis tcalaba	*Nokos Hadjutci* ("Little Bear *Hadjo*) (Deer)
oīdjawalgi	1. *Fus Yaholotci* ("Little Bird Yahola") (Bird)
	2. *Hotalgutci* ("Little Wind") (Bear, father Wind)
	3. *Halak Hopai* ("Potato Hopai") (Panther, father Raccoon, Raccoon and Potato belonging to the same phratry)
hilis hoboia	1. *Itco Hutci* ("Little Deer Foot") (Raccoon, father Deer)
	2. *Talsi Yahola* (Bird)
ta'pala	1. *Halak Yahola* ("Potato Yahola") (Bird, father Raccoon)
	2. *Hotalgi Hadjutci* ("Little Wind Hadjo") (Bear, father Wind)
tutka oktididja ...	*Itcoili Imała* ("Deer Foot *Imała*") (Raccoon, father Deer)
yahaikas	1. *Pahos Fiksiko* (Raccoon, father Deer with which the Pahosa is affiliated)
	2. *Miko Yahola* (Bear)

If one town wished to play a match game with another, said my *Pakan Tallahassee* informant, they sent a man to that town with a ball stick, and when the people of town number two had readied an agreement they sent the ball stick back. My informant said that he {just} then had a ball stick hanging up in his house which had been sent by the Alabama.

In the women's dance, the *atasa* held by the leading woman is red and has an eagle feather attached to it; that of the second is white and has a feather of the *fus hatki* ("white bird"), a bird found down by the creeks, attached to it. They used from 12 to 14 terrapin rattles. During the women's dance the two *ta'palas* stand about where the two pots nearest the west bed are in the plan. Each carries a wand called *si'dik-kika* having a white feather fastened to the end.

The dog whippers used in this dance are taken from any clan. [24]

About 54 men were present at the last preceding busk and 25 women and girls participated in the dance.

At the top of the *pokabi* in this town was a horse skull. In scoring for this game they draw a line from the ball post to the nearest corner of the south cabin. When the skull is struck, 4 are scored; when the pole under the skull is struck, it counts 2 on the way out and 1 on the way back. They may count it as a game, however, by agreement when they reach the corner post. The women's tallies are marked on one side of the line, the men's on the other.

There is little difference except in detail between the above plan of Pakan Tallahassee and the several I recorded in 1912.

WIOGUFKI

The plan of Wiogufki is given in Figure 6 and a view of the ground from the southwest in Plate 3, Figure 2.

There is a little log house on the grounds in which the pots are stored when not in use to keep them from being broken. There never was a north cabin so far as my informant knew. On the upper end of the ball post is a cow skull.

The women walk four times around the fire; then their leaders stop opposite the singers and they begin to dance.

The *hilis tcalaba* holds office for four years. In this town the place of the *miko*'s *heniha* is taken by a *tastanagi*. Indeed all of the *tastanagi*s are considered the same as the *heniha*s. They are called "the people who are named" and are of the nature of lawmakers and assistants to the *miko*. The *miko's tastanagi* is also the same thing as the *yatika*. There are no *islatcagagi*s (retired leaders who acted as councillors), and no Creek town now has a *hotibonaia*. There are five water boys picked at random. At the front posts of each cabin are four poles with feathers tied to the ends for use in the "feather dance."

The two leading women in the women's dance carry *atasa*. The principal function of the *ta'palas* is to call the women up for their dance which they do four times. Each has a wand with a little white feather at the end. Their official positions do not end with the women's dance but continue to the end of the busk.

No medicine is now put in the fire-sticks but it was formerly done. The only medicine they use at the busk is the *miko hoyandja*, to which nothing is added.

The *Hathaga*s and *Tciloki*s were the same as in *Hilibi*. They were exogamous, and if the exogamic law was violated the ear's of the culprits were cut off. [25]

The towns of *Wakokai*, *Tukpafka*, and *Talahasutci* were all one with this. In regular ball games they always played against Alabama. Comparison between the plan given above and the two obtained in 1912 shows considerable differences, but since one of the former was obtained from the same man, I think the explanation lies in the smallness of the town and the weakness of many of the clans which has resulted in many changes within a comparatively short time. Nevertheless there is a general correspondence and the allocation of clans to the moieties also agrees except in the case of [26] the Panther clan. This is explained by the fact that the Panther was anciently considered a White clan and later came to he regarded as *Tciloki*.

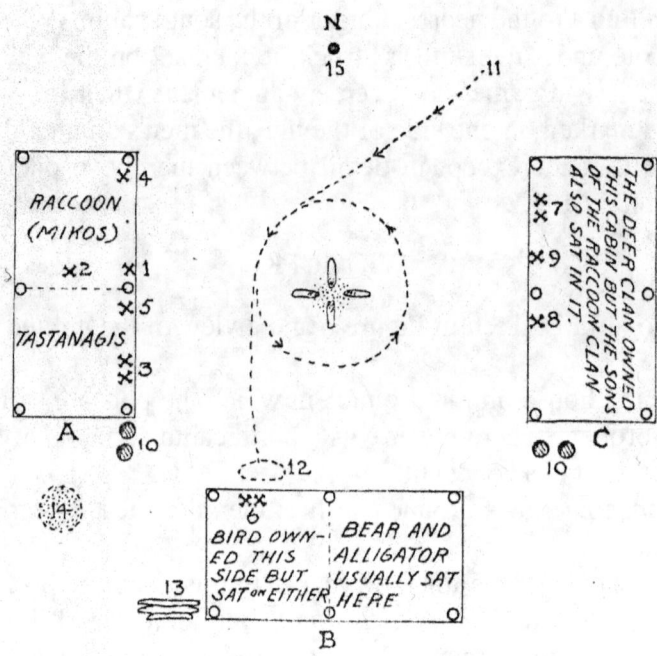

FIG. 6. — Square ground of Wiogufki.

A. Chiefs' Bed: 1, *miko* (Alligator); 2, *hilis haya*; 3, *hilis tcalaba* (Bear and Deer); *hilis hoboia* (Panther); 5, a tastanagi (instead of heniha) (Raccoon).

B. Whites' Bed: 6, *yahiaikas* (Deer).

C. Warriors' Bed: 7, *ta'pala* (Raccoon); 8, *hilis hoboia* (Deer); *tutka oktididja* (Deer).

10, medicine pots (near bed A for men; near bed C for women and boys); 11, point where women enter to dance); 12, point where women begin dancing); 13, woodpile; 14, ashes of old fires; 15, ball pole.

OKCHAI

Figure 7 shows the arrangement of this square and Plate 4, Figure 1, shows a view of it taken in winter.

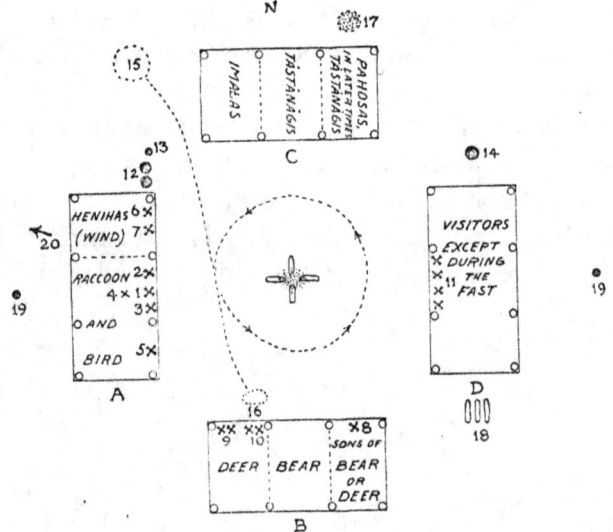

FIGURE 7. – Arrangement of square ground of Okchai.

A. Chiefs' Bed: 1, *miko* (Raccoon formerly, Bear in 1929); 2, *heniha* (Deer); 3, *yatika* (Deer formerly; Wind in 1929); 4, *hilis haya*; 5, *ta'pala* (any clan); 6, *hilis tcalaba* (Bird);
  7, tutka *oktididja* (Wind).
B. *Henihas* Bed: 8, *ta'pala* (any clan); 9, *hilis hoboia*; 10, *yahaikas* (any clan)
C. Warriors' Bed.
D. Youths' Bed: 11, *oidjawa* (any clan)
  12, medicine pots; 13, medicine pot for boys; 14, medicine pot for women; 15, point where women assemble preparatory to the dance; 16, point where women start dancing; 17, ashes of previous fires; 18, woodpile; 19, ball post; 20, a spring lies in this direction.

The *hilis tcalaba, ta'pala,* and *tutka oktididja* changed every four Years. The *hilis haya* was reappointed every four years.

Wiley Buckner, an old informant {teacher} of mine, was the former *yatika*. The *tutka oktididja* in 1920 was *Hotalgi Miko*. [27]

The medicine was pounded up just in front of the pots at the north end of the chiefs' bed.

The fire was brought from Alabama in the great migration and new fire was lighted from it. They dug in the earth as deep as the arm would reach, put the fire in there, and made the new fire on top. This is the very spot at which they first placed their square in Oklahoma and it has not been moved. The squares of the kindred towns, *Łałogalga* and *Asilanabi*, are not so old.

There were two poles with feathers on the ends at each of the front posts of the cabins all the way round.

Atasa were borne by the two women who led in the women's dance.

The *tastanagis* were law makers. They had charge of the rules governing the taking of medicine and if any one broke one of these regulations they made him stay in the square ground all night without eating instead of breaking his fast that evening as was usual.

In the various beds of this square ground the "sons of the clan" can sit with their fathers.

The *Hathagas* and *Tcilokis* were the same as at *q*.

Their principal opponents in the ball games years ago were the Hilibi.

This arrangement agrees substantially with that obtained by me in 1912 (BAE-AR 42nd: 234), the principal difference being in the location of the Bear and Bird clans. My earlier informants placed the Bird and *Aktayatci* in the middle of the south cabin and the Bear at the east end of the same, while the later one said nothing of the *Aktayatci* but placed the Bird clan in the southern section of the west cabin and the Bear clan in the center of the south cabin, the sons of the Bear being located next to them on the east. The arrangement of this square must be taken in connection with the plans of *Łałogalga* and *Asilanabi*.

ŁAŁOGALGA, OR FISH POND

For a plan of this ground, see Figure 8.

The *tutka oktididja* is appointed every four years but always from the *Aktayatci* clan. The *hilis hoboia* are chosen every four years and ordinarily from the *Aktayatci* and Bear clans but this is not necessarily the case. However, if one dies before his four years have expired he is replaced by someone of his clan. The *hilis hoboia* also act as the *hilis tcalaba*.

Ta'palas are appointed only when needed. There are no special water carriers, the *hilis hoboia* calling upon any boys for this purpose whenever water is required. [28]

The two leaders among the women carry *atasa*, that held by the first being colored red, that by the second white.

One of the two medicine pots contains *pasa*; the other the *miko hoyanidja* along with *witana*, *tutka hiliswa* ("fire medicine"), which grows in wet places in swamps and has red flowers, *tcato hatkutci* (four "little white rocks"), and *tutka-tcok-hissi* (green moss from an old fireplace).

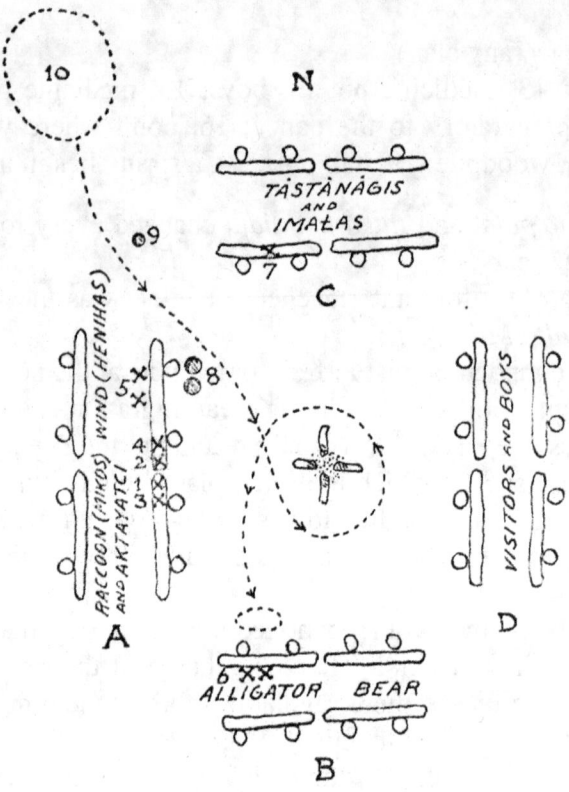

Fig. 8. – The square ground of Łałogalga, or Fish Pond.

A. Chiefs' Bed: 1, *miko* (Raccoon); 2, *heniha* (or 2nd chief) (Wind); 3, *asimbonaia* or *yatika* (head speaker, drawn from any clan); 4, *hilis haya* (any clan); 5, hilis hoboia.

B. Citizens' Bed (*Tasikaialgi intupa*); 6, *yahaikas* (no fixed clan).

C. Warriors' Bed; 7, *tutks oktididja* (*Aktayatci*).

8, medicine pots; 9, boys' medicine; 10, point where women assembled preparatory to the dance.

If one has eaten new roasting ears he is given a little *pasa* root to chew and then a little *pasa* in cold water of which he must take four drinks. Then he can take all of the medicines like the others. [29] Some of the medicine is swallowed, the rest spit out. The doctor sees that the medicines are taken and fines those who neglect to do so.

There is a town policeman called *istikona'ha* who carries out the orders of the *miko* against those who have refused to obey him, and collects fines from them. The incumbent in 1929 was *Maxcy Alakotci*.

When I interviewed them they were using the *tastanagi* as the town *miko*.

The *Hathagas* are the Bear, Wind, Bird, and Alligator; the *Tcilokis* are the Raccoon, *Aktayatci*, Deer, and Potato.

The *Aktayatci* are said to have formed one phratry with the Raccoon.

In match games, they played against *Tukabahchee, Atasi, Łapłako, Eufaula, Hilibi,* and *Kealedji. Alabama* was formerly of the same fire but later drew away.

This year (1929) they did not use the *pasa*. The *Asilanabi* square ground is arranged just like this one, but the *Okchai* differ from these two a little in the use of their medicines. It is thought that *Asilanabi* is older than *Łałogalga* and that the latter branched off in order to get the extra money that was paid to its six representatives in the national assembly.

Except that there is more detail, the arrangement given here differs only slightly from that which I recorded in 1912 (BAE-AR 42nd: 236). The only noteworthy divergence is in the position assigned to the Deer clan by my earlier informants, but this may be attributed to the fact that the *miko apokta* was then a Deer and his clan was probably brought over to the west cabin for that reason. As we should expect, the agreement is also close with the arrangement of the Asilanabi ground though there are minor divergencies in the allocation of clans to the south cabin. All of my authorities agreed well in assigning clans to the two moieties, but the oldest of all of them thought that the Bear and Allligator were probably *Tciloki*. This may have been the ancient arrangement.

TUKABATCHI

The plan of Tukabahchee square appears in Figure 9 and a view of it as it looked in 1912 is given in Plate 5, Figure 1.

The number of *tastanagis* is indetermined. The *toba mawidine* were officers not otherwise named who always remained in the cabins. There is one in each of the 12 beds except a part of the southeast cabin as indicated. They were selected from any clan, given names taken from the father's clan, and seated with the latter, Thus, if [30] a man were a Deer and his father a Raccoon, they would give him a name from the Raccoon clan's names and seat him with them. After being so seated these officers were not obliged to do any further work connected with the busk.

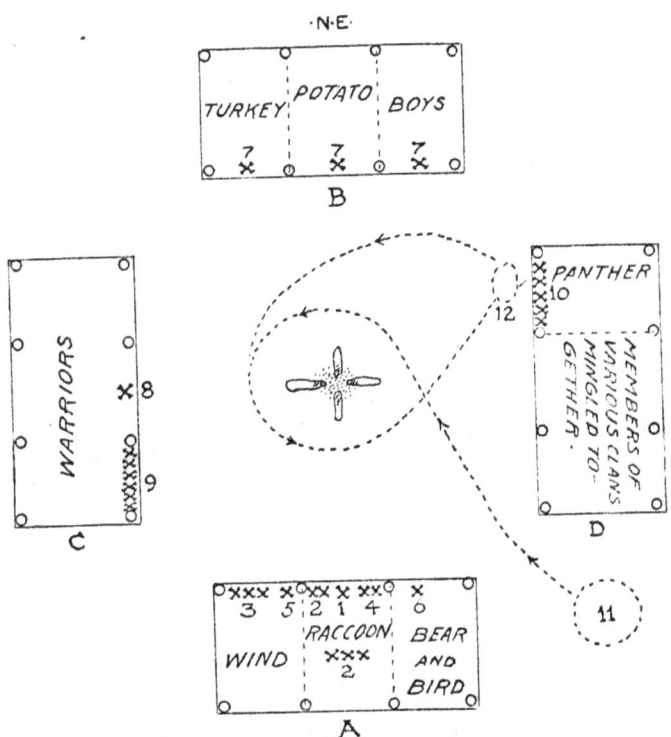

Fig. 9. — Tukabahchee square ground.

A. Chiefs' Bed: 1, *miko* (Raccoon); 2, *mikos* (substitutes (Raccoon); 3, *henīha*s (Wind);

4, *henīhas* and *yatikas*; 5, *hilis haya*; 6, *ta'pala*.
B. Potato Bed; sometimes also called Youths' Bed: 7, 7, 7, *toba mawidine*.
C. Warriors' Bed: 8, *ta'pala*; *tastanagi łakalgi*
D.   Youths' Bed (*Tcibanagalgi intupa*): 10, *yahaikas*; 11, point where women assemble preparatory to the dance; 12, point where the women start dancing.

The *istatcagagis*, most of whom sat in the southeast bed, were like a jury, or like a committee, to settle matters of routine. They comprised both men and women. The admittance of women to this select group is something which I heard from no other informant. [31]

A man was picked out of the bed of the *henihas* to speak for others, *i.e.*, the *yatikas* were selected from the *heniha*s. None was used in the stomp dance. As payment for his services the *yatika* was given a deer hide and a ribbon. When he was wanted by the *miko* he was summoned four times, but he did not start until he had received the fourth call. He set a basket on the ground into which all of the *tasikaia*s threw bits of tobacco to be taken to the singers for the women as payment for their services.

The *hołibonaia* was a special speaker used in the ball game and in war. The term *asimbonaia* was about equivalent to that of *yatika*. He was a head man chosen from among the *tastanagi*s for almost any purpose. He listened to any message which the *miko* wished to give out and then repeated it aloud.

There were two *hilis tcalaba* who sat with their clans and were summoned whenever needed. One was a Raccoon and one a Bear.

There were two *oktididja* who sat with their clans or wherever they belonged until summoned to attend to the fire.

Four *hilis hoboia*, selected from any clans, were sent to gather the medicine.

All of the *tasikaias* shared in getting water.

The famous Tukabahchee plates were taken out and cleaned four years in succession and then left covered for four years.

The feather dance was discontinued at Tukabahchee when my informant was a small boy.

The three leading women in the women's dance carry *atasa*. The leading woman has an eagle feather on her *atasa*, the second a white crane feather, and the other the feather of a third bird, perhaps a goose. They start one at a time and when the third moves all the rest follow. After they have walked round the fire four times they begin to dance and circle the fire again six times.

The *Hathagas* were Bird, Wind, Bear, and Beaver; the *Tcilokis* were Turkey, Alligator, Raccoon, Deer, Panther, and any others.

In olden times the moieties were exogamous. The Raccoon and Potato were then brothers, or rather half brothers, but intermarriage between them is now common. Even today, however, the Beaver and Bird will seldom intermarry. The Bird was the "uncle" of the Beaver and the Beaver the former's "nephew."

A man's children called his father's clan "fathers." One can say anything he wishes to, however disrespectful, about his own clan, but he must not speak against his father's clan or permit anyone else to. [32]

The general arrangement is the same as that obtained from the father of my informant in 1911-12 (BAE-AR 42nd: 244), but the stations here assigned to some of the individual officers are probably more nearly correct, particularly the locations of the *mikos*.

KEALEDJI

Figure 10 shows the Kealedji square.

The *hoktagi immiiko*, "women's chief," supervised the women's dance. There are now no regular water carriers. The *imałas* formerly sat in the north cabin, but now there are no officers so called. The beds are called by the names of the clans which occupy them. If the *asimbonaia* is wanted to deliver a speech, he is called over to the *miko*'s seat for that purpose. For *tastanagis* the best men are chosen. The *ta'palas* are changed every four years. In former times they had a regular four days' busk, but now it lasts for but one day and there is no feather dance.

In the match games they played against *Okchai*, *Wiogufki*, and *Tulsa*.

The *Hathaga*s are Wind, Bear, Panther, and Turkey; the *Tciloki*s are Raccoon, Deer, and *Aktayatci*. In ancient times these moieties were exogamous.

The names of the present officers are as follows:

miko	*Kasilita Yalwia* (Raccoon)
henīha	*Henīha Imałutc*i (Wind)
miko apokta	*Kayomulgi* (Raccoon)
hoktagi immiko	*Wiwohka Yahola* (Raccoon)
henīha	*Oikas Hadjo* (Wind)
asiinhonaia	*Kosa Fiksiko* (Bear)
ta'pala	*Talmutcas Hadjo* (Bear)
..... "	*Alak Hadjutci* (Turkey)
hilis tcalaba	*Kan Tcati* (Wind)
" "	*Itco Imała Fiksiko* (Deer)
tutka oktididja	*Ahali Imała*
hilis hoboia	*Tałkona Hadjo* (Wind)
" "	*Hotalgi Fiksiko* (Wind)
tastanagi	*Tastanak Tcapko*
"	*Tastanakutci*
"	*Inhenīha* (= *henīha*)
"	*Tatkona Hadjo*

The plan of the revived square ground of the *Kealedji* agrees in all essentials with the one given me in 1912 from memory by a very old man, except that in recent times the Deer clan seems to have lost its importance or died out. It is interesting to find that old [33] and recent informants agree in assigning the Panther clan to the White moiety. They differ, however, regarding the position of the Turkey, which the earlier informant considered *Tciloki* and the later White. But this clan, together with the Alligator and *Tami*, is known to have been on one side in some towns and on the opposite in others. [34]

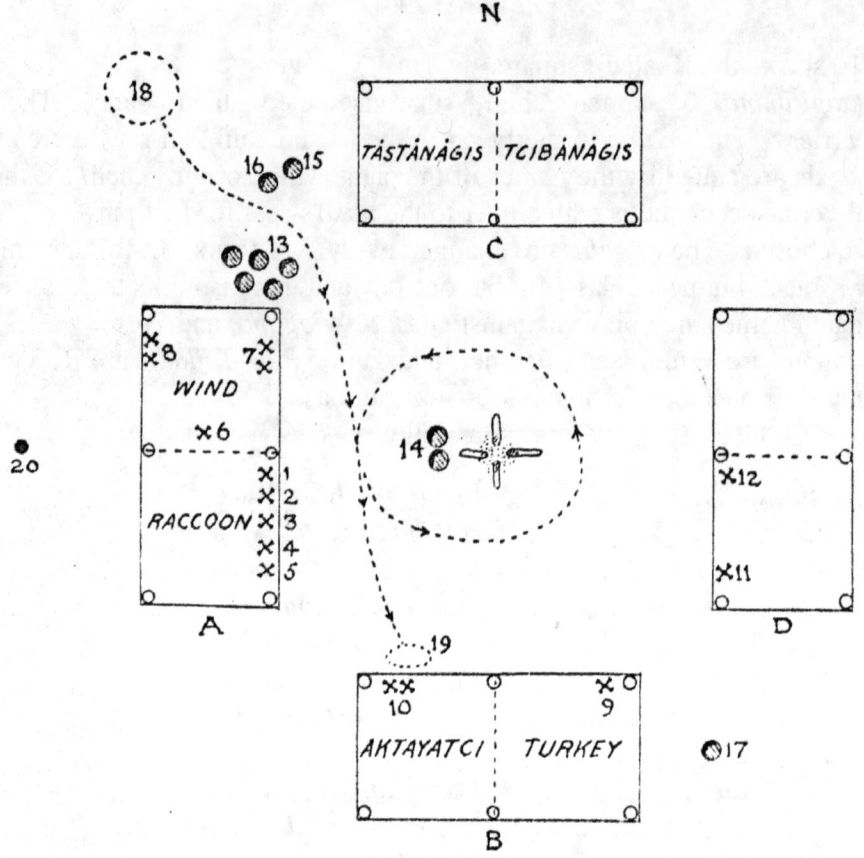

FIG. 10. — The Kealedji square ground.

A. Chiefs' Bed: 1, *miko* (Raccoon); 2, *henīha* (Wind); 3, *miko apokta* (Raccoon);
    4, *hoktagi immiko* (Raccoon); 5, *henīha* (Wind); *hilis haya* (usually Raccoon;
    Wind in 1929); 7, *hilis tcalaba* (Deer and Wind); 8, *hilis hoboi*a (Wind).
B. Youths' Bed: 9, *ta'pala* (Turkey); 10, *yahaikas*
C. Warriors' Bed.
D. White Bed: 11, *asimbonaia* (Bear); 12, *ta'pala* (Bear).

   13, medicine pots (1st position); 14, medicine pots for those fasting (2nd position); 15, medicine pot for boys (2nd position); 16, medicine pot for girls (2nd position); 17, medicine pot for women (2nd position); 18, point where women assemble preparatory to the dance; 19, point where women start dancing; 20, ball post.

ŁAPŁAKO

Figure 11 shows the plan of this ground.

The two pots of medicine were prepared where they are shown (nos. 4 and 5) and remained there all of the time. The Bird clan sat anywhere.

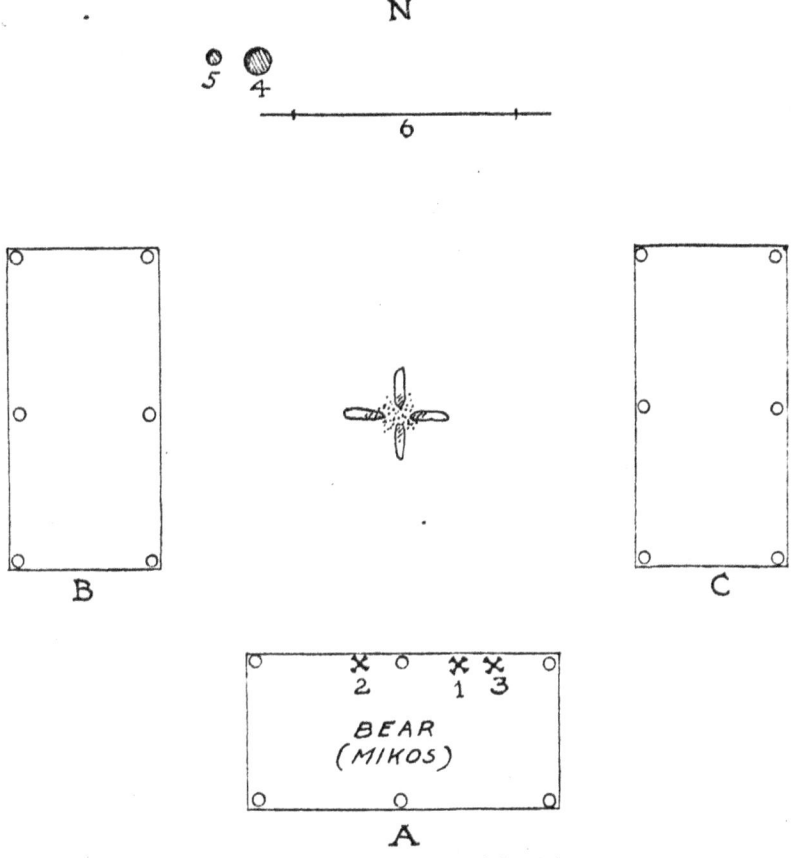

FIG. 11. — Square ground of Łapłako.

A. Chiefs' Bed: 1, *miko* (Bear); 2, *heniha* or *miko apokta* (Bird);
     3, *yatika* (sometimes seated here).
B. Warriors' Bed. This was usually occupied by middle aged men of various clans.
C. Citizens' Bed (*Tasikaialgi intupa*). Occupied by various classes, including persons not properly citizens of the town but taking medicine here, men married in the town or adopted into it, and men whose fathers belonged to it.

     4, a large pot of medicine for the fasters; 5, a small pot of medicine for the women and children; 6, rack for ball sticks.

The *yatika* belonged to no regular clan, and at the present time there is no such officer. There are two *hilis tcalaba* who occupy no special seats, and one *hilis haya* who is taken from any clan of a friendly town. Towns belong to the other town moiety do not [35] take medicine with them and in fact are not invited except in the case of individuals married into the town.

The *Hathagas* are the Bear (the most important of them), Bird, Beaver, and Wind; the *Tcilokis* are the Raccoon, Deer, Potato, *Aktayatci*, Panther, Alligator, etc. Here the Alligator, Turkey, and Beaver can intermarry; in Eufaula they could not. But probably this means that the Beaver could intermarry with the other two, as the Alligator and Turkey were seldom allowed to marry under any circumstances. The Bird and Beaver were classed together in *Łapłako*, but this group does not include the Bear or Wind. The *Hathaga* clans had the reputation of being progressive while the *Tcilokis* were full-bloods and reactionaries. This characterization probably followed the coming of the white people.

The towns of the opposite group were called *Talipoła*, which means "foreign but not unfriendly."

The word *Łapłako* indicates a place where there are many marshes filled with canes. This town square, which had been discontinued, was revived in the year 1903 in this way. They had to prepare a ground in order to take medicine before a game with the Nuyaka Indians next year. Later this was improved with regular cabins, but it must have been inconspicuous or have been considered unimportant, as I heard nothing about it in 1912.

Łapłako and *Atasi* are now nearly fused on account of the number of intermarriages between individuals belonging to them. Before the Civil War the *Łapłako* had an *Atasi* Indian named *Holalgi Hadjo* married among them as their *hilis haya*. One of the great men of Łapłako in former times was Jim Boy (*Tastanagi Imała*)[66] whom my informant remembers to have seen. He thinks he died just before the Civil War broke out. McKenney and Hall (*History of the Indian Tribes of North America*, vol. 2, pp. 71-74) give a portrait of this chief and a considerable account of his life. He was born in what is now Alabama in 1793 and accompanied the warriors of his town during the Creek War of 1813-14, but was too young for active participation. In the war with the Seminole he was one of the leaders of the Creek contingent which aided the Americans. The exact date of his death seems to be unknown.

The arrangement of the modern ground differs more from those described to me in 1912 (BAE-AR 42nd: 254 and 255) than any of the others. The first of the latter was obtained from a very old man who should have known the ancient arrangement well, but of course my interpreter and I may have misunderstood him. The cabins are at different points of the compass [36] and more confusion is shown in the later organization, but they agree in stating that the *miko* belonged to the Bear clan and in placing that clan in the south cabin. My older informant allocated this clan with the *Tciloki*. This was probably an error on his part but he seemed to insist upon it.

They have had no busk since the Civil War and no women's dance, and the *pasa* is no longer used, only the *miko hoyanidja*. The dances in the square are three stomp dances. Seven days before one of these the "broken days" are sent out and on the day when the sixth stick is thrown away they are all to be at the ground, while on the seventh they are supposed to be taking medicine. Seven days before the dance they also meet and pick out four clean young men, called *hilis hoboia*, men whose wives are not pregnant, who are not given to intoxicants, and who have not attended to the digging of a grave during the preceding month. These men gather four bundles of medicine (*miko hoyanidji*) which they lay down with their tip ends toward the west. First they spread out a bed of leaves called *lodja issi*, "turtle leaves," which should be taken from hickory trees. The medicine is laid on top of these and more leaves are spread over it. On the morning of the last day all of those who are to take medicine are supposed to present themselves at the square ground. The fire is built up so that it will not go out all day. Early in the morning the two *hilis tcalaba* prepare the medicine, first the medicine for the women and children and then that for the adult men. This is taken four times during the day, the fourth time between one and two o'clock. Before they take the medicine the *yatika* announces, on behalf of the chief, that each of those intending to take it is to get a stick and throw it into a blanket. These sticks are counted and the *yatika* announces the number. Four times (or sometimes twice) during the day the men who are to take medicine with the exception of the officials (the *mikalgi*, *yatika*, *hilis haya*, and the two *ta'pala*) go out to get firewood so as to be ready for the dance that night. Four men are selected to keep watch of the fasters during the night, to see that no one sleeps or breaks

---

[66] <See p113, front cover herein>

his fast, or drinks or goes with a woman. That is why the numbers are taken. These four men are called *istikonā'ha* = "men taking away," because they take away the hat of anyone found sleeping (and treat similarly anyone who breaks the taboos in other ways). The hat they carry to the miko and when the owner comes to get it, he is fined.

After they have taken medicine for the fourth time, they go to the creek for a bath and then return to the square. The *yatika* [37] talks to them telling them to take care of themselves all of that night, and then they scatter to the camps to eat. Before sundown, however, they are supposed to be back on the ground. The *yatika* calls to them four times and by the fourth time they are to be in their seats. When all are in their places, the two *ta'pala* are selected. The *yatika* makes a speech on behalf of the *miko*, calling upon his hearers not to act in an unfriendly way toward the outside friends who are about to be admitted to the dance, not to take liquor, to behave themselves all through the night, not to fight, and so on. This speech is addressed to the town people and outsiders alike. After it the fasters dance four times and then the visitors are admitted. That "kills the fast." All through the day the square is to be kept clean with the idea that the fasters will in consequence be clean. They go up to take the medicine two by two, and those who are ceremonially unclean take the medicine last. They dance until about daybreak. Then all belonging to the town go down to the branch and bathe, after which they return and sit in their respective beds. Then a collection may be taken to defray their expenses and they settle other matters. The night before, the chief of a friendly town may have announced a dance, and, if so, the announcement is now made and advice given as to how they are to help their friends. This advice is uttered by the *yatika*, speaking for the *miko*, and he then gives a general talk, advising his people not to use liquor, not to break the laws, and to be good citizens in every sense of the word. Then they disband for the year.

HILIBI

A plan of Hilibi square is shown in Figure 12 and a general view of the ground as it appeared in the winter of 1911-12 in Plate 5, Figure 2.

Two poles with white feathers attached were at each front post. These were used in the "feather dance" and were called "the path," because the path was to be white.

When there are visitors the owners of the east cabin move elsewhere in order to make room for them. When the south cabin is overcrowded, some of its occupants move into the east cabin. In this town the clans were always considerably mixed up in the beds. The *ta'palas* can sit anywhere. The *tutka oktididja* does not have a particular seat on account of his official position, he is appointed every four years. The *tutki didja*, who starts the fire, is identical with the *hilis haya*. [38]

If a man whose father is of the *Aktayatci*, the *miko's* clan, is given a busk name, he is brought to the *mikos'* bed and given a seat there.

The *Hathaga*s are the Bear, Bird, Alligator, Beaver, Turkey, and Wind; the *Tciloki*s are the Panther, Potato, Deer, *Aktayatci*, and evidently the Raccoon. The Alligator and Bird are considered as practically one clan.

The two leaders in the women's dance carry *atasa*.

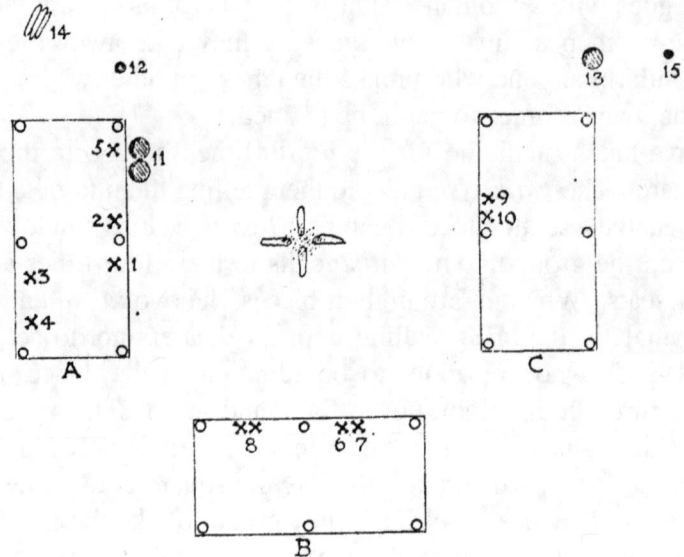

FIG. 12. — Square ground of Hilibi.

A. Chiefs' Bed: 1, *miko* (Aktayatci); 2, *heniha* (Alligator); 3, *hilis haya* (Raccoon in 1920);
    4, *ta'pala* (Bear); 5, *hilis tcalaba* (Bear in 1929).
B. Raccoons' Bed: 6, *hilis hoboia*; 7, *tutka oktididja* (Raccoon in 1929); 8, *yalaikas* (any clan).
C. Cabin used by visitors: 9, *ta'pala* (Alligator); 10, *hilis hoboia* (Alligator).

11, medicine pots; 12, medicine pot for boys; 13, medicine pot for women; 14, woodpile; 15, ball post.

The history of this town is as follows. It was founded by a man of the *Aktayatci* clan who went off to live by himself and then put up a ball post. Many women belonged to his family and he had numerous visitors, some of whom married these women so that it soon grew into a large band of which he was probably the first *miko*. Anyhow that is the way the *Aktayatci* came to have the town. After stomp dances had been held there for some time, more visitors came [39] to join them and it grew still larger. Because it was built up very rapidly, its founder called it Hilibi, which means "hurry" (*hila'pkis*, "I make haste"*). Since it was an "illegal" band, a *talwa fatcasīgo* ("town deviating from correctness"), all the clans do not have regular places, having been drawn from so many other bands.

The following notes on some personal names continued in the town roster give an interesting insight into the manner in which totemic names were bestowed:

Fos Hatki Imała ("White Bird *Imała*"), so named because he belonged to a White clan, the Wind.

Halak Hopaie. He belonged to the Bear clan, but his father belonged to the Raccoon, hence the name *Halak* or *Ahalak* ("Potato"), since both these clans are *Tciloki*.

Pahos Fiksiko. He belonged to the Wind clan, but his father was a Deer and the *Pahosa* is of the same phratry as the Deer.

As shown by the native story above given this town was not supposed to be ancient or to have a firmly fixed town organization, and, while it was older than the Hilibi people themselves believed, it seems to have preserved the irregularities which might naturally be associated with a new town. Not improbably the tradition of irregularity preserved the fact. At the same time there is a general agreement between the plan here given and that which I obtained in 1912 (BAE-AR 42nd: 258). The *mikos'* cabin is to the west, and the *mikalki* and *henīhalgi* were of the same clans, *Aktayatci* and Alligator respectively. The Alligator and Turkey were classed as Whites from association with the Bird by my later informants, but the earlier ones gave them as *Tciloki*.

ALABAMA

This was a very simple square of exceptional arrangement as shown in Figure 13.

The Alabama were one of the incorporated tribes with a language distinct from Creek. The clan names in Alabama are: *Mahaleha* (Wind), *Sawaha* (Raccoon), *Aktayaciha* (*Aktayatci*), *Hatcuntcobaha* (Alligator), *Konoha* (Skunk), *Nilaha* (Hear), *Koīha* (Panther), *Fociha* (Bird), *Filoha* (Turkey), *Ofataha* (Beaver).

All of the officers were brought over to the chiefs' bed. Men of the Alligator, Bear, and *Aktayatci* have been *mikos* and a man of the Skunk clan was once the *heniha*. There is no regular rule for either position.

The *Hathagas* were the Wind, Bear, Panther, Skunk, and Raccoon; the *Tcilokis* were the Bird, Beaver, Turkey, Alligator, and *Aktayatci*. The Wildcat was the same as the Panther. [40]

One of the greatest Alabama Indians now remembered was *Kantcati Yahola* (Alabama name *Tcīsōki*), who was the *hilis haya*. He was born in Alabama and came west with his tribe. He lived until about 1866.

The {below} above plan and the three others I obtained in 1912 and the years immediately following (BAE-AR 42nd: 263-264) show considerable minor variations but all agree in locating the chiefs' bed in the east and the warriors' bed in the west. Most of them also place the Bear and Panther clans in the latter and the Wind, *Aktayatci*, and Deer in the former, where they are noted at all. In allocating the clans the above informant agrees with the older ones except regarding the Panther which the men first consulted asserted was *Tciloki* while it is here given as a White clan, but this is a clan which has been placed on both sides.

FIG. 13. — Alabama square ground
A. Chiefs' Bed: 1, *miko* (Wind); 2, *henīha* (Raccoon).
B. Warriors' Bed.

KASIHTA

For the plan of *Kasihta* square ground, see Figure 14. There should be two *hilis tculaba*, drawn from the Alligator clan, but they are not employed now. Four *hilis hoboia* for the pasa, four for the *miko hoyanīdja*, and one *tutka oktidīdja* are chosen by the *miko* without reference to clan. There is no definite body of water carriers. Two *ta'palas* are selected from any clan to serve just for the night. They carry sticks called reeds, and their function is to invite the dance

leaders to lead dances and see that all take part. There is only one singer for the women's dance.
He sits behind the *miko*. [41]

In 1901 the old square ground was given up and the new one was established in June,
1920. Because the new generation was weak, one cabin was cut out. The *Coweta* square is said
to have been the same as that of *Kasihta*.

Every time anything is brought in or anything repaired they dance all night because thus
the two things are joined together, just as two days are united by the night on which they dance.
Formerly dances were held every Saturday night, but hard times have put an end to them. The
dance which was being held when I paid my visit was because they were then putting up a
{new} ball post.

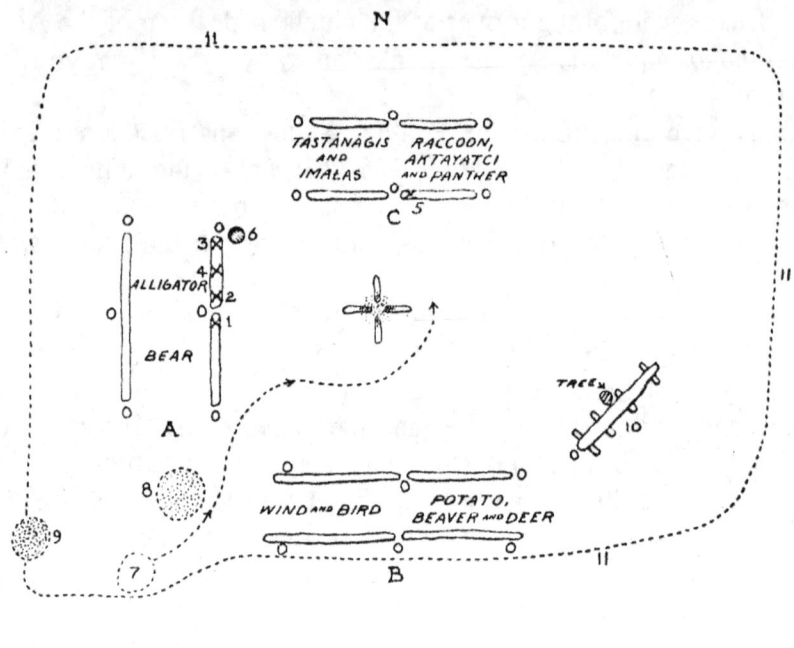

FIG. 14. — Kasihta square ground.

A. Chiefs' Bed: 1, *miko* (Bear); 2, *heniha* (Alligator); 3, *hilis haya* (seat when on duty);
4, *asimbonaia*.
B. Whites' Bed: (*Henihalgi intupa*), or "Cabin of the Greater Kings."
C. Warriors' Bed: 5, *asimbonaia* (*Aktayatci*).

6, medicine pot; 7, point where women assemble before dancing; 8, trash heap; 9, where
ashes of old fires were placed; 10, split log where are seated those young men who have broken
the rules and are in consequence placed here as a punishment before being allowed to mix with
the rest of the people; 11, line of sweeping (*tadjo*) marking limit of square ground; 12, ball post.

The *Hathagas* are the Wind, Beaver, Bird, and Deer; the *Tcilokis* are the remaining clans,
yet it is said that the Bear, Alligator, and [42] Wind were of the same "class." Under the present
law they can all marry outside of third cousins.

The *Kasihta* defeated the *Coweta* three times in the ball game, the last time in 1878, and
after that they took them under their jurisdiction and they have played on the same side.

Comparison of the plan of the new *Kasihta* with the plans of the earlier grounds secured
by Gatschet and myself (BAE-AR 42nd: 266-268) shows that the old order has been fairly well

maintained allowing for the disappearance of some clans, particularly the Fish clan. Incidentally I wish to correct an erroneous statement in my report in which I misquoted Gatschet to the effect that the *Kasihta miko* belonged to the Alligator clan. While the Alligator clan occupied half of the chiefs' cabin, the *miko* himself has always been taken from the Bear and was stated to have been so by Gatschet {??}. The allocation of clans to the moieties by my recent informants contains a number of difficulties, for they seem to have placed the Bear among the *Tciloki*, which is unlikely, especially as it was said to belong to the same "class" as the Alligator and Wind. My own earlier authorities also classed the Beaver and Deer as *Tciloki*.

The following information will be interesting to those who wish to study acculturation processes in intangibles. It was told me by the Indian considered best able to speak for the town.

> The original four cabins represented the New Jerusalem with its 12 gates. The busk goes back to the time when Jacob set up the altar at Bethel and is traced from him and his 12 sons. All of the Indians in America entered in two migrations, one at the time of Jacob (1500-2000 B.C.) and the second 600 years later, at the time when Jerusalem was destroyed by Nebuchadnezzar. Then they talked face to face with the Great Spirit because they were more obedient to God than any other tribe, but about 700 years after the Messiah they got away from the original law on account of desire for riches. Then they lost the old law and asked for a new government, and by holding a ceremony in midsummer, in the month of July, it was given to them. That new law taught them to tell the truth and be honest with their fellow men and to raise their children in such obedience, not to touch anything that did not belong to them, not to make a false statement. That is the law which we are trying to follow.

He added:

> We have a hard time because the white men have failed to fulfill their part of the agreement. They have strong laws that we can't begin to understand and our customs are about choked out through grafters who claim to have bought the claims of the allottees on which our squares are located. In order to hold their grounds several towns have to pay rent year after year. If the law makers would cooperate with us and give us full privileges we would raise more substantial, law-abiding young men and young women. That was the custom and the wish of our forefathers. [43]

OCHESEE SEMINOLE

This is the only Seminole ground from which I obtained information during my recent trip. The plan of it is shown in Figure 15.

There are two pots of medicine for the *miko hoyanīdja* and *pasa* respectively, but the latter is introduced only at the busk. The women, however, use wormseed ("*wīlana*"). After they are through with the medicines, whatever is left is poured out at the place where they have been taken.

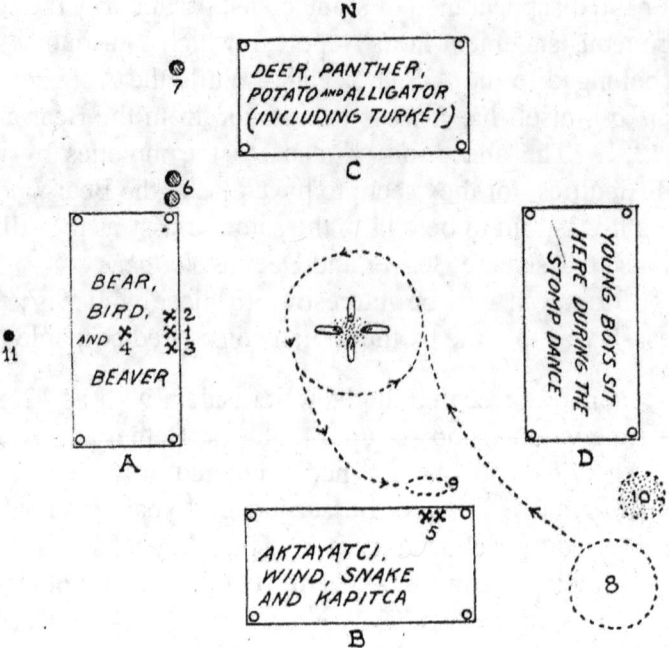

Fig. 15. — Ochesee Seminole square ground.

A. Chiefs' Bed: 1, *miko* (Bear); *2, heniha* (Bird); 3, *yatka* (Deer in 1929);
4, *hilis haya* (Wind in 1929).

B. Warriors' Bed: 5, *yahaikas*.

C. Warriors' Bed:

D. Youths' Bed.

6, medicine pots; 7, medicine pot for boys (continuing red root); 8, point where women gather before dancing; 9, point where women start dancing; 10, ashes of old fires; 11, ball post.

The *miko* is chosen if possible from the Bear clan, but if they do not find a suitable man of that clan, they select someone from the Beaver clan. [44]

The *yatika* and *hilis haya* may be selected from any clan, the former being chosen for his oratorical gifts.

There is now no *heniha*. The last they had went to live with the Creeks and did not come back.

Two *ta'palas* are used in the women's dance and hold their position for four years. Other *ta'palas* are chosen temporarily for the other dances. In the stomp dances they change these *ta'palas* several times during the night.

There are four *hilis boboia* taken from the west, north, and south cabins but from any clan. They keep their positions as long as they choose to serve.

There is one *tutka dīdja* who can be of any clan.

Five or six boys bring water to the ground.

The two leaders among the women carry *atasa* which are painted with white clay annually just before the dance. Women do not take the *wīlana* internally; they merely wet their faces and other parts of their bodies with it. The boys use only the *miko hoyanīdja*.

The ashes of the old fire are removed from the square and the new fire lighted on the morning of the fast day.

The *Hathagas* are the Bear, Bird, Beaver, Wind, Otter and Skunk; the rest are *Tcilokis*.

The Bird and Beaver belonged in one phratry, and so did the Wind, Otter and Skunk; the Alligator and Turkey; and the *Aktayatci, Kapitca*, and Snake.

The name of the present *miko* is *Nokos Miko*, and his father belonged to the Deer clan. The last *henīha* was named *Henīha Miko*, and his father was of the Bear clan. The busk name of the *yatika* (my informant {source}) is *Pahosa Tastanagi*; his father belonged to the *Aktayatci*, and his father's father to the Bear.

They have a ball post surmounted by a wooden fish. A hit on this fish counts = 4, and on the post above a certain mark = 2. There have been no regular match games between towns in the lifetime of my informant, but about two years ago the old men and the young men played against each other.

The above plan of the Ochesee ground agrees closely, naturally enough, with that which I obtained from the man whose advice was particularly resorted to in reestablishing it some years ago (BAE-AR 42nd: 283), for in 1912 it had been given up. The main differences are in the seating of the Potato and Alligator clans. In the matter of the moieties the only change is in the case of the Raccoon clan, which I previously set down as White. This is so exceptional, however, that I have always believed that I must have misunderstood my informant. [45]

The two brief genealogies which follow will illustrate in some measure the influence of the clan system on marriage. The first is the genealogy of Jeff Canard of Łapłako; the second that of Earnest Gouge[67] of Hanna, the latter of especial interest because it includes the famous orator *Hobohił Yahola*.

paternal grandfather (Bear)	paternal grandmother (Alligator)		maternal grandfather (Wind)	maternal grandmother (Beaver)
	father (Alligator)		mother (Beaver)	
		self (Beaver)		

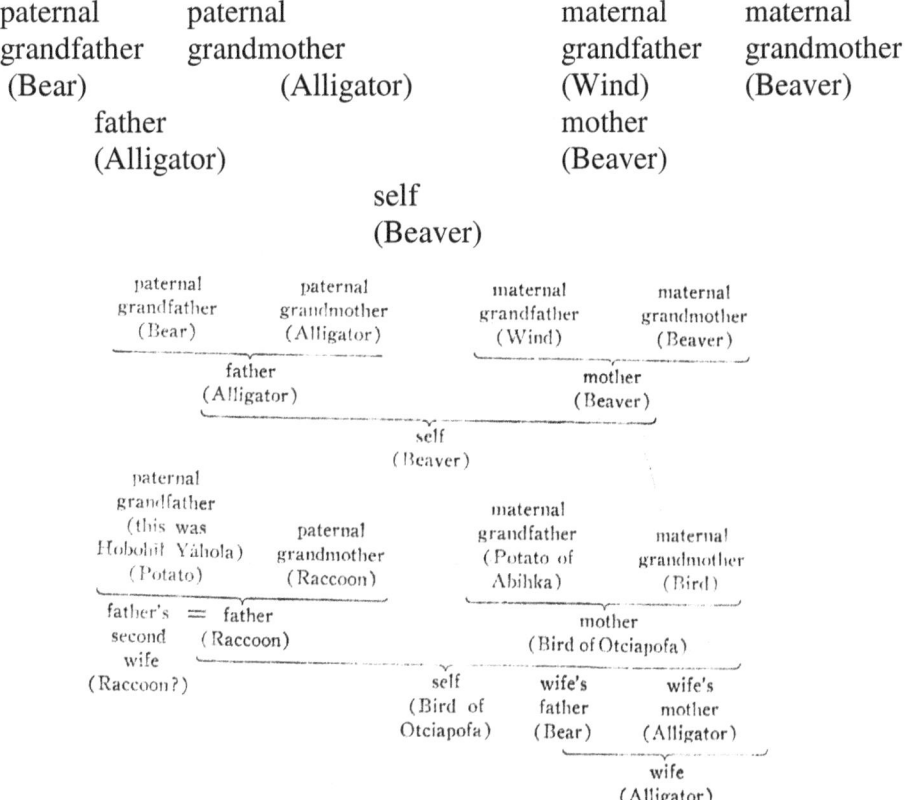

[67] Earnest Gouge 2004 *totkv mocvse ~ New Fire: Creek Folktales.* Jack Martin & Margaret Mckane Mauldin, eds. Norman: University of Oklahoma Press.

paternal grandfather	paternal grandmother	maternal grandfather	paternal grandmother
(this was *Hobohił Yahola*)	(Raccoon)	(Potato of *Arbihka*)	(Bird)
(Potato)			

father's	father		mother
second wife	(Raccoon)		(Bird of *Otciapofa*)
(Raccoon?)			

self	wife's father	wife's mother
(Bird of *Otciapofa*)	(Bear)	(Alligator)

wife
(Alligator)

CONCLUSION

The busk undoubtedly represents a long period of development, and as the stages through which it passed and the elements entering into it have been lost, we can never understand it fully. Its main purpose, however, {is} was evident. It was to restore the connection of the tribe with the universe which a year of civil or profane living had tended to rupture. Hence the new fire, extracted from its abiding place in the wood and not as yet sullied by contact with humanity. Hence the rigorous fast accompanied by administration of medicines divinely revealed to the ancestors, the general pardon of offenders, the sabbath calm prescribed for that period of regeneration, the use of white paint, and the employment of the term white — "the white day," "the white smoke," "the white drink" — in various parts of the ritual. The one discordant note seems to have been provided by the women's dance, since the leaders [45] of that dance carried representations of war clubs {*atasa*}, which there is every reason to believe were anciently adorned with scalps, and some of these were painted red. But I suspect that this dance was an attempt to represent war as a protective institution and to thank the being or beings who preside over human destiny for having so well defended them against assaults of the — as usual — perfidious foe. Possibly some element of propitiation also entered into this dance.

The universe with which the Creeks sought reconciliation was not, however, a material one. What they had in mind was rather the **mind** or **minds** believed to be operant there. While we know of some supernatural beings connected primarily with the busk and numerous spirits associated with natural objects were anciently believed in, it seems fairly certain that the peculiar patron of the ceremony was a solar, or rather celestial, being generally called *Hisagita-immisi*, "the breath controller," and also *Ibofanga*, {Above} "the one above," and that the busk fire was in some way an earthly representation of the great solar fire overhead. While it is probable that *Hisagita-immisi* was not in ancient times the monotheistic deity he has now become, there is every reason to think he was already, before White contact, the supreme being of the Creeks.

TUSTENNUGGEE EMATHLA.

THIS is a fine looking man, six feet and one inch in height, of manly and martial appearance, and great physical strength, who seems well calculated to command the respect of a band of savage warriors. Our brief sketch of him is framed from memoranda taken from his own lips. He is a full-blooded Creek, and was born on the Tallapoosa river, about the year 1793, which would make him forty-five years old at the period to which we bring down his biography. He is most generally known by the familiar name of Jim Boy, but is properly entitled to that which we have placed at the head of this article, *Tustennuggee*, meaning *warrior*, and *Emathla*, {*imała*} which signifies *next to the warrior* {aide}.

When the war broke out in 1811, between the Creeks and the American people, he was too young to wield the tomahawk, but was permitted to follow the warriors of his nation to the field; and he thus witnessed the capture of Fort Mimms, a fortress which the Indians surprised at the commencement of hostilities, and where they basely massacred all who fell into their hands, without regard to age or sex. He was also present at the battle of Cahawba, but took no further part in that war. He afterwards accompanied General Jackson, under the command of McIntosh, towards Florida, but was not in any fight.

When the Creek nation became divided into two parties, one of whom were friendly to the American people and government, and disposed to yield to the settled and inevitable policy which demanded their entire separation from the white race, and the other [72] hostile to our country and unwilling to emigrate, Tustennuggee Emathla attached himself to the former party. He has continued, since he reached the years of maturity, the undeviating friend of the Americans; and it affords us great pleasure to recognize, in the steady attachment of this individual and many others, the most intelligent and best disposed of their race, some proof that, whatever abuses may have corrupted and disgraced our intercourse with that unfortunate people, the general policy of our government towards them has been of a kind and liberal character.

In the late war in Florida, Tustennuggee Emathla seems to have rendered some service. General Jessup sought his services to lead a party against the Seminoles, and he accordingly raised a band of seven hundred and seventy-six warriors, whom he conducted to the seat of war. He descended the Chattahooche to Tampa Bay, having instructions from General {Thomas} Jessup not to engage in hostilities against the Seminoles until he should first have endeavored, as a mediator, to induce them to abandon the bloody and fruitless contest in which they were unhappily engaged. In this attempt he was not successful; and we find him, soon after his arrival at Tampa, joining the camp of Colonel {Ichabod} Lane, by whom he was sent, with two hundred of his warriors, to look after the Seminoles. He fell in with a party of the latter, and drove them into a swamp, from which they opened fire and wounded several of his men. He was then sent to meet Governor Call, and arrived at the spot where General {Edmund} Gaines was surrounded, soon after that officer had been relieved. On the following day he joined Governor { } Call, and proceeded to Fort Drane. Thence they moved on one of Acee-Yoholo's towns, called Weecockcogce, or little river, about sixty miles from Fort Drane, where the Seminoles, though numerous, refused them battle, fled, and were pursued. The Creeks were unable to overtake them; but the Tennessee horse fell in with them on the following day, and a fight ensued, in which several were killed on each side. [73]

Tustennuggee and his party joined the army again at Fort Dade, and the Seminoles being in a Swamp hard by, an attack was planned, in which the Creeks were invited to go foremost, an honor which they promptly declined, while they cheerfully agreed to advance side by side with the white men. In this fight the Creeks lost four men, besides one who was accidentally killed by the whites; but the Seminoles were beaten. He was afterwards sent to a place towards Fort Augustine for provisions, and was in several skirmishes not worth recording.

This chief states that he joined our army under a promise made by the commanding general, that in the removal of the Creeks to the west of the Mississippi, which was about to take place, his family and property should be attended to, and that he should be indemnified for any loss that might happen in consequence of his absence. These stipulations, he alleges, were broken by the removal of his women and children while he was absent in the service of the government, whereby his entire property was destroyed. Nor was this the worst of his misfortunes. His family, consisting of a wife and nine children, were among the unfortunate persons who were on board the steamboat *Monmouth* when that vessel was sunk by the mismanagement of those to whose care it was intrusted; and two hundred and thirty-six of the Creeks, including four of the children of Tustennuggee Emathla, were drowned. Melancholy as such an occurrence would be under any circumstances, the catastrophe is infinitely the more deplorable when happening to an ignorant people while emigrating unwillingly under the charge of our public agents, and to a people whose whole intercourse with the whites has tended to render them suspicious of the faith of civilized men. The more intelligent among them will doubtless attribute the misfortune to culpable negligence, if not design, while the ignorant will see in it, with superstitious awe, another link in the chain of fatal events entailed upon the red men by their contact with the white race. So far as the chief before us [74] has any claim upon the justice or benevolence of our country, there can be no doubt that the government will maintain its faith inviolate. Whatever may be thought of our policy towards the Indian tribes, as such, we are not chargeable, as a people, with any backwardness in the discharge of our obligations to individual claimants.

McKenny and Hall 1870 #2: 71-74.
History of Indian Tribes

John Napoleon Brinton Hewitt
(16 December 1859 – 14 October 1937)

Born among Tuscaroras near Niagara Falls, JNBH was the oldest of five born to Harriet Brinton and David Brainard Hewitt, a revered country doctor. David had been orphaned as a boy, adopted into a Tuscarora family on the Tuscarora Reservation, and raised as an Indian. Both parents spoke fluent Tuscarora, but JNB had to learn it from schoolmates on the playground before he studied classics at Wilson Union and Lockport Union academies, pressuming a medical career. Overwork and severe sunstroke, however, ended his studies and in 1876-78 he turned to farming, newspaper work, and teaching night classes for other Tuscarora young men.

Tuscarora homeland had been North Carolina until they were attacked by the colony and fled north, where they were taken in by the Seneca and made non-voting members of the League of the Iroquois, now of seven rather than six nations. They were settled near Niagara Falls.

After Hewitt moved to Jersey City, he was recruited in 1880-84 by Erminnie Smith to help with her collecting and translating of Iroquoian folklore for the BAE while he also worked as a street car conductor for Jersey City Railways and Adams Express. When Erminnie died 9 June 1886, JNB volunteered to complete her work, especially their *Tuscarora-English Dictionary* (finally published 2015 in Toronto) and was accordingly hired by the BAE seven years after it began, and worked there for 51 years.

At the bureau Hewitt studied Indian languages and myths, especially those of the Iroquois, begun under Smith. He worked with native delegations visiting DC, such as the Creeks who provided the information in the following report. A year after joining the bureau, Hewitt clearly established the relationship of Cherokee among the Iroquoian languages, a connection long suspected but not fully proven. His best-known article, "Orenda and a Definition of Religion"; appeared in the American Anthropologist. After Powell's death, much of the attention of the bureau staff was directed at completing the bureau's two-volume *Handbook of American Indians North of Mexico*, for which Hewitt wrote a number of entries. He was also charged with replying to questions in letters send by the public. His responses were both thorough and glacially slow.

Hewitt's most significant contributions are his transcriptions in the Iroquois languages, and corresponding English translations, of the ritual speeches and traditions the great oral texts that were to define the cultures of societies such as the Iroquois much as do written texts in "literate" ones. These include the Iroquois origin myth (cosmology), traditional accounts of the founding of the League of the Iroquois, and speeches of the Condolence ceremony held for the purpose of mourning and installing chiefs of the league. The two major publications resulting from Hewitt's interest in mythology are "*Iroquois Cosmology*" and "*Seneca Fiction, Legends, and Myths.*" Both appeared in the Annual Reports of Bureau of American Ethnology; the later work, a collection compiled by Jeremiah Curtin and Hewitt, was edited by Hewitt.

When Hewitt was hired by the bureau there were no anthropologists holding a Ph.D. in the discipline. This changed in 1900 when John Swanton was hired, and Hewitt found himself an "amateur" (without formal training) in a field now dominated by "professionals" with graduate training). By continuing to study Iroquois languages and cultures, but not publishing his results, Hewitt solved after a fashion the dilemma of his being a native in such a situation. By recording Iroquois traditions, he preserved them; by not publishing them, he preserved them and himself from criticism by others.

Hewitt was a devout Christian concerned with Indians' own sense of self-esteem. He was a member of the Ingram Memorial Congregational Church until 1923, when he joined All Souls

Unitarian Church. He married twice, both times to non-Indian women. In 1913, to Catherine C Stuart Hewitt (1858–1918), then in 1925, Carrie Louise Hurlbut (1870–1951).

Hewitt joined the Anthropological Society of Washington a year after moving to Washington, D.C.; he served as its treasurer from 1912 to 1926 and as its president from 1932 to 1934. He was a charter member of the Society of American Indians, founded at Ohio State University in Columbus. From 1918 until his death he was the Smithsonian Institution's representative on the U.S. Board of Geographic Names. Hewitt died at the age of seventy-eight, and is buried in Rock Creek Cemetery, District of Columbia.

NOTES ON THE CREEK INDIANS[68]
By J.N.B. HEWITT

EDITED BY J.R. SWANTON

CONTENTS

ILLUSTRATIONS

[121]

---

[68] John Napoleon Brinton Hewitt *Notes on the Creek Indians*. John Swanton, ed. Bureau of American Ethnology, Bulletin 123, Anthropological Papers #10 1939.

Introduction

By J.R. Swanton

In the administrative report of Dr. J. Walter Fewkes, Chief of the Bureau of American Ethnology, for the fiscal year ended June 30, 1921, Mr. J.N.B. Hewitt reported that he was "at work on some material relating to the general culture of the Muskhogean peoples, especially that relating to the Creeks and the Choctaw." He went on to say that —

> In 1881-82 Major J.W. Powell began to collect and record this matter at firsthand from Mr. L.C. Perryman and Gen. Pleasant Porter, both well versed in the native customs, beliefs, culture, and social organization of their peoples. Mr. Hewitt assisted in this compilation and recording. In this way he became familiar with this material, which was laid aside for lack of careful revision, and a portion of which has been lost; but as there is still much that is valuable and not available in print it was deemed wise to prepare the matter for publication, especially in view of the fact that the objective activities treated in these records no longer form a part of the life of the Muskhogean peoples, and so cannot be obtained at first hand. In addition to this material, it is designed to add as supplementary matter some Creek tales and mythic legends collected by Mr. Jeremiah Curtin.

At that time I was preparing my extensive Creek material for the press and suggested to Mr. Hewitt that he print his own notes first so that I could refer to them. But although the administrative report for the year following indicates continued work by Mr. Hewitt on his manuscript and it appears that he took it up again in 1926 for a time, it remained unpublished at the time of his {1937} death.

Although Choctaw is mentioned in the administrative report of 1920-21 as well as Creek, the material is practically all Creek. The greater part of this Hewitt had copied, in a somewhat amplified form. I have checked his copies by the originals and have completed the copying. The material is not very extensive and in considerable measure it duplicates what I published in the Forty-second Annual Report of the Bureau, but there is some information which is unique. [124]

The greater part of this material was obtained from Legus F. Perryman of the Okmulgee or Big Springs town and the remainder from Gen. Pleasant Porter, also of Okmulgee. Porter was at one time head chief of the Creek Nation and Perryman probably accompanied him as his "interpreter", though both appear to have been able to speak and write English, and most of these notes were originally written down by them. Mr. Hewitt states that they were obtained at Jersey City in 1881-82, but on one sheet appears the address "Tremont House, Washington, D.C.," and so it is probable that some additions were made in Washington. This would seem to be implied by Hewitt's reference to Powell's part in obtaining them. In 1881-82 Hewitt was working over Iroquois material with Mrs. Erminnie Smith, generally in New York State, but the place of residence of both was Jersey City. Some notes were evidently added in 1883. The editor met Mr. Perryman once in 1912, not many years before his death. In the 30 years that had elapsed between these two dates it is evident that much had dropped from Mr. Perryman's mind. Be that as it may, many of the items in this paper have never been printed before and add some valuable details to our knowledge of the ancient Creeks, and this in spite of the fact that *Okmulgee* was one of the towns most rapidly affected by European influence. It was formerly one of those affiliated with the *Hitchiti*, speaking the *Hitchiti* language which was nearer to Choctaw than to

Creek.

The editor has preferred to risk some repetition of material already published in the Forty-second Annual Report of the Bureau and other papers rather than the omission of material that might be of service for a fuller understanding of the ancient Creek organization. Wherever the pronoun "I" appears it is the editor who is speaking, but it will not be difficult to separate the few comments that he has added.

TOWNS[69]

At the time when Porter and Perryman were interviewed (1881-82) they stated that there were 49 towns, each occupying a distinct territory, but that they had increased greatly after white contact and that tradition said there were originally but 18. These were all divided into two classes, one called the *Italwalgi* (*Itulwuiki*) and the other the *Kipayalgi* (*Kipayuiki, Kipoywuiki, Kupahyuiki*)[70] This [125] last is also given as *Tipayulki* but this form seems to be erroneous. The towns called *Italwalgi* had control of important matters relating to civil government. Their badge was white, the emblem of peace and wisdom. The towns (or tribes) called *Kipayalgi* had charge of military affairs, and their badge was red, the emblem of war and prowess. In many respects the former had executive functions, while those of the latter were legislative and judicial. The colors mentioned were painted on doorposts and on various articles, and were used in bodily decoration. All of the people of a town, whether of White or Red clans, belonged as a whole to one of these two classes. Although the White towns were entitled to the civil offices, sometimes the Red towns obtained such dominion and power during war that they kept them when peace came. For instance, the White towns had civil control of the Creeks from time immemorial up to the Revolution of 1776, and then the Red towns obtained power and kept it until 1861. Since the Civil War, 1861-65, the White towns have again been in control. The White towns took sides under McGillivray with the British and this may have caused the change of power to the Red towns. The following list of the eighteen original towns with their daughter towns and the division of the nation to which each belonged is given by Perryman, but the more usual spellings of the town names have been substituted.

WHITE TOWNS

{	1. *Otciapofa* ("In the hickory grove").
{	2. *Tulsa Atclna-hatchee* ("Cedar Creek Tulsa" or "Little River Tulsa").
I. *Tulsa* {	3. *Tulsa Kaniti* ("Tulsa Canadian").
	4. *Lutcapoga* ("Turtle Place") { *Łučapoka* '3+ turtles dwell' }.

NOS. 2 and 3 represent a division which took place after they migrated west. There is a note to the effect that the Tuskegee came from Tulsa but this is erroneous.

---

[69] See BAE-AR 42nd, Washington, 1928; also F.G. Speck, *Ethnology of the Yuchi Indians*, Anthropological Publications of the University of Pennsylvania Museum, vol. I, No. 1, Philadelphia 1909; and F.G. Speck, *The Creek Indians of Taskigi Town*, Memoirs of the American Anthropological Association, n.s. vol. II, pt. 2.

[70] *Italwalgi* seems to mean "his own towns" and *Kipayalgi* or *Inkipayalgi*, "his opposites," and it is believed that the applications of these would change with the individual. Perryman and Porter belonged to a White town and therefore their *Italwalgi* were Whites and their *Kipayalgi* were Reds. Had they belonged to a Red town the appellations would have shifted accordingly.

	1. *Oltcadi Tuskegee* ("Red Water Tuskegee")
II. *Tuskegee*	2. *Kaniti Tuskegee* ("Canadian Tuskegee").

These two towns had divided only a short time before.

	1. *Tallahassee* ("Old Town").
	2. *Tukpafka* ("Spunk Town").
	2a. *Koasati.*
III.	3. *Wakokai* ("Blue Heron Town" — the place where they nested).
	4. *Wiogufki* ("Muddy Water").

No. 1 is said to have been "the first." No. 2a was inserted later and the insertion is erroneous. The name of No. 4 is also that of the Mississippi River.

	1. *Okfuskee.*
	2. *Tcatoksofka.*
IV.	3. *Abihkutci.*
	4. *Nuyaka* [126]

"These four were all one and this one was called *Okfuskee*. Before that they were all *Tulsa* and the *Tuskegee* were also at first *Tulsa*;[71] all the White towns were originally *Tulsa*. All came out of the ground at the Rocky Mountains." No. 2 is said to have been modern, only 50 years old in 1882.

	1. *Talwa łako.*
	2. *Okmulgee* (or "Big Spring").
V. *Hitchiti*	3 *Sawokli* (extinct).
	4. *Okitiyakani* (extinct).

The first three were originally one town called *Hitchiti*. This is somewhat confusing for *Hitchiti* is also given among the numbered towns.

VI. *Kasihta.*

VII. *Łałogalga* ("The fishery — fish pond").

VIII.	*Wiwolika* ("A-wo'-ka") ("Roaring Water").
	Okchai.

No. 1 separated from No. 2.

IX. Asilanabi ("When the tea stem is green" or "Place of green leaves." The "tea" is said to have been from wintergreen leaves but this is doubtful).

	1. *Abihka.*
X. *Abihka*. The gate	2. *Talladega.*
of the nation.	3. *Kantcadi.*

There was only one square at first but "of late they have had three squares."

XI. Pahan-tallahassee. From what town lately sprung is not known.

RED TOWNS

	1. *Coweta.*
I. *Coweta*	2. *Łikatcka.*

These two towns were formerly one.

II. *Tukabahchee.*

III.	1. *Holiwahali.*

---

[71] This is certainly wrong. The *Tuskegee* were connected with the *Alabama* and *Koasati* rather than the true Creeks.

2. *Łapłako*.
1. *Kaialedji*.
2. *Hatchee tcaba*.

These were one and came from *Tukabahchee*.

1. *Atasi*.
2. *Talmuchasi*.

These were one.

1. *Eufaula*.
VI   2. *Eufaula hobai* ("*Eufaula* far away").
1. *Chiaha*.   These three were one.
VII   2. *Osochi*.
3. *Hotalgihuyana* ("Whirlwind Track").

Towns confederated with the Creeks but speaking other languages were the following:
1. *Yuchi* (adopted by the *Kasihta*).
2. *Alabama*.
3. *Koasati*.
4. *Hitchiti*. [127]

The Yuchi language was very different from the Creek. The others resembled one another and were similar to Choctaw.

The following tribes were conquered by the Creeks or were remnants of peoples incorporated with them:
1. *Apalochicola*.
2. *Yamasalgi*.
3. *Nokfilalgi*.
4. *Natchez*.

These four were thought to be extinct but the first continued under the name *Talwa łako*, and there are a few *Natchez* even today. Perryman thought that the *Alabama*, *Hitchiti*, and *Koasati* had sprung from the *Apalachicola* and he is, indeed, supported by their languages. A note says that *Alabama*, *Hitchiti*, *Koasati*, and *Natchez* were like Choctaw but that is not true of Natchez, though Natchez is remotely connected with the Muskhogean tongues.

The information above given corresponds in almost every detail with that which I obtained 30 years later, but, as already stated, *Koasati* was in no way connected with the *Tukpafka* group of towns, and the same may be said of *Tuskegee*. I did not learn of a town corresponding to *Tallahassee* from which the *Tukpafka* group are supposed to have come, and Perryman was clearly wrong, or misunderstood, in separating *Łałogalga* from *Okchai* and *Asilanabi*. The relationship of these three is so well recognized that not a suggestion of any difference in origin reached me. On the other hand, I am not certain that *Wiwohka* belonged with them, though the connection is probable. It will be noticed that, although the group to which *Kaialedji* and *Hatchee-tcaba* belongs is made coordinate with *Tukabahchee*, it is stated specifically that the former came from the latter, but the information I received regarding *Talmuchasi* would separate it from *Atasi* and align it with the *Okfuskee* towns. This I believe to be correct, because the connection is stated by Hawkins. *Atasi*, as well as *Kaialedji*, is commonly believed to have sprung from *Tukabahchee*. Either Perryman did not know that *Apalachicola* and *Talwa łako* were names for the same town or, what is more probable, he was misunderstood. The *Yamasee* were connected with the *Hitchiti* in language, and Gatschet was given to understand that *Nokfilalgi* was a name for the *Timucua* of Florida.

A town was usually designated as a "fire," for a council fire was always kindled in it in a prescribed place, and the houses of the village had to be built within a drumbeat of that. The man who had charge of the fire was an important official and was called *Tutka-titca*, signifying "fire maker." Each town had a certain amount of land under cultivation and whenever a child was born it was proportionately increased, an extra allotment being made. At the annual festival [128] a census was taken by means of sticks (the "broken days") and if it showed an increase in population, more land was taken in. This, of course, applies to the time when there was plenty of waste land around the towns. If they found they were decreasing — I suppose this means decreasing seriously — they attributed the calamity to the tythe (tie) snake and removed.

Towns, like clans, were perpetuated matrilineally, each person belonging to the town of his or her mother.

CLANS[72]

Among the Creeks the clan was a body of kindred, actual or by the legal fiction of adoption, which did not embrace the entire body of persons represented in a community having a kinship system. The persons who belonged to a clan might be regarded as the descendants of a common ancestor, a woman, through women. Only the descendants of the women belonged to the clan. The descendants of the males belonged to the several clans with which they had intermarried. Thus, a group of brothers and sisters belonged to the clan of their mother; but only the children of the sisters remained in the clan; the children of the brothers belonged to the clans of their wives, as has just been said.

The organization of the clan was based on kinship. The unit of the organization of the tribe was the clan, since each tribe was composed of a group of clans. The town was usually constituted of a number of segments of clans, each segment retaining its blood kinship rights and duties. Each household or fireside, of course, consisted of members of two different clans.

The clans were separated into two divisions, one called *Hathagalgi*, "People of the White," and the other *Tcilokogalgi*, "Foreigners," who were enemies, fighters, bloody, red. One authority called the second of these "*Olumhulkee*", probably intended for *Lamhalgi*, "Eagle People," the Eagle clan, although now nearly extinct, having at one time been important. Each of these is said to have consisted of four principal clans from which the others had, theoretically, become separated, and these, along with some of their subdivisions, were given by Perryman as follows:

HATHAGA (WHITE MOIETY)

I. *Hotalgalgi,* Wind Clan.
    a. *Konalgi,* Skunk Clan.
II. *Itchaswalgi,* Beaver Clan.
III. *Nokosalgi,* Bear Clan.
    a. *Yahalgi,* Wolf Clan.
IV. *Fuswalgi, Bird Clan.* [129]

---

[72] BAE-AR 42nd: 1928, pp. 114-119; F.G. Speck, *Ethnology of the Yuchi Indians.*

TCILOKOKO (RED(?) MOIETY)

I. *Aktayatcalgi*, said to be the old name.
    a. *Tcolalgi*, Fox Clan.
II. *Katcalgi*, Panther Clan.
    a. *Kowakatculgi*, Wildcat Clan (all Cat clans came from it).
III. *Ahalagalgi*, Potato Clan.
    a. *Halpatalgi*, Alligator Clan.
    b. *Wotkalgi*, Raccoon Clan.
    c. *Sopaktalgi*, Toad Clan.
IV. *Itcoalgi*, Deer Clan.

The arrangement by fours falls in line with a tendency noteworthy in Morgan's treatment of clans among various tribes and might be attributed to him since his influence was all-powerful in the Bureau of Ethnology in its early years. This, however, would be a mistake. The number four is the cardinal ceremonial number among the Creeks and use of it may readily be attributed to that fact. Again, so far as the White clans are concerned, the data I got agrees precisely with that of Perryman. Even in this moiety it was probably a convention, as I learned from two or three good sources that the *Katcalgi* — of all clans — had formerly been on the White side. The arrangement of clans in the Red moiety is still more doubtful, outside of what has already been said of the *Katcalgi*. The *Aktayatcalgi* and *Ahalagalgi* were sometimes put together. More often the *Tcolalgi* were associated with the *Ahalagalgi*. On the other hand, the *Wotkalgi* were usually made one of the leading clans, or the leading clan of its group, and the *Halpatalgi* were generally given an independent position though classed with the *Itamalgi*, given by Perryman as an unclassified clan, and the *Pinwalgi* or Turkey Clan. The *Sopaktalgi*, however, I never before heard of associated with this group. They were always placed with the *Takosalgi* or Mole Clan and the *Tcokotalgi*, and sometimes these were put in one phratry with the *Itcoalgi*. Besides those clans already given, Perryman knew of two others, one called the *Atcialgi* or Corn Clan, of unknown affiliations. The other, the *Panosalgi*, is probably intended for *Pahosalgi*, a clan closely connected with the Deer.

THE SQUARE GROUND[73]

The Square or Yard was called *Tokfi'tta* (or *Tokfi'kta*), but sometimes *Paskofa* (Perryman spelled it "Pas-cofar" or "Pars-cofer").

Three plans of Creek Squares are given, two of them evidently intended to represent the same, while the third seems to be distinct. As the descriptions given in the text and the notes accompanying the [130] sketches disagree in some particulars, it is somewhat uncertain how many Square Grounds are in question. The third plan (fig. 13) bears a rather close resemblance in its arrangements to what we know of *Kasihta* and is probably intended for it.[74] The four cabins erected toward the four cardinal points are indicated by A, A, A, A, and, in front of each, split logs are shown (B, B, B, B). The Chiefs (*Mikalgi*) who belonged to White clans sat in the west cabin, the

---

[73] Ibid., pp. 170-241; also cf. Smithsonian Misc. Coll., vol. 85, no. 8. *Tokfi'tta* contains the word *fi'tta*, "yard." *Paskofa* means "the swept area."
[74] BAE-AR 42nd: p. 266.

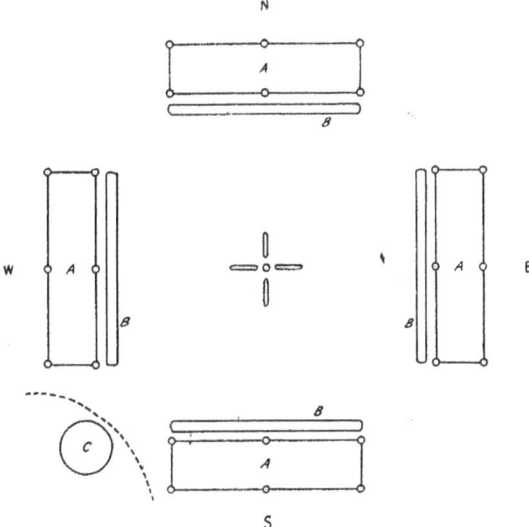

FIG 13. — Creek Square Ground or "Big Home", probably that of Kasihita.

Warriors (*Tastanagalgi*) and Aspergers (*Yaholagi*), the former at least from Red Clans, in the north cabin, the Chief's Advisers (*Taski henihalgi*) and Burden-bearers (*Imałałgi*) or Warriors' Assistants in the south cabin, and the women and children in that to the east. The four cabins together were called the Big House (*Tcoko łako*). C is the "round or Steep House" (*Tcoko faski*).

The other plans, combined in figure 14, may be intended to represent the *Okmulgee* Square to which Pleasant Porter and Legus Perryman [131] belonged but the only other plan of that Square I have been able to obtain resembles that of *Kasihta*.[75] This also has four cabins but there is more detail regarding their construction. Each measured 30 by 10 feet and consisted of two long seats, one behind the other. The roof was raised on nine posts (though only six are shown in figure 13) and the ends were separated into two sections — in the minds of the Indians

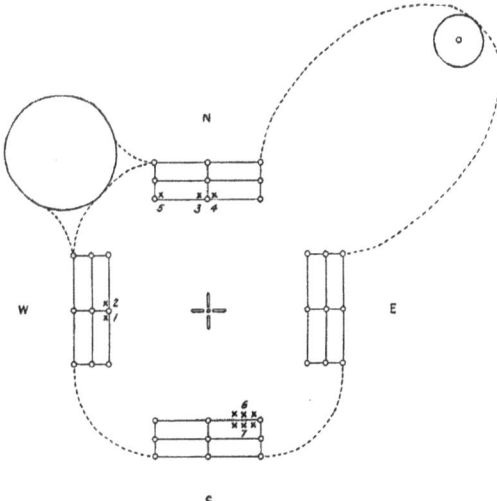

FIG 14. — Creek Square Ground or "Big House", perhaps that of *Okmulgee*.

if not otherwise — by a median line from front to back inward, and twenty feet apart between the nearest posts.   connecting the three center posts. The cabins were oriented so as to form a

---

[75] /7 BAE-AR 42nd: p. 208.

perfect square facing The fire was kindled in the exact center of the enclosed space, and, as indicated in the diagram, at the inner ends of four main logs arranged in the form of a cross and oriented also toward the cardinal points. Close to the front posts of all the cabins except that to the east, which was for the women and children, were four seats for men of rank. The west cabin was that of the Chief (*Miko*) and in it sat, as numbered, (1) the Town Chief (*Talwa* [132] *miko*), and (2) the Speaker (*Simiabaya*). The Warriors (*Tastanagalgi*) sat in the north cabin and their leaders at the places numbered 3-5. The *Henihalgi* sat in the south cabin and on the fourth day of the annual busk the women (6) began their dance in front of the east end of this cabin facing the singers (7) placed there for them. The circle to the northwest marks the location of the "Round or Sharp House" said to be 100 feet in diameter and 50 feet high. The sweepings from the ceremonial ground made ridges of earth called *tadjo* which are indicated by the broken lines. The circle to the northeast represents a mound of earth heaped about a tree and derived from the dirt and rubbish in the Square which was scraped up annually and thrown there. The space intervening between this tree and the Square is evidently the Chunky Yard, though it is not so designated. The location of this was different in the different towns.

According to the notes in the text the Sharp House was made around a tall tree or, if no suitable tree was available, a pole erected for the purpose. Other poles were leaned against this and we are here told that it might be carried up to 60 feet. This was to furnish a shelter in case of rain. A fire was maintained there and there is where they danced in bad weather. By an evident error the text locates this at the "southeast" corner.

In the construction of all of these buildings, certain persons were assigned to the duty of procuring each of the timbers, and every clan had to provide a special number of poles for the Sharp House. This assignment was never varied.

Every person knew his place in the Square. The west and south cabins were generally occupied by men of the White clans, but in one town we are informed that they used only part of the south cabin and had some seats in the east cabin instead. This exception may have been due to the fact that the *Imałalgi*, assistants of the Warriors, were seated in the south cabin in the first plan given.

All of these Squares were arranged in accordance with certain measurements and the Indians were as precise about these as if their lives depended upon it.

GOVERNMENT[76]

Perryman said that each town consisted of a number of clans or rather a number of segments of clans, and the Town Chief (*Talwa Miko*) was chosen from the principal one. Whenever another clan increased in numbers and importance so as to exceed that of the principal clan, a part or the whole of this clan would separate from [133] the village and establish a new one. This happened only when the people were so numerous and the leading men so popular that they could induce members of the other clans to unite with them in the enterprise. In this way the chiefs of the several tribes came to be widely distributed among the clans. This statement must, however, be taken with some qualification since a number of related towns are known to have been governed by the same clan.

In the Red towns the leading officers were selected from the military line by the civil moiety, and the leading officers of the White towns (?) were selected from the civil moiety by the people of the military moiety, in whom inhered the military government and who to some

---

[76] BAE-AR 42nd: pp. 276-333; *Smithsonian Miscellaneous Collections*, Vol. 85, No. 8.

extent took part also in civil affairs, as in a similar manner the civilians took part in military affairs. But questions of peace were decided by the people of the White towns, and civil officers were chosen from their body. Questions relating to war were settled by the people of the Red towns, and the military officers were chosen therefrom.

There was yet another class of people in the state, namely, the prophets and medicine men or shamans. These constituted a priesthood, and performed important functions. Every act of the Muskogee government, or of the officers thereof, was considered a religious act. Councils were always convened with religious ceremonies and the installation of officers was always opened similarly. In the charge given to the officers at their installation, the religious customs were enjoined and the importance of these shown. The festivals held by the people were all religious festivals, were opened with religious ceremonies, and were intended to inculcate religious ideas, so that when a festival was held religious truths were always taught. Whenever punishment was inflicted, the religious reasons therefore were always explained to the culprit and to the people. All punishment was explained as a washing away of the wrong. Every officer of the government was also a religious officer and was virtually a priest, and these officers were supposed to be repositories of religious truth, so that the doctrines were handed down from officer to officer of the government from generation to generation, and the method of selecting officers long in advance of their installation was needful in order that the men might be trained in the governmental, and especially in the religious, duties. In fact, governmental and religious duties were held to be one and the same.

The principal chief of a town, called *Miko* or *Talwa Miko*, was chosen out of the domestic or White clans by the executive or Red clans. One class selected the leader from the other class. In making the selection they considered the matter for a long time. They studied the character and qualifications of the best men that the [134] particular group of clans had, and talked about the matter sometimes for a week or more, finally selecting the man they regarded as wisest and best. They did not, however, take a formal vote. The names of a dozen men might be mentioned at first, and the number then narrowed down to one. Afterwards one of their number was chosen to deliver the decision. He might be called a member of the Executive Council. These Town Chiefs never held a higher office but the Executive Chiefs could be promoted. New members were added by the Executive Council itself, but a great many clans had no man fit for the position. They might number as many as 24 but were often fewer. The name of the new chief having been announced by these men, including a list of his virtues, a committee of these same clans notified him in a speech which lasted all night. He might refuse the honor absolutely. If he did they approached him again, but if he refused the third time they left him alone. However, a man of great prudence would refuse until the third time. He would not consent at once, but if he finally accepted he would say: "If it is your will, then it must be so." When he had accepted the office the opposite line of clans was notified of his acceptance. When it was thought to be necessary to change a chief, the matter was taken under consideration a long time. They would say: "This man is getting too old; his thoughts are getting short, and he cannot finish an idea; he cannot rule wisely. Let us select some younger man to learn the duties of the position." Then, after a long conference, another man would be selected and notified. A man's son was never made chief in his father's stead. His uncle was the nearest kin, being his mother's brother, and having the same blood as his mother.

The installation of chiefs. — When they installed a chief they put in his hand a white wing or a white feather. White was the emblem of civic rule. Sometimes they used the wing of a large white bird or white feathers from the wing of a turkey. The fan was placed in his left hand, and in his right hand he held a white staff.

A long ritual speech was made by the celebrant to the officer who was being installed. The first idea presented to him was this: "We put you on your bench and put in your hands the white fan and the white staff of authority and we also put in your care our women, our children, and people without number." They always used these ceremonial expressions, and also said, "We put the laws of our government in your hands." Then they told him that he must not occasion strife nor permit it, that he must not allow the "crossing of sharp instruments," meaning any kind of internal tribal strife, and added, "We are under you; you must see to it that this great calamity does not take place." They told him that he must not govern by sharp instruments, that is, by war, but he must govern by the law [135] of wisdom. They told him that his eyes must look downward, but that he must not see the ground. This meant that he must keep his people in view and not be influenced by anything around him. There is a great deal involved in the idea. He must look downward toward the ground but should see nothing crawling, crawling things being evils or dangers to the public welfare. He must consider only the interest of his people. The speech of installation was very lengthy.

Two persons out of certain clans were appointed by the chiefs of the towns to install officers, and the people followed them two or four deep. They followed them about until they came and stood before the candidate, when these two men walked out before him, conducted him to his bench, and proclaimed the law to him.

To be considered a person of great wisdom a man must be able, it was said, to discuss fully and completely four lines of thought. There appears to be some confusion in the statement of these, but it seems that the speaker first (a) gave all the objections raised by the opponents of the solution he favored, then (b) he answered those objections, (c) stated all the other objections to his own ideas he could think of and (d) finally outlined his own position on the matter in hand. Usually this was done very elegantly by a skillful speaker, setting forth in succession as convincingly as he could the cases for the negative and affirmative, and often he did it so well that one would believe he advocated the position opposed to his own.[77]

Rather brief mention is made of "the Chief or Superintendent of the Council Square." He seems to have been the man called in one place *Tcoko-łako-miko*, "Big House (i.e., Square) Chief." His duties were mainly confined to matters within the Square Ground, as his name implies, but he was also a kind of lieutenant to the Town Chief and took his place on occasion. Therefore he was usually called *Miko Apokta*, "Second Chief," and generally belonged to the same clan as the *Miko*.

The chief's adviser and spokesman was called *Heniha* or *Taski Heniha*. In one place it is said that he was "the Chief or Head Herald or Speaker whose duty it was to declare the decrees and judgments of the Principal Chief acting as the spokesman of the Council and through whom said Principal Chief always conveyed to the people the knowledge of the laws and decisions of the Council in the establishment and enforcement of law and order." He had charge of certain feasts and festivals. He was supposed to be an old man thoroughly versed in the laws and traditions of the people. Sometimes there was a fiction of age, for this office might be held by a [136] young man. After a decision had been reached by the Council, the Town Chief called this man to him, and informed him of it, telling him just what he must say to the people, and then the other announced, the decision in a loud voice to all present. *Taski Heniha* seems to have been

---

[77] The four lines of thought are recapitulated right afterwards and in a somewhat different manner.

the name of the principal speaker to distinguish him from the rest of the *Henihas*, for there were usually several, all drawn from one clan or one phratry.

As defined by Perryman, the *Heniha* appears to have performed the functions elsewhere assumed by the *Yatika*, "Interpreter." It is possible that in the Okmulgee town, or perhaps among the Lower Creeks generally, this was usual, or it may have come about through a breakdown of the organization. In the *Okchai* town, at least, the *Heniha* and *Yatika* were two different men, one sitting at the right hand of the *Miko*, the other at his left, but it was the *Yatika* who spoke. The position of *Heniha* was, however, hereditary in a special clan, usually the Wind, and at least a White clan, while that of *Yatika* seems to have been attained by merit. It is possible that a *Yatika* was gradually introduced owing to the fact that the *Heniha* would not always be endowed with the necessary eloquence.

The *Tastanagi* was a Military Chief whose duty it was to organize and have in charge the warriors in the town, i.e., the men who were fit to take part in warfare. In one place there is mention of two *tastanagis*, and we know that there were sometimes more than one, and that in such cases the principal warrior was called *Tastanagi łako*, "Big Warrior." He was the Sheriff or Chief of Police within the town as well as the Head Warrior outside of it.

The *Imałas* {aide, ensign} are called "burden carriers" and are said to have had certain duties to perform in the festivals. They were in fact a warlike grade below the *Tastanagis* and acted as their lieutenants and messengers. Like the *Tastanagis*, they were selected from Red clans.

The name *Yaholagi* is given to several messengers, evidently those selected to administer the Black Drink to the members of the Council. In these notes a more general function is indicated, "that of a crier or herald, or one who announces or conveys to others the decisions or orders of his superiors," but their specific and original duty was probably as just given.

The Chief Priest, Fire Keeper, or Fire Maker of the town (*Tutka-titca*), was also known as Medicine Maker (*Hilis-haya*). In making a fire he bored one stick into another until the fire started. Sometimes 12 men cooperated, one boring at a time. At every Council the fire must be kindled by means of the fire drill and by the Fire Maker. He did not sleep on the night before he made the fire, being supposed to work upon it all night. He is said to have had as one of his duties that of calling the Council together by beating upon a drum at the [137] town house. He was selected on account of his recognized abilities and appointed his own subordinates. However, he seems usually to have belonged to the same clan as the Town Chief and I was told that this was due to fear of treachery.

There was a Councilman or Elder Man who represented in the town council his clan or that segment of it which dwelt in his town. At times it became necessary for all the segments of a clan to assemble to discuss and adjust affairs which concerned the entire clan. So many new towns came into existence in later times that it happened that the jurisdiction and authority of the Elder Man or Head Man of a segment in an important town came to extend over two or more segments dwelling in contiguous towns, especially when these towns were only short distances apart. Usually each segment of a clan in the several towns had its special Elder Man but in some cases, where an original town had been divided into two or more, and such divisions occupied adjacent sites, there might be a common Elder Man for such segments, but the Elder Man of the entire clan was supreme over all, and an important case might be submitted to him from any segment.

The clan regulated its own affairs, that is to say, the conduct of its members in relation to one another. The Elder Man was the chief and usually the oldest man, but if the oldest man had become incapacitated by reason of senility, the next in age became the Elder Man. This officer was the teacher and counselor of the clan, and his authority was great. When minor offenses were committed complaint was made to the Elder Man, whose duty it was to advise and warn the offender. When offenses were more flagrant, or had been repeated after warning, complaint was made again to the Elder Man and the offender was punished in accordance with his judgment.

Elsewhere it is said that this officer was called "the Ancient." Though this office might be held by a person of any age and was sometimes occupied by a mere boy, yet he was always called the Ancient One. Nevertheless, an old man might lose his position on arriving at his dotage. When matters of importance to the segment of a clan arose, this Ancient might call a Council of the clan of all those who had arrived at years of maturity. The government and teaching of the youth of the clan belonged to this Ancient. It was his duty to instruct them, from time to time, in their duties and obligations to one another and to their elders and to the members of the clan. Punishment for even childish derelictions could not be meted out "without his advice and consent, which was usually given in a formal manner. The boy or girl, the young man or young woman, was charged with the offense and the Ancient heard the evidence. He might decide that the charge was not well founded, and state [138] that the offender had never been advised to shun the conduct charged against him. But if he decided that the offender had been duly advised regarding such evil conduct as was specified in the charge, then the offender might be whipped by members of his own clan. If matters of grave importance arose in the segment, the Ancient might call a large Council of the clan, composed of the members of two or more of the segments. At this Council the Ancient, or the one among the Ancients who was regarded as the wisest, presided and rendered judgment.

A man's status was indicated by his war or busk name. To the name of a chief was appended the word *Miko*, to that of a warrior of the first class the word *Tastanagi*, to that of an individual belonging to a privileged peace clan the word *Heniha*; and to the name of one of the second grade of warriors the term *Imathla*. According to the informants there were two grades beneath these, one indicated by the word *Yahola*, and a lowest which carried the name *Fiksiko* or *Hatco*. The arrangement is given as follows, reckoning from the lowest grade up:

(1) *Fiksiko* and *Hatco*, (2) *Yahola*, (3) *Imathla*, (4) *Henihe*, (5) *Tastanagi*, "warrior," "leader of warriors," (6) *Miko*, "chief," or "town chief."

And the following explanation is added:

A lad on coming to maturity received his first name. He might be raised subsequently to the second grade, especially if he early manifested wisdom. The word employed for the second grade signified a crier or herald or one who announced or conveyed to others the decisions or orders of his superiors. If a lad belonged to a Red clan he might be raised to the third grade, and if to a White clan to the fourth grade. Later he might be raised from the third grade to the fifth or from the fourth grade to the sixth.

The above statements are in line with those obtained by myself, except that my informants did not define the two lowest grades clearly and I do not feel certain that they were universally distinguished. The names *Fiksiko* and *Hatco* were usually given to men known as common warriors (*Tasikaya*). In another place it is said that the *Yahola* title was higher than *Imathla*, and that is quite possible since the functions of the *yahola* criers were important and were concerned with the cult of a being supposed to preside especially over the busk. The later statement is also evidently correct in claiming the *yahola* title particularly for the White clans.

The Ancient of the clan or Elder Man seems to be confounded sometimes in the material at hand with the *Simiabaiya* (or *Isimia-baya*), which means "he who adds to," or "he who keeps (a body of [139] people) together." In common usage it meant "a leader," and he was usually described as "a chief who represents national interests," one "who represents the town in the council of the confederacy and who represents the town council in matters relating to the confederacy." This is borne out by what is said regarding the manner in which he was selected. We are told that the *Simiabaiya* came from the same section as the Chief of the town, and that when he attended the General Assembly he usually took with him one of the *Tastanagia* from the other bench. This is evidently on the assumption that the town Chief belonged to a White clan. In the contrary case, a leader among the Whites would probably be selected. Considerable is said about the manner in which new *Simiabaiyas* were selected but it leaves one in doubt whether the position was retained in the same clan or whether it was retained in two clans of opposite moieties and alternated between them. We read that if the *Simiabaiya* "is of the clan of the Deer, they will take another man from the Deer clan that has been schooled under him, or some old man of the same clan, and he will be taught under that man. The young man steps into his place from the same clan and the same family as the reigning *Simiabaiya*. Sometimes they have two or three in training at one time." And yet some of the preceding sentences seem to imply that there was an alternation between the Red and White sides. Just above the *Simiabaiya* is identified with the Ancient of the clan and it may be imagined that the two offices were often combined in one man.

Again, it is said that the clan chiefs were selected by agreement within the clans on the ground that the individuals so selected were the best and wisest men in the clan and therefore able to represent their interests and assert their rights before the chief. "They are selected usually without any vote, but by general consent of the constituents in consultation."

THE COUNCILS[78]

The Council was called *Intałaka*, *łałaka* being a word which signified "great men" or "officers." The town council is said to have been composed of the Town Chief (*Miko*), the Square Chief (*Tcoko-łako Miko*), the "Speaker to the Chief," who in this case seems to be identified with the head *Tastanagi*, and a Councilman from each of the clans, that is, its Ancient. Although it is not so stated, I feel that it must have included the other speaker for the chief, the *Taski-heniha*, though he may have been admitted to it as Ancient for his own clan. This, indeed, appears to be indicated in another place. [140]

It is said that town councils were called together by the Fire Maker, presumably at the instance of the Chief. The Fire Maker would go to the town house and beat upon the drum, and then summon the Town Chief, the Square Chief, the man who had charge of the Square Ground ceremonies, and three or four other Councilman called "lawmakers." These last (?) would then call the people together and state the case to them. If a trespass, for instance, had been committed against some other town, the latter would appoint two persons to meet the others and agree upon some definite method of adjustment. Representatives of both parties would meet and settle the difference.

It was the duty of the Ancient to call the clansmen together in council. If they dwelt near one another, he sent a messenger to notify them. If they lived far apart, he broke up a number of sticks and sent to each a bundle containing as many {broken} sticks as there were days between that time and the date of the Council. The one who received the sticks threw one away each day, and when he threw away the last one he went to the place of meeting. In the town they all lived within sound of the drum but they did not use it in calling the clan together.

---

[78] ** See footnote 8.

At least some of the people were privileged to petition the Town Chief to summon general gatherings. On such occasions the *Taski-heniha*, or the several *Henihas*, were also consulted. After the Council had assembled the Chief would set before its members the reasons for calling it, and tell them to take the subject matter into consideration. This was communicated to them directly by the Chief's Speaker.

In the case of a Council of the Confederation, the *łałakas*, or "officers," included the *Simiabaiyas*, but it is uncertain how many others were added. It was their duty to bring with them the officers of their respective towns, but these were usually only listeners. There was commonly one presiding officer of this Council with a second chief under him, but sometimes there were two of each. The first usage was probably the original one, but it may have been changed to the second "owing to some difference of opinion." The two principal chiefs had equal power and so did the subordinates, but the latter had no duties to perform, being merely in line of succession to the leadership. They would choose two others to succeed them when they became principal chiefs. The presiding officer of the Council informed the Town Chief of any decision that had been made, whereupon the latter would go over the matter with his own speaker in a low voice and the speaker would announce the decision to the officers of the town there met together. It was the duty of the officers to pay strict attention to this so that they could repeat it substantially [141] as it had been announced to them. The speaker would instruct them that on their return to their respective towns they must call their people together and communicate to them the laws or other matters that had been resolved upon at the General Council. They were also to say what the result of disobeying these would be.

There was no set time for the meetings of the Confederate Council. Whenever these great men thought it necessary to call it together, it was summoned by direction of the Chief. This apparently means the presiding officer of the Council, who would then send the broken or split sticks to every town in the nation which was expected to attend the Council.

NAMING[79]

The first personal name was given to a child at birth in commemoration of an important event which might have occurred then, or in remembrance of some good or ill fortune that had befallen one of the older clan people, some one of the mother's brothers or sisters or their children. That is, it might refer to an event which was connected with the person's immediate family or members of his clan. For instance, if some person, perhaps the father or mother, ran away or was thrown down, or if the father was on an expedition and a remarkable event happened, the child born soon afterwards was named from that occurrence. This was the first name. It was a baby name, and it did not amount to anything. It simply denoted the time of the child's birth. Sometimes, when nothing unusual had occurred, the child was named from some peculiarity of the mother or father.

But when the child reached puberty it became necessary to give it a new name, and the right to select this inhered, not in the members of its own clan or moiety, but in the members of the paternal clan or moiety on the other side of the Council Fire. Certain persons within that clan had the matter in charge because of their relationship.

The proper notification of the need for giving one of their offspring a name having been made to the officers of the paternal clan, a suitable name was chosen. A new name was not coined on each occasion, for each clan had a large number of names peculiar to it which were

---

[79] See BAE-AR 42nd: pp. 87-106.

constantly in use, being bestowed again after the death of the bearer. On occasion two or more persons might have the same name.

And so at the annual festival called *poskita* the Elder Man of the paternal clan stepped forth at the proper time and called out loudly a certain name four times in succession. The person to whom this name was to be given did not know that it was to be bestowed upon [142] him, and he was then informed. Thereupon he stepped forth in front of the said Elder Man and received the name along with a present. Sometimes the name indicated the rank conferred because certain names became attached to certain official positions, as has been explained elsewhere, and installation into an office carried with it the name attached thereto. If a young man was of great promise he might also receive a name belonging to the highest rank of clan chiefs, or the highest to which he might be entitled by reason of his clan relationship.

A youth was likely to receive first the names *hadjo* or *fiksiko*. *Hadjo* signifies "excited," "enthusiastic," "mad," "crazy," and *fiksiko* "without a heart," "brave." *Hadjo* denotes a lively or active person, an athlete. *Fiksiko* means brave, courageous, literally "without feelings." Bestowal of the first name meant that the youth was now worthy of manhood.

The titles given subsequently, *Imałthla*, *Tastanagi*, and *Miko*, have been described elsewhere. They carried with them official functions and special seats on the Square Ground.

Often men acquired two names or titles.

Hopayuki was the highest name of all. The bearer of it combined the qualities of a warrior and prophet and it was derived from *hopayi* which signifies "a prophet." Perryman added that it signified a traveled warrior, one who had been in foreign lands. A Civil Chief might also have this title. Those who had it "did the thinking and the predicting," but the warriors carried out their matured plans.

MARRIAGE[80]

When a man was considered by his clansmen entitled to a wife, a conference was held by the elder men of the clan. The prospective groom must, however, have the following virtues. He must be a good hunter, a brave warrior, and an athlete. Having decided that he was old enough and fully capable of becoming the parent of children, a decision which gave him adult status, the elder men conferred with the elder women of the clan, saying to them in substance: "Our young man," giving his name and qualifications, "should now have a wife. He is now a man. He should have the orderly opportunity of having offspring and strengthening our people thereby."

They and the women debated the question seriously and in the best possible spirit, and the women took the matter under advisement. It was naturally supposed that the women knew the qualifications of the marriageable women of other clans better than the men. They selected some family in a clan which had a cousin relationship [143] with their own and could intermarry with theirs and in which there were marriageable women.

They asked this cousin clan to give them a wife for one of their men. At once the members of the cousin clan took the matter under consideration, the elder women consulting with the elder men, saying: "Our cousin clan so-and-so asks us to give them a wife from among our young unmarried women. What do you think of this request?" The men thereupon considered the matter carefully, and if they concluded that the young man was worthy of one of their daughters they permitted the women to return on their behalf an indefinite answer but nevertheless one of encouragement. Thereupon the young man was privileged to make a present

---

[80] BAE-AR 42nd: pp. 368-383.

to the clan of his prospective bride. It was not necessary to send the present directly to her very house, because the suitor was not supposed to know, and usually did not know, the woman who had been chosen as his spouse. If the clan elders accepted the present they sent it to the woman's house. The suitor was notified and was then privileged to visit in that house. The woman's maternal uncles then talked with him confidentially but frankly. Finally they told him to return to his own home and say that when they were satisfied that he was the right kind of man they would send for him. That meant that he had been accepted.

On the appointed day they harangued him at length, telling of the duties he was about to assume in his new relation as husband. They made him understand the customs peculiar to the clan in which his children would be brought up, and they made him understand what position he would occupy with regard to the people of their clan. Finally they said: "You will find your wife in that house," or "You will find your bed yonder," indicating it with a gesture. She had purposely been placed there already.

In former times it was customary to give away the oldest girl in the family first, however undesirable she might be, especially if the suitor was not considered a very desirable husband, but if he was liked she might be passed over. Sometimes a young man of great force of character would circumvent all the finesse of matchmaking and would manage his case so adroitly as to obtain the girl of his own choice. It depended upon his strategy. After that, being a married man, he could go and come whenever he pleased.

The groom was expected to leave his wife's house before sunrise every morning until his wife became pregnant. He might then remain, but he must suspend sexual relations with her. In the interval before the birth of the child he was expected to build a house for himself, that is, if the house of her mother was not big enough to accommodate another family. He might erect it near the home of his parents-in-law or some distance away, depending upon his [144] inclinations. Just before the child's birth the young husband was expected to go off on a hunting trip. He was not supposed to be at home on that occasion. But each clan had customs that were peculiar to itself.

If the betrothed woman eloped, and was not retaken before the next annual busk when all offenses except murder were forgiven, she was free. But if she was recaptured within that time the penalty imposed was very heavy. If the offence was committed within the same clan it was not forgiven and meant death for both man and woman.

When fornication occurred between individuals of different clans, the matter was compounded by the clans concerned. Certain demands were made for the loss of the woman and these must be satisfied, but the abductor seldom gave the woman up. Generally the penalty was a heavy fine as an equivalent for the loss of the woman and breach of the common law of marriage. The clan of the offender must pay for the offence.

If adultery had been committed and the guilty pair were captured, they were severely punished. The people of the man's clan were called together to exact the penalty. The offenders were beaten with rods until they were insensible, and then the end of the nose was cut off or it was slit lengthwise, or one of the ears of each culprit was cut off or it was sawed with a dull knife, so that no one would be attracted by either in future. Mr. Perryman says that for the first offence both ears were cut off and for the second the nose.

In reply to a question regarding the punishment for the violation of a widow, Mr. Perryman said that the violator of a widow was punished exactly as though her husband were living. She belonged to his clan.

After the death of a married man the clan elders assembled and, after consultation, chose someone from their clan who was in duty bound under clan custom to marry the widow. If he did not wish to marry her he must nevertheless take her as his wife for one night, after which his claim to her was extinguished. Then the clan elders chose another man. One member of the clan had the right to select him. Although the man chosen already had a wife, clan law nevertheless required him to take the widow. The old men said that the man who did not intend to marry a widow took her to his home and kept her there for a single night without having sexual relations with her. That would have been unjust, they said, if he had intended to turn her away immediately afterwards. Still, he could have such relations with her and then release her.

When a man married a woman who had a sister or sisters younger than herself, he might claim the right to marry them, and if he had [145] done well by the first he was entitled to the others, but he had nothing to say about giving them away.

EDUCATION[81]

The father had no more to do with the discipline and education of his children than an alien. He could not punish their misconduct in any way, but he had such a right in some other man's family, i.e., in the family of the man who had married his sister. It was the mother's clansmen who might punish the children of their sister. The husband might sit around and talk in his wife's house but he had no authority there. He had full authority if he wished to exercise it in the house of his sister and her husband.

When children arrived at a certain age the sexes were kept strictly apart. This age was not definitely fixed, but probably it was when there might be danger that the children would think of having carnal intercourse with one another. The girls were controlled by the elder women. They had to sleep apart and to bathe in pools separate from those used by the boys. The girls had to bathe in streams of flowing water below the point at which the boys and men were bathing if necessity compelled them to use the same stream. The boys and men must not cross the path by which the girls and women went to the stream. The boys were kept strictly from the girls until they obtained wives or until they had passed the age of indiscretion.

In every town there was an old man who taught the children. It is implied that there was only one in a town, but it is evident that he was identical with the Ancient or Elder Man mentioned above and that he was a clan functionary or functioned over a group of related clans. He went from house to house, gathering the children around him and telling them tales, singing songs, instructing them first in their duties at home, obedience to their superiors, their mothers, their uncles (the fathers were not often present), instructing them that they must not tell falsehoods, must not steal, must not injure anyone, must not fight, must not quarrel, must not kill, and so on. As soon as they were 6 years old the boys were instructed to bathe in a stream every morning before sunrise, especially in winter. They were taught to play ball, and once every year they were "scratched," that is, the muscles of their calves and their thighs in front were scratched until the blood ran out in order to make them grow and to harden them. This was continued until they were 15 and it was regarded as an honor for a young man at the ball games to show his scratches in regular order on his arms and legs. [146]

When he was 15 a boy on attendance at a night festival would hear a strange name called out several times and then his own name, after which some friend would come for him, take him from the shed {bed}of the women and children in the Square Ground, and conduct him to one of the men's sheds, and after certain ceremonies an old man would give him some token, make him

---

[81] BAE-AR 42nd: pp. 358-367.

an address, and tell him that he was no longer a child but a man. The boy then waved the token over his head and uttered his first war whoop, shouting "*Hi-yo-ke-toh*," the war whoop.

The object of all instruction was to develop a fine body and a good character. The girls were instructed in their duties by the same old man, but they were not required to bathe every day. There was a girl's game of ball, different from that of the men. It had a single pole and the ball was thrown by the hand at a mark on the pole, every hit counting one.

When a boy had been detected in an offence, let us suppose it to be theft, he was brought up for trial and the question was put to the old man, "Has he been taught not to steal?" The reply might be, "Yes, over and over again. He is a bad boy and would not heed instructions." And then, if he was proven guilty, he would be punished severely, generally with the "long scratch," a deep and ugly incision extending from his arms down over his breast and down each leg, or down his back, or both. These scratches were readily distinguishable from those given boys at the annual festivals.

But if the teacher said that the boy (or girl) had never been taught, no punishment would be inflicted.

These teachers taught young people about the laws and the penalties attaching to the infringement of them, for though the children would hear the laws proclaimed at every festival, they would not understand them, and so the teacher had to explain them carefully.

If it became evident that a teacher was neglecting his duty another would be put in his place. There was no formal appointment. The people simply sent for him to come and instruct their children. He was usually a medicine man.

Sometimes a woman would study medicine and become a doctor but no woman held any office.

Boys were early instructed in the ball play, as it was considered the best means of developing their muscles, since it was accompanied by running and wrestling. The old men said it was invented at a time when there was no war and therefore there were no enemies to fight. They called it the "Little War." The name of it was *Po-ko-its it-ten*, "Hitting at a ball," and sometimes *Ah-fats-kee-tah*, "Amusement." (Related by L. Perryman, December 14, 1882.) [147]

Crime[82]

The fundamental idea regarding punishment was that it cleansed the culprit from the guilt of his crime. Criminals carried no guilt with them out of the world. After undergoing the prescribed punishment the culprit was innocent. It mattered not what he had done. If the law and custom had been enforced against him (or her) he was thereafter, to all intents and purposes, as innocent and as honorable as any other man in the community.

If a person of one clan killed a member of another it was held that the crime had been committed against the entire clan, and it was the right and the duty of every member of the aggrieved clan to seek reparation from the other.

The Ancients of the injured clan formally demanded satisfaction of the other. Two persons were generally selected to carry the news and make the demand. They dressed in a certain way and put certain marks on their persons. They always dressed in haste. Before they reached the edge of the town they rushed forward shouting and were perfectly safe when coming in this manner. No person might then interrupt them. No one might touch them. While on such missions they were sacred. They then had a right to deliver the message, and no person could

---

[82] BAE-AR 42nd: pp. 338-357.

question them. If there was no dispute as to the facts, the clansmen adjusted the matter without an appeal to the higher authorities, by one of the following methods:

Atonement by adoption and substitution. — If the murderer was a man of consideration, a fine ball player, a valiant warrior, or a successful hunter, and an excellent man in every way, the clan of the murdered man, when they held their council, might say: "Had we not better save this man? We cannot bring back our own kinsman. Here are his mother, his family, his sisters who are dependent on him. Let us, then, save this man's life." Thereupon, he would be adopted to take the place and position of the murdered man. It was not always necessary for a prisoner of war to run the gauntlet before being adopted by some member of the clan. Sometimes the wife of the murdered man accepted the murderer as her husband after he had been adopted into the clan. In like manner, the mother of the murdered son or daughter might adopt the murderer in place of such a child.

Atonement by heroic deeds. — If the injured clan had lost one or more of its members in war with another tribe and such injury was still unavenged, the murderer might volunteer to become the avenger, in which case, if the proposition was accepted, he might at once [148] proceed to perform his self-imposed task. To this usage Muskogee tradition attributed the origin of the custom of taking scalps as evidence of victory.

Atonement by *payment of wergild.* — If the murdered man was a person of low standing in the tribe, a warrior of no renown, a poor hunter, a generally worthless fellow, and the murderer was a man of high standing, and if the latter had a brother or cousin of the same standing as the murdered man, the brother of low degree was usually substituted for the real murderer.

Atonement by death. — If the murderer himself was a man of small repute it often happened that his clansmen consented to his death, and then the clansmen of the murdered man were permitted to execute the sentence. If the members of the clans interested failed to settle the difficulty speedily the matter was usually brought up before the Council of the Town and settled there. Generally three men, but sometimes six, were selected to hear the evidence. The fact that a murder had been committed was sometimes called to the attention of the clan by the Town Chief. In case the parties to the murder belonged to different towns and the clansmen failed to adjust the difficulty the case was brought up before the Council of the Confederation. But if a man killed one of his own clansmen the matter was settled wholly within the clan. No compensation or other satisfaction was made by the clan itself; in this case, the only question that arose concerned the advisability of killing the murderer. The friends of the murdered man might claim their right to take his life, and they might proceed to the killing; but if the murdered man was of less eminence than the murderer, an attempt was usually made by the most closely related clansmen to placate with gifts the anger of the nearer relatives and friends of the murdered man by repeating to them what an injury to the clan it would be to lose a man of such high standing.

When the murderer was a man of distinction he was executed with arrows, but the old women finished a man of no consideration with a war club, and a woman was also executed with a war club. Time was given before the execution to prepare for the death ceremonies. Sometimes the criminal was sent to a hostile town where he was executed by those who did not know him. If his own town decided to execute him it was done by certain officers who had this among their functions.

It may be mentioned as a curious fact that if the executioners failed to kill their victim at the first attempt it was held that some mystic power had interposed, and the offender was adjudged in consequence to be innocent. It sometimes happened that another circumstance was interpreted as involving mystic interference. [149]

If a serious personal difficulty arose between members of different clans it was settled simply by agreement between the clans. All difficulties of this nature were settled by calling the town together. In case a member of one clan lost an eye by the act of a member of another clan, one of the other clan must also sacrifice an eye if reparation was not otherwise made.

With respect to a very troublesome man, his own kinsmen, his own clan would kill him unless, after due warning, he mended his ways, for they had determined that he was not worthy of life, that he would corrupt the young men and cause them to do evil, and that he was not capable of raising good children, for these children would be bad like him. If a man were outlawed no individual might kill him, but after they had related to him his evil deeds as a warning to others, he was executed by the collective body.

If a man or woman stole an object, the injured clan through its own spokesman notified the clansmen of the culprit. After hearing the evidence the accused clan was obliged to bring forward a return or payment of equivalent value. Twofold was the custom of the Creeks; they never attempted to deny the theft if they were satisfied with the character of the evidence. The clan as a whole examined the evidence brought forward to support the charge. If they found the charge true (and their own honor made it necessary for them to find out the truth about it), they decided what should be done under the circumstances. Sometimes in making reparations they turned the culprit over to the offended clan for punishment, where he might be whipped or otherwise punished, although his own clan could pay for the stolen object. But if he was a good man in other respects they willingly paid for the stolen object. If the clan made the reparation by returning the object stolen with a good-will offering or by paying the equivalent of the stolen property, in making reparation the clansmen declared to him the law of theft, pointing out the different steps in wrongdoing which had brought him to this culpable act and the evil consequences of the act as well. The restitution or reparation being made, the offender was considered just as good as any other member of the clan, his physical punishment had the same effect.

CEREMONIES[83]

A number of festivals were hold during the year determined by certain phases of the moon. Anciently it was customary to hold such meetings every month to give and receive counsel and also for enjoyment. There were two principal festivals, a lesser and a greater.

The former took place in the spring, usually early in April, and [150] in the south generally at the time when berries, such as mulberries were getting ripe. The town chief notified his people, and particularly the medicine man, when it was time to hold it. Then the people assembled at the busk ground after dark and danced all night — men, women, and children. In the morning the men swallowed the medicine (*pasa*) which soon caused violent vomiting, but the women and children merely washed their hands and faces in it. This was prepared during the night, the medicine man blowing into it and a weak solution of *miko hoyanidja* (red root) was prepared and carried home for those unable on account of sickness to be present. During the morning the people all went home carrying some of this medicine with them to the sick who were not required to take the strong emetic (the *pasa*). The assembly was dismissed after the rehearsal of the several duties which devolved upon each one.

---

[83] BAE-AR 42nd: pp. 534-613.

The great festival, called *Poskita* or Busk, which signifies "to fast," was held when the corn was large enough for roasting ears, generally in July or August, and at a certain time of the moon. Towns differed as to the time of the moon but each always held it at the same time annually.

The town chief first called a meeting to dance and during the night of the dance he delivered bundles of sticks of seven each to the *Tastanagi*, who then proclaimed that the "broken days" were made, i.e, that the time was appointed and the sticks ready for distribution, and that the people must prepare to hunt before the great ceremony took place. This was perhaps the assembly called *Hills-cinet-kita*, "Medicine overnight," at which they took medicine to prepare their bodies for the reception of the maturing crops and the ripening fruits. At these meetings the same ritual was observed, an important feature being the rehearsal of the chief points of their laws, in the nature of an epitome. The speakers would point out in what respects they feared the young and unruly among them were going against the provisions of their laws, and the penalties that must follow such infractions.

Each of the principal men for whom the bundles had been prepared took one, threw a stick away the first day and continued doing so until the seventh day, when all assembled at the Square Ground again and danced all night. They could hunt during the entire intervening period or at any time within it. On the next day, the eighth, the town chief again delivered bundles of sticks to the *Tastanagi* and he announced that the broken days were "made" for the Great Festival, they threw away one stick as they began to clean up the Square around, a proceeding which generally took them not more than an hour, and then they went home to breakfast.

On the next day, the second of the busk series of "broken days," all remained at home making preparations to move to the Square Ground. [151]

On the third day the people assembled at the Square with the game {meat} which they had killed already prepared, like the rest of the provisions, so that it would keep during the busk. That night there was an ordinary dance, lasting about two hours, participated in by men, women, and children. There were no important dances on that night.

On the morning of the fourth day a fire was kindled in the Square by the medicine man with the use of two sticks rubbed together, medicines also being used. The men then assembled in the Square and sat around, and the women brought provisions there and laid them down. The men ate in the Square that day but the women had to eat at their camps. The best of the provisions were supplied but no new vegetables, no new corn. If persons from other towns were present they were also invited to eat. At midday, while the men were eating, the women danced the *Its-hopunga*, "Gun Dance," each woman standing alone and circling about the fire. Before they began, a speech was made by the Great Tastanagi of the town, in which he rehearsed briefly the traditional history of the people, emphasized the importance of the festival they were observing, and informed them that it had existed from immemorial times. He gave the traditional story of the founding of the town and the origin of the festivals, detailing briefly the rules governing them. He called the attention of the people to the importance of preserving them because they tended to preserve their health and prolong their lives. He exhorted his people to follow their leaders and keep in the ways of their fathers. He also told them that this was the right time for the festival. These speakers always referred to a long-past home in the east where the sun rises. This form of expression was used even when they lived in Georgia.

In preparation for their dance the women put on their finest costumes, with plumes, shells around their necks and ankles. There were three leaders who wore terrapin shells. Three men were stationed in the south cabin, and when the women leaders were ready these musicians began to sing, accompanied by drums and rattles made of terrapin shells or a coconut filled with pebbles and provided with a handle. The women danced around the fire four times. Then they retired and rested, returned and danced around the fire four times more, and continued in this way until they had danced four several and separate times, making four circles around the fire each time. The men sang and kept time to the music of the drum and shells, and the women kept time with their feet and by rattling their shells. It took about two hours to complete this dance.

Meanwhile, after the chief had finished his address, a number of young men, who had been standing about a hundred yards away, around the mound in the *tadjo*, gave a whoop and ran away to the prairie to obtain the medicine. In about an hour they returned bearing this on poles and delivered it to the chief medicine man. This [152] medicine was the *pasa* (button-snake-root) and it is a very violent emetic.

That night there was another ordinary dance by the men, women, and children. The men sang as they danced but the women and children only whooped.

On the fifth day no woman and no man who was not undergoing the purification was allowed to enter the Square Ground. The medicine being now ready, the fasting men drank it, beginning at daylight, certain chosen men bringing it to them. Each drank until he was full and vomiting was induced. That night the fasters danced and kept it up all night. They ate nothing all that day. Many different dances were performed and if anyone fell asleep he had to pay a fine.

On the sixth day the men drank a decoction made from the leaves of the *asi (Ilex vomitoria)*. This was taken at intervals until mid-forenoon, perhaps 9am o'clock, and they danced the Feather Dance. Then they ate, or rather drank, a thin gruel made of corn called *sófki*, the water and corn being simply cooked together. No salt must be used. They could now eat the new corn, but without salt, and melons and similar food might also be eaten. They continued to dance the Feather Dance during the rest of the day, but remained in the Square Ground and might not touch anyone who had not partaken of the medicine (*pasa*?). That night they slept in the cabins or on the Square Ground.

On the seventh day they began dancing the Feather Dance early in the morning. Each dancer bore a pole decorated with feathers, half of them, belonging to the White Clan Cabin, having white feathers, and half, belonging to the Red Clan Cabin on the north side of the Square, having black feathers. There were two dance leaders and all followed them in two rows, a white-feathered pole being followed by a black-feathered pole, and so on. The men sang while they danced. After this the ground was swept clean, preparatory to admitting all the other people.

The notes are confusing at this point, but I understand that the women now brought provisions into the Square, but nothing that had been cooked with salt.

Two men were then sent out to tell the women to prepare to dance the Red War Dance, the War Dance, the Paint-Up Dance ("to paint up for war"), the native name of which is *Its-atitska*. Both men and women painted up but only the women danced. The singers painted one side of the face black and the other side red. This was the "War paint." Just before the women began dancing another long speech was made telling of their wars, of their great warriors, and of their great deeds, in order to encourage the young men to become great warriors and leaders. If a war was on foot the warriors [153] would be ready to set out, being now purified. Then the women, without any men, came out and danced this War Dance. The three leaders had boards made in the shape of tomahawks, painted red, and decorated with black and white feathers, and they shook them as they danced. They danced around the fire and then rested, repeating this four times. In modern times some of the women have had guns or pistols which they discharged while dancing. This dance was like the first women's dance. It was controlled by the Red Clans while the other was controlled by the White Clans. The great Feather Dance, however, was controlled by both jointly. This one dance lasted several hours.

Then followed a Buffalo Dance by the men, stripped naked and wearing only their breechclouts, ornaments on their arms, tiger tails, and ornaments and buffalo horns on their heads. It followed the war dance by the women. One man sang and the rest grunted like buffalo, and they stooped down as they danced. They pretended to paw the ground and bellow. They feasted afterwards.

Then came a rest until sunset. After nightfall they began the night dances with singing and whooping — no war dances — only peace dances. First they danced the Old Dance, participated in by men, women, and children who danced first around the mound in the *Tadjo* and then inside the Square. It was followed by common, amusement dances or "stomp dances" which lasted all night. In these they imitated the cow, horse, quail, etc. They came to an end at daylight and then all left for their homes.

Mention is made elsewhere of the Crooked Arrow Dance and the Dance with Knives. It is also said that they took medicine for four days while the above schedule allows for but three.

Late in the autumn it was customary to assemble the people for the purpose of performing Medicine Dances which were like those performed in the spring.

All these dances were not solely for the old men or solely for the ball players, but as well in order to give the young men and the young women enjoyment. One group of social units commonly sent a challenge to their opponents in ball-play in the following words: "Our young men have become lonesome for the lack of pleasure and for this reason we are sending to challenge you to a game of ball." At all meetings there was dancing and enjoyment for young and old, and when it was time to separate a speaker of known ability addressed the assembly with words of good counsel.

First the speaker would say that they had assembled for amusement and instruction and then he would follow with an outline of the general law of morals observed by the people. He pointed out [154] the great danger to the peace of the community involved in forgetting or overstepping that law. The penalty for these transgressions was set forth in brief but forcible terms. Afterwards he announced any new law or regulation adopted by the chiefs and councilors with the injunction that it be carefully observed. He summarized the reasons which had moved their leaders to enact it after having given the matter due consideration, telling the people that their chiefs had discussed it at length. He admonished all to obey their leaders without question, for it was intimated that they knew best the principles of their moral law. The people thus received an outline of it and were instructed to carry it out.

Usually the kindred towns were invited to these assemblies. Their representatives were assigned certain places in the Square and took part in the ceremonies performed there. It was merely a matter of courtesy to ask them to take part in the ceremonies. They had nothing to do with the internal affairs of the town that entertained them.

In emergencies these kindred towns were sometimes asked in to aid if the town itself could not decide on the proper measures to take. Their decision was then accepted as the law of the town in question.

There is a note to the effect that the women danced on each of the four days on which the men took medicine, but this seems to be an error.

GUARDIAN SPIRITS

Innutska is said to have been the name of the tutelary deity which came to a youth when he was fasting at the time of puberty. It seems to mean literally "What-comes-to-him-in-sleep." The girls are said to have acquired their guardian spirits "through the medium of remarkable dreams" and so there may not have been much difference between the two. Indeed, our text continues, "both male and female persons may acquire fetishes through such dreams or by adopting an object or a portion of an object which has impressed the partaker as exhibiting magic power, such as a fierce animal or striking rock, or an element of some weird experience." The editor has no parallel to this in his material.

MEDICINE[84]

When a person was taken ill his near kindred appointed one of their number to take an article he had worn to the prophet who subjected it to a searching examination (by means of certain drugs?) or the purpose of ascertaining the cause of the illness. If he succeeded [155] he told his clients the name of it but he himself gave no medicine.

Diseases were carefully classified, and as soon as the disease was known the remedy was known and recourse was had to a medicine man or a medicine woman. This person possessed a pouch, usually made of the whole skin of some animal, which was well filled with the remedies known to him or her. Some were compounded from roots, leaves, or herbs as well as pebbles, shells, or other strange objects, each of which had been acquired in accordance with certain esoteric formulae known only to an inner circle of the medical fraternity of the community. Each drug was prepared during the singing of a song peculiar to it, and it is added that this took place during a meeting of the medicine men of the community, but I feel uncertain regarding this. Usually the words of this song describe the preparation of the medicine in great detail, although in terms which are largely metaphorical.

Many diseases were attributed to the influences of animals, such as the bear, buffalo, beaver, and deer. If a person had stomach trouble it might be said that the beaver had built a dam across it {cf p20ff herein}. If he was afflicted with boils it might be said that ants had raised small anthills on his flesh. Another animal was said to cause diarrhea. If a person touched an eagle without using the proper medicine he would have a wry neck. Rheumatism was caused by a fabulous monster. When one sneezed it was said someone was talking about him.

In order to become a medicine man or a medicine woman a person must fast a certain number of days, must learn the prescribed songs, must prepare medicines (and charms) according to well-established formulae, must remain in seclusion at times, and must then use the medicines which had been thus prepared when called to minister to the sick. This process of instruction and initiation continued four moons in each year for four successive years. Each medicine must be learned in four days. Some practitioners would refuse to administer remedies for certain diseases and would send the patient to another who was regarded as a specialist in that subject.

Four was a sacred number among the Creeks. It will be remembered that the novice in medicine fasted for four days. One must sing a song for four days detailing the virtues of the medicine and teaching what it would do. Thus the number four appeared in numerous places. There were four days assigned in which to learn each remedy and four months in each year of a four-year period for completing the medical course. Again, a man might not have sexual relations with his wife for four months after the birth of a child. A sick man must use a remedy during four consecutive days. Mr. Porter said that certain herbs were collected one at a time on

---

[84] BAE-AR 42nd: pp. 614-666.

four [156] successive days, and successively on exposures toward the east, the south, the west, and the north.

The medicine man or woman was exempt from all manner of work except the preparation and administration of remedies. The head medicine man of the town must prepare and kindle the council fire, although, in a figurative sense, this was supposed to be burning always.

The chief prophet of the tribe (or town), who might be at the same time the medicine man, had charge of the war medicines, which are said to have been prepared at a secret conclave of the medical fraternity. He was much feared because of his supposed power to cure or cause fatal illnesses. It was believed that he had one medicine potent enough to make the ground quake, another to cause the enemy to lose their way, another to make the ground swampy, another to bring on a rainfall that would obliterate all tracks, others to lengthen or shorten distances, another to bring on heavy fogs, another to make arrows go straight to the mark, another to transform men into certain animals such as the wolf (fox) or owl, so that they might spy out the enemies' camp without being detected, and still another, the greatest of all, to cause the warriors to have an aspect terrifying to their enemies.

This great medicine man would stanch the flow of blood and heal wounds received in war. The first thing done to such a wounded man was to have him eat certain kinds of earth, one of which was the clay or mud (*fakkitali*, literal "raw dirt") brought up by the crawfish. This crawfish earth was also applied to the wound externally. Then he was secluded so that no woman might see him, lest one in her catamenial period should lay eyes on him. It was believed that, if such a woman should lay eyes on him, his cure would be impossible.

Grayson added that the medicine man could make a medicine capable of transforming the human body into a sieve so as to allow an arrow or bullet to pass through him without occasioning injury. This condition of the body was known as *E-sar-la-weatch-e'toh*.

It was commonly believed that a man who killed another was haunted by the latter's spirit and would become insane, meaning "troubled by the spirit," unless he was purified. It was also believed that a person who merely associated with an unpurified murderer must himself be purified lest he lose his sanity.

Insanity was treated as follows. First, four clear white pebbles were selected and placed in a cup of clear water. Over this certain ceremonies were performed and certain songs sung. Then the medicine man took some of the water into his mouth and spurted it violently upon the head of the insane man, also causing him to drink from the cup four times. It was believed that this performance gave the medicine man power over the insane person who thereafter was [157] compelled to do his bidding and was treated in various ways until finally cured.

WITCHCRAFT[85]

One of the duties of the medicine man was to apprehend sorcerers, witches, or wizards who had committed some offense against the welfare of the community, using arts and craft superior to theirs. When a person was convicted of such an offense — by well-established, many, and severe ordeals and tests — he was condemned to death. He was then placed in charge of the medicine man. It was said that a person under charge of witchcraft must show that he had greater powers than the medicine man, thereby proving, I suppose, that he had been falsely accused. "He would try to show a great fire and then vanish out of sight."

It was believed that wizards could take out their intestines containing their life spirit and

---

[85] BAE-AR 42nd: pp. 631-635.

transform themselves into owls, flickers, etc., after which they would fly through the air to perform their misdeeds. Therefore owls and other birds of ill omen were held in great terror.

The owl referred to is commonly the great horned owl.

SOULS[86]

A man was believed to have two souls, first, the spirit which goes with him through life and talks to him in his dreams and is called the good spirit, being named *inu'tska,* which signifies "his talent," "his ability," "his genius." It was thought to be seated in the head. There was also the spirit or soul of the dead person, *yafiktca,* literally "his entrails." Sentiments, passions, feelings of good and evil, are said to come from the latter; thought, planning, devising from the former. There seems to be some confusion in the text between heart and head, the former being *fiki,* the latter *fiktci.* It was declared that the "life spirit" resides in the intestines and does not leave them until after a person's death. (See Witchcraft.) Some, however, believed that the life spirit could leave the body without bringing on death, as in sleep and dreams.

The term *hisakita,* "the breath," was applied to the agency of the great prophet above, but, according to one statement, was also applied to the life spirit.

STORY OF THE MAN WHO BECAME A TIE-SNAKE[87]

Among Mr. Hewitt's papers was a version of this story of which I have published five more. It was written down at Washington, D.C., June 24, 1883, perhaps by Porter or Perryman but more likely [158] it was one of the tales collected by Jeremiah Curtin to which Hewitt refers in his report to the Chief of the Bureau. It runs as follows:

Two Indians, one of whom was named *Kowe,* went upon a hunting expedition and were singularly unsuccessful. Before they killed anything their supplies of food became exhausted and they had nothing to eat. One evening, as they were walking along through the forests, feeling very hungry and dejected, *Kowe* noticing nearby the hollow stump of a tree which had been broken off near the ground, approached it and found that it contained water. Upon closer examination he found a few small fishes swimming about in this which he captured in order to use them as food.

When night came on and they could not well proceed farther, the hunters halted and established a camp or resting place for the night. Dressing the fish and preparing them for the evening meal, Kowe invited his companion to join him in eating them. The latter, however, declined, saying that, as the fish had been caught in a very unnatural place, he feared that they had become in some way unfit for human food, and would have a bad effect on anyone eating them. He advised Kowe himself not to eat them but the latter was very hungry and was not deterred by his friend's fears.

At the time they retired to rest no ill consequences showed themselves, but late in the night Kowe was heard to groan and make sounds as if he were in great misery, so that his friend was awakened. On inquiring the trouble, Kowe replied: "You cautioned me last evening against eating those fishes, but I did not heed you and ate them, and that, I apprehend, is the cause of my present calamity. I am now spontaneously and steadily taking on a hideous form, an end which I can neither avert nor control, and it is distressingly painful. I wish you to get up and look at me,

---

[86] BAE-AR 42nd: pp. 510-514.
[87] BAE-B 88: pp. 30-34, 97, 154.

but I hope you will not be afraid of me, for no matter what my form proves to be, I shall never forget our friendship or harm you."

Upon this the friend got up and, lifting the covering from his unfortunate friend, found that he was gradually being metamorphosed into a snake, a large portion being already coiled up in the bed. He replaced the covering and bore his grief in silence. When morning came and it was light *Kowe* had turned into a fully developed snake of hideous appearance. He was, however, able to converse with his friend in human language and he solicited him to follow him back to a lake or pond of water which they had passed the day before. On their way thither the snake requested his friend to return home and inform his wife and all of his relations of the occurrence, and to tell them that he desired they should all come out to the pond to see him for the last time. He further directed that he should bring back a *saoga* or rattle to rattle on the bank so that he would know that his wife and relatives had come to see him, whereupon he would appear to them. [159]

Having given these directions to his friend, he disappeared in the depths of the lake which they had now reached. The friend immediately returned home and reported what had happened to him, delivering also his message to his wife and relatives.

As soon as possible the relatives and many others went to the pond to view the strange sight, the news of which was uppermost in everyone's mind. On reaching the pond the friend began to shake his rattle and sing, calling "*Kowe*! *Kowe*!" as he had been instructed to do. Thereupon the waters of the pond began to roll and bubble and show considerable commotion, and presently an enormous snake appeared. Coming up to the shore where stood a great crowd of spectators, it laid its head on the lap of the woman who had been its wife during the days of its humanity. Its head was now surmounted by a pair of horns. It happened that the woman was provided with a sharp instrument and with this she cut the horns off as mementos of him who could no more be her companion.

These horns were found to have value to anyone who had a portion of one, giving him luck and success in the hunt. It is said that a song or chant something like the following must be sung before going out with the horn to hunt:

> He coiled himself up
> He loosed himself out of his coil
> He straightened himself out
> He went in a zigzag way
> He glittered toward the sun
> He disappeared in the water
> The water bubbled.

On account of the virtues attributed to it, this snake's horn at once became a charm greatly desired by every hunter, and in course of time it was broken up into very minute pieces in order that its virtues might reach and benefit as many men as possible. I (i.e., the recorder of the story) have been informed by a friend who has a minute fragment of this so-called horn that it is a little red particle which will float if placed in water.

THE ORIGIN OF THE NATCHEZ INDIANS

The Natchez have a tradition that they came from the sun, that the sun is a woman who has monthly discharges, and that one of these dropped upon the earth and turned into a man. They think that when they die the sun will expire, and that it shines only for them.

This origin story is identical with the origin myth of the Yuchi and it would be of very great importance if we could be certain that the Yuchi were in no way responsible for it. It is in keeping with the solar worship of both Natchez and Yuchi.

NOTE ON CONTRIBUTOR

Dr. Morris E. Opler (May 3, 1907 – May 13, 1996) is Professor of Anthropology at the University of Oklahoma. Before joining the University of Oklahoma faculty he taught at Reed College, Claremont Colleges, Harvard University, and Cornell University, where he is Professor Emeritus. He holds an M.A. degree in anthropology from the University of the State of New York at Buffalo and the Ph.D. from the University of Chicago. He is best known for his contributions to anthropological theory, for his studies of the Apachean-speaking tribes of the Southwest, and for his research and writings on peoples of India, but he also has long-standing interests in other areas, as this monograph attests.

The author wishes to thank Ned Jacob for generously providing the exciting cover design, Mary Haas for supplying correct phonetic transcriptions of the names of Creek Towns, Lucille R. Opler for assistance in preparing and checking the manuscript, and Harold N. Ottaway for his careful editorial work.

To the memory of

Felix S. Cohen and H. Scudder Mekeel, associates who demonstrated their concern for the welfare, rights, and prospects of the American Indian long before this became fashionable.

THE CREEK INDIAN TOWNS OF OKLAHOMA IN 1937
MORRIS E. OPLER

ABSTRACT

This monograph, which contains a good deal of historical and ethnological material about the Creek Confederacy and the Creek Towns composing it, describes the research carried out in 1937 by Morris E. Opler as a member of the applied anthropology unit of the Bureau of Indian Affairs. His studies, which are reproduced here, were part of an effort to make the benefits of the *Indian Reorganization Act of 1934* and the *Oklahoma Indian Welfare Act of 1936* available to the Creek Indians of eastern Oklahoma.

INTRODUCTION

When Franklin D. Roosevelt was inaugurated as President of the United States on March 4, 1933, and proclaimed his New Deal policies, the economic health of the nation had been sapped by the great depression. No section of the population was in worse straits than the American Indian. Even before these national difficulties reached crisis proportions, their lot had steadily deteriorated. Their lands and resources had dwindled, their health and educational problems were acute, and their morale was at low ebb. The general economic collapse served to make a bad situation desperate for them.

That there would be an attempt to inaugurate a "New Deal for the Indians" was virtually guaranteed when President Roosevelt named Harold L. Ickes to the post of Secretary of the Interior, an office which Mr. Ickes held all through the Roosevelt years and from which he resigned in 1946 during the administration of President Truman. Mr. Ickes and his wife Anna, who died tragically in an automobile accident in New Mexico [2] in September, 1935, were known to have a deep and long-standing interest in the American Indian. The direction in which events were moving was made obvious when Secretary Ickes promptly appointed forceful and eloquent John C. Collier, who had been Executive Secretary of the American Indian Defense Association since 1922, to be Commissioner of Indian Affairs. Mr. Collier, like Mr. Ickes, enjoyed a long tenure and served as Commissioner throughout the Roosevelt administration. He resigned his post on March 14, 1945, less than a month before President Roosevelt's death.

During the first months following his appointment, Commissioner Collier worked feverishly with solicitors of the Interior Department, Indian leaders, and congressmen to shape legislation that would embody his conception of what should be done to arrest and reverse the erosion of Indian prospects. Early in 1934 a draft law was ready, and Collier concentrated on efforts to win support for it from Indian groups and from congressmen. The bill called upon Indian groups to organize and gain charters of incorporation enabling them to apply for the financial aids provided by the legislation. For this reason the bill is often called "The Indian Reorganization Act." Alternately it is known as the Wheeler-Howard Act, after its cosponsors, Senator Burton K. Wheeler of Montana, who was Chairman of the Senate Indian Affairs Committee, and Representative Edgar H. Howard of Nebraska, who was Chairman of the Indian Affairs Committee of the House of Representatives. Though Indian organization was an important feature of the bill, flexibility and self-determination were to be the guidelines in accomplishing this. In his memorandum of explanation to members of the Senate and House of February 19, 1934, regarding the Wheeler-Howard Act, Collier wrote: "The bill contemplates that the charter powers of different communities may differ profoundly."

On March 22, 1934, Collier and his chief aids met with the Indians of the Five Civilized Tribes of Oklahoma at Muskogee, Oklahoma, to discuss the proposed Wheeler-Howard bill and to answer any questions concerning it. Again he emphasized the right of the Indians to organize in ways agreeable to their views and traditions, saying: "This bill does provide to the Indians who want to organize, the power to do so and Government aid in the organizing. It does not prescribe how they shall organize. They may use any form used by anybody in the United States in building up wealth, self help; they can organize as they will and the Government stands to help them." This vision of Commissioner Collier, as will appear, was in contrast to the views held by many of the long-term Indian Service officials in Oklahoma and, for that matter, throughout the nation.

The Wheeler-Howard Act (Public Law Number 383, 73rd Congress; 48 Stat. 984) was passed by both houses of Congress by June 14 and was signed by the President on June 18, 1934. In essence, the Act ended the allotment system through which so much [3] Indian land had been lost; it extended the trust period for lands held in trust for Indians by the government; it provided for the return of Indian lands that had been declared surplus but had not yet been sold; it halted the sale or transfer of restricted Indian lands except for the purpose of consolidation; it empowered the Secretary of the Interior to purchase land for Indian occupancy and use; this land to remain in the name of the United States and to be exempt from state and local taxation; it authorized a revolving fund of $10,000,000 for loans to chartered Indian organizations; it also authorized up to $250,000 annually in reimbursable funds to be used for educational tuitions and fellowships; by its terms civil service requirements were to be waived, and Indians were to get preference in applying for positions in the Bureau of Indian Affairs.

Though many of Collier's policies were thus incorporated into the bill, a number of others fell by the wayside before it became law. For instance, a section was deleted which would have given Indians much more control over their judicial affairs and law enforcement. The Indians of Alaska were excluded from some of the main features of the bill, and, at the insistence of Senator Elmer Thomas of Oklahoma, the Indians of Oklahoma were excluded from most of the benefits of the Act by Section 13.

For over a year there was no real difference in the fortunes of those who had been included in and those who had been excluded from the Act. Though Congress had authorized funds for organizing Indian tribes and cooperative groups and for the other purposes central to the Act, no funds were actually appropriated until mid-May of 1935, and no funds were available for use until after July 1, 1935, the beginning of the fiscal year. Moreover, in no case did the amount appropriated come close to the amount authorized by the bill.

Nevertheless, once some resources were in hand, Commissioner Collier pressed forward to implement his plans. Since most of the benefits of the legislation could be enjoyed only by Indian tribes and groups which were formally organized and chartered under the Act, he began to recruit personnel to aid in this work. One of his innovations was the establishment of an applied anthropology unit under the leadership of Dr. H. Scudder Mekeel. It was this development that brought me into the Indian Service during this interesting period and which made possible the observations and reports contained in this monograph. [30]

REPORT ON THE HISTORY AND CONTEMPORARY STATE OF
ASPECTS OF CREEK SOCIAL ORGANIZATION AND GOVERNMENT

It is the purpose of this report to give as much ethnographic and historical background as is necessary for an understanding of contemporary Creek social and political organization and to describe the existing social segments in terms of number, alignments, and functions. The emphasis throughout will be on the reality situation, and not on arbitrary terminological distinctions which officialdom or white neighbors have found useful in their dealings with the Indians in question.

The history of the Creek Confederacy has been so tempestuous, government policy in regard to its membership has changed so many times, white pressure, removal, the Civil War, Reconstruction, allotment, and statehood for Oklahoma have led to so many special organizations and movements, that there exists today an undue amount of specious labelling which acts as a serious barrier to clear thinking concerning Creek problems. Because Indian Service employees who stand in a special relationship to the Creeks have not been uninfluenced by such talk, it is of the utmost importance to clarify the most obvious current misconceptions.

An example or two may indicate the degree to which mere shibboleths may distort the picture of Creek society. Early in a conversation with one of the most important government officials in Creek country, when the subject of Creek Tribal Towns was mentioned, this gentleman said in a tone of finality and dismissal: "Oh, they're just the 'Snake' Indians." Thus, by identifying those Creeks interested in the organization of Creek Tribal Towns with an anti-government movement of the time of allotment, he set the tenor of his attitude toward Creek Tribal Town organization. Yet the basis of his disdain is decidedly in error. I have attended two meetings of the so-called "Snake" faction and have found them, though not hostile to, certainly indifferent toward Tribal Town organization under the Oklahoma Indian Welfare Act. The reasons are obvious. The extremists of this faction believe that the government should be forced to honor the terms of the removal treaty of 1832. If and when this occurs they expect to be so rich in land and resources that they will have no need for the small parcels of land which they could secure under the terms of the Oklahoma Indian Welfare Act or for the credit which may be thus secured. On the other hand, those interested [31] in Creek Tribal Town organization are concerned with 1937 rather than with 1832. They desire that the land acquisition program be related to Town needs and that it aid in consolidating membership and providing for the young landless Indians of their organizations. They desire that credit facilities be utilized for the cooperative or individual needs of their membership. Through organization under the Oklahoma Indian Welfare Act and in cooperation with the government they hope to usher in a new and progressive phase of economic and social history for themselves. Leaving aside the question of whether or not they can accomplish all they conceive, their view of things is quite different from that of the "Snake" sympathizers, and they should not be confused or identified with them.

The words "Snake" "conservative," "stomp dancer," etc., have been used in such accusing and patronizing contexts by missionaries and white officials that the average Creek, especially one who professes Christianity, bends backward to keep his name clear of such associations. He is not unaware that, in the eyes of many whites, anything distinctively Creek is termed "Snake" and "pagan." He knows that the Creek Tribal Town, because it ordinarily has a cleared space or "square" where ceremonies are performed by those who still find solace in them, is considered in this light. Therefore he is wary about professing membership or interest in his Town unless he is sure that the one to whom he is speaking has a clear understanding of what a Tribal Town is. I was several times told by white officials of a young Creek who was "not interested in his Town" and who "scarcely knew" to which Town he belonged. This example was given to illustrate that the young, progressive Creek element could not be expected to show interest in such an outworn tradition. Later I had the opportunity to see this man in the company of other Creeks. It turned out that he knew very well to which Town he belonged. Moreover he was far from indifferent concerning political and economic problems as they confronted his Townspeople. He explained quite explicitly that when he was questioned about his Town, he felt that he was in reality being asked whether he was interested in the green corn dance and the "stomp-ground ceremonies" which are ever associated in the minds of the whites with the Towns. Being a Christian and a "progressive" and not wishing to set himself in an unfavorable light, he thought it best not to show too much enthusiasm about the Town. In other words, where we have misconceptions in regard to Indians, we are likely to invite misleading reactions. And since we wanted them and invited them, we are happy to act on a basis of them, frequently moving in the wrong direction.

Not long ago I was invited by letter to attend a meeting to be held at Haikey Chapel in the northern section of Creek territory. When I arrived there, I saw at once that whatever this group might be on the social and political side, on the [32] physical side the arrangement of the church and surrounding buildings suggested the square of the old Tribal Town. The-meeting was called to order in the church. The chairman of the meeting was C.B. Haikey. After prayer and introductory comments he called upon a younger man, the secretary, to read the correspondence and to introduce the speakers. These people were ostensibly gathered to discuss the possibility of organizing, by which they meant the forming of a credit association. For some reason they seemed to have no idea that organizing as a band or tribe was a possibility. When Mr. Hagerty of Indian Organization talked on that aspect of the Oklahoma Indian Welfare Act and asked what type of organization it was in which they were interested, Amos Beaver, the secretary, remarked: "I think that the credit association is the only one they had in mind; I never heard of the other, of organizing by band or tribe." Not long afterwards he asked: "Is that a new one, or has it always been there, this organizing by band or tribe?"

The meeting continued. I inquired concerning the name of the informal organization which had been created and which was then meeting with us. "Well, we were told that we would have to have a name, and so we decided we would call our organization *Lochapoka*." *Lochapoka*, "Where the Turtle Lives," {*Łočapoka*} is the name of a Creek Tribal Town, an offshoot of the ancient Creek Tribal Town of *Talsi* [Tulsa]. I then asked whether the use of that name had anything to do with the Creek Town. Yes, most of them belonged to *Lochapoka*. I asked whether a list of prospective members of the organization was at hand. A list of the names of twenty-six Creek family heads who had already signified their interest in the organization was handed to me.

Analysis gave the following results. In eighteen cases of the twenty-six, husband, wife, or both belonged to the Creek Tribal Town of Lochapoka. In three other cases husband or wife belonged to the neighboring Tribal Town of *Kanchati*, which belongs to the same moiety as *Lochapoka* and whose members are therefore on very friendly terms with the people of *Lochapoka*. In two other cases the persons involved belonged to "friendly" (same moiety) Towns, but to Towns whose concentration of population was a little farther removed. It was evident that membership in this particular Town and the relation of this Town with others was exceedingly important in the developments which were taking place.

Next I asked whether Lochapoka still existed as a Tribal Town. "Well, we don't have our fire any more. We haven't had our square grounds since the Civil War. But this church acts as our meeting place and we stick together around here," was the reply. When I asked where the people of *Lochapoka* lived, I received the following answer: "Most of us live around here. This is the north end of the Creek Nation. North of us are the Cherokee. South of us, due south, is *Kanchati*. [33]

West are the Yotchi [Yuchi, Euchi]. On the east side, in Wagoner county, is Kawita." In this description of locality, the feeling of the Creek for the Towns is evident. *Kanchati*, Yotchi, and Kawita are all Towns which belong to the Creek Confederacy.

I next left the meeting place and visited with the people at the homes which surrounded the church. Almost without exception these people identified themselves as members of *Lochapoka*. When I returned to the meeting, I found occasion to ask whether the internal organization of the Town had been maintained. I was informed that the Town still had officers and that Haikey, who acted as the preacher in the church, was the *miko* or Chief. Interestingly enough, Joe Bruner is considered a *tastanagi* (another officer) of this Town.[88/13] I asked C.B. Haikey whether he knew who the members of his Town were, and he answered in the affirmative. He claims to have a roll, which he keeps fairly well up to date. When I asked him why this was necessary, since the Town no longer retained its square, he replied that the Town felt that it had claims against the government.

The question now arises, "Does *Lochapoka Talsi* exist as a Creek Tribal Town?" Formally, the answer depends on one's criteria, of course. For those who are convinced that the Creek Town exists only as long as its members gather at a stomp ground to participate in the annual Busk, *Lochapoka* no longer exists. For those who are interested in the Town as a social and political entity, for those who are more concerned that a group whose members are linked by heredity and tradition should maintain its solidarity than they are that a church, rather than a Town square, act as its focal point, *Lochapoka* still flourishes. If the people involved are casual neighbors, with nothing more in common than that they happen to be individual farmers in the same district, one kind of a program will suffice. If they represent a group which recognizes itself as distinct from others, which acknowledges bonds of tradition and blood, which evidences a feeling of common responsibility, and which has organized leadership, a great deal more can be planned in terms of political, social, and economic activity.

A number of people to whom I have spoken lately have expressed surprise and even disappointment that the ancient concept of Tribal Town should play such an important part in contemporary Creek affairs. They know that the Creeks are referred to as one of the Five Civilized Tribes, and it seems incongruous to them that an Indian population which has earned the title of "civilized" should be at all interested in types of organization of the past. Of course these people use contemporary white American society as the measuring stick in regard to what is "civilized," and since they have not heard that whites have Tribal Towns, they assume that such forms can do the Creeks no good. A great deal of nonsense [34] has grown up around the use of the term "civilized" as applied to the American Indians who formerly occupied the Southeast. Since they farmed and were more or less sedentary, they contrasted markedly with the nomadic tribes of the Plains, but in their social forms, their war complex, and their beliefs they closely followed patterns which are well known from other regions. The current conception that

---

[88]/13 Mr. Bruner was a severe critic of the Indians Reorganization Act. At the meeting of March 22, 1934, with Commissioner Collier he several times tried to bring the gathering to a premature close by interrupting to make a motion for adjournment and to call for a vote on the question.

they are somehow innately more susceptible to the white man's views, beliefs, and social forms than any other Indians of the continent is simply not justified. What differences obtain in white-Indian relations between members of the Five Civilized Tribes and other Indians can be easily explained in terms of length of contact, intermarriage, type of contacts, and plain force.

Again, it has been expected that since we were good enough to grant the title of "civilized" to all five southeastern tribes, their response to American institutional life should be uniform. I have heard it argued that since the Choctaws or some of the other tribes in question were able to give up their Towns without much struggle, attachment to Towns must show stubborn backwardness on the part of the Creeks. The truth is that the Creeks are as they are in respect to this matter and the Choctaws are as they are in respect to it for definite historical and developmental reasons. Without an understanding of the initial historical differences, the situation cannot be fully grasped.

It is essential to realize that the Creeks were not and, strictly speaking, are not now a tribe. The Creek Nation is a confederacy of tribes, and as a political phenomenon the Creek Confederacy stands as the most important and advanced of its kind in aboriginal America north of Mexico, with the possible exception of the Iroquois Confederacy. Most of the tribes which were welded together by this political consolidation spoke languages belonging to the Muskogean linguistic family, but some of these dialects, such as *Hichiti* and *Alabama*, diverged considerably from the others. In addition, people such as the *Yotchi*, who spoke a language totally unrelated to Muskogean, were also incorporated into the Confederacy. The evidence is that most of the tribes which became members of the Confederacy entered the Southeast from the west and that, as they settled down to agricultural pursuits, were conquered by the dominant Muskogee, or sought membership in the Confederacy for the purpose of military safety, they assumed the characteristics of the Creek Town. Such Towns were formed not only by separate tribal incorporations, but by the splitting up of one Town into two when the growth of population put too much of a strain on the land or resources of the vicinity.

Since many of the units had separate historical origins and distinctive languages or dialects, it was inevitable that each Town would insist on a generous amount of autonomy and independence. And this was actually the case. The Confederacy [35] was the loosest of organizations. Compared to it, the American colonies before the formation of our federal government was a paragon of integration. Such cooperation as existed was mostly for defense against a common enemy. One Town would not infrequently attempt to punish another for real or fancied injuries.

The independence of each Town was based on the following factors: Each Town had its own body of officers and their advisers, each had its own land, public buildings, town square or ceremonial grounds, its own traditions, and its own ceremonies, which were, to some extent, distinctive. Moreover, membership in the Town was not a matter of choice or caprice, but a circumstance of birth; the child belonged to the Town of the mother. Then, too. Towns could and did act alone in military affairs, and no Town accepted as valid treaties or agreements affecting it unless ratified by its own officers, as well as by those who presumed to speak for the Confederacy. By all the rules of social analysis a Town comes very close to the concept of a tribe or a fairly autonomous segment of a tribe, such as a band.

My observations incline me to believe that some of those whose very work brings them into daily contact with the Creeks fail to understand the historical situation and the modern extension of it. Not long ago when I was seeking some information which only a Muskogean speaking Creek could give, a teacher in a school situated in Five Civilized Tribes country advised me to seek out a certain "Creek" boy. After I failed to elicit the information which I was certain any Creek of his description must know, I learned that he was a Yotchi [Yuchi], and, while he spoke excellent Yotchi, he knew no Muskogean at all. On another occasion, at the same school, a Yotchi girl was telling me some interesting details concerning her people. During the recital one of the schoolteachers happened to join us. When I told her that I was in the process of learning something about the Yotchi, she seemed much astonished. "Why, I thought you were a Creek," she said to the girl who was helping me. "No, I'm down on the rolls as a Creek, but I'm Yotchi, and that's different," was the firm reply. Both parties to the exchange were to some extent correct. The Yotchi became members of the Creek Confederacy and established their own Tribal Town. They were removed with the Creeks and have been enrolled with the Creeks. They have responded to the pattern of Creek culture closely, and the structure and nature of their society bears marked resemblance to that of other Creek Tribal Towns. On the other hand, they have retained distinctive features, including their own language, and they have taught their children to regard themselves as Yotchi, no matter how others may classify them.

The relations of one Town to others and to the Confederacy must not be ignored, however. In the first place, most of the Tribal Towns either spoke or adopted a generally similar dialect of the Muskogean language. Thus most of them had a [36] mutually intelligible language in common. Moreover, as tribes joined the Confederacy, they were influenced and assimilated culturally, and so the Towns of the Confederacy formed a cultural unit when compared as a whole to neighboring peoples. Naturally this greater ethnic similarity was felt by the Towns themselves. As has been mentioned, some Towns owed their origin to division within an older, overpopulated Town. When this happened the older Town would be regarded as the "Mother" Town by its offshoot. Relations between the two and among any others which might originate from them were most friendly. Such Towns would belong to the same moiety, or dual division, of the Confederacy. Marriages would be encouraged between unrelated members of such Towns. These Towns would cooperate most often for attack, defense, and for the inevitable ball game, the most important ceremonial game of the Southeast.

In connection with the relation between Towns the concept of moiety must be understood. Throughout Southeast culture there is no more pervasive idea than that of the dual division. Its influence is noticeable in every branch of thought and endeavor, not only in Creek society, but among other peoples of the region as well. The Choctaws, for instance, were divided into two great sections. These divisions functioned at the time of death. When a person of one moiety died, his remains were cared for by a member of the opposite division.

As far as the Creek Towns were concerned, the dual division meant this: When a group joined the Confederacy and established itself as a Tribal Town, it had to become affiliated with either one of the two divisions known anciently as the "Whites" and the "Reds." Each side had two "foundation Towns," Towns which are traditionally supposed to have been the earliest and strongest of the Confederacy and from which other Towns are said to have sprung. While not all Creeks agree concerning the identity of these "foundation" Towns (another evidence of local Town patriotism), in general it is conceded that *Tokipahchi* and *Kawita* were the leaders of the "Reds," and *Apihka* and *Kasihta* for the "Whites." Today a Town is often referred to as being on the "*Tokipahchi* side" or the "*Apihka* side." Ordinarily newcomers to the Confederacy, when they were not offshoots of existing Towns, became attached to the Confederacy because of some friendly relations or alliance with a Creek Tribal Town, and when they became a recognized member of the union, they became attached to that side of the dual division to which their sponsor belonged. Or, a defeated tribe would be recognized as a member of the moiety to which a Town that had taken an interest in it and saved it from total destruction belonged.

The degree of rivalry which existed between Towns of opposite moieties is scarcely appreciated. A Creek refers to a Town of the opposite moiety from his own as "my enemy Town" or "my unfriendly Town." A Town on his side of the [37] moiety is "my friendly Town." Nor was this just a matter of speech. Anciently a Creek who walked into an "unfriendly" Town uninvited was likely to get a good beating. When Towns of opposite moieties held some grudge against each other, one would challenge the other to a "match game" of ball (lacrosse). Friendly, practice games were played between Towns of the same moiety or between teams from the same Town, but these "match" games were so rough and dangerous that they were and are known as "little brother to war."[89] What is more, towns of the same moiety aid each other in these match games; by mutual agreement players can be drawn from Towns of the same moiety.

The most important religious symbol of the Southeast and the Creeks is fire; it takes much the same place as tobacco-offering does on the Plains or as the use of cornmeal and pollen does in the Southwest. In the perpetuation and division of Towns, the sacred fire has a prominent position. Therefore Towns of the same moiety are said to belong "to the same side" of the fire.

The function of the dual division in Creek society is not difficult to fathom. The Creeks were a warlike, expanding people at the time of first white contact. The dual division of Towns, with its rivalries, its rough-and-tumble games, its challenges, and its appeal to patriotism kept the men in fine fettle and kept the spirit of competition aflame, even in times of peace. The Creeks made no mistake when they named their match ball games "little brother to war."

Since relations between Towns of the opposite moieties usually carried an undertone of rivalry and mild enmity, marriage between members of "unfriendly" Towns was rare.

I have discussed the implications of the moiety division at some length because it cannot be ignored in any well-considered plans for organization or other procedure in Creek country. A meeting was held at *Okemah*, Oklahoma, to consider the organization of a credit association. One moiety was represented by members of the Towns of *Laplako* {*Łapłako*} and *Atasi*. The other moiety was represented by members of the Towns of Fishpond, Greenleaf, and *Nuyaka*. Much of the time was consumed by voluble disagreement between members of the two factions. Since the speeches were made in Creek, the officials present had little clue to what was actually happening. Finally an important official of Fishpond announced that whatever happened, the members of his Town would have nothing to do with the organization. Later, when I asked a man from *Laplako* why this officer had taken such a stand, he said:

> "Oh that's the way those people are – they always disagree on everything," which simply amounts to saying that the people of *Laplako* and Fishpond find difficulty in cooperating for specific programs. [38]

I am sure that while these Creeks were dividing along moiety and Town lines, those whites present who were urging organization were thinking solely in terms of county organization. In other words there was no meeting of minds between officialdom and the Indians. Neither comprehended the motivations of the other. Yet I am quite certain that if the

---

[89]/14 Dr. Mary Haas has published a paper (1940: 479-489) in which she provides evidence that a Town which is defeated in match play by another on three or four successive occasions (the number is in dispute) is forced to become a member of the moiety of the victor.

question of organization by Towns had not been raised, despite the factional dispute and the divergent Towns involved, enough signatures could have been secured to make possible the formation of a credit association on a county basis. And this would have meant one of two things: a constant struggle for control, or the nonparticipation and disinterest of a large section of the population.

The dual division among the Towns of the Creeks does not now have the extreme implications of hostility which once was the case. Yet it certainly still possesses some vitality, and in a delicate situation where the utmost in cooperation and receptivity on the part of the Indians is required, it will prove a valuable guide to action. I am perfectly aware that considerations like this receive scant attention and scant respect in some quarters. There are always people ready to say that even if such social forms as Town moieties exist and exert some weight, such rivalries and antagonisms are out of place in twentieth century living, are a vestige of the past, and deserve little official recognition.

Yet whether or not we approve of the particular alignments within Creek society, we cannot ignore them any more than we can will out of existence comparable opposition groups based on region, race, and religion in American society that often form a basis for political and social action. What can be done, of course, is to utilize the existing alignments to beneficial ends. Perhaps the competition between Towns which flourished on the ball ground can be translated as well into raising better crops, having a superior record of land utilization, or showing a better record in the repayment and utilization of government loans. The more friendly bonds between Towns can likewise be made to serve modern political and economic ends.

Why is it that in spite of long decades of government opposition, white contact, war, and removal, the Creek have retained so much more of their ancient internal organization than the Cherokce, Choctaw, and Chickasaw? I have heard the usual explanations which circulate in the region. Some put it down to a difference in innate ability. Some see in it evidence of too much mixture with the Negro. Some attribute it to the larger percent of full bloods in the Nation. Few have put a finger on the fundamental causal factor, the essential difference between Creek social organization and the social organizations of the other southeastern tribes mentioned. [39]

In aboriginal North America, economic organization, law, social obligation, education, and most institutionalized aspects of life were inextricably linked with the concept of kinship. In most hunting tribes a family or a group of related families formed the economic unit. The elders of the unit trained and educated the young. When a member of the blood group was injured or killed, this unit acted to exact vengeance. In larger, more sedentary tribes, the principle of kinship prevailed but was still more greatly elaborated. Clans (extended bodies of real or reputed relatives claiming descent in either the male or female line) appear, and these may have economic, educational, ritual, legal, and political functions. It was rare indeed that kinship groups were subordinated to a larger, more strictly political unit. We know, however, that this occurred among the Aztecs of Old Mexico. For the Southeast such an advanced political development existed only for the Creeks.

In many ways the Creek Tribal Town is one of the most significant and interesting achievements of the American Indian. It became the hub of all Creek activities – social, political, military, economic, and ritual. Strong clans existed, but they were perfectly subordinated to the needs and organization of the Town.

In the first place, the Town was the land-owning unit. All the agricultural land surrounding the Town was considered the property of the Town. Arable land was assigned to clans, whose members ordinarily lived together in definite sections of the Town.

When it came to political organization, the clans were again subordinate to the Town and were expected to make fixed and definite contributions to the leadership of the Town. One clan was expected to furnish the _miko_ or chief secular officer of the Town. Another clan was required to name his assistant. Each Town had its council house where the officers and their councilors met to discuss Town affairs. Each Town had its village square also, the scene of all important rituals and acts of public importance. Adjoining it was the Town ball ground.

All noteworthy events in the life of a Creek were inseparably connected with his Town. Until initiation, when a meeting or ritual was held in the square, he took his place on the side designed for the young people of the Town. When he was initiated and given a name, it occurred in the Town square on a public occasion. After initiation he took his place, according to his clan, in one of the arbors bounding the village square. Beginning in the spring he participated in a cycle of Town rituals which continued, at intervals, until fall. At harvest time, before he dared eat of the green corn, he felt that he had to partake of the "black drink" in company with his own Townspeople at their annual _buskita_. [40]

He saw to it, too, that the fire in his home was extinguished at this time and rekindled with a brand that had been lit at the sacred fire of the Town. Any crime that he had committed during the year was forgiven if he returned from hiding at the time of the Busk ceremony and came to the Town square. In the ball game he was expected to represent his Town unless permission was granted him to play for some friendly Town. In other words, the Town had become the predominating force in Creek society, because all activity passed through its channels.

Compare this to the Towns or settlements of other southeastern tribes — the Choctaw, for instance. There is no evidence that membership in the Choctaw Town was hereditary. The Choctaw settlements were more numerous and less compact than those of the Creeks. Early observers remarked on their tendency to be scattered over a large area. The Choctaws lacked a greatly developed annual green corn dance and the Town sacred fire-kindling rite that attended it. We may suspect that the strong feeling of Town solidarity which accompanied the rite for the Creeks was not present among the Choctaws. Moreover the Choctaws were more homogeneous linguistically and culturally than the Creeks. While there were dialectical variations among the Choctaws, there were not incorporations into the Choctaw Nation of peoples speaking widely separated languages. The Choctaws were a true tribe rather than a confederacy, and Choctaw settlements never achieved the political autonomy which the Creek Town demanded.

What we are in a position to see now is this: The Creeks have not transplanted and retained their Towns in the face of removal and allotment because of some inconsiderate stubbornness or ingrained conservatism, but simply because the Town was so carefully wrought an instrument, so involved with the life of the individual and the maintenance of other institutions, that it could not be easily surrendered. The Creek has declined some aspects of the white man's conception of how he should live because he has had the most advanced political form of aboriginal North America to oppose to it. The Creek's political genius and advancement have been the causes of much of his suffering at the hands of the whites.

Viewed in historical perspective, it is hard to see where the Creeks who wished to hold to their Town economy rather than be allotted were so far in error or were even so unprogressive. As it has been already pointed out, the old Creek custom was for the Town to act as the land-owning body. Plots were assigned to individual use. Today the government has a land acquisition program under the Oklahoma Indian Welfare Act. The land acquired is not to be given outright to individuals, but title is to remain in the name of the United States and assignments for use are to be made. After years of talk about individual enterprise, "Snake" Indians, and conservatives, we seem to be remarkably close to time-honored Creek usage. [41]

Cooperative group work in farming was a part of the Creek economy. A number of individuals would work together, passing from the field of one to the field of another as they finished the necessary labor. While the work was cooperatively done, the proceeds from the individual plot belonged to the family to which it was assigned. In our present cooperative enterprises, in the pooling of costs of machinery, etc., we are much closer today to former Creek methods than we realize.

For every Creek Town there was a common plot of land, cultivated by the contributed labor of those who could find free time. Most of the produce of this field went to the support of the sick, orphaned, and widowed. Such a concept of collective responsibility has found its way into modern American thinking, as civic community chests and social legislation attest.

What I am suggesting here is that the Creek Town has been maintained not only because its organizational framework was so strong, but because it embodied values which had their roots in Creek economy and morality. An intelligent and sensitive Creek expressed this when he said: "We lived well then because we helped each other and advised each other. It is since we have been separated that we have gone downhill."

In a previous report ("Memorandum in Regard to Creek Towns") I have traced in outline the long-term attempt of the government to reduce the independence and importance of the Town and to encourage the development of some central body which could speak for all the Creeks. Since then I have compiled much additional evidence on the subject, but the trend is so clear that it is hardly necessary to introduce new material of this nature. The attitude of the government was crystallized by the inevitable plans for removal and by the difficulty in obtaining the signatures of all Town representatives to any treaty. Despite the continual pressure, nothing that approximated a Creek national government was organized before 1860. In that year a constitution was adopted which provided that the Nation be known as the Muskogee Nation; that there be a Principal and Second Chief and general council; that the nation be divided into four districts with one judge for each district. It likewise provided for five supreme judges for the Nation. Before the constitution could become effective, the country was plunged into civil war and the Creeks were divided into two warring camps. There was no recognized government for the Creeks from 1861 to 1866.

In 1867 another attempt was made to form a national government. The delegates met at Deep Fork and decided henceforth to meet at Okmulgee. In the constitution which was adopted the hand of the white advisers and sophisticated mixed bloods can be plainly detected. Most of the provisions [42] and even the preamble are modelled after the United States constitution instead of being shaped out of Creek background or political consciousness. A council of two houses, one the House of Kings and the other the House of Warriors, patterned after the United States Senate and House of Representatives, respectively, was established. Each Town was entitled to one representative in the House of Kings, elected for four years, and one representative in the House of Warriors, elected for a two-year term, for each two hundred people. The Principal Chief, who had to be thirty years old, was to be elected by a majority of male voters for a four-year term. A bill which passed both houses was to be submitted to the Principal Chief and, if approved by him, was to become law. If rejected by him, it could be passed over his veto by a two-thirds vote of both houses. Even in the most minute details the constitution aped white American forms. Thus charges of impeachment were to originate in the House of Warriors, the Creek equivalent of the United States House of Representatives, and the members of the House of Kings were to act as judges in impeachment trials. Nothing flatters white sensibilities as much as imitation where Indians are concerned. The adoption of this constitution was hailed as a great forward step, and the adjective "civilized" was tossed about more recklessly than ever before.

Still, the new government set up under this constitution did not convene without opposition. A prominent Creek, known to the whites as Sands, refused to come to the councils of the Nation, and his followers refused to recognize the new government. On the other hand, the United States government recognized the new organization and paid all money to it. As the historian has put it: "The new government involved prejudice among the less progressive" who were "dissatisfied with the decreased number of executive officers" (Morton 1930: 55). In other words, the rank and file of the Creeks recognized the threat to the Towns which the new centralization of power offered. Most of the people of the Towns of *Nuyaka*, *Taskigi*, *Atasi*, *Kayaleychi*, *Tokipahchi*, and some others were highly antagonistic to the new development. The dissatisfaction broke out in overt form in 1871. When Chief Checote tried to convene the national council at *Okmulgee* in that year, three hundred of Sand's followers marched on the capitol and broke up the meeting. Civil strife was narrowly averted, and only the strong support of the United States government made possible the continued existence of the central Creek governing body.

By 1875 a second major disturbance threatened the stability of the Creek central government. *Lachar Harjo*, the candidate of the Upper Creek Towns, was elected Principal Chief. The followers of the ex-Chief and favorite of the Lower Creek Towns, Sam Checote, still dominated the legislature, however. The legislature immediately proceeded to impeach the newly elected Chief, and much bitterness was generated as a result. [43]

That the attempt at centralization of power was not proceeding too smoothly is recognized by Meserve, and despite his typically white bias and impatience with those who defied "progress," the unsatisfactory conditions can be sensed from this excerpt:

> The Creek Indians who clustered among the hills of *Nuyaka* and contiguous Indian villages ...declined to acknowledge the Creek National Government under the constitution of 1867; they ignored its autonomy by refusing to send representatives to the National Council ... As time progressed these Indians assumed a posture of defiance toward the Creek Government ... The *Nuyaka* Indians were well-intentioned, hospitable and Godfearing but unyielding in their attachment to the primitive rites and usages of their race (1932a: 57-58).

By 1880 a still more serious defection from the national government was in full bloom. A rival independent government with *Nuyaka* as headquarters was formed. The constitution of 1867 was denounced and dismissed as not binding upon the Creeks. A program was announced whereby the former type of government was to be reestablished. *Isparhecher*, a former principal judge of the Okmulgee district, acted as the leader of the movement. In 1881 a clash occurred between the rival forces north of Muskogee. In the summer of 1882 two men were killed in a fight resulting from the arrest of a follower of *Isparhecher*. By this time the recognized government was attempting to secure United States military intervention. The recognized government raised a considerable sum of money for military purposes. After an engagement or two a large body of *Isparhecher*'s followers fled west to the Kiowa jurisdiction. By 1883 Creek affairs were in serious disorder and the schools of the Nation were closed. The *Isparhecher* faction which had fled from Creek territory was escorted back by the military in the summer of

1883.

Shortly afterward United States commissioners were sent to mediate between the two sides. A general amnesty was declared. *Isparhecher*'s request for a separate government was denied, and his group was required to take the oath of allegiance to the regular government. Checote, the Chief of the regular government, resigned, and a new election was called for September, 1883. In this election Checote, Perryman, and *Isparhecher* were the candidates. No one had a clear majority, but *Isparhecher* held a plurality of votes. He assumed that he had won the election and actually served in office for a few days. Then Secretary of the Interior Teller intervened and instructed the Indian agent to recognize Perryman as the successful candidate. The interference of the United States government was bitterly resented by the Creeks. Thus did the government demonstrate that it had no intention of allowing the whims of the Creeks to interfere with the type of central government it had sponsored. [44]

The reasons why the United States government acted to unseat *Isparhecher* can be inferred from the platform of the *Isparhecher* party. In a ringing sentence the committee of the party declared: "We desire the preservation of our nationality; to hold our lands in common, as the treaty of 1866 provides" (Morton 1932: 204.). This was no empty political phrase but a declaration made necessary by an unpromising chain of events which had been forming since removal. The Creeks who valued their separate existence were beginning to fear pressure from within and without. The whites were increasing in numbers and impudence within Creek territory, and a growing body of mixed bloods and educated Creeks were becoming convinced that autonomy would sooner or later be an impossibility and that assimilation and acceptance of white culture in full was the only answer.

A review of the most prominent milestones of Creek history will indicate how serious the matter appeared to those who hoped for the persistence of Creek culture.

The removal treaty of 1832 guaranteed that no state or territory should ever have a right to pass laws for the government of the Creeks in their new homes. General Cass, Secretary of War, in a message to the Creeks in January, 1832, promised that the lands to which they would remove in the West should be theirs "as long as the grass grows and the rivers run." By the treaty of August 11, 1852, ownership to the land they occupied was guaranteed to the Creeks "so long as they shall exist as a nation and continue to occupy the country hereby conveyed to them." Long before this, by the Indian Intercourse Act of 1834, which forbade unauthorized entrance into any reservation, the Creeks were apparently safeguarded from white encroachment.

But by 1866 a decided change in Creek-United States government relations was taking place. Because some of the Creeks had signed an understanding with the southern representative, Albert Pike, at the beginning of the Civil War, the Nation was treated as a belligerent, and a harsh treaty was forced upon the Creeks in 1866 in spite of the fact that almost half of the population had sided with the North during the struggle. By the terms of this treaty the Creeks ceded one-half of their entire domain, the land to be used by the United States for the settlement of "other Indians and freedmen." Other demands of a foreboding nature which were incorporated in this treaty stated that the Creeks were to allow a railroad, authorized by the United States government, to pass through their territory and that they were to take steps toward the formation of a territorial government and an intertribal council.

It was not long before the fruits of this treaty were being reaped. By 1870 the first railroad — the Missouri, Kansas, and Texas line — was passing through Creek country. White men [45] came to operate the railroad and the stations. Towns sprang up. Soon there were hundreds of white families within Creek borders. In order to fulfill another section of the treaty an intertribal council was called at Okmulgee in 1870. After two sessions a committee of twelve was authorized to draw up a constitution for the organization of Indian Territory. Two Creeks acted on this committee. The resulting constitution was adopted by a 52 to 2 vote of the delegates. Because the Okmulgee constitution did not give the United States a share in the proposed Indian government, it was never ratified by Congress, nor was it ratified by the tribes whose delegates had framed it.

In 1871 another bill was passed in Congress which aimed at the destruction of the Indian governments. This bill destroyed the treaty-making rights of the tribes by providing that "no Indian nation as a tribe within the territory of the United States shall be acknowledged or recognized as an independent nation, tribe or power with whom the United States may contract by treaty."

Another attempt at an intertribal conference was made in 1871. At this time the Kiowa were on the warpath and were indifferent to the proceedings, and the gathering broke up without permanent accomplishments. During June of the next year representatives of the Five Civilized Tribes met at Okmulgee and selected delegates to meet with those of the "wild" tribes. The meeting took place later in the year at Ft. Cobb, but again the results were negligible.

In 1873 the Creeks relinquished another parcel of land to the United States government, this time to house Seminoles with whom a long-standing quarrel had been going on. The stipulation was made that the Seminoles were not to alienate the land without the consent of the Creeks.

By 1874 a marked restlessness was evident among the Creeks. That they feared they were to be dispossessed of their lands is shown by the fact that the Commissioner of Indian Affairs in his report for the year complains that they were making "most strenuous resistance to a survey and the apportioning of their lands in fee." In July of the same year the agencies of the Five Civilized Tribes were consolidated and managed under the direction of the Union Agency at Muskogee. In 1880 it is estimated that there were 6,000 whites on the reservations of the Five Civilized Tribes.

This was the state of affairs when the *Isparhecher* or Green Peach revolt broke out. Viewed historically it is seen as an outbreak against a "kept" central government which was doing little to protect Creek interests from white invasion. *Isparhecher* and his followers have been pictured as unprogressive and superstitious Indians. The course of events soon proved that they foresaw what was in store for their people much more accurately than the group which basked in government favor. [46]

After the Green Peach uprising one occurrence after another pointed to the final extinguishment of the Creek national government. At an intertribal conference held at *Eufaula* in June, 1886, representatives of the Five Civilized Tribes agreed to reject all offers from the government for the purchase of land for use of citizens of the United States. This action was ratified by the legislature of each tribe. Yet in 1889 a Creek delegation, headed by Pleasant Porter, went to Washington and offered to remove all restrictions on the western lands which had been reserved for Indians and freedmen by the treaty of 1866. This opened the way for white settlement in the former Creek lands to the west, and by 1890 there were 140,000 whites out of a total population of 210,000 inhabitants in Indian Territory.

The presence of so many whites in a region governed by Indian authority and courts raised serious questions of peace and order. In 1889 a United States court was established at Muskogee. By an act of May 2, 1890, the laws of Arkansas, as far as applicable, were extended over Indian Territory until Congress should otherwise provide.

Now matters came rapidly to a head. Under an act of Congress of March 3, 1893, a commission headed by Senator Henry L. Dawes was appointed by President Cleveland and instructed to negotiate with the Five Civilized Tribes for the extinguishing of the national title to the land and for its allotment in severalty. No authority was given to the Dawes Commission except to negotiate and report. In June, 1895, an intertribal meeting was held at Eufaula, and to it the Creeks sent five delegates, including *Isparhecher*. After a two-day session the meeting went on record as opposed to the proposed agreements.

The general election for Principal Chief of the Creek Nation was held in September, 1895. In this election *Isparhecher* and Pleasant Porter were the opposing candidates. General Porter was a Creek of part white extraction and was married to a white woman. He had acted as the military arm of the recognized national government whenever it had been threatened by internal difficulties. It was he who had broken up *Isparhecher*'s Green Peach revolt and sent the disaffected elements scurrying to the west. Throughout his life he demonstrated extreme pliancy in the hands of the United States government and the whites. He died a 33rd degree Mason. In this election *Isparhecher* won handily. As Meserve has put it: "The elevation of *Isparhecher* to the position of Principal Chief at this particular time clearly indicated the posture of the Creek Indians toward the allotment of their lands and the extinguishment of their tribal government" (1932a: 73).

In 1897 a committee headed by Porter reached an agreement with the Dawes Commission. By it each Creek citizen and freedman was to receive a patent to 160 acres of land in [47] lieu of common ownership. It provided for jurisdiction of United States courts over allotment controversies and the trials of Indians and whites alike. It granted citizenship to the Creeks after expiration of the tribal government. This agreement was not to be effective until ratified by both Congress and the Creek Nation. In ratifying this agreement Congress stipulated that the Creeks would have to accept it by September 1, 1898, by a majority vote. The Creeks were reluctant to bring the matter to a vote. Meanwhile, the United States government, impatient at the little headway made to persuade the Five Civilized Tribes of the benefits of allotment, resumed the right of protection and control. In June, 1898, Congress passed the Curtis Act, which provided for the termination of tribal jurisdiction, abolished tribal courts, extended jurisdiction of the Dawes Commission over citizenship, made allotments compulsory, and prohibited payments to tribal governments. The provisions of the Curtis Act were embodied in the United States-Creek Agreement of 1897, and on November 1, 1898, *Isparhecher*, who had hesitated as long as he could, allowed the question to go before the Creek people. The agreement was defeated at this general election.

Nevertheless, under authority of the Curtis Act, the Dawes Commission opened a land office at Muskogee in April, 1899, and began to allot the use and occupancy of the land surface. *Isparhecher* had failed to stop allotment, and his followers fell away. In 1899 General Pleasant Porter was elected Principal Chief over *Isparhecher*. By 1900 Porter had convinced a large section of the Creek population that further resistance was ill advised. A Creek delegation entered into a new agreement with the Dawes Commission which provided for the dissolution of the tribal government on or before March 4, 1906. This agreement was ratified by Congress on March 1, 1901, on condition that the Creek council accept it within ninety days. In advocating a committee to deal with the Dawes Commission anew, Porter had told the Creek council:

> It is true and it is admitted that the title to the lands cannot be segregated without an agreement with us so to do. The lands of the tribe were patented to the nation in fulfillment of treaties mutually agreed upon by and between the United States and

the Creek Nation and their partition cannot be lawfully made except by mutual agreement of the contracting parties; therefore a treaty or agreement in this usual manner will be seen to be of the highest importance (Meserve 1931b: 329).

Porter headed the commission, and the subsequent agreement was ratified by vote of the Creek Nation on May 25, 1901. [48]

An Act of March 3, 1901, had declared all Indians of Indian Territory citizens of the United States. After that date the Creek Nation ceased to exist "except as sort of a financial corporation to take care of tribal funds" (Morton 1930: 218). The tribal government was still maintained, but had few functions except in acting as agent in managing the business of the Nation. There were no courts to enforce tribal law, and the Indians were under the jurisdiction of the United States government.

It must not be thought that all the Creeks sat supinely by while these events were in progress. A large and powerful section of the population was openly dismayed and angered by what was transpiring. The change in the system of land tenure was the bone of contention, for upon the Creek system rested much of their social, political, and religious organization as well as their economic life. By 1900 unrest was so prevalent that Chief Porter appealed to the United States government for protection.

Early in 1901 occurred the movement known as the "Crazy Snake" uprising. *Tcito Hadjo*, "Crazy Snake," known to the whites as Wilson Jones, was a prominent Creek, a former member of the House of Kings, who had been a leader of a dissenting faction ever since the arrival of the Dawes Commission in Indian Territory. When it became apparent that the government intended to allot the Indians in defiance of former treaties, Jones and three friends made a trip to Washington. There they found the removal treaty of 1832 and brought back a copy of it. Jones held that the United States had no right to disturb the status of the land or to interfere with the Creek government. Therefore he proceeded to set up a government to take the place of the one that was being dissolved, and he threatened all those who accepted allotment certificates with dire penalties. Crazy Snake recognized the Creek Tribal Town of Hickory Ground as his capitol. Again the United States took action. The "Snakes" were notified by the U.S. agent, in 1900, of the illegality of their government. In 1901 the new government disclosed its intention of carrying on and sent notice to the President of the United States to that effect. After a few clashes between those who were accepting allotment certificates and the "Snakes," the agent and marshall asked for cavalry. Forces from Ft. Reno were dispatched in January, 1901. Jones and his secretary, John Timothy, were captured, and the records of the "Snakes" secured. From the rolls of the officers and citizens of the rebel government, ninety-four names of prominent men were selected, and these persons were captured as an example to the rest and charged with conspiracy. They were tried and convicted and given the choice of being peaceable or of going to jail. Finally they were all liberated. Thus ended the first "Snake" uprising. [49]

The allotment of the Creek Indians went on for the next five years, but the "Snakes" were merely observers. They declined to make selections, and selections were arbitrarily made for them. They refused to accept the allotments assigned to them. In the process of allotment these "conscientious objectors" came out very badly, of course. In the first place, freedmen, those under the influence of intermarried citizens, mixed bloods, and those without scruples concerning the issue were in an enviable position to make a first choice and obtain the most desirable lands. Again, since the "Snakes" were considered nuisances anyway, there was a tendency to assign less desirable parcels to them. Since the allotment went on without the cooperation of the "Snakes," some of them received allotments which would have taken them far from their Towns, relatives, or friends.

In the election of 1903 Porter was again elected Principal Chief. His office was divested of almost all power by this time. He now observed the rudderless state of his people and became a strong advocate of a state government for Indian Territory. His efforts and those of others culminated in a constitutional convention called by the chiefs of various tribes. The meeting took place in Muskogee in August, 1905. The convention framed a constitution for a State of Sequoyah, which was to embrace the old Indian Territory. This constitution was adopted by the people by a large vote in a general election. It was never favorably acted upon by Congress, however.

The agitation of the former followers of Wilson Jones against allotment and against the provisions of the Creek Agreement and the Curtis Act still continued. In the fall of 1906 a Senate Investigation Committee came to Indian Territory, and Jones addressed them in Tulsa, pleading that the United States honor its treaties.

The duties of the Principal Chief of the Creek Nation were now little more than a matter of form. Porter was mainly occupied with attaching his signature to thousands of allotment deeds. The governments of the Five Civilized Tribes were to be terminated on March 4. 1906. But Creek allotment was not completed by that date, and because it was necessary for the Chief to continue in office to execute conveyances and other legal documents, it was found impractical to abolish the tribal government. Therefore, at the last moment, by an act of March 2, 1906, Congress continued the existence of the tribal government "until otherwise provided for by law," taking good care, of course, to strip the governing body and officers of all fundamental powers. By this act it was provided that the council should not be in session more than thirty days in the year, that no act except a resolution of adjournment be valid until approved by the President of the United States, and that no contract involving [50] payment or expenditure or affecting property of a tribe be valid until approved by the President. Collection of tribal revenue and disbursement of tribal funds were placed in the hands of the Secretary of the Interior; tribal taxes were abolished, and tribal schools were placed under the control of the Secretary of the Interior. Tribal officers in office on the date of the approval of the measure were continued, and it was stipulated that in case the chief executive refused to perform his duties he could be removed by the President of the United States. On April 30, 1908, the documents, records, and papers belonging to the Creek Nation were turned over to the United States office at Muskogee, and the Secretary of the Interior took charge of all tribal property.

Though the State of Oklahoma was admitted into the Union in 1907, the whites were still apprehensive about the attitude of the Indians who had opposed allotment and the termination of their own government. Rumors of another uprising began to be spread. The newspapers did much to induce panic and inflame public opinion. The white people called for military protection. The story circulated that Crazy Snake was leading a full-blood revolt. The settlers appealed to the sheriff of McIntosh County, who in turn called on the governor for military aid. The State militia marched to put down this fictitious uprising. Meanwhile Crazy Snake was in Cherokee country and knew nothing of his "military venture" until he learned that the militia was seeking him. Martial law was proclaimed in McIntosh County, and the militia advanced on the Creek Town of Hickory Ground. They found no armed resistance and no evidence of an uprising. It turned out that a group of Negroes and Creeks, some of them followers of Crazy Snake, had established themselves at Hickory Ground in a shanty and dugout village. Some of them were accused of minor depredations in the neighborhood, and somehow they became implicated in the destruction of a smokehouse. In an attempt to make arrests in connection with the affair fighting occurred. Soon the incident became magnified out of all reasonable proportion, and the ludricous interpretation described ensued. Because of its amusing origin this "uprising" is known as the "Smoked Meat Rebellion."

But Crazy Snake's difficulties were not yet over. The sheriff had secured a warrant for his arrest and went to his home to take him into custody. When he came upon Crazy Snake, he fired without warning. Crazy Snake escaped with a bullet in his hip. He made his way to Choctaw country, where he secured a haven with a Choctaw friend, Daniel Bob, until his death in 1911.

I have offered so full an account of the inception, life span, and termination of the Creek national government because from such a survey certain indisputable but little appreciated facts emerge. It is plain that the centralization of power [51] was first sponsored and encouraged by the United States government, that the Creek central body and officers were then used as instruments in the whittling away of the rights and lands which they were theoretically supposed to administer, that a large section of the Creek people were hostile to the recognized government and would have upset it on more than one occasion had not our moral support and military aid been forthcoming, and that even as much of the Creek governmental machinery as has been allowed to persist was retained for the convenience of carrying out the intentions of the United States government.

I emphasize this particularly because some people to whom it has been suggested that the Creeks organize initially in terms of their Tribal Towns have expressed the fear that such a move would do damage to Creek unity and to the central government of the Creeks. These expressions seem strange in the face of the long and determined attempt to undermine and liquidate that same Creek national government. Leaving aside the question of the good faith with which the argument is put forth, the truth is that the unity extolled was largely artificial and extremely precarious. A government which is called upon to weather six grave crises in a scant forty years of its existence cannot be accepted as too stable.

The situation is still less promising today. By the act of 1906 the body of officers then existing was allowed to continue in office when the life of the government was extended. But, with the exception of the executive officers, no provision was made for future representation or for the functioning of the legislative body. Representation had been by Towns, but, through allotment, it was expected that the population of the Towns would be scattered and the Towns, in fact, cease to exist as such. So firmly accepted was this view that after allotment Creek enrollment no longer was kept by Towns, though before allotment Town rolls had been in order.

The Towns have not been definitely recognized since the time of allotment, and a queer medley of usage obtains in respect to their representation today. Some Towns send no representatives because they see no use in doing so and are uncertain whether they have any authority to do so. Some Towns have permitted those men who represented them at the time of the act of 1906 to continue to do so. As the years have gone by some of these representatives have died, but no step is taken to replace them. Presumably, when the last of these representatives expires, the Towns in question will be without a representative. There are other Towns which were entitled to a certain number of representatives according to their populations. The relative populations have changed considerably, but these Towns seat the same number of men as they did when the legislative body was ossified by Congressional edict. There are cases where a Town is practically exterminated, but survivors come to represent this nonfunctioning [52] unit simply because the Town was entitled to representation in times past. Again, other Towns take care in selecting representatives and scrupulously fill places that are vacated. In other words, this national council about which some individuals are so solicitous is in a sad state of disorganization in a formal sense. The Creeks feel this and have come to look upon its monthly meetings as a general gathering to which anyone may come and at which anyone may voice his opinion. I have been expressly told this, time and again, by Creeks. The executive officers, the Principal Chief and the Second Chief, are chosen in a regulated manner and have more definite functions.

A council for the Creek Nation which could consider matters which affect all Creeks is eminently desirable. But in order to function properly and to be more than a sounding board for the Bruner vs. anti-Bruner factions, it must be more realistically related to existing and functioning natural units. I have not the least doubt that if the Creek Towns were to organize in terms of their present existence and functioning and were recognized by the United States government, a central federated body of representatives would result. Such a federal body cannot possess much vitality and promise, however, unless it represents the Towns as they exist in number and strength today, and not as they were in the days preceding allotment. The semblance of central organization which exists now, though it may nominally serve for official purposes, can have no other than a deleterious effect on the self-respect and independence of a people. In other words, I cannot agree that organization by Towns for local purposes of credit, cooperation, land acquisition, etc., could have anything but an ultimately beneficial influence on Creek federation and solidarity.

In the materials summarized thus far and in previous reports I have traced the rise and the decline of the importance of the Creek national government. We have seen that its star was late in rising and that its descent was equally precipitous. We have now to inquire into the history and fate of the much older political and social units, the Tribal Towns.

In the first place, when removal was forced upon it, the population of a Town, whenever it could, removed as a unit. One of the vivid memories of my Creek work is the recital of a *Laplako* Creek as he narrated how, according to the tale of his grandfather, the people of his Town came away together, were loaded on a rotting hulk of a ship that floundered on dark night, and how his grandfather and other men saved the Town from extinction by rescuing panic-stricken women and children. [53]

Long before any individual could recover from the effects of that tearful journey, in fact, the first act performed when a group of Townspeople reached their destination in Indian Territory was formally to reestablish the physical characteristics of their Town. One of their number would put down ashes from the hearth of the old Town square which he had brought from the south, and the nucleus of a new Town square was established. The city of Tulsa bears its name because on its present site the Creeks of ancient *Talsi* placed the ashes which they had brought from their southeastern Town. The gesture is of definite psychological import; we may assume that if, despite dispossession and this difficult journey, the Creeks' first thought was for the reestablishment of their Towns, these Towns must have had tremendous meaning for them.

The extent to which the Tribal Towns were recognized by the United States government after removal for the purpose of compiling census rolls, making per capita payments, etc., has been covered in a former report, and the material will not be duplicated here. The key position and vitality of the Towns can be gauged by the fact that all new developments had of necessity to be related to the Towns. For instance, the first neighborhood schools located by the Creeks in Indian Territory bore such names as *Concharty* (*Kanchati*), *Thlob-Thlocco* (*Laplako*), *Tuckabatchee* (*Tokipahchi*), *Hillabee* (*Hilapi*), *Cusehta* (*Kasihta*), etc. – the names of Tribal Towns.

As time went on and the presence and institutions of the whites made more of an impress, other innovations which accompanied the white influx became attached to the Towns. The most important of these was the growth of Christianity and the establishment of churches. We have already seen the close nexus existing between the hereditary members of *Lochapoka* Town and the Haikey Chapel. From our analysis it is demonstrable that the chapel in no wise crushed or crowded out the Tribal Town but simply displaced the Town square as the hub of its activities. The *miko* slipped into the position of the preacher of the church, homes sprang up around the church instead of around a Town square, social work and aid to the distressed went on under the auspices of the church instead of under the name of the Town.

In outline this is what happened. The war against the political autonomy and social independence of the Tribal Town was a long and aggressive one, as we have seen. It ended in allotment, when, as far as the United States government's scheme of things went, the Towns ceased to be of significance. As the repressive steps were taken, it became more and more difficult for the Towns to discharge the social and communal functions of the past. But though Creek government of the ancient order was discouraged and ridiculed, churches were, of course, regarded with approval. A section of the Creek population took the path of least resistance. [54]

Under the aegis of the church they carried on meetings of Townspeople and the distribution of goods among Townspeople which would have been frowned upon under any other auspices. Much of this adaptation of a new institution to time-honored purposes was unconscious on the part of the Creeks themselves, of course. Nevertheless the transfer of functions from the Town to the church and the" incorporation of the churches into the existing Towns are perfectly apparent. At the Town squares in times past an all-night dance called *saiyakida* used to take place. Today the Creeks use this same word to designate an all-night song and prayer meeting which often takes place at a church.

In many cases the association of the church with the Tribal Town is indicated even in the name. There is a church called *Laplako* which acts as the headquarters of a section of the population of *Laplako* Town. Almost without exception those who belong to this Methodist church are by birth members of the Tribal Town of the same name. The few exceptions can be accounted for by intermarriage or relationship to Town members. The meetings at which the people of *Laplako* discussed the question of organizing as a Town were held at this church. Important officers of the Town are leading members of the church.

Even when two Towns utilize the same church there is usually a reason which goes back to former modes of social organization. The church called "Greenleaf" (*Asilanapi*) is shared by the people of the Tribal Town of Greenleaf and by the people of the Tribal Town of Fishpond (*Lalokalka*), as well. But Greenleaf and Fishpond are not only neighbors, not only members of the same moiety (i.e. the same fire), but claim to be offshoots of the same parent Town (*Okchayi*). They are expected to help each other in ceremonial ball games and in other practical or ceremonial matters.

It can be assumed, then, that if Tribal Towns were to organize, the church situation should offer no serious obstacle, since the churches are arranged and organized in terms of the Tribal Towns themselves.

It is necessary to mention this because some have assumed that because there exist Christian churches with religious functions and Town squares where ceremonies are performed, two irreconcilable elements are present which would clash over the question of organization by Towns.

This view rests on the assumption that the average Creek thinks of the Town and the church as two rival religious organizations and throws his loyalty with one to the exclusion of the other. In the eyes of the Creek, however, the Town has many other legitimate functions besides those of a ritual character. In the first place, he recognizes it as a social body to which he belongs by birth, and he further accepts that it should have political, social, and economic [55] functions as well as religious ones. Therefore, whether he goes to the Christian church or participates in the rites of the Town square, he will acknowledge the Town as a suitable instrument for political organization.

As a matter of fact, the distinction between those who attend the Christian church connected with their Tribal Towns and those who go to the Town's square at the time of the annual green corn dance is not nearly so sharp as some seem to believe. There are a few ardent church members in each community who say that it "is a sin" to go to the Busk and accordingly stay away. And the people who have charge of the ceremony at the Busk are likely to have little use for the Christian church. But the great majority of Creeks manage to participate in the activities of both church and Busk without conflict. One of the most ardent participants of the Busk explained to me that the four arbors which surround the square grounds are each divided into three compartments to symbolize the twelve apostles of Christ. A prominent member of the Town of Alabama has been one of the most consistent proponents of organization for his Town. On the last day of the green corn dance (Busk) of his Town, I came to the square to interview him. He was engaged in other activities at the time and was not available, but I was told that if I would come to the Salt Creek Church (the church of the people of Alabama) the following day (Sunday), I might see him there. Most of the Creeks are in a comparable position. They see no inconsistency in the double role, and, considering the basic Creek ideology which has found its way into the church and the amount of secondary Christian interpretation which has become attached to the ceremonies, it is small wonder.

The point to be emphasized is that all members of the same Town recognize themselves as such whether or not they believe in Creek rites or take part in the annual Busk. On the committee of ten which drew up the constitution for the Tribal Town of *Laplako* all shades of belief were represented. On this committee sat the minister of the church, the man who has a most important function at the time of the Town's Busk, and a number of persons who make use of the church and the Busk grounds with equal felicity. At a meeting to discuss Town organization at Hickory Ground, I addressed myself to two young men who came together, sat together, and seemed much interested in the discussion. I learned that they were neighbors and friends. When I asked them whether they attended the green corn dance of their Town, one answered:

"I never miss it"; the other replied: "I haven't taken the medicine [participated in the rite] for six years." I asked whether this difference in attitude toward the Busk had altered their relations or would make it impossible for them to work together on a common Town committee. They claimed that they were as good friends as they had been and that they considered religious preference a personal matter which [56] would not be injected into work on a social and political program for their Town.

This plain statement of fact, which I have heard repeated again and again by Creeks, will not prevent those who see in any expression of genuine Indian patterns a danger to "civilization" and "progress" from announcing that "savagery and superstition" are being encouraged if Tribal Town organization is permitted. This attitude toward Indian institutions comes from within as well as without the Service. One extension employee among the Creeks, an Indian of another tribe and an ex-minister, confided to another employee that organization by Towns would "set the Creeks back one hundred years." The same person is credited with having foretold the end of the Christian church if Creek institutions are encouraged. There is no doubt that the same cry will be duly taken up by others.

This feeling that the Creeks will be retrograding at a rapid rate if the institutions they have maintained are brought out into the light of day is based on a series of naive beliefs in respect to the Creeks which have a hold on the imagination of outsiders, especially of whites.

The first of these is that the Creeks are so thoroughly acculturated and at ease in white American society that Creek institutions which have no parallel among the whites are unnecessary anachronisms. The existence of a number of Creeks who have entered the professions is pointed out in this connection. But despite these specific cases, the fact remains that a very small percentage of the population is in any position to compete on equal terms with white professional and business activity. Time and again when I have been told that a certain Creek has moved to a white neighborhood, is well educated, and is getting along with great success, the post which the "progressive" lad holds turns out to be nothing more dazzling than that of a clerk in a store. The blunt truth is that most of the Creeks keep to themselves in their own communities. They go to their own churches. They provide their own amusements and social life. Their contacts with surrounding whites are mostly a matter of trade and barter.

As far as the whites of Creek country are concerned, they have no intention of accepting the Creeks into the mainstream of their social and political life. The history of white-Creek relations in Oklahoma is a story of the decreasing influence of the Creeks in the territory which was once theirs, of a gradual pushing of the Creeks into the background economically, socially, and politically. When the Constitutional Convention met at Muskogee in August, 1905, and drew up a constitution for the proposed State of Sequoyah, Creeks such as Porter and Posey acted in important capacities. That the Creeks could prove a dominant force in State issues [57] is unthinkable today. Socially the Creek is at just as much a disadvantage. The whites make much of alleged Negro admixture among the Creeks, placing the estimate of Negro blood much higher than it could possibly be. Thus the intense discrimination against Negroes found in Oklahoma (which the Creeks themselves practice, incidentally) indirectly affects the social status of the Creeks. Of course, a very wealthy Creek or a Creek of marked white admixture has a much easier time of it, but the rank and file of the population who are typically Creek in physical characteristics or interests have little opportunity to become identified with white culture.

Not long ago I stopped at a garage in the heart of Creek country. The young mechanic and I began a conversation about the Creeks. I asked him whether he had managed to get acquainted with any of the Indians personally. He replied: "No, and I don't want to. I don't like them." He went on to characterize these Indians as "dishonest" and "shifty." It turned out upon inquiry that despite long residence in the neighborhood this young man had had none but formal business relations with the Creeks. They did not attend the places to which he went; they simply were not represented in the circles in which he moved. One gets the same story from the Creeks. At Alabama Town I was told that the Creeks do not like to send their children to schools with white children because, if they are numerically inferior, they are ridiculed and molested.

To understand and feel at home in a culture one must be actively associated with its processes. The marginal position of the Creeks socially and economically does not admit of that large-scale successful acculturation which some pretend to see. I should like to offer one or two examples of the other face of the coin, a face which, I am afraid, is even more characteristic.

During my Creek field work I had occasion to attend, with a representative of Indian Organization, a meeting of the Tribal Town of Hickory Ground. One of the members of that

Town was working on the construction of a schoolhouse in the neighborhood, and I was sent to make arrangements which would permit him to attend the meeting. When I arrived I found my man busy plastering. He had no idea whether his services could be spared and sent me to see the man in charge of construction. When I explained the nature of my errand to this individual (this was a piece of government construction), he smiled broadly and said: "Sure, take him along. That fellow deserves some time off. I get here early in the morning, but no matter how early I come, he is always here ahead of me, working. I don't know what time he does come. And he works till I tell him to stop. Do you know, I don't believe he knows he's supposed to work only eight hours a day, and this was actually the case." This Creek, a relatively young [58] man, living out his life in the rural environs of Hickory Ground, had scarcely any conception of the world of American industrial relations, of wages and hours, of the relative obligations of employee and employer. All he knew was that as long as he worked he was paid. He supposed that as long as he performed satisfactorily he would be retained, and so he worked hard and long, to the evident amusement of his superior.

Not long afterward I was speaking with an intelligent, English-speaking Creek about a trip which he and two others had made to Washington as representatives of a Creek faction. These men were by no means dull. In Washington their sincerity and directness made a most favorable impression on the Assistant Commissioner of Indian Affairs, whom I have heard refer to their visit. The trip was made by automobile. During the course of his description of the journey I was startled to hear my Creek friend say: "Tennessee is a nice state all right, but it sure costs a powerful lot of money to go through it." When I asked for an explanation of this remark, I received the following account. The three Creeks were about to enter the State of Tennessee when they were stopped at a bridge by a man. They didn't know who he might be, but he wore an official-looking cap. He told them they would have to pay a cent and a half a mile to cross Tennessee and proceeded to collect the requisite sum. The story concluded ruefully, "And we were crossing Tennessee the long way. It just about cleaned us out."

One has a picture here of a dishonest and officious white man realizing that he is dealing with Indians and determining to victimize them. Yet the revealing thing is that he was able to perpetrate so palpable a fraud. The trick would have been challenged by any average white person. Nevertheless these above-average Creeks were not certain enough about the manipulation of authority in white society to risk an outcry. I emphasize that this episode does not justify the assumption that these Creeks are more gullible than comparable white men. I have been with the narrator of this tale long enough to know that in his own familiar setting he is shrewd and subtle. Still, despite his Europeanized clothes, his ability to speak English, and his occasional contact with whites over a long term of years, he is not equal to the nuances and inner understandings of white culture. Most of the Creeks are in this man's shoes or in shoes remarkably like them. They move in the world of white activities gingerly and with circumspection. They never know when they will discover that they have paid a dear price for "going across Tennessee." I suspect that here lies one of the reasons why a section of Creek society wishes developments in organization to take place within a framework which they understand without reservation, in which the subtleties are, for once, their own. Then if the white man does not know what "being on the same Side of the fire" means, let <u>him</u> take .the pains to find out. [59]

If he doesn't understand what a Tribal Town is, let <u>him</u> blunder along until he learns. Despite the bewilderment and contempt of the whites, there are a large number of Creeks who would like to carry on their political and social life in a manner congenial and comprehensible to themselves.

A corollary of the idea that the average Creek is the perfectly Americanized individual is the claim that even where some attachment to distinctly Creek institutions exists, the parties to the attachment are a few lingering old people who will soon be gone. The emancipated youth must not be tied to their whims, the argument goes.

I tried this argument on a group of Creeks myself to see what the reaction would be. I was at a meeting in the Town square of Talwalako with Mr. Hagerty of the Indian Organization. Old Creeks and young were present. When an auspicious moment presented itself, I recited the little piece I had so often heard. "It's true that some old people think much of their Towns," I said, "but I understand that the younger Creeks who have been to school are not interested in them." After a painful pause I had my answer. "I am interested in _my_ Town," one of the younger men told me with spirit, and others who sat around grunted assent. "Why, you don't even know what a Town is," one young fellow declared excitedly, and it took me some minutes to quiet the storm I had aroused.

Anyone who bothers to read the old reports will discover that ever since 1850 the officials in Creek country have been waiting for those few hoary intransigents to depart this life so that the last links with the past will have been broken and progress can be accelerated as never before. The assurance with which white Americans persist in believing that an Indian, as soon as he has had some formal education, embraces white culture in toto as something far superior and more satisfying than anything he has known before borders on the pathetic. Some of the best-informed Indians I know consider white culture to be one of the least attractive weeds in the garden of history.

This summer I had the opportunity to witness a number of the Busks of the Creek Towns. Preparation for the Busk entails a considerable amount of manual labor. The Town square has to be cleaned of all brush, the arbors in which the participants sit are repaired, etc. Young people of both sexes did more than their share of preparatory work as far as I could observe. At the rituals which followed, young people and even children participated in large numbers and with enthusiasm.

The same is true for the political personnel of the Towns. The _miko_ or Chief of Alabama Town is a very young man. Many of his fellow officers are young or middle-aged. The committee which drew up the _Laplako_ constitution consisted of individuals who were far from being superannuated. [60]

It will not do to believe that a few years of training in a government school obliterates centuries of tradition and cultural history. One of the most interesting experiences of my Creek work was a long talk with a man (a man with some white admixture, incidentally) who is now just entering upon middle age. He introduced himself as a graduate of Haskell. While away at school, he married an Oneida woman who bore him children. His wife died and he returned to Creek country. Since clanship is established through the mother, his children were without their proper place in Creek society, and he was accordingly troubled. He consulted the officers of his Town, and it was decided to have the children adopted into a clan which had been diminishing in numbers and which was likely to pass out of existence in that Town unless the trend was reversed. This man was immensely pleased. His children were assured of status and a place in Creek society, and a clan which had important functions within the Town was fortified by the inclusion of his kin. This man speaks excellent English. He is one of the few Creeks who have entered a field of endeavor usually reserved for whites, the real estate business. Yet this is his story substantially as he related it to me. One of my colleagues in the Indian Service once addressed this question to him: "Are the Creeks really concerned with Tribal Towns?" The answer returned was impressive and earnest: "As long as there are Creeks there will be Tribal Towns." Despite what some expect in regard to the attitude of the younger people, many older Creeks told me that when they become discouraged by the state of affairs and by the expense and labor required to continue with the Busk and other Town activities, it is the insistence and cooperation of the younger people which encourage them to go forward.

Another point of view acknowledges the existence and even the vitality of the Creek Tribal Town but treats the matter indulgently as evidence of a sentimental attachment to the past on the part of some of the Creeks. According to this view, the Towns are a formal residue of the past, are without significant possibilities or functions for the future, and are indeed, a dead weight of conservatism at the present time.

I imagine it will amaze those who have accepted this idea without question to learn how functionally important the Towns still are. Anyone who becomes closely identified with the Creeks senses this sooner or later. A white lawyer in Creek country married a woman of part Creek extraction. He told me that for business reasons he had tried to get his wife to transfer from the Tribal Town to which she belonged by birth to another Town in whose territory he was carrying on his practice. The woman did make formal application to the officers of the Town to which her husband wished her to belong, but the application was rejected on the grounds that she had no valid reason for making the change. If modern business and economy are so closely correlated with these loyalties, certainly an organizational and credit program which aims at success cannot afford to ignore them. [61]

When I was discussing the land acquisition program with some of the members of *Laplako*, it came out that before the people of this Town had known anything about the United States government's program, they had a land acquisition program of their own under discussion. The Town was trying to raise a fund with which to purchase land in the name of the whole Town. "We didn't want it to be as it was with the oil found on Creek land," one Townsman told me. "Then a few people got rich, and the rest stayed as poor as ever. We wanted this land to belong to all of us. We wanted it to be as it was with the Osages." The land was to be used for the young people of the Town who were never allotted any land and for those who had lost their lands. "We have been trying to raise some money for the purpose. But most of us are very poor; just a very few are well-to-do. Some of these wealthier people promised to help out, though." Here we get an expression of the feeling of common interest which marks the Creek Town. The concept of individual riches is definitely subordinated to the needs of the social body.

A further indication of the vitality of the Town in the realm of economy and social service occurs in this quotation from a *Laplako* Creek:

> They used to help a person if he had a hard time or needed something. If he needed a house built, the *miko* could tell the officers to get people to help him, and they would all get together and do it. And if a man was sick or had hard luck, an accident, they would work in his field for him. They are more social and try to help their fellowmen more. For instance, my uncle's house burned down. It was the house in which I was raised. People of *Laplako* Town were called on to move a little house near to where the old one had burned down. They cleared away the wreckage. They began to build him a new house, cut the logs. It's not all finished yet.

That the Town exercises considerable control over its members in social and even personal relations came out in the course of work with members of this same *Laplako* Town.

When they wrote the first draft of their constitution, they inserted a clause to the effect that the children of any Town member and a Negro would have no rights in the Town. When the committee was going over the draft with Mr. Curry, the latter asked whether this clause was necessary, whether *Laplako*-Negro marriages occurred so frequently that parental and social disapproval did not provide a sufficient check. The answer was that no marriage of this description had occurred within recent times for "We'd just about kill a *Laplako* girl who did it." It is apparent that the Town is solicitous concerning the activities of its members and [62] exerts moral pressure as a Town when it feels that its mores are being disregarded. I have used *Laplako* as an example since it is a Town which has already drawn up a constitution and therefore is, so to speak, in the limelight. But the principles and functions illustrated are equally true of other Towns.

Admittedly the Towns do not carry out all their former functions with the consistency and authority with which they were once exercised. Their poverty, the scattering effects of allotment, the lack of recognition by the United States government, etc., could not fail to make sharp inroads on their activities. Since the Towns have functioned quietly and, as it were, under cover, most whites – and this includes officials – have failed to notice that, except for staging the green corn dance, they have functioned at all. How many have known, for instance, that over twenty Tribal Towns have maintained a full roster of officers to this day? Since the Busk or green corn dance has been the only event spectacular enough to catch the attention of the great majority of non-Creeks, they have concluded that it is the sole concern and function of the Town. Even if this were true at the present time – if, after decades of attempts to eliminate the Towns and to elevate a central government at the expense of the Towns, the expression of religious values were all that was left to the Town – it would prove exactly nothing. To block all other avenues of expression and then complain that too much attention is devoted to ritual matters is hardly a fair test of what a Town might do for its members. It is the equivalent of holding fast to a person's windpipe while observing that he does not breathe easily. The question is not what the Towns accomplish now, for obviously they are not in a position to work wonders. The question is, given encouragement in organizing and given credit facilities and a place in the land acquisition program, what they will be inspired to do.

Some indication of what could be expected under such conditions was furnished by the Tribal Town of Alabama-Kowasati. When I learned that this group wished to organize as a Town under the Oklahoma Indian Welfare Act, I happened to mention it to an Indian Service employee of the region. "Oh, that bunch!" was the rejoinder, "all they want to do is dance and have a big time." Later I was present at some of the meetings at which the Townspeople discussed the subject of organization. At the decisive meeting when the people agreed to go ahead with their plans, I was especially interested in watching the movements of a white employee of the district. This individual went around with a black look on his face and greeted all white visitors with a perfectly audible whispered, "It's a shame to allow these Indians to organize." When the Alabamas began to dictate what they wished to include in their constitution, I heard him say wrathfully: "There is only one man in this whole outfit who [63] is willing to do a decent day's work." My thoughts went back to the accounts of the people of Alabama as they lived before removal. I remembered how they were described as being among the most industrious and hard working of the Lower Creeks. I remembered the passage in which it was said that they were the "granary" of the region in which they lived, raising not only enough corn for themselves, but a surplus which they sold to the early military posts of the district. And here were their descendants, a likely enough looking group, labelled as being unwilling to do a decent day's work!

I left that particular meeting at about five o'clock. It never occurred to me that the discussion would pass on to anything other than the wording of the constitution. But these "shirkers" and "dancers" and "ritualists" evidently had something else on their minds. A few days later I met the Creek (a member of another Town) who had acted as interpreter at the meeting. "You should have stayed on," he told me.

> They just began to get busy after you fellows cleared out. That meeting lasted till ten o'clock that night. They wore me out. I had to go to bed about nine. They said that now that they are going to organize, they ought to do something about it. They said they ought to show they mean business by getting together and doing something for the Town, something that will build up the treasury so that they can help some of the poor ones among them. They went right to work. One woman of the Town offered to let them use twelve acres of good land which she owns if they will put a crop in. She has no men folks to farm it. They are going to put in a cotton crop, and they picked out a man to watch out for it and take charge of the work. He has to get others to work on it when they haven't got something else to do. They are taking up a collection for the seed money, but the money from the sale is all going to the Town. Then they began talking about putting up some buildings at their square for the use of the Town, sort of a community house. They bought one small building very reasonably from a member of the Town. Then they were given another building and the lumber from a barn that isn't being used any more. They are figuring on putting up a commissary with this; they'll buy groceries at wholesale and pass them on to the members at cost. [64]

At a meeting of Indian Service employees held a little later I ventured to mention the information which had been given me. From an important Indian Service official of eastern Oklahoma I drew a pitying look. "They haven't done any of this yet, and they probably won't. They get great ideas and enthusiasms, those people, but they disappear just as fast. I wish I could remember all the great things they were going to do that never were finished." And he dismissed the subject with a resigned glance which plainly told what the hardheaded administrator has to contend with from the various dreamy specialists sent to plague him.

A few weeks later I was asked to come to the home of one of the officers of Alabama Town. He wished to know what had become of the constitution which his group had sent in for approval. We discussed the mechanics of organization for a while, and then I remembered the story of the Town enterprise. I mentioned that I had heard of that part of the meeting which took place after my departure and asked whether any of the plans discussed had ever been put into operation. Very quietly, and not without pride, he told me that they had. The crop had been planted and was already above ground. The working schedule of volunteer labor was functioning smoothly. "And that is not all," he went on to say. "The women of our Town got together, too. They said, "We belong to this line as well as the men. We can contribute something too." So they have formed a sewing club. They do any kind of sewing for whites. Creeks, or other Indians and charge for it. All the money goes into a fund for the Town. Just now they are making patchwork quilts." I asked whether there was any evidence of their handiwork around. He called his niece, who lives with him, and she brought out an adequately made quilt which she said was the seventh one which the club had made since the work had begun.

Something had happened to these people. Human energy is like any other kind of energy. The proper conditions must obtain before it can be expressed and tapped. Qualities which could not be awakened when the people felt isolated and divided were evoked when the opportunity for common action and renewed integration seemed possible. An attitude which even the best of Indian Service employees could not stimulate became manifest as soon as Creek leaders saw some opening for their talents.

A number of times I have been asked: "What percentage of Creeks belong to Tribal Towns?" The question is irrelevant. Every Creek, at least every Creek whose mother is also a Creek, belongs by birth to some Town. A child's Town membership follows that of his mother. When the mother is a white woman or a woman of some other tribe, the children are normally adopted into the Town of the father. [65]

Some people with whom I have conferred have thought that only those who actively participate in the affairs 'of the Town should be considered members. Such an interpretation is a new departure in the classification of Indians, as far as I know. Cheyennes are not considered Cheyennes because they become politically conscious but because they are born Cheyennes. In like manner members of Tribal Towns are members by virtue of birth or adoption.

It has been further argued that because only a small percentage of the members of Tribal Towns have been politically active in the affairs of the Nation, interest in the Towns is at low ebb and that therefore they should not be organized under the Oklahoma Indian Welfare Act. Superintendent Landman came dangerously close to this argument in his letter of March 29, 1937, to Mr. Monahan.[90] In that letter he stated that in the last election to choose a Principal Chief of the Creek Nation only 25 per cent of the eligible voters cast ballots, though the ballots were distributed through members of the Creek legislative body, who are nominally supposed to represent Tribal Towns. The inference drawn from this circumstance, by a logic which I confess I cannot comprehend, was that not more than 25 per cent of the Creeks are interested in Towns.

In the first place there is a whole section of Creek population, whose members belong to various Towns, which will not participate in any election for Principal Chief of the Creek Confederacy or Nation. The members of the Four Mothers Society are in this group. Here is an excerpt from a statement I took from one of the prominent members of that organization.

> One half of the Creeks meet at Okmulgee according to the old law that has been withdrawn, [i.e., the old law which permitted the Creeks to have their own government]. And one half of us stand on the 1832 treaty. The others have no right to have a Chief, no right to have a capitol house. They have nothing to stand on. But they still hold meetings. They have a Creek general convention. They elected a Principal Creek Chief. I didn't vote. They had no right to elect a Chief. We only had our own Town Chiefs long ago.

It can scarcely be held that this man's interest in the election of a Principal Chief and his interest in Tribal Towns are synonymous. And he is one of the leaders of a powerful section of

---

[90]/15 This letter, which is introduced to indicate the type of official resistance that developed, appears as Appendix E. Both A.C. Monahan, the Regional Coordinator of the Indian Service, and A.M. Landman, the Superintendent of the Five Civilized Tribes, were extremely lukewarm toward the organization of Creek Towns, probably because they had been very active in planning for county associations in eastern Oklahoma and saw any other development as a challenge to their scheme.

Creek opinion. Moreover, bearing in mind that the centralized Creek government with its Principal Chief was established largely to arrest the power of the Towns, the election of the Principal Chief is hardly the issue on which to test the interest in the Tribal Towns. At a meeting of [66] members of the Tribal Town of Alabama, attended by approximately seventy adult Creeks, I asked how many present had voted in the general Creek election for Principal Chief. Less than 10 per cent of those present indicated that they had done so.

But even if it could be proved that only 25 per cent of the total membership of the Towns was politically active, it would not automatically follow that too little interest to warrant organization exists. Throughout organizational work in the Indian Service it has been assumed that the group actively interested in organization will be relatively small. The participation of 30 per cent of the eligible voters has been deemed sufficient justification for continuing with the program in any tribe. In Oklahoma, in specific cases, it has been ruled that this percentage may even be reduced. If Mr. Landman's argument is sound, it is a criticism of the whole Indian reorganization program rather than a questioning of Creek Town organization. However, there is no need to judge participation in Town programs by the number of votes cast in the last election for Principal Chief. In that election less than two thousand Creeks voted. Yet I have evidence that over five thousand individual Creeks participated, throughout the year, in the rituals, games, dances, or meetings at over twenty Town squares.

It has also been asserted that the members of any one Town are too scattered for concerted action, that most Towns have some members in various parts of Creek territory. This assertion seems to me to be as strained as some of the others. Even if a Town's members were as scattered as has been pictured, I doubt that the difficulties would be insurmountable. Creek country is not so vast that vitally interested members could not manage somehow to get together. We tend to forget that Town members come together now for meetings and rituals and that these occasions bring scattered individuals to the Town square even though their homes are some distance away. This summer a Creek of my acquaintance told me when the Busk of his Town was to take place. Since the dates change each year and this individual was living at some distance from the center of his Town's population, I asked him how he knew of the coming event. He answered that "the word had been passed on to him." Of course he succeeded in getting to the square at the appointed time. In other words, it is my strong conviction that if the Towns are given something tangible for which to get together, the members will not fail to gather.

This preoccupation with the scattered condition of the Towns seems peculiar in the face of developments in organization elsewhere. A tribe in the north of the state whose membership is greatly scattered was organized with no qualms. Ballots to absentee voters were mailed out. No one questioned the procedure or thought the tribe too diffuse to lend itself [67] to organization. The Cheyennes and Arapahoes live interspersed among white farmers, in parts of seven different counties. But no one said that they should not be organized for that reason.

Yet the depiction of the scattered Town has been somewhat overdrawn. It is true that there is some scattering. Allotment, for which the Creeks are hardly responsible, accounts for much of it. Those who would not take allotments initially were given tracts without their consent, and these unfortunates were likely to find themselves far from their Townsmen. Sometimes young people, who were never given allotments, are forced to go far afield in search of employment. Some who have lost allotments which were once theirs find themselves far from their Tribal Town home. Occasionally a well-educated Creek obtains employment in the government service or in a profession and must go where his work takes him.

But in almost every case, the solid majority of the members of a Town reside in the immediate vicinity of the Town square and church. At Hickory Ground Town I was told that 80 per cent of the membership lives within McIntosh County. At most of the Towns it was proved to my satisfaction that most of the members of the Town lived within a five-mile radius of the Town square, thus forming a rural community of Townsmen with headquarters at the square grounds or church. The Creeks themselves are eager to keep the Town membership as compact as possible. To this end they wish the land acquisition program to be connected with the organized Towns, so that their young, landless members will find land to till at home. This is one of the most earnest objectives behind the desire of the Alabamas to organize under the Oklahoma Indian Welfare Act.

Very little official attention has been given to the Towns since the days of allotment, and so the question of how many Towns have maintained their internal organization and at least some of their functions is a most important one.

In what follows I have arranged the Towns according to the moieties or side of the dual division of Creek Towns to which they belong. Only the Towns which still maintain their Town squares and their Busk as well as a church are here enumerated.

Of those anciently called the "Red" Towns or those on the same side of the fire as the important "Mother" or "Foundation" Town of *Tokipahchi*, the following exist today:

Tokipahchi, with square grounds 7 miles north and east of Holdenville.
Laplako, with square grounds 10 miles southeast of Okemah.
Kayaleychi, with square grounds about 6 miles northeast of Hanna. [68]
Hilapi, with square grounds 2 miles east of Hanna.
Yofala Kaneyti, with square grounds west of Eufaula.
Alabama, with square grounds 9 miles east of Wetumka.

Of the "White" Towns or Towns sometimes said to be on the Apihka side of the fire, the following carry on full functions:

Apihka, with square grounds southeast of Henryetta.
Asilanapi, or Greenleaf, with square grounds 4 miles southwest of Okemah.
Lalokalka, or Fishpond, with square grounds near those of Greenleaf.
Kasihta, with square grounds southeast of Okmulgee.
Nuyaka, with square grounds 12 miles northeast of Okemah.
Okchayi, with square grounds 6 miles east of Hanna.
Pakantalahasi, with square grounds 3 miles east of Vernon.
Oyokofki, with square grounds 4 miles west of Hanna.
Ochiapofa, or Hickory Ground, with square grounds southeast of Henryetta.
Talwalako, or Big Town, with square grounds 7 miles east of Henryetta.
Talmochasi, or New Tulsa, with square grounds 2 miles from Spaulding.
Talahasochi, or Old Tulsa, with square grounds 6 miles southeast of Holdenville.
First *Yotchi* Town, with square grounds 5 miles west of Kellyville.
Second *Yotchi* Town, with square grounds south of Bristow.

Thus we find a nucleus of twenty Towns, scattered in all parts of Creek country, which have adhered to their ancient mode of organization in every detail.

Returning to the Towns on the "Red" or *Tokipahchi* side of the fire, we find that there are other Towns, which, although they have not continued the upkeep of square grounds of their own, have preserved, by one means or another, their identity and group characteristics. The Tribal Town of *Kowasati* Number 1, whose members lived near the people of Alabama, have thrown their lot in with the Alabamas and the two Towns have formed one unity known as Alabama-Kowasati. These two groups were historically related in years past in the southland. At one time they spoke slightly varying dialects of one language, and it is possible that they represent offshoots of one stock.

Atasi is another Town on this side of the fire which discontinued its own square grounds and Busk. But, through church affiliation and social service work, a certain amount of solidarity has been maintained among its members. The people of *Atasi* live mostly around Weleetka, and those who [69] are interested in Town ritual go to the square grounds of *Laplako* at the time of the Busk. If organization by Towns is initiated, *Atasi* may be reestablished in a formal sense or may choose to make some sort of an organizational alliance with *Laplako*.

Liwahli is another Town which today lacks a Town square but whose members still feel a strong central bond. This Town formerly had its square southeast of Wetumka. *Liwahli* is said to be the "Mother" Town of *Laplako*, that is, *Laplako* was formed by the division of *Liwahli*. Since the people of the two historically allied Towns live in the same general region, it may be possible to unite them once more for the purposes of organization. *Liwahli* still has officers and a skeleton of internal organization of its own.

Kawita (*Coweta*) and its offshoot, *Likachka*, were Towns of former importance which have suffered loss of membership and prestige in recent years. Most of the people affiliated with them live north of *Eufaula*. *Chiyaha* is another Town of the *Tokipahchi* side or moiety which was closely allied with *Kawita* but which no longer maintains a separate "fire" or square grounds. These Towns, allied as they are by former bonds of origin and contact, might very well unite to perfect a single strong organization.

It should be remarked, too, that the three Tribal Towns of *Kayaleychi*, *Hilapi*, and *Yofala Kaneyti*, though each now has square grounds of its own, are close geographically and close also in terms of contacts and friendly relations. It is not impossible that common problems and interests will bring these groups still nearer together and that an organizational coalescence may finally take place.

On the "White" or Apihka side of the fire, in addition to the Towns already listed as having their own fires, there are a number of others whose survival and vitality should be noted. The first of these is *Akfaski*, whose members live northwest of Okemah. *Akfaski* has had a varied history. At one time it was one of the most thriving Towns of the Creek Confederacy. It is credited with having had a number of branches or offshoots, one of which was the Town of *Nuyaka*. *Akfaski* suffered much disorganization and havoc during the Civil War period and declined to the point where it did not preserve all the characteristics of separate political existence. For some years its members have been going to the square grounds of Nuyaka for the annual Busk, but lately the population of *Akfaski* has shown an upward trend, and there has been revived interest in reestablishing a Town square. It is fairly certain that this group will have its separate grounds by next year. [70]

The revival of *Akfaski* refutes a very popular fallacy concerning these Towns, namely, that they are all "dying out." For a while the decimation which attended removal, the active hostility of the missionaries, and the discouragements of the allotment period threatened the existence of a number of Towns, but, if anything, a revival of interest is taking place in regard to them today. This is a fact that some of the workers in Creek territory cannot seem to see, in part because they are reluctant to admit the existence of the trend, no doubt. It brings to mind an incident which occurred during my Creek researches. After the close of a meeting in the vicinity of Hanna, I was sitting in an automobile, talking to a farm aid of the region. He was telling me, "The Indians of this district are not interested in these Towns," when, at that most inopportune moment, there was a rap at the window, and an Indian interrupted to say that the Creeks of the Tribal Town of *Okchayi* were interested in organizing as a Town and wished to have a meeting to discuss the subject.

Another indication of the vigor of the Towns is that the process of creation of new Towns by the division of older Towns into two parts is still taking place. At the time of allotment the Yotchi had but one Town. Today they have two Towns, each with its separate square grounds. In the same way, within the last eight years, the Tribal Town of Talsi (*tulsa*) has split into New Tulsa and Old Tulsa.

Of course, there have been adjustments in the other direction as well. *Tokpafka*, an offshoot of *Oyokofki*, has been absorbed again by *Oyokofki*. The Towns of *Taskigi* and *Oywohka* diminished in numbers and importance and have just about been absorbed by other Towns. The father-in-law of one of my informants was born a member of *Oywohka*. When that Town seemed on the verge of passing out of existence, he transferred over to *Pakantalahasi*. *Tokpafka* and *Oywohka* were both on the *Apihka* side of the dual division. Another Town on this side of the fire which no longer has square grounds of its own is *Hichiti*, which was once located northeast of Henryetta. The survivors from *Hichiti* are now closely allied with *Kasihta*. Still another Town of this moiety which is still in existence, though without square grounds of its own, is *Apihkochi*, or Little *Apihka*. The people of this Town are now in closest touch with the people of *Nuyaka* and *Akfaski*.

To summarize the relations between the Towns of this moiety, the following observations are in order: *Asilanapi*, *Lalokalka*, and *Okchayi* are traditionally and practically bound together by various ties. They are supposed to assist each other in the ball game and on other occasions.

Kasihta, *Hichiti*, and *Talwalako* have pretty much fused forces. It is possible that these three would even welcome a joint organization. [71]

Tokpafka and *Oyokofki* have merged for all practical purposes.

Nuyaka and *Akfaski* are closely related also. More remotely these two are supposed to be connected with the *Talsi* Towns.

Lochapoka is an outgrowth of *Talsi* and its closest affiliations can be looked for in that direction. Traditionally Hickory Ground is credited with being the "Mother" of the *Talsi* and *Akfaski* Towns. In any organizational work it is necessary to keep these alignments in mind.

The picture we get of contemporary Creek Town organization is this: The Towns are divided into two major divisions or moieties. The member Towns of each of these moieties have their closest relations with each other and are expected to help one another in ceremonial and practical contexts. Therefore the people who may be expected to work best together today are those who belong to Towns of the same moiety. Within each moiety there are clusters of Towns, which, because the Towns were derived from a common source or are in some way historically or traditionally related, cooperate for work, social occasions, or ritual. Twenty of these Towns still have Town squares. Another one is about to renew its square grounds (*Akfaski*). A number of other Towns share the square grounds of neighboring Towns of the same side of the fire (e.g., *Kowasati*).

It need not surprise or perturb anyone to learn that the Towns are not precisely as they were in 1895 in number, individual importance, and alignment. Social change is continuous; we cannot bid it stop. We know that the Seminoles are a southern offshoot of the Creeks.

Nevertheless they are recognized as a separate people because they differentiated enough in interests and geographical position over a period of time. A number of separate Apache tribes I studied in previous field work are without question the result of the division of one parental stock. And we know that many of the tribes which the United States government considers a unified whole have reached their present condition by the amalgamation of a number of formerly diverse peoples. I inject this train of thought at this point because I would consider it calamitous to have it ruled that only Creek Towns recognized by the government in 1895 (the date of the last official census of them) may be organized. We cannot permanently arrest Creek social organization as of 1895 and frown on unions and divisions which have occurred since. Since the discovery of America, whole tribes such as the Carriso and the Karankawa have disappeared, while other tribes such as the Navajo have increased in numbers. This flux is no less true of Creek Towns. The manner in which to proceed, if we are to proceed in this direction at all, is to determine whether a group with the characteristics of a Town should be organized and [72] then to go ahead with the organization of groups which exhibit such characteristics at the present time.

Mention has been made of the transfer of individuals from one Town to another by adoption. It is well to know how this is accomplished. When a Creek feels that he has sufficient reason to ask for the transfer, he consults the _miko_ or Chief of the Town to which he wishes to belong. If this officer feels that the action is justified, he consults the _miko_ of the Town to which the person belongs by birth. If objections are raised at that end, the adoption cannot take place; the consent of the Town of one's birth must always be obtained. The _miko_ of _Kasihta_ told me of a recent case involving a woman named Katy Yardy, who wished to transfer from _Hilapi_ to his Town of _Kasihta_. This man had a talk with the _miko_ of Hilapi, and the Hilapi _miko_ agreed to release the woman. Accordingly she was adopted into _Kasihta_. This mechanism may be important in two ways in organizational work if it proceeds by Towns. When there are but a few survivors of a Town, they can no doubt be adopted into Towns where they are well known. And when work on his allotment keeps a person so far from his Town that he cannot take part in its activities, he may be able, if he is willing, to transfer to a Town more conveniently situated for his purpose.

That the organizations and alignments which have been here described have meaning for the Creeks is beyond cavil; otherwise they would not have been retained for hundreds of years and into the present. It may be that the system of Creek social organization that exists is not the most logical one that an administrator, organizer, or student can conceive as he sits at a desk. But it happens to be the one that the Creeks have evolved and understand. There are always individuals who are genuinely inspirational when it comes to ordering the social life and philosophy of others. Once when I was discussing the problem with an Indian Service employee, this man exclaimed in a tone of pleasant discovery: "Why don't we organize the Creek Towns into one big council?" He simply cut through all Creek concepts concerning moiety, foundation Towns, etc., to what seemed to him to be the simplest solution. The answer is that we could do as he suggested, and it would not at all surprise me if we did. It is possible, considering the straits of the Creeks and the prestige and authority of the United States government, to set up almost any kind of an organization we choose. But if we do seek a solution unencumbered by moieties, individual Towns, and the like, we shall have to instigate it and we shall have to manage it. The Creeks will simply regard the scheme as another of the white man's toys and will never move to use it as a lever for social, political, and economic betterment. What is not of a people is simply window dressing. It may be of formal use, but it is bound to be a functional loss. [73]

As I see it, there are two chief obstacles to organization by Towns. One is the skeptical and even hostile attitude of individuals within the Indian Service. The facts — and it is useless to try to dodge the issue — are these. For a long time aid to Indians moved along on an individual merit basis. The government employee advised, taught, and demonstrated. When he found an Indian who listened to him and followed instructions, that Indian was encouraged and rewarded. Today we see the futility of dealing with each Indian as an individual case. We see the necessity for evoking Indian leadership, for freeing social forces, and for organizing cultural values which are stronger than any words of a coldly regarded white man. But most of the Indian Service employees were trained in the first school of thought and are strongly suspicious of the second. Their knowledge of social dynamics is not too vast. Organization is something to accomplish simply and with dispatch so that the real work of the morrow may go on. Time and again I have heard such persons tell the Indians at an organization meeting: "This is a strictly business proposition." With this I profoundly disagree. No economic plan which does not have reference to social forces can succeed unless it constitutes slavery.

To a government employee of a certain outlook, concern over Creek Towns will seem particularly useless and provoking. In the first place, the Towns were liquidated by the United States government for all practical purposes long before he came into the Service, and so the issue comes to him as an unfamiliar surprise. Since the Town rolls have been allowed to lapse, he sees work ahead to bring records up to date, etc. An employee who works in a county of Creek country asked me sourly how many Towns there were in his particular area. When I gave the count as six, he said with feeling: "That means that I'll have just six times as much work to do as I would have if we had one credit association for the County." I answered that the idea was to have the Indians and not him take the responsibility and do most of the work. But my words evidently did not carry conviction, for he returned: "Oh, I know who will do all the work. I know just how much they can be expected to do."

The other obstacle to organizing by Towns is the well-founded suspicion among the Indians that it will do them no good to permit governmental interference with their Towns. From long experience the Indian has learned that when the government takes a native institution under its wing, the Indian is rarely able to recognize what is left of it when it is handed back. An incident connected with the Alabama-Kowasati constitution will serve as an example. These Creeks said that they wished to have their *miko* or chief political officer elected for life, his term to be ended only by resignation, impeachment, or death. This aroused a mild storm in organizational circles. It appeared that the tenets [74] of democracy were being violated; too much power was being concentrated in one man's hands. Now it so happens that we elect our chief executive in a general election every four years, but it is also true that another high officer, quite as important in many respects, the chief judicial officer of our country, is appointed for a life term. Therefore the appointment of officials to high offices for long terms is not foreign to our political life. What was being insisted on in the case of the Creek Town Chief is that the mechanics of his elevation exactly duplicate the procedure followed in the election of the President of the United States. The Creeks did not suggest a long term for their chief executive because they wished to flout the sensibilities of those who admire the way white Americans do such things. Their request had direct relation to their social organization. As has been noted before, each clan or important group of lineages within a Town has particular functions to perform in the political economy of that Town. From one clan the Chief is selected. Other clans contribute other officers and care for other duties. These Creeks wished their organization to function smoothly and traditionally. The possibility of having the office become a political football did not intrigue them. In fact, they would feel uncomfortable and insecure if a person of the wrong social segment held the office. My feeling is that Indian organizations should be truly Indian in character or that a different terminology should be employed. Some of the Creeks with whom I had contact seemed to feel that their Towns, struggling and incomplete though they were, were still their own, and they hesitated to make them the focus of the government's attention.

It has been said that, even though organization by Towns may take care of a section of Creek population, there are other mixed-blood Creeks who are totally divorced from Town activities and who would wish to obtain credit through other channels. It is also said that since the mixture of races will continue, this will be increasingly the case. It is undoubtedly true that there are Creeks, particularly mixed bloods, who are totally disinterested in their own culture and Towns. Educational and missionary work which aimed at this result have not been entirely in vain. Before one of the Town rituals took place, I met such a Creek. I asked him something about the music I might expect to hear at the ceremony. He answered: "They don't have any music; they just run around in a circle and yell. I wouldn't *go* across the street to see them make fools of themselves." I went to the ceremony, nevertheless, and heard some of the most interesting Indian music to which I have ever listened. It is apparent that a man with the views of this Creek would not be likely to seek credit through his Tribal Town.

But it must be realized that approximately two-thirds of the Creeks are listed on the rolls as having one-half or [75] more Indian blood. It is unlikely that there will be in the immediate future as much Indian-white mixture as there has been in the past. In the first place, the Creeks of an appreciable degree of Indian blood are resisting intermarriage more strongly than they have before. In the second place, the peculiar conditions which encouraged mixed marriages no longer exist. Under frontier conditions there was an influx of unattached white men who established permanent or temporary attachments with Indian women. Later, when it became apparent that allotment would take place, many whites deliberately married Indians for little other reason than the material gain that was forthcoming. Today the Creek Indian is submerged economically and accused by some whites of having Negro blood.

It can be expected, if present conditions prevail, that those who have a heavy percentage of white blood will continue to mingle and marry with whites and gradually pass completely out of the orbit of Creek culture. It is also likely that the number and percentage of Creek full bloods will increase. It is a question, considering the large number of Creek full bloods living today, whether we have not, when considering matters of organization and credit, been too solicitous concerning the Americanized fringe of mixed bloods. Very often when I mention Tribal Towns or kindred matters, I am told: "Only the full-blood element is interested in that." The full-blood element, after all, constitutes the predominant sector of Creek society.

It may be that there will exist enough individuals uninterested in Towns and unable to work through them to make it advisable to form a credit association or several such associations to take care of their needs. However, it seems to me that we are obligated to attempt an intelligent organization of all viable American Indian institutions before deciding to supplement these with other social or fiscal structures. If Creeks exist who are unwilling or unable to work through their own institutions, they may be considered as individuals par excellence, and the individual loan provision of the Oklahoma Indian Welfare Act would be particularly suited to their needs.

Morris E. Opler
Assistant Anthropologist 1937

Opler

PAPERS IN ANTHROPOLOGY

A Scholarly Journal
For Professional Anthropologists
And Others Interested In General Anthropology
And Its Various Subfields

Volume 13 | Spring 1972 | Number 1

Editor
Harold N. Ottaway

Re-printed 1977

PAPERS IN ANTHROPOLOGY is a publication sponsored by the Department of Anthropology, University of Oklahoma. It is devoted to the dissemination of papers based on research in all areas of anthropology. Individuals wishing to submit papers for possible publication and/or those wishing to subscribe to the journal should write to:

PAPERS IN ANTHROPOLOGY
Department of Anthropology
University of Oklahoma
455 West Lindsey
Norman,
Oklahoma 73019

*Published
Semi-Annually*

The University of Oklahoma is an Equal Opportunity Institution.
This publication has been prepared and distributed at no cost to the taxpayers of the
State of Oklahoma

181

TABLE OF CONTENTS

APPENDICES

BIBLIOGRAPHY

Adair, James
1775 *The History of the American Indians*. London.

Anonymous
1907 "Creeks." Handbook of American Indians North of Mexico, Part 1, edited by F.W. Hodge. *Bureau of American Ethnology Bulletin* 30, pp. 362-365. Washington.
1910 "Upper Creeks." Handbook of American Indians North of Mexico, Part 2, edited by F.W. Hodge. *Bureau of American Ethnology Bulletin* 50, p. 872. Washington.

Bartram, William
1955 *Travels of William Bartram,* edited by Mark Van Doren. Dover Publications. New York. First published in 1791.

Callacombe, Doris
1933 "Alexander Lawrence Posey." *Chronicles of Oklahoma,* Vol. 11, No. 4, pp. 1011-1018.

Cohen, Felix S.
1941 *Handbook of Federal Indian Law*. U. S. Government Printing Office. Washington.

Davis, Edward
1937 "Early Life among the Five Civilized Tribes." *Chronicles of Oklahoma,* Vol. 15, No. 1, pp. 70-101.

Davis, Mace
1935 "Chitto Harjo." *Chronicles of Oklahoma*, Vol. 13, No. 2, pp. 139-145.

Dawes, Anna L.
1907 "Commission to the Five Civilized Tribes." Handbook of American Indians North of Mexico, Part 1, edited by F.W. Hodge. *Bureau of American Ethnology Bulletin* 30, pp. 332-333. Washington. [114]

Foreman, Carolyn Thomas
1929 "Alexander McGillivray, Emperor of the Creeks.'" *Chronicles of Oklahoma*, Vol. 7, No. 1, pp. 106-120.

Foreman, Grant
1934 *The Five Civilized Tribes*. University of Oklahoma Press. Norman.

Gatschet, Albert S.
1884 *Migration Legend of the Creek Indians*. Philadelphia.
1901 "Towns and Villages of the Creek Confederacy in the XVIII and XIX Centuries." *Publications of the Alabama Historical Society, Miscellaneous Collections* Vol. 1, pp. 386-415. Montgomery.
1907 "Lower Creeks." Handbook of American Indians North of Mexico, Part 1, edited by F.W. Hodge. *Bureau of American Ethnology Bulletin* 30, p. 776. Washington.

Gatschet, Albert S. and Cyrus Thomas
1907 "Alibamu." Handbook of American Indians North of Mexico, Part 1, edited by F. W. Hodge. *Bureau of American Ethnology Bulletin* 30, pp. 43-44. Washington.

Haas, Mary R.
1940 "Creek Inter-Town Relations." *American Anthropologist* Vol. 42 (3): 479-489.

Menasha.

Haas, Theodore H.

1947 *Ten Years of Tribal Government Under I.R.A.* Tribal Relations Pamphlets – 1. United States Indian Service. Washington.

Hall, Arthur H.

1934 "The Red Stick War: Creek Indian Affairs During the War of 1812." *Chronicles of Oklahoma*, Vol. 12, No. 3, pp. 264-293.

Hawkins, Benjamin

1848 A Sketch of the Creek Country. *Collections of the Georgia Historical Society.* Savannah. [115]

Lambert, O.A.

1926 "Historical Sketch of Col. Samuel Checote, Once Chief of the Creek Nation." *Chronicles of Oklahoma,* Vol. 4, No. 5, pp. 275-280.

Meserve, John Bartlett

1931a "Chief Opothleyahola." *Chronicles of Oklahoma*, Vol. 9, No. 4, pp. 439-453.
1931b "Chief Pleasant Porter." *Chronicles of Oklahoma*, Vol. 9, No. 3, pp. 318-334.
1932a "Chief *Isparhecher*." *Chronicles of Oklahoma*, Vol. 10, No. 1, pp. 52-76.
1932b "The MacIntoshes." *Chronicles of Oklahoma*, Vol. 10, No. 3, pp. 310-325.
1933 "The Plea of Crazy Snake (Chitto Harjo)." *Chronicles of Oklahoma*, Vol. 11, No. 3, pp. 899-911.

Milford, L.L.D.

1956 *Memoir or a Cursory Glance at My Different Travels*, edited by J.F. McDermott. Chicago. First published in 1802.

Morton, Ohland

1930 "The Government of the Creek Indians." *Chronicles of Oklahoma*, Vol. 8, No. 1, pp. 42-64; Vol. 8, No. 2. pp. 189-225.
1931 "Early History of the Creek Indians." *Chronicles of Oklahoma*, Vol. 9, No. 1, pp. 17-26.

Nathanson, Jerome (editor)

1946 *Science for Democracy.* King's Crown Press. New York. (See remarks by Morris E. Opler and Felix S. Cohen regarding Creek Towns, p. 118 ff.)

Opler, Morris E.

1952 "The Creek 'Town' and the Problem of Creek Indian Political Reorganization." *Human Problems in in Technological Change*, edited by Edward H. Spicer, pp. 165-180. Russell Sage Foundation. New York. [116]

Speck, Frank G.

1907 "The Creek Indians of Taskigi Town." *Memoir of the American Anthropological Association*, Vol. 2, Pt. 2, Dec., pp. 99-164. Lancaster.
1909 "Ethnology of the Yuchi Indians." *Anthropological Publications of the University of Pennsylvania*, Vol. 1, No. 1. Philadelphia.

Swanton, John R.

1907 "Koasati." In Handbook of American Indians North of Mexico, Part 1, edited by F.W. Hodge. *Bureau of American Ethnology Bulletin* 30, pp. 719-720. Washington.
1922 "Early History of the Creek Indians and Their Neighbors." *Bureau of American*

Ethnology Bulletin 73. Washington.

1928 "Social Organization and Social Usages of the Indians of the Creek Confederacy." *Forty-Second Annual Report of the Bureau of American Ethnology*, BAE-AR 42nd: pp. 23-472. Washington.

1931 "Modern Square Grounds of the Creek Indians." *Smithsonian Miscellaneous Collections*, Vol. 85, No.8, pp.1-46. Washington.

1932 "The Green Corn Dance." *Chronicles of Oklahoma*, Vol. 10, No. 2, pp. 170-195.

1934 "Introduction." The Five Civilized Tribes by Grant Foreman, pp. xiii-xiv. University of Oklahoma Press. Norman.

Thomas, Cyrus

1907   "Five Civilized Tribes." Handbook of American Indians North of Mexico, Part 1, edited by F.W. Hodge. *Bureau of American Ethnology Bulletin* 30, pp. 463-464. Washington.

APPENDIX H ~
CREEK TOWNS TO WHICH REFERENCE IS MADE IN THE MONOGRAPH

Name of Town	Phonetic Transcription	Remarks
Akfaski	ákfáski	County of Okfuskee
Alabama	alipa•ma	named after this
Apihka	a•pihka	
Apihkochi	a•pikoči	"little Apihka"
Asilanapi	assila•napi	"green leaf"
Atasi	a•tasi	
Chiyaha	či•ya•ha	
Hichiti	hičiti	Town of Hitchita
		Named after this
Hilapi	hilápi	
Kanchati	kanča•ti	"red ground"
Kasihta	kasíhta	
Kawita	kawíta	
Kayaleychi	kayaleyči	
Kowasati	kowassa•ti	
Lalokalka	łałokalka	"fish pond"
Laplako	ła•płakko	
Likachka	łi•ka•čka	"arrow breaker"
		or "broken arrow";
		town of Broken
		Arrow name after this
Liwahli	łiwa'hli	
Lochapoka	ločapo•ka (or)	"where the turtle lives"
	ločapo•ka talsi	[108]
Nuyaka	no•ya•ka	town of Nuyaka
		named for this
Ochiapofa	oči•apo•fa	Hickory Ground
Okchayi	okča'yi	
Oyokofki	óyókófki	"muddy water"
		(Wiogufki)
Oywohka	oywo•hka	"roaring water"
Pakantalahasi	pakantalaha•si	
Talahasochi	talaha•soči	Old Tulsa
Talmochasi	talmočasi	"new town", New Tulsa
Talsi	talsi	Tulsa named after this.
Talwalako	talwałakko	"big town"
Taskigi	ta•ski•ki	
Tokipahchi	tokipahči	
Tokpafka	tokpa•fka	
Yofala Kaneyti	yofa•la kaneyti	Town of Eufaula
		named after this
Yotchi	yo'tči	

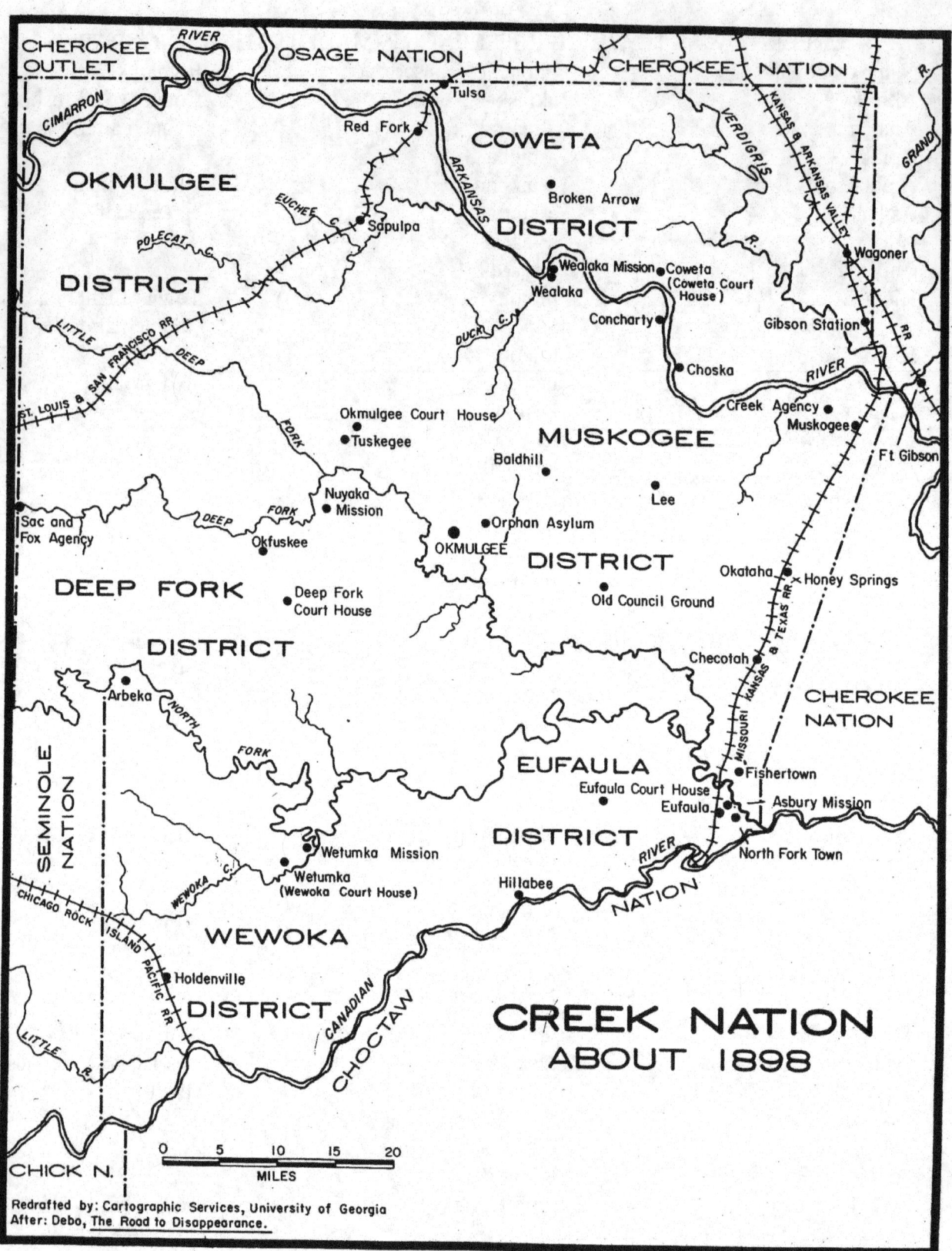

CREEK NATION
ABOUT 1898

Redrafted by: Cartographic Services, University of Georgia
After: Debo, The Road to Disappearance.

KARL SCHMITT
(1915-1953)

By Fred Eggan

COLLISION with a train while driving near Magdalena, New Mexico, on August 6, 1952, resulted in the death of Karl Schmitt and serious injuries to his wife, Iva. He was on the threshold of a brilliant career in anthropology and all who knew his warm personality will feel a deep sense of personal loss.

Karl was born December 20, 1915, in Albany, New York, the son of Karl and Beatrice Schmitt, but the family soon moved to Washington, D.C., where Karl attended William McKinley High School and George Washington University, obtaining his B.S. degree in geology. During his youth he had become interested in local Indian artifacts and had spent much of his time in making archeological collections in the Tidewater area. As a result his interests shifted from geology to archeology. He entered the University of Chicago to study under Dr. Fay-Cooper Cole in the autumn of 1938, after a summer with the U.S. National Museum archeological excavations in western Missouri.

At Chicago his range of activities broadened but archeology remained his central interest. He took part in the Kincaid excavations, but also maintained his relations with the U.S. National Museum, participating in its excavations in Kansas and Virginia. From March 1941-March 1942 he served as archeologist at Ocmulgee National Monument, Macon, Georgia. During this period he married {3 August} a fellow student, Iva Osanai; their twin children, Sigrid and Kirk, were born February 18, 1944.

Soon after receiving his M.A. in the spring of 1942, he was inducted into the army. His background in natural sciences led to his assignment to the meteorological school at the University of Chicago from which he received a certificate of professional competence in meteorology and a commission in the Air Force. He served at various stations in the United States and then was sent to Morotai in the Southwest Pacific. After separation in March, 1946, as a major in the Air Force, he returned to the University of Chicago to continue his studies.

Karl served as a teaching assistant in the department of anthropology while completing his doctoral dissertation on "Archaeological Chronology of the Middle Atlantic States" which was summarized in J.B. Griffin (ed.), *Archeology of the Eastern United States*, University of Chicago Press, 1952. He received his Ph.D. in 1947 and accepted a position as assistant professor of anthropology at the University of Oklahoma.

When he went to Oklahoma his area of specialization again shifted, this time from archeology to ethnology. The large Indian population, with its opportunities for ethnological and social anthropological research, offered a new challenge. With his wife and children, he spent weekends and summers in the field, primarily among the Wichita and Caddo, but also with other groups. He retained his archeological and historical interests but the problems of contemporary change and development began to take precedence. The new "pan-Indian" culture in Oklahoma, the development of factionalism, and the study of changes in social organization and kinship became the major foci around which he organized his researches.

His published papers reflect the variety of his interests. Some, such as his "Notes on Morotai Island Canoes," were by-products of war-time assignments. Of his more recent studies, only his and Iva Schmitt's *Wichita Kinship: Past and Present* had gone to press. This is a notable addition to our knowledge of Plains social organization and an important contribution to the study of problems of social and cultural change. It combines historical and comparative studies in admirable fashion, and develops hypotheses which are both important in themselves and as stimuli to further research. Several manuscripts on various archeological sites, Caddo kinship, Factionalism, and Pan-Indian culture in Oklahoma are largely completed and it is hoped that they can soon be published. His M.A. thesis is to appear in revised form in T. Dale Stewart's *The Historic Indian Village of Patawomeke, Stafford County, Virginia.*

Karl loved his work and he and Iva made many friends among the Indians whom they studied. At the Memorial Service held in Norman, October 5, 1952, a great many Indians came long distances to attend, and the Caddo family which had adopted them spoke of their love and esteem for him. A few days later the Caddoes presented a radio program dedicated to his memory. The University had also recognized his worth and promise. He had recently been promoted to associate professor of anthropology and was to have taken over the chairmanship in September. Karl was a member of the American Anthropological Association, the Society for American Archaeology, the Texas Archaeological and Paleontological Society, and the Oklahoma Archaeological Society, and has been elected to Sigma Xi.

Karl's many friends, both white and Indian, will feel his loss deeply. Their [239] sympathy goes to his wife and children, with a hope that Iva Schmitt can carry forward the research which she and Karl had been pursuing so fruitfully.

UNIVERSITY OF CHICAGO
CHICAGO, ILLINOIS

BIBLIOGRAPHY
Compiled by Robert Bell

1942 "Patawomeke, An Historic Algonkian Site," M.A. thesis, Univ. of Chicago.

1943 "A Dated Silt Deposit in the Ocmulgee River Valley, Georgia," American Antiquity, Vol. VIII, pp. 296-297.

1947 "Notes on Morotai Island Canoes," Man, Vol. 47, Article 127, pp. 119-122.

"Notes on Some Recent Archaeological Sites in the Netherlands East Indies," American Anthropologist, Vol. 49, pp. 331-334.

1949 J.S Slotkin and Karl Schmitt, "Studies of Wampum," American Anthropologist, Vol. 51, No. 2, April-June, pp. 223-236.

1950 "Two Creek Pottery Vessels from Oklahoma," The Florida Anthropologist, Vol. 111, Nos. 1-2, May, pp. 3-8.

1950 "The Lee Site, Gv-3, of Garvin County, Oklahoma," Texas Archaeological and Paleontological Society, Vol. 21, Sept., pp. 69-89.

1950 "Wichita-Kiowa Relations and the 1874 Outbreak," The Chronicles of Oklahoma, Vol. XXVIII, No. 2, pp. 154-160.

1952 "Archaeological Chronology of the Middle Atlantic States," in Archaeology of the Eastern United States, edited by J.B. Griffin, pp. 59-70.

1952 "Wichita Death Customs," The Chronicles of Oklahoma, Vol. XXX, No. 2, pp. 200-206.

1952 Karl And Iva Schmitt, Wichita Kinship: Past and Present, Univ. of Oklahoma Book Exchange, Norman.

KARL SCHMITT pp237-239 AMERICAN ANTHROPOLOGIST 55, 1953

https://anthrosource.onlinelibrary.wiley.com/doi/pdf/10.1525/aa.1953.55.2.02a00070

ARBEKA

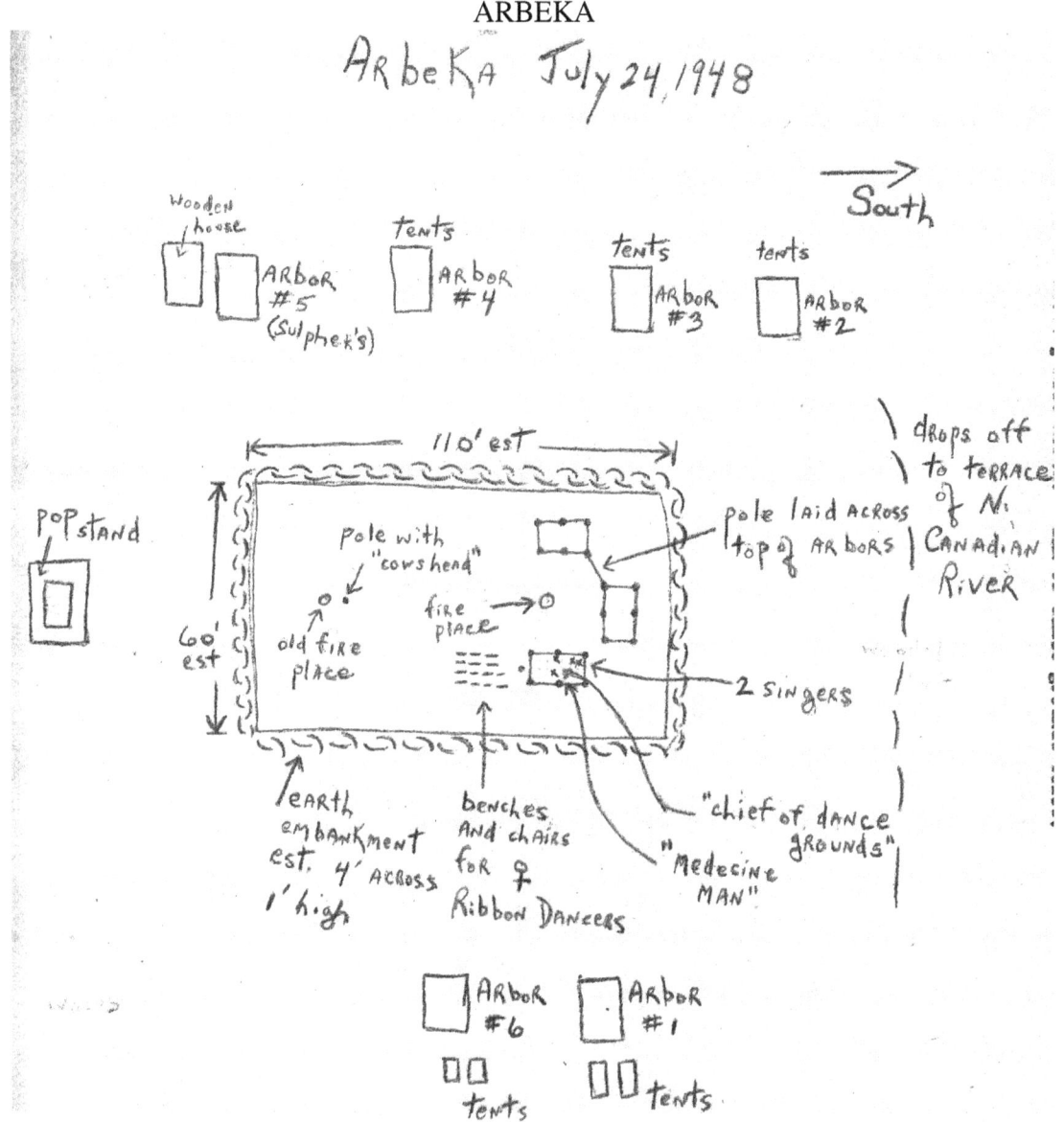

July 24, 1948 [Page. 112] Sometime previously I had called Don Whistler and asked about Green Corn Dances. He told me that the Yuchie were having one near Sapulpa in July, and that the Creeks were having one this week-end at Arbeka. Don said it was supposed to start at 10:00 a.m. We left Norman at 10 and arrived at Arbeka about 1:30 p.m. — no dance had started. Arbeka is 8 miles west of Henryetta and about 9 miles south. On our arrival people were sitting under arbors, and eating, back from the dance ground. We parked under a tree – an Indian family was parked under an adjacent tree and somebody from camp # 5 asked them to come over and eat (at least that was the result of the talking). No one asked us. There was no town in our sense — no houses nearby, except a farm house about a mile north. Plan of dance grounds {above} below: [Page 113]

About 2:30p.m. some men came out and started sitting under the arbors in the dance ground. A big, fat man (Joe Hicks) — came out in front of the west arbor and said something in Creek — later found out it was equivalent of "hurry up." During the afternoon he repeated this on a number of occasions. Joe Hicks was apparently a sort of master of ceremonies, or the equivalent of a Samoan talking chief — he also had an assistant. During the afternoon Joe Hicks and his assistant made circuits of all the arbors and associated camps — about 5 or 6 circuits in all. They would start with arbor #1 (see plan) and go counter clockwise ending with #6. A Creek man of about 40 yrs. told me they were telling the women to hurry up and get ready for the dance. On these circuits they carried short sticks 3 or 3 ½ feet long with one end split, and a downy feather (chicken feather ?) [egret] tied in the split — this apparently is a badge of office.

The "chief of the dance ground" {*mikko*} sat in the front center of the west arbor. He was a young fellow of about 26 yrs. Dresses in army suntans (GI). Sitting around him were a number of men who were his advisors. Sitting in back center of the same arbor was the "medicine man" (later I found out this was Alex Sulpher). The "chief of the dance ground" directed the ceremony with the help of his advisors. This information (except identity of Alec Sulpher) was furnished by my fellow spectator, the approximately 40 yr. old Creek. Joe Hicks did all the audible talking. He would get up and say something very loud in Creek and various men would come over and then go perform errands. Once two men went and got a large iron pot and took it down to the woods south of the dance ground — most, if not all of the men, went down there at some time or other during the afternoon. At another time a number of men were sent to the various camp arbors and got benches and chairs for the women dancers to sit on. Several of the men doing these errands had two short slanting red dashes painted on each cheek. One young fellow with the paint marks looked incongruous with a cigar sticking out of the side of his mouth and a nap brim felt hat.

People kept arriving during the afternoon — including many white people. Heard one white man say that the reason they hadn't started yet was that the men hadn't finished taking medicine — later Mrs. Sulphur and Mrs. Fields said no, they didn't take medicine until the next day.

Somewhere around 3:30, the man in the west arbor made a drum by tying a piece of skin over a can about the size of a two-pound Crisco can. When they tried it out, it sounded like a water drum. At about that time, a man took two cocoanut shell rattles, with wooden handles and holes cut in the shells, and laid them on the ground a little SE of the fire. Later a man (the same one ?) came out and took them back to the west arbor. [Page 114]

Finally about 4:00 the dance started. The women came trooping out of the various camps and arbors, and sat on the benches and chairs to the north of the west arbor. The women were dressed in long (to the ground dresses), and had many ribbons hanging down from their shoulders. A number of young girls (aged 6 - 8 years) had on short dresses. Four "shell dancers" (two real shells and two with cans) sat in front to the left or north. Joe Hicks gave the dancers a talk and then lined up in the order he wanted them — this was almost by apparent age, but there were a few exceptions of older women further back in line. Hicks used his feather-stick as a pointer to tell which woman to get in line next. The four shell dancers were in front. Hicks got a feather ornament which was hanging in the front center of the west arbor and gave it to the leading woman — she also had a wooden knife (or was it a miniature war club) but I'm not certain whether Hicks gave it to her or not. Hicks then got the head of the single-file line of women and his assistant got at the rear — carrying their feather-sticks. Hicks led the line past the west arbor and three times around the fire (big circuits) in a counter-clockwise fashion and then stopped in front of the west arbor. I believe he then gave a speech or talk, but I'm not sure. The shell dancers were facing the men with rattles in the west arbor, and the other dancers were facing in the same direction. Then the men with rattles started rattling and singing very low.

The shell dancers got in time by jumping up and down. The south rattler held his rattle extended to the south (I call it a side rattle) and the dancers turned and did a slow skip dance counter clockwise around the fire and back to the west arbor. The south rattler gave a side rattle as a signal for them to turn and stop. When the dance stopped, the men in the arbors gave what must be a sign of approval — what sounded like a long groan, starting high and gradually descending. The slow dance was repeated, as far as I could see, identically three times. Then came a series of fast dances with identical features (including step, rattle signals, groan of approval, etc.). The difference was the greatly increased tempo and the men giving peculiar yelps (of encouragement) while the dance was going on. At the end of the third fast dance, Hicks led the women counter clockwise around the fire (once) and back to their seats. He then got a bucket of water and a dipper and gave women, who wanted it, drinks.

After a rest period, Hicks and his assistant led the women out past the west arbor and around the fire and back to the west arbor (just one circuit, not three as for the first set of dances). Then the same set of dances (three slow, three fast) was repeated as before — including singing, rattling, groans of approval, yelps of encouragement. Then the dancers were led back to the benches and chairs for a rest and water furnished by Hicks. The dances were repeated twice more — with a rest between. This made a total of four sets of six dances (3 slow, 3 fast). During one rest period two men went out among the spectators and passed hats, taking up a collection. No one said what it was for — I asked my approx. 40 yrs. old neighbor. He wasn't sure, but thought it was to buy tobacco and other things for men conducting the ceremony. Also during the rest period somebody passed out hand bills advertising an Indian Powwow to be held at Sand Springs, Oklahoma [Page 115]

Following the "Ribbon Dance" Joe Hicks got up in front of the west arbor and gave a speech in Creek. Then the "medicine man" (Alex Sulpher) got up and started walking around the fire clockwise and the men sitting under the arbors fell in line in back of him. The four "shell dancers" (women) got in back of Sulpher. This was a version of the "stomp dance" which I learned later from Mrs. Sulpher is called the "Old Dance." This dance was very pleasing to watch and listen. Alex Sulpher had a good voice, and the responses from the other dancers had a practiced air. The dance had walking intervals, parts where Sulpher did a stiff-kneed shuffling step with the shell dancers, and other dancers falling into step with him. There was also occasionally a sort of side hesitation step. This last was the only apparent difference from the stomp dances, which were danced later in the evening. During the walking phase of the dance, the men gave shrill, high-pitched yelps. The "Old Dance" lasted about five minutes, and at the end everyone went off to supper.

After the Old dance, Iva and I and the twins drove down to the N. fork of the Canadian River. There we met an Indian woman and two girls in a big Buick car. We ate our supper and went back to Arbeka. This time we parked beside the big Buick and got to talking with the owner — name of Mrs. Fields. The twins went out into the dance square and played with the Indian kids who were chasing around the pole. Mrs. Fields left and later came back and told us "Those people want you to come over and eat." We (all four Schmitts) went over to the Sulpher's arbor and were fed. The amount of food put out was rather tremendous — the table set about 14 people, and they must have fed continously for almost two hours — when someone got up, someone else sat down. Food was good — fried potatoes, fried pork, boiled beef, bread, jam, cake, "sourcake", coffee, tea, sofke, and more I can't remember. I had never tasted *sofke*, so I asked for it — it was sour and I couldn't drink much. [Page 116]

About 9 p.m. dancing started again. First thing was a "War Dance" by some "Western

Indians" — these turned out to be Caddos. During the afternoon my 40 yr. old. neighbor had mistaken Iva for a "Western Indian" — this led to his telling me that he had heard some were coming to put on a dance. After the "Old Dance" I had gone up and met Joe Hicks and he told me that some "western Indians" — the Caddos — were going to dance that night. Told him that I had "been at Moreau's dance (July 10) and he said Moreau was here. Moreau was sitting under the east arbor so I went over and said hello. Moreau said they were going to "show them some war dancing" that night. The War Dance went on as follow: Moreau and two other men sat on benches just to the north of the same arbor; Joe Hicks got up and made the announcement that the "western Indians" — Caddos — were going to put on a war dance — the announcement was both in Creek and English; Moreau and the other drummers started singing and the little dancer of about five or six years started first, and then his four older (teen aged) companions joined in; later a sixth dancer showed up. The dances were in the now familiar pattern of a song followed by a pause, then a short sort of encore during which the dancers danced back to their seats. There were several such dances. Then each dancer did a solo — Joe Hicks was told the name and he announced it to the crowd — then the song started, the boy got up and danced, was applauded by handclapping, and sat down. The youngest had to do an encore — a real American-European type. Following this Hicks announced that there was to be a collection to pay transportation expenses of the dancers. A couple of men went through the crowd passing hats. The crowd was in a big semi-circle from the west and east arbors. After the collection a "Round Dance" was held. This was also in the now familiar pattern — dancers in a big arc, side by side going clockwise about the fire. The six war dancers were the nucleus of the Round Dance. A lot of the Creeks joined in — evidently in the spirit of fun and curiosity. Joe Hicks joined and got a big laugh. It was rather a poor spectacle — half of the dancers in one step, half in the other, and both halves changing step. However the Creeks and whites enjoyed it. Iva and Sigrid got out and danced.

Concerning War and Round Dances in general. They were not good by Anadarko standards; the drumming and singing was not polished — sort of hesitant (remember at Moreau's Caddo dance, Kiowa drummers and female singers helped for War and Round dances); the War dancing itself was not good — dancers made several mistakes in timing the end of the song; the Round Dance was bad — largely because the great majority didn't know the step. However, I heard many favorable comments both from white and Indian spectators. Mrs. Fields later told me she was thinking of having her boy (apparently an adopted son of four or five years) learn to War Dance — she had heard that someone in Tulsa gave lessons in War dancing. [Page 117]

Following the Round Dance came a series of stomp dances. Joe Hicks walked around the fire (counter clockwise) talking in Creek all the while. Finally a man started walking counter clockwise around the fire, and others fell in line behind, the shell dancers got in behind the leader, and the "stomp dance" followed. I got between the south and east arbors, and sat on the ground and watched. While we were watching some women brought up a wooden bench and set it down just behind me (but within the square grounds.) Mrs. Sulpher and Mrs. Fields came over — they had been looking for us in the dark. They got us to dance a number of dances and told us a lot of things as well. We were told Joe Hicks was picking out the next leader and telling the people about him when he walked around the fire and talked — he carried his feather-stick. His assistant also walked around with his stick but never said anything. Hicks did not dance himself (with one exception to come). Mrs. Fields and Sulpher said "Some leaders are better than others" — people would crowd, to get in when they were leading, Mrs. Sulpher said her husband was good — that he sang in the old way — he led a dance that night, and it was very good.

There was one man of about 55 years who sat under the south arbor who was also good, he wore an old (a few small holes and general wear) shirt but brightly colored. It reminded me of a Seminole shirt even though it was not of the shingled ribbon effect. Mrs. Fields and Sulpher didn't know who he was — when I said he looked like a Seminole because of his shirt, they said that's what it was. One young fellow about 22 years old, was not so good — they said he was from New Tulsa (?) — said when he sang it wasn't the way they used to sing, more like an American song — implied there was too much melody in his singing. Also told me there used to be two white fellows who led dances. The "shell dancers" were of two kinds — one with regular shells of land tortoises made into leg rattles, the others with about 12 Carnation milk cans soldered and wired together in each leg rattle. The real shells have a higher pitched sound — when the cans get in their deeper metallic sounds overpowers the real shells. Both kinds were present at Arbeka — Mrs. Fields said that at Tukabachee they didn't allow cans — only real shells. One of the stomp dances had no shell or can dancers — the woman were tired —— and Mrs. Fields said that dance wasn't so good — missed the shell dancers. [Page 118]

The stomp dance itself always formed a spiral going counter-clockwise. It always stayed the same with the leader in the middle — it never unwound as at the Caddo dance. The dance starts as the picked leader starts walking around the fire —— often at this time the followers gave high pitched yelps. The leader sings phrases — often in a port of yodel — and the followers respond, sometimes with the same phrase, sometimes with a stereotyped short response — the response of the followers is lower than the leader (dropped an octave?). The leader walks and then starts a stiff-kneed shuffle and the can or shell dancers quickly get into the same step — then he may stop the shuffle and walk awhile, and again break into the shuffle. The dancers on the inside of the spiral move rather slowly but those on the outside have to almost run to keep up. Some leaders raise their hand in the air while singing, others put one hand to the mouth, others do neither. Some turn sideways (I thought so that those in back could hear the singing better, Iva thought they were singing to the fire {yes, see p202}). Some vary the stiff-kneed shuffle with a walking squat or duck-waddle step. Some sing slow, some faster — Mrs. Sulpher said the latter was better, made livelier dances. Often the leader ends the dance with a rising *iiiiii*. Joe Hicks led the last dance which was very good. In spite of his tremendous stomach, he got down and danced the duckwaddle with no apparent effort — would move like that well ahead of the shell dancers, would turn sideways and sing. Hicks put some Creek words in his song (Mrs. Fields and Sulpher said most had no meaning) — he sang "old ones are all gone, just you young people left, I'm carrying on."

After leading the last dance, Joe Hicks sat in the west arbor and gave a long oration in Creek — for about ten minutes. Asked Mrs. Fields what he was saying — he was telling the men who were going to take part in the ceremony on the following day to come down and sleep in the arbors and dance place, to come there and not to sleep with their wives, and that tomorrow they were going to take medicine. This is obviously only the gist of what Hicks said since he talked for ten minutes, and it took Mrs. Fields only a minute to tell me the above — she prefaced the statement with something to the effect that they (the Creeks) were different from whites. [Page 119]

Misc. Information volunteered by Mrs. Fields and Sulpher: The Creeks are still divided into towns and membership to a town is inherited through the mother's line. Mrs. Fields belongs to New Tulsa and lives in Henryetta; Mrs. Sulpher belongs to Tukabachee and lives in the town of Eufala (modern white town), I asked about "Red" and "White" towns but they didn't seem to understand what I was after. I also asked about "clans" sitting under certain arbors, but again they didn't seem to comprehend.

The dance we saw was not the "Green Corn Dance" — that would start the next day (Sunday). We saw the "Ribbon Dance". On Sunday the men would take medicine and do the "Feather Dance" — they would wear the shell leg rattles then (I had asked if men ever wore them) {No}. It was permissible for whites to dance the night we were there — the next night they wouldn't allow any whites to dance at all (unfortunately I didn't ask about visiting Indians —something Mrs. Fields said made me think they couldn't either — she said at one time she had to get her dancing in tonight — I'm not sure whether she couldn't dance Sunday, or whether she just wouldn't be there). Told us that they were very strict who dances — if anyone had been drinking even a little, they wouldn't allow then to dance. They knew who had been drinking, (the man in charge knew) — even if only a little — it was implied that there was something mystical about how they told. If someone was suspected of drinking they took them out of the dancing. They were strict how they danced — don't dance holding the waist of the person in front — The Cherokees did that at their dances, and people got drunk, too. Even at this dance they were not as strict as they used to be. They let that "colored man" dance (during the afternoon an obvious Negroid individual with kinky hair and very dark skin sat under the east arbor — later went over to the west arbor and shook hands with everybody sitting under it — apparently talked Creek — he danced in the Old Dance in the afternoon, and in the stomp dances at night.)

During the afternoon the 40 yr. old man told me there would be a "ball game" on Monday — he also said he had been away for 15 or 20 years. I asked Mrs Fields and Sulpher about the ball game — they said it wouldn't be until the end of July or beginning of August. Was told by the 40 yr. old that they tried to hit the "cows head" with the ball — that's what scored the points. They also played the ball game between villages on some occasions — then it took place down in the flat to the south of the dance ground. Inter-village ball games were rough, and often the players got into fights.

One of the dances on Saturday night was different from the Stomp Dances. This, I was told, was a "Double Header." There were two leaders who sang, and two lines of dancers who followed them. In this dance, the dancers held hands and the leaders led the lines around the dance ground.

Whenever a stomp dance started Mrs. Fields and Sulpher would go to the center and break into the line — would take Iva along. I didn't notice men doing the same thing. I asked about it and was told that it was a woman's privilege to break in near the center — it was better to dance there, didn't have to run to keep up with the dance. [Page 120]

I met Dwight Beaver (Caddo) a few day after the Arbeka dance, and asked why he hadn't been at Arbeka. Said Moreau came by his house after him, but he had been at his sister's (Dorothy) house near Cement. Also told me that Moreau had had a group of Caddo war dancers (including Dwight) at a Creek dance the week before (was this the Yuchi affair at Sapulpa?) Moreau had made arrangements there for the Caddos to dance at Arbeka. (Remember Moreau s wife is at least one-half Seminole and owns land with oil wells in the eastern part of the state). Dwight asked me in a very intense manner if they had had a "stomp dance" at Arbeka. Apparently he is very much impressed with them.

In talking to Don Whistler on the phone asking the way to Arbeka, I told him about the Caddo dance – said Billie Johnson and his son were good stomp dancers — Whister said the sons were "good war dancers, too."

195

June 17, 1949, Arbeka Green Corn Dance [355]

The evening that we went to Ralph Morrow's (Caddo) we talked about going to the Arbeka dance. AS a result they decided to go also — Hank Weller had a post card from Joe Hicks (Arbeka Creek) asking them to come over and bring some war dancers. I went and saw Hank the morning of the 17th and he said that he and Ralph and others were going to come on Saturday. So, we went into Anadarko (I already had Dwight Beaver and tried to pick up Bobby Lee Thomas, another teen-age Caddo war dancer). He was at bible school so we went off without him.

We arrived at Arbeka about 6:15 pm. The women's "Ribbon Dance" was still going on. They were dancing and sat down on the benches which had been placed again just north of the west arbor in the square ground. There were relatively few dancers this year — perhaps 15 women and girls. When they sat down a man brought them water — not Joe Hicks this time, but I think his ass't. What I saw of the Ribbon Dance seemed the same as I saw last year.

When the Ribbon Dance was over — there was a short lull. This was followed by the "Old Dance" led by a man named Nichi Gray from the town of New Tulsa (I found out who he was later.) I think some of the women got in the Old Dance, but my memory is poor here. After the old dance two men went to the east and cut oak branches and swept the square ground where the dancing had been going on (around the fire). Both started in front of the west arbor — one going north, and the other south — they met in front of the east arbor and threw their branches on top of that arbor. Each man swept half of the dance circle.

I had seen Don Whistler under an arbor to the east and went to say hello — turned out to be the arbor of Joe and Amy Kinnard. After the Old Dance, Joe Hicks came out of the east arbor and recognised me — called me 'Smitty'. He went around telling visitors to eat under certain arbors — this was to distribute the crowd so that one family wouldn't get all. Most of the visitors were Indians. Iva, Dwight, myself and twins and Pen Whistler and his son were assigned by Hicks to the Kinnards. Supper was primarily weenies and kraut, peaches — not too special.

After supper the men went back to the arbors — sat around and talked. As it got dark they sang a few songs — I was told that they were "ball game" songs. During the evening a few cars were coming in until a small crowd had arrived. Finally about 9 or 9:30 a stomp dance started. This was nearly the same as we saw last year. Joe Hicks and his ass't walked around with the feathered sticks. Joe talked at great length in Creek — picking out the leader for the next dance. Iva and I danced a number of times and nothing was said. This year they unwound the spiral a number times and rewound it to the north but still well within the square. In the unwinding everyone held hands and the long line was led along in front of the west arbor on the way to rewinding. When the rewound spiral was complete, the leaders and crowd would really sing — as the end of the song approached the leader would greatly speed up the time (gradually) and end up with a high-pitched yell.

June 17, 1949, Arbeka Green Corn Dance. [356]

At one time in the evening 3 clowns showed up and led stomp dances. One had on a rubber face mask which was a charactiture {caricature} of a very black, big red-lipped Negro (this was worn by the "chief"), another was that of an Indian (this along with a Seminole shirt was worn by Alex Sulpher), the other was that of a white man (I don't know who wore it.) First the Negro led a stomp dance followed by a shell dancer, then the Indian, then another shell dancer, then the white fellow. In the dance the two other clowns did the same hand and feet actions as the leader. The dance following was led by the Indian clown, the next dance by the White clown. All three dances were well received and caused considerable laughter. In the dance led by the white clown I got out in the circle of men before the singing started — the clown said, "looks like my brother" when he got opposite me.

After the last stomp dance which I think was led by Joe Hicks the crowd dispersed. The men stayed down in the square under the arbors. Joe Hicks gave a long oration in Creek again —-probably telling the men about taking medecine tomorrow and having to sleep in the square ground. Following the speech these men sang a few songs.

The twins slept in our car — Iva and I on the ground in back of the car. We woke up about 6:00am — others were awake also but nobody made a move to get breakfast. We sat around and sat around — there was intermittent activity down in the arbors. Various men were sent on errands from time to time. Some men came back with various plants — the medecine man had others in a burlap sack. The chief took a cotton chopping hoe from the roof of the west arbor and spent about 20 minutes hoeing and patting in the area of the fire place. I couldn't see but I am fairly certain that he was making a low mound for a new fire place. A short while later a man in the west arbor took a bundle of thin sticks, cradled them in his hands and swung them from aide to side rather briskly — undoubtedly bringing some coals to a blaze or a burn. A new fire was laid in the center and the bundle of sticks was taken out to start the new fire. Once it was burning the women in the various arbors started up their fires and started cooking breakfast. (No coals were brought from the new fire).

While the above was going on, other man went to the wooden building where the Sulpher's stayed and got out some paraphernalia. There were 4 graduated grey crocks, some dippers, and other things I didn't make out. The medecine man (Alex Sulpher) was working on the west aide of the square but north of the arbor. He had a wooden billet about 2" square which he used to beat various roots and plants which he had and which were brought to him. Some men took Joe Kinnard's pick-up truck and drove off for water — when came back they parked it back of the west arbor and inside the square. The plants, roots etc were put in the crocks and water was poured in — the details I didn't notice. [357]

June 18, 1949, Arbeka Green Corn Dance.

After the medicine was mixed some men took the next to the smallest crock and placed it just to the east of the middle of the square. Women from all the arbors took dippers and pails and went and lined up raggedly facing the crock and the west. (The above "just to the east of the middle" etc — is not right — it was outside of the square to the east). Joe Hicks faced them and the east and gave another long oration in Creek. Finally two old women stepped out of the line, went down to the crock, faced the east, took a dipper full of the medecine, tasted it very slightly and then started to wash the hands, arms, face, hair and feet with the medecine. The sequence was to pour some medecine on the hands, wash up the arms, pour some over the arms, then lift feet and pour over the legs and feet. First (I think) poured some in hands and put over the face and poured some over the hair. This sequence was performed several times by all women. After the first two were through the rest of the women went through the same thing. Quite a few women had young girls {who} which they washed in the medecine. I noticed some of the women carefully kept some kind of big green leaves which were floating in the medecine —

197

Amy Kinnard {Conard} took some up to her arbor and put them away.

I was eating breakfast at what I thought was the Sulpher's arbor (it turned out to be a coalition of three families), while I was there the women finished washing in the medecine (there were a number of women in the arbors who did not participate). The women then left and went to the west — Mrs Sulpher said to wash in the lake (stock pond?) which was only a short distance away. Mrs Sulpher's daughter decided to go and wash her hair — she had not washed with the medicine.

Following the women and girls — the smallest crock was placed some distance north of the west arbor and young boy children were taken by adult males and washed with the medecine of that crock. Approximately the same procedure was followed — they did not drink the medecine. After washing in the medecine the boys were taken to the arbors and were scratched with a needle on the arms and legs. Mrs Sulpher said that they were scratched 4 times on each limb. However I looked at one small boy (not walking yet) and he had 5 scratches on each forearm and the back of each calf. He hadn't cried at all. Mrs Sulpher said that a member of the same clan as the boy had to do the scratching — that was why they were taken to different arbors. The purpose of the scratching is to "make them stout" — so they will grow up big and strong. Some of the men apparently scratched themselves. We were told that when the Indians served time in the army — they were not found to have high blood pressure — it was because they scratched themselves.

June 18, 1949, Arbeka Green Corn Dance [358]

Following the scratching of the boys, the men got ready to take the medecine. I think Joe Hicks gave another talk before they took it. Two crocks were placed just north of the west arbor. The men took medecine two at a time. In doing so they first tasted it — washed their face and hands, poured it over their hair — then each drank 4 large gourd dippers of the medecine. It did not make them sick immediately — they either stayed along the west embankment or walked across the square to the east embankment and vomited. In doing so they always faced east. Most seemed to have to put their finger down their throats to make themselves vomit. With four dippers of medecine down them they vomited profusely. After all the men had had their turn they sat under the arbors and rested for perhaps an hour. Mrs Sulpher told me that here at Arbeka they didn't make the town members take the medecine — that it was voluntary — she said it was potent stuff (not her words) and that you had to get it out of you or it would "work on you". She also said that it wasn't as bad as white people thought it was — it didn't make you deathly sick.

The men took the medecine once more that morning — seemingly the same as the first time. About lunch time they got ready to take it again. The women had just started to fix lunch when the men got ready — one woman in the Kinnard arbor said something to the effect, "Wouldn't you know they would start while we're eating." Of course, the men taking the medecine didn't eat lunch — they had been fasting since the night before. Visitors, women, and some Creek man who didn't want to take medecine were the ones who ate. Lunch consisted of pork in several forms, peaches. Early in the afternoon the men took the medecine the 4th and last time — I noticed this time that a number of man drank only one dipper — some, however, took all four.

Following the last drinking of the medecine the men rested for a long time. I had heard from Mrs Sulpher that they were going to try to finish up early — that they were going to dance some dance instead of a longer one. I said something about it to Amy Kinnard — she didn't understand — said that last night (17th) they should have danced the Buffalo Dance but didn't.

Finally about 4:00pm or later the men started the "feather dance". As part of the paraphernalia from the wooden building they had brought a large bundle of sticks — about 8 feet long. There were some whitish feathers which the men tied on the end of the sticks — I later heard they were "crane feathers". Some of the men went around to the arbors and stuck the feathered sticks along in front of them. Finally the men came out of the arbors and followed the chief and another man about 4 times around the fire place (counterclockwise). Then the dance started — couples {pairs} of men side by side with the chief leading on the inside. Most of the men just ran in step for the dance — but the "chief" did several varieties of sort of a skipping step — very energetic. My impression was that the men did the same sort of sequence the woman did in the Ribbon Dance — three sets of four dances — with variations in the speed or time. [559]

In the feather dance the men hold the long sticks with the crane feathers tied on them. After each man had taken one and gotten in line there were still some sticks left over — so Joe Hicks and his ass't gave than to the dancers — so that some men carried two feathered sticks.

I had to take Amy Kinnard to town to buy groceries — I also took an older woman who turned out to be the chief's mother and a little girl — perhaps the chief's daughter. We left for Henryetta while the feather dance was going on. Iva said I missed other parts of the dance — one part where the men went to four corners of a small square just to the north of the fire. The chief led the singers to each corner of the square. There was also another dance where the "chief" led the men in single file in a sort of "snake dance" (sinuous line) in the part of the square north of the fire place (total square). Before each part of the dance the chief led the dancers around the fire several times (notice this is pattern for Creek dances we have seen — even the "stomp dance" starts with the leader walking around the fire several fines.)

When I got back from Henryetta the men were sitting under the arbors. Than they got up and the chief led them around the fire about 4 times and than off into the woods to the west — I was told they were going down to take a bath in the lake (where the women had gone that morning). After perhaps 20 minutes they came back in single file — emitting shrill whoops. They sat under the arbors for a few minutes — then somebody started circling the fire — it turned out to be the Old Dance again. Somewhere here they washed with medecine again — either before the Old Dance or after it. Then the dance was over — the women had a big supper ready and the men scattered off to their arbors to eat supper and break their fast.

At one time in the morning — while I was eating at the Sulpher's — Joe Hicks came over and stepped just out of the square ground — he asked me if I had some paint — he wanted some signs painted. I told him no, but that we could use my wife's lipstick. So he said that he would get some paper. Later in the morning he came to the outside of the square and motioned to me again. This time he had some sides of a large cardboard box — he wanted signs made to tell people not to drink — I let him furnish the words — he finally decided on NO DRUNKARDS ALLOWED followed "by order of Arbeka Chief." So Iva and I made 3 such signs and one saying NO DRINKING ALLOWED (latter because of space limitations). Sometime during the afternoon some of the men went from the west arbor (carrying out instructions) and tacked them on the pop stand and trees north, east, and west of the square. (We found some kids crayons in the car and used them instead of lip-stick).

At supper we had a large variety of things — hominy of squaw corn cooked with a pigs head, "*abuski*" cooked with dried squirrels, fried pork, cooked loose hamburger meat with onions (the latter possibly for our benefit) — and other things I don't remember — heavy on starch and fatty pork — no green vegetables. [360]

June 18-19, 1949, Arbeka Green Corn Dance.

During the afternoon Hank Weller (Caddo) showed up with his wife, children, and Bill Bedoka (Caddo-Delaware). Then a little later Ralph Murrow, wife, Bobby Lee Thomas and Reitha (Mrs Murrow's Daughter) also showed up. Joe Hicks came over after supper and made arrangements for the War Dancing. It had rained hard at supper and the Caddos didn't want to dance in the square and ruin their moccasins in the mud. Finally they decided to dance under the Kinnard's arbor — people could gather around and watch. It was decided that they dance at 9:00 because the stomp dance would start at 10:00. The dancers were busy fixing their costumes for what seemed like hours — they were very fussy — had the feathers drying in the hot tent.

Finally just before they got to dancing Hank and Ralph sat down to figure out a program — they sort of included me in it also. It was decide to start out with slow war dances — about 4 songs. Then a fast war dance — about 4 songs. Then each dancer was to solo — Dwight first, Bobby Lee second, and Warnie Weller last. That order was justified by starting with the oldest and ending with the youngest. Then was to come a Round Dance, then a Squat Dance as a finale. I was asked to announce but tried to slide out in favor of Joe Hicks. It ended by me reading what was to come next and Joe Hicks saying it in Creek — I had to make an announcement asking for contributions to help pay the expenses of the dancers. Seven dollars plus was contributed into the hat Kinnard passed. The money was divided (by me) into 5 portions — one for each dancer. Hank Weller, Ralph and Bill Bedoka did the singing — and sounded good this year.

By 10:00 a large crowd had collected — I have no way of guessing — there were cars and cars. Probably 5-600 people were there, including quite a few white spectators. The dance started about 10:00 and I watched a while — Iva went off with Reitha and danced a number of dances. I sat under the east arbor with Bill Bedoka and Hank. Nobody said anything. Finally Hank and I decided to get in a dance — when the leader got up and started walking around we got up and got in — he sang about two lines when one of the officials with a feathered stick got ahold of my arm and told me I had to get out. Took me over to the Aide and said that the chief didn't want me to dance — that if they let me dance, other white fellows would get in too and cause them trouble.

The above incident was somewhat embarrassing at the time — and got more so as the night went by. Later in the night Joe Kinnard asked Hank Welter why he wasn't dancing — he said that he and his friends had come down here to have a good time and than you "ruled my friend out." Joe Kinnard was apologetic — said he didn't have much to say what went on here, that he didn't belong to this town, that those who did were divided on what to do, that some people would go ahead and do things without consulting the rest. Alice Weller was mad — said. they ruled me out and let "an old niggah" dance — "they love niggahs here." (He was part Indian, part Negro school kid with a bus load of Indian school children) [361]

June 18-19, 1949, Arbeka Green Corn Dance.

Alice Weller also lectured Mrs Sulpher and some other Creek woman about it. Mrs Sulpher acted surprised about it and said that she would say something to her husband — it was stronger than that — more that she was going to tell her husband something. Nothing much more was done. Next morning Joe Hicks came over to ask me to take his son to Anadarko since he was in the army and stationed at Ft Sill. Hicks was very apologetic about it and said that the man who pulled me out shouldn't have — that I should have been let dance after I had done so much for them (making signs and taking the chief's mother to town). Probably if I had said something to Joe Hicks before the dance nothing would have happened.

The Stomp Dance lasted all night — crowds and crowds of people danced. The singing actually sounded better from a distance of perhaps 100 or more feet. Somewhere just about daylight (not dawn) the dance ended — with the Old Dance.

After breakfast which was served about 6:45 or so there was a wait of perhaps an hour or more. Then two or three young fellows got down in the square with ball sticks and a white (rubber?) ball — it wasn't an "Indian ball" and started throwing it to each other. More men and boys got in — then several girls also. Then the games got started — men and boys against women and girls. The men with ball sticks and the women with bare hands. Both sides were trying to hit the "cow's head" on top of the pole in the northern part of the square ground. I think the men had to hit the head to score a point while the women could hit the pole also above a black line 4 or 5 feet below the cow's head. The game got rather rough after a while — girls would shove the boys down when both were chasing a lose ball. The men would use their sticks to block off girls chasing a ball — It's a wonder to me that none of the woman got their fingers mashed. I watched them play for perhaps an hour and then decided to get on back to Anadarko. Joe Hick's boy was playing — his father got him out. I noticed Alex Sulpher and one of his daughters playing.

On the way home I asked Hick's boy how they became proficient with ball sticks — he said that they used to live near the square ground and would play ball every Sunday. I noticed in the field east of the square that one goal was still standing — like a soccer goal only smaller — perhaps 10' wide and 8' high [362]

June 18-19, Arbeka Green Corn Dance.

At one time in commenting on the amount of food that was put out by these people, Joe Kinnard {Conard} volunteered that they had slaughtered 3 hogs and split them among the six arbors — each arbor getting half a hog. I didn't find out who got the hogs but got the impression that it was a group affair.

At one time Amy Kinnard volunteered that she had a home that cost $38,000 — back in the 1930's at that. She showed us a picture of it. Was brick bungalow sort of style — couldn't get much idea of the size.

The home personnel of the Kinnard arbor were Joe Kinnard and his wife Amy. Joe's sister whose name we didn't know. She worked hard at cooking and generally helping, Lena — was the wife of the medecine man's ass't — she worked very hard cooking and taking care of a large number of her children. Mattie was Joe's niece and dressed considerably better than the others (she was quite young 18 or 19) — she didn't do any cooking but waited on table and washed dishes. Mattie may be quite wealthy if she is the Mattie we heard about later.

The cooking was done over a wood fire. Two large logs were laid parallel and a fire built between them. Of course the large logs would catch fire also. Iron kettles of several sizes would be set on the large logs — also large iron skillets. Meals were prepared in an amazingly short time by this method.

In talking to Mrs Sulpher it came out that she didn't belong to this town — she belongs to New Tulsa. Her husband, Alex Sulpher the medecine man is not from Arbeka either — he is from Nuyoka. It then came out that there are not very many medecine men left and that Alex is in demand to serve at a number of different towns. The reason that Arbeka had the Green Com Dance early this year was so they could get him to mix the medecine — he already had done so at two other busks in June. In all he will serve 5 or 6 towns. Mrs Sulpher said that this year two towns got together for the Green Corn Dance — that is members of one town decided to take the medecine at the other's busk.

The "chief" is a youngish looking man in his thirties. He is not a veteran but was a 4F. He has been chief for 2 or 5 years. When they decided to make him chief, he didn't want to be. But the others of the town thought that he would be a good chief since his mother is a conservative old Creek woman who had been bringing her son to the busks for all his life. When he was first made chief he was very serious and apparently afraid of making mistakes — now they said he was getting used to it and beginning to "cut up a little." He seems to have been the one to get the masks for the clowning during the stomp dance — also in leading the stomp dances he seems to cut up and unbend.

In the stomp dances when they get going good the leader often steps fast and gets several paces ahead of the line — then they turn to the fire and dance in place and sing loudly and emphatically till the line catches up. When singing to the fire (Iva is right*) they hold the palms up to the level of the head and facing the fire and move them from side to side — or up and down.

June 18-19, 1949 Arbeka

While I was sitting under the arbor with Bill Bedoka and Hank Weller listening to the singing — Bill said something to the effect that wasn't it amazing that a fellow could take a "beat up old song and make it sound good." It turned out that the song was a real old stomp dance song but that the fellow was singing it in the new style — the style that Hank and Bill call "the blues".

I asked Bill Bedoka if he remembered the first time he led a stomp dance — he said yes. He was about 21 at the time and had been going to school (I think at Chilocco) and during the evenings a lot of them would go down to the park and take turns leading — for rattles they used Prince Albert tobacco cans with pebbles in them. After school was out he went down to New Tulsa — some of the Creeks there had been practicing with him at school. He was picked to lead a dance. I asked if he was nervous — he said yes. "I had 17 shell dancers behind me!" Then he said that after the first few times around he wasn't nervous anymore.

I asked Bill Bedoka how he learned so many songs — he didn't have a very definitive answer — something to the effect that if he heard a song and liked it, he remembered it.

Stories by Ralph Murrow.

Dream of Hank Weller's father: Ralph said that Hank's father went to sleep and dreamed that he was traveling east over a wide straight road. He traveled (walking) for a long time. He was going downhill but didn't notice it because the grade was so slight. Finally he saw a grass house ahead — he walked in through the floor (a Wichita grass house has a door to the west and east) and saw a man sitting in a rocking chair. The men looked at him and said, "What are you doing here? You're on Indian." The Indian than looked closely and saw that the man in the chair was the Devil. The Devil told him to go back where he came from. So the man turned and went out the west door and was home in a flash. (conveyed home by mystical fashion — he walked down very long and slowly.) When he got home he woke up. Hank's father said that after that he didn't worry about dying because now he knew that hell was for white people only and Indians didn't go there.

Dream of John Loco (Apache): Ralph said that John Loco dreamed that he had died and was traveling on a road with two other men. They were white men and he followed them. Finally they came to a place and were met by the Devil. The Devil asked the first white man, "Do you want to stay here or go back where you came from? The man said yes, so the Devil told him it would cost $5.00. The first white man took five dollars from his pocket and gave it to the Devil — he was told to go back and did so. Than the devil looked at the second white man and said "Well, do you want to go back or stay." The second man said he wanted to go but that he only had $4.98. The devil picked him up and started to throw him in the fire and said that wasn't enough. The man said that the Devil should wait a minute, he might find some more money. He looked all through his clothes and found a penny and gave it to the Devil and said that ought to be close enough. But, the Devil picked him [364]

June 18-19, 1949, Arbeka.
Stories by Ralph Murrow., cont.

up and started to throw him in the fire again. The Jew (for that is what he was) begged again for a chance to look and see if he could find the other penny — he finally did and the Devil sent him back. The devil then looked at the Indian and said, "Do you want to go back, or do you want me to throw you in the fire?" John Loco said, "I'm just a poor Indian, I don't have any money." So the Devil picked him up and started to throw him in the fire. John Loco said, "I think I've got some money back there were I came from — you call Mr Gillette at the agency and maybe he'll give you an order for five dollars." John Loco says the Devil must have done it, too, because he came back to life.

Wichita man: There was a Wichita man who gambled a lot and stuck to the old ways. Finally he was converted to the Baptist church. For seven years he was a very good Christian — didn't gamble, run around with women — in all ways a model Christian. Finally after seven years he went to Tawakoni Jim's place. There were Indians gambling all around. He stopped and watched a game of three card Monte — watched for a long time. Finally he reached into some pocket and pulled out two bits {25¢} — he gave it to one of the players to bet for him — the player tried to get him to bet it himself. Finally the player took the two bits — the man said bet it on that card. The card won and the player started to pick up the money — the man said leave it there — it won again. Finally the man broke the game and won $500. He stopped being a Christian then — said that he had been a good Christian for seven years and what had it got him — he wore old worn out clothes, didn't have enough food to feed his family — then in a few minutes he won $500, being a Christian hadn't done anything like that. So, he went back to the old Indian ways.

203

September 8, 1951. Arbeka Creek Dance

The Wellers (Caddo friends) came by shortly after noon on their way to Arbeka — so we fed then and took off about 2:00pm. Iva, Kirk, Warren Weller, and I arrived first — it was about 5:00. There were no other cars parked around the square — some parked by arbors. People were eating — no one came to see who we were so we just sat for maybe 50 minutes. Finally Joe Hicks went by in a car (on his way to town) and recognized us. He had the driver stop and then shook hands with us and told us to go eat at his arbor. As we started over to Joe's arbor, a younger man came up and shook hands — he seemed most glad to see us. Turned out his name was __ Field {or Fixico, p219}. He insisted we go down and eat at his place. He and his wife had no arbor — but had a table and boxes, etc. around. They fed us a wonderful meal — fried chicken, pumpkin, *abaski* and meat, hominy and meat, pie, doughnuts, green peppers — and many other small side things.

Things looked a little deserted compared to the times we had been there before as there were not as many camps in use.

Joe Hick's family was camped. The arbor of family from which the chief came (he drowned last year) was in use. The camp of Amy and Joe Cannard {Conard} was in use, but was being run by Amy's sister – Amy died last spring. The camp to the south of Amy's was also in use. Then Field and his wife had an incipient one started south of the square – we were told that this

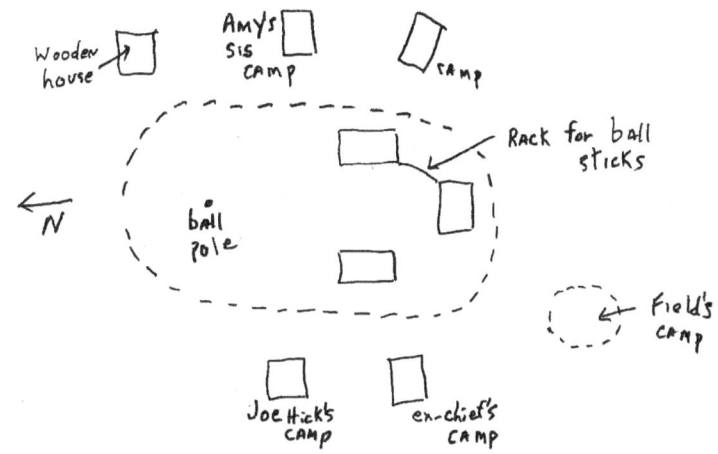

was the first year they had had a camp of their own. The camp by the wooden house where ceremonial paraphernalia is kept was not in use — this is where Mrs. Sulpher and Mrs. Fields fed us once before.

Misc. Items noted: The set of graduated crockery vessels (like my F used to make beer in) were on the ground to the north of the of the west arbor. Obviously the men had taken medicine in the afternoon. The stringer of wood between the south and east arbors was there again — this time I found out what is was for — the men hung their ball sticks and breech cloths over it before the ball game. The pop stand was gone — but after dark a truck loaded with pop came in — the young freedman that I saw at New Tulsa seemed to be partially in charge of the pop. [2]

After supper and very late — must have been almost ten o'clock — the evening's activity got started. John MacIntosh (Creek married to Pawnee) had brought a number of Pawnee war dancers with him. Turned out to be mainly from the {Moore} family. They dressed in their feathered costumes and danced in the area between the west arbor and the ball pole. A bench was placed for the dancers to sit on there — and the drummers also sat on benches. Two Pawnee young men who sang at Camp Creek at the Wichita-Pawnee give-away in 1949 were the main singers. They

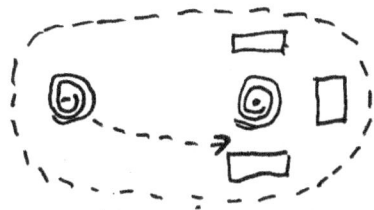

got Hank Weller (Caddo) to help. Warren Weller (Caddo) also dressed and danced. A series of standard "war dances" were performed. Then a very small boy (less than 2 yrs.) was carried out by his mother and he did a war dance — then he did an Eagle dance (much like the pueblo one put on by Taos — and finally did a hoop dance with one hoop. Two Pawnee teen-age girls were in costume — one with a cut-down buck-skin dress — so it was just above her knees — it was like a drum majorette's costume. They danced the war dance and finally one did a solo. For this she twirled a baton and war danced at the same time – then the gas lanterns and car lights were turned out and she twirled a baton with red lights on the end. Warren Weller did a solo dance also.

Finally a round dance was held — and perhaps a total of 40 people got out to dance.

During the costumed war dancing a Pawnee woman did the conventional woman's step — Alice Weller also got out with shawl and danced with the same step. La Crete Weller got a shawl and did the same step — she has a costume and can do the fancy step, but without the costume she danced like a lady. Alice W got Iva a shawl and got her to dance also.

When the Round Dancing was over the Creeks started their affaire. First some talking was done by Joe Hicks and then the Old Dance was performed. This was started around the ball pole. It was led by a young man I don't know. It, of course, was counter-clockwise. After a number of songs the leader unwound the spiral and led the line around the fire in a counter-clockwise fashion. The Old Dance was ended here.

From then on it {was} almost one "stomp dance" after another for the rest of the night with occasional talks by Joe Hicks from time to time. Two men were in "charge of picking leaders — Joe Fite (the man who yanked me out of the dance a couple of years ago was one*). Joe Hicks did not act as a leader-picker. About ½ way through the night they changed leader-pickers.

About 1:30 in the morning the Fox Dance was performed. I was sitting in the west arbor and heard them plan to do it "next dance" — it actually came about 5 dances later. Nichi Gray was asked to lead the songs and his daughter was asked to lead it. A chair was placed in the east portion of the ground and Nichi Gray sat in it, facing east with a coconut rattle. Several other men stood with him and helped him sing. [3]

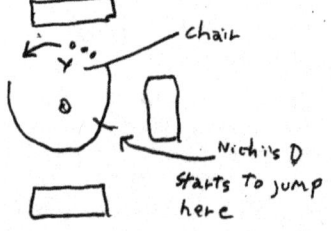

One beat a small water drum. A line of women got behind Nichi's daughter so that about 2/3 of a circle {formed} about the square — perhaps 40 women. About 10 had shells or cans on. Nichi would start a song and than hold the rattle out in front of him at arm's length and shake it hard as a signal for the dancing to start. The women danced the two-beat with each foot step. When Nichi's daughter would get between the west and south arbors she would start jumping with both feet. The idea being that she would be in front of her father at the end of the song. For the first dance it was not timed just right. She wound up about 8 feet short. The dance was performed 4 times in all. In jumping the dancers would not jump just straight forward along the circle but turn from side to side — Nichi's daughter even jumped around and then backward a couple of times. After the dance was over, I heard Nichi's daughter tell her father that he sang too fast — some of the women had dropped out before it was over — it was too hard.

Then about 3:00 in the morning a "double-header" dance was performed.

The last dance in the morning was the Old Dance led by Nichi Gray. During this, and several of the last stomp dances, a couple of younger men did some clowning with a rubber mask. They would try to scare girls with the mask by surprising them – some young fellow also yelled and played, they were a little drunk.

Following the Old Dance a man of about 60 with a large black, droopy hat got in front of the west arbor and gave about an 8 minute talk in Creek. He talked the fastest I've ever heard – his name was William Jones {*Hilibi* ?} and he is some kind of a leader at Hickory Ground. A Creek man told me he was saying "it was all over except the ball game," and that people should go from here and "not get in trouble."

Following Jones' speech the men got ready for the ball game. Joe Hicks went over by the ball pole and started pairing off players. The men assembled around the area. Joe would indicate two men — one for each side and then they would lay their ball sticks on the ground opposite each other. The final result looked like this:

pole. ॥ ॥ ॥॥ ॥ ॥ ॥ ॥॥॥ ⟶
॥ ॥ ॥॥ ॥॥ ॥ ॥॥ ॥

and so on to about 25 opposing pairs of sticks

I learned later that a moiety-like division still exists — players belong on the "east" or "west" sides. During the game I heard male spectators saying things like "the east's my side", "I belong to the west". The players were from many towns besides Arbeka. Six kids between 8 and 11 were paired off against each other. There were finally about 25 players on each side – a great deal of recruiting was done by men walking out among the spectators.

After pairing off the players, they picked up their sticks. The east side went off into the woods south of the square ground. Joe Hicks led the west side in the ball game song and dance around the ball game pole. Joe's young son "Red" did the long drawn out siren-like yell that accompanies the dance — "Red" has red hair and is about 11 years old. During parts of the dance the players yell, whoop, and shake their sticks in the air. After [4] Joe and his side finished their dance they went off into the woods and changed their clothes — as they were going I could hear the east team singing the same ball game song in the woods to the north.

The players and the spectators went up to an open field east and a little south of the square ground — it was contoured for farming. One man not playing had taken an axe and cut some oaks in the woods for goals – 3 pieces for each goal. A group of men at each end of the field tied them together, dug holes and put them up.

The goal at the north end of the field had the top piece slanting — by accident I'm sure. This was the goal the west team was attacking. The goal at the south end was a proper rectangle. Distance between the two goals was about 110 yards.

Joe Hicks and his team sang the ball game song around the north goal — duplicating the performance around the ball game pole in the square. The dance is counter-clockwise. The dancers whooped and shook their sticks at the other team to the south. They "gobbled" as a challenge to the other side. While Joe and his group were dancing the other side started the same dance around the south goal. Mrs. Sulpher told me they should dance at the same time — the singing and whooping was like they were "fighting" each other.

  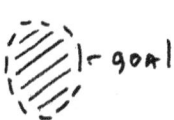

Then the two teams went to the center of the field and lined up facing each other — I don't remember for certain if they laid their ball sticks down in opposing pairs – I think they did. William Jones, the Hillabi man, talked in Creek to the teams — a mile a minute again. I caught the opening words — he started with the names of a series of Creek towns – *Arbeka*, *Hillubi*, etc. One of my neighbors said he was enumerating the towns from which the players came. Jones talked about 4 minutes. Suddenly the players broke into several groups – a group of guards for each goal, a group as attackers for each goal. Each team left a number of players in the center of the field and Jones kept right on talking. He talked for maybe a minute and tossed the ball in the air — still talking. Then the center group of each team fought for the ball. The person getting it clear would throw the ball toward the goal his team was attacking – sometimes he would run part of the way if there was an open field. The six kids stayed in the same area as indicated – when the ball went near them the other players let them fight for it without interference.

The players wore G-strings but most had shorts of some kind also – some regular underwear shorts, some basket ball shorts. A couple had nothing decernable {discernable} under the G-string. Most had paint line on their faces and feathers tied in their hair – most players had tennis shoes on. [5]

This game was not as rough as the one we saw at New Tulsa last year. There was little if any purposeful hitting of an opponent with the ball sticks. No person was bloodied up as we saw at New Tulsa. As the game went on it got somewhat rougher. Several times a player running with the ball in his sticks would be tackled (as in football). When we talked to our host (Fields) after the game he had a 2" cut in his scalp and caked blood in his hair — somebody had hit him with ball sticks. Quite often the players would give the challenge that Hank Weller calls the "gobble."

One of my male neighbors told me that he has seen many games in which the players just get into a fight at the beginning and never get around to playing ball. Another said sometimes 2 players get in a fight and just about kill each other — if the others let them fight it out, and they sometimes do. Someone said when Nichi Gray was younger he got into a fight every game. This game today was called a "Match game" — though a "real match game" is between teams from 2 different towns.

Many of the older men not playing stood in the playing field near the center — I was told they were supposed to be there. Some women had water buckets and gave players drinks when the ball was at the other end of the field.

The west team was better and scored the 20 pts. — the other team maybe got 8 or 10. Babe Hardjo was a leading scorer for the west. At the end of the game Joe Hicks led his team in the ball dance around the north goal. They really whooped it up — gobbling, yipping, and shaking their sticks at the other goal. The loosing team did not dance.

The ball players then went off and bathed and dressed. The women cooked breakfast. Joe Hicks told us to stay for breakfast. Finally breakfast was ready after a long wait — we were told that they had decided to "eat on the ground" since they could share out the food better that way.

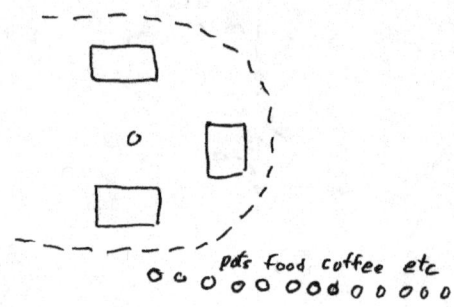

pds food coffee etc

The food was lined up oriented in a line N-S and people just came up and helped themselves. There were no plates — except Joe Hicks's people gave Alice W and Iva plates to eat from. Standard procedure was to take a piece of bread and pile on fried potatoes, a piece of pork, pumpkin, and other food as available. There were some "blue dumplings — dense blue corn meal with a few reddish beans in them. Both men and women ate together here at Arbeka — not separate as after the ball game at New Tulsa last year. [6]

Field told me that this was the 2nd dance of the year for Arbeka – they had not had a green corn dance. Field said it was because they had lost their chief – they hadn't picked a new one yet. ([handwritten] Their chief drowned in the river last year, or last spring.)

Joe Hicks also volunteered to me that this was only their second dance of the year. I asked why – Joe said it was because what happened last year – "about that woman." (Mrs. Sulpher shot her husband's girl friend at the Arbeka green corn dance last year.)

Alex Sulpher was medicine man again this year. During the evening's dancing he sat in a chair in the center of the west arbor and watched the dance. He was picked to lead at least one dance. His chair was the only one under the arbors.

NEW TULSA LITTLE RIVER CANADIAN

New Tulsa Medecine Dance June 17-18, 1950

Outline notes ~
men filed in from woods ("both")
Old dance – several leaders
talks by Bennie Davis Tiger
visited by Deer Medecine Dance 3 before corn dance *trouble with {finding} med men
men eat – then visitors
then 2 ball games
supper
ball games
talks – war dances
stomp dances Double Header, 4 women dances , drunk dances
breakfast
ball games

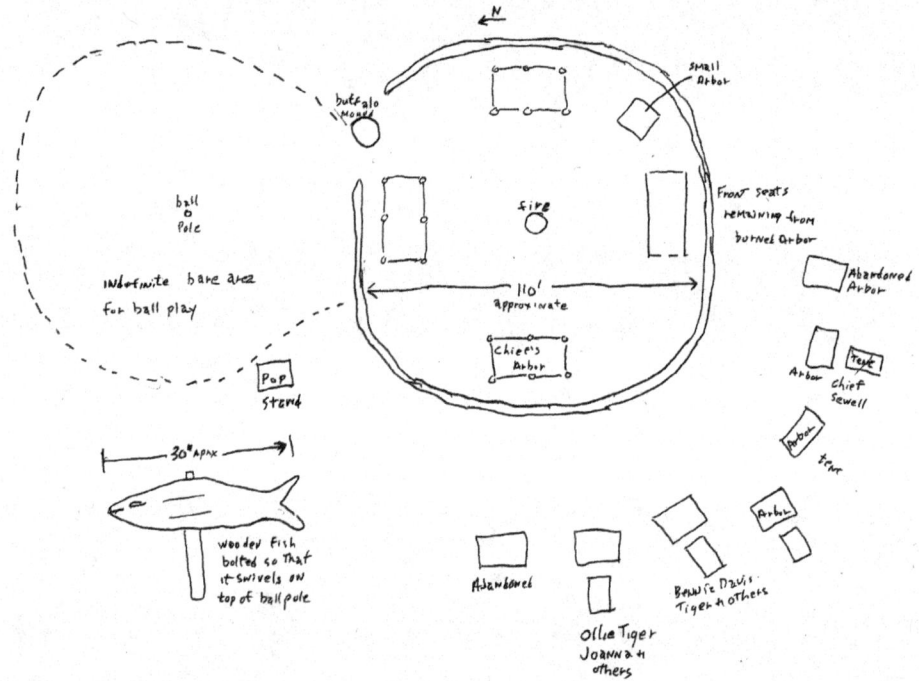

We got to New Tulsa, which is between Holdenville and Sasakwa, Oklahoma, about 2:30pm. There was little activity except for women sitting or cooking under the arbors. Hank Weller took us over to Ollie Fixico's arbor (other families also) and we met a number of women. While we were talking the men came out of the woods in single file from the north. I believe they had been down taking a bath. They sat under the arbors for a short time – Benny Davis Tiger gave a talk in Creek. Then the men got around and did several "stomp dances" c-clockwise {counter- clockwise} around the fire. The dances came one after the other without a break – there were different leaders for each song. Then they sat under the arbors some more and Benny Tiger talked off and on for some time (all in Creek of course).

While the talking was going on a Creek man named Thomas Deer came over to our cars and told us that we would be fed as soon as the men who had taken medicine finished and ate themselves – he said something about eating a little fruit. He reassured us several times we would be fed, but that we had to wait awhile.

From Thomas Deer we found out that this was not the "Green Corn Dance" but a "medicine dance". He said they had to have three of these dances and then the fourth is the "Green Corn Dance". He also said they were late this year because of trouble getting a "medicine man", then they got another and he got sick – now they have one from their own town (New Tulsa). However, the trouble finding medecine men put them behind schedule. This town has also lost its chief [2] since last year. He was run over by a train. Deer says the authorities think it was murder, but he doesn't think so. The new chief is a very light-skinned individual – at first glance looks like a white man. His name is Old man Sewell.

Thomas Deer is a deputy US Marshall. He said he has held the job for 30 plus years. He really takes it seriously. For the dance he has to deputize a number of men to help him police – he really takes his job to heart and is proud of it.

Following Bennie Tiger's talks the men went off to various camps and we could see that only men ate at the fixed sitting. When they finished we were told to go eat – 6 at the fixed arbor, 6 over there. There seemed to be no other visitors and with Bill Bedoka there were only 11 of us. There were beef ribs, stewed squirrel, weenies & sauerkraut, dutch oven bread, white store bread, green beans, canned baked beans, coffee, and a small amount of cake – probably a couple other things I missed. I ate at the Tiger's & companion's arbor.

After the women had eaten and cleaned things up, they had a ball game. First a couple of teen-age boys got their ball sticks and some young girls got out around the ball pole and started throwing the ball around. The men got under the north arbor and played a variety of pitch – either took part or kibitzed. From time to time Benny Davis Tiger would shout in Creek toward the camps – to get the women to hurry up. Finally some women came over and one of the men got a lot of ball sticks and the regular game followed. For this the men used sticks and the women their hands. The small girls helped the women. The small boys used their hands and when they got the ball both men and women would try to get them to throw it to them – sometimes a little boy would throw it to a woman, sometimes to a man. The idea was to hit the fish or the pole above a mark near the top of the pole. To start the game Benny D Tiger would stand on the west side of the pole and throw the ball almost straight up with his sticks – everybody gave shrill shouts as the ball went up. Then men and women fought for possession of the ball. Shoving, tripping, etc was fair. The men sought to get free to throw with the sticks and the women with their [2a] hands. Women would block for each other – a favorite trick was for women to hold men's belts so that another woman could throw. Women in particular, and some men, would push opponents when they were going after the ball. There were a number of pile-ups and fights for the ball – this caused much amusement. We were told of an incident which once happened in a game. A woman sat on the ball and wouldn't get up. Finally a man well known for his joking said "I don't care I'm going to run my hand in there and get that ball." Then he walked toward the woman – she got up and ran. In the pile-ups today men would haul women off and women, men.

Sometimes in the excitement men would give a peculiar sort of yell which was called a "gobble" – this we were told was a challenge. After the men got behind in the score they didn't "gobble" any more.

After each point made, Benny D Tiger threw up the ball again and people would yip. A different ball was used after each point – there were 3 or 4 lying near the base of the pole.

The women won the first game. Then after a short rest a second game was played. Again the women won. There was less team work on the part of the men – men would fight each other to catch a ball coming down – women would {not}. I forgot to ask how many points made a game.

After the second ball game the women went back and finished getting supper. We were told they could seat 12 at Ollie Tiger's et al table. There was a much larger supper, but along the same line as at noon. Even the cooks said it was sour *sófki*.

Following supper the men went back and sat under the arbors. There were a number of talks, mainly (if not all) by BD Tiger. He also yelled at the women who were cleaning up dishes, etc. Finally 2 more ball games ensued. [3]

After the ball games, the men sat under the arbor and it got dark. From time to time Tiger would talk. It had been decided the Caddos would dance. So Warren Weller, Gene Beaver, and Paty Carter got dressed. Ralph Murrow, Hank Weller, Bill Bedoka, Leon Carter, Buzzie Carter and myself got around the drum. The fire keeper got a large fire going in the center of the square & benches placed for the dancers. Then followed a number of War Dances, slow War Dances, a Two-Step, a series of Round Dances, a Shield Dance by Warnie and Gene, and a final War Dance. Hank would tell the Creek man what was going to come next and he would tell Bennie Davis Tiger in Creek, then Tiger would announce in Creek and in loud oratorical style what was going to happen. After this was over Tiger gave another talk and for 5 to 8 minutes people came up and dropped coins at the chief's arbor. Everytime someone gave something, the men under the arbors would sing MA•do ... MA•do ... MA•do ... Creek equivalent of "thank you". Afterwards I heard that each war dancer got $1.15 and Lucreta Well who two-stepped got all the pennies which came to .60¢ plus. A number of people got out and round danced, including Creeks.

After the Caddos were through Creeks talked some more. Finally Willy Gray whose job was that of "finding leaders" started walking around c-clockwise. He led an assistant who followed him. He picked the "chief" Old Man Sewell and he led the first "stomp dance." Then they came in rapid succession. Gray would talk in Creek – one of the things he was doing was telling the people they couldn't dance if they had had anything to drink.

Thomas Deer had said that he would have to appoint deputies to help him. During the evening there were 6 men who went round and round with flashlights and looked for people who had been drinking. After the stomp dancing started a rather tremendous crowd arrived. The marshall and the deputies also took charge of parking cars. They were very fussy – would park a car and then make the driver get in and move it six inches. The deputies would spot someone who had been drinking – who were not directly drunk, just smelled of liquor or beer – and go in the circle and pull them out of the dance. I noticed that they took them outside the square and talked to them for some time and let them go. Deer said [3a] that if they got rough he would send them to town to jail. About 4 women in a row were pulled out of the dance {at} first – finally some men.

The singing for these dances was very fine. There were 9 shell dancers. Only for a very short period did Nichi Gray's daughter get in with can rattles.

Our attention was called to two styles of singing – the old style and the "blues". I'm not too sure yet that I can always tell the difference. The blues start off with a series of low grunts – the singing is not as loud as the other can be. Ollie Tiger who is renowned as one of the finest singers let me dance – a blues. Later we found he left early when his son got drunk – took him home.

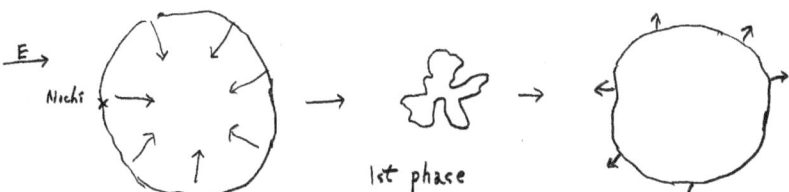

1st phase

Alice Weller kept trying to get me to stomp dance – I wouldn't go. Hank didn't dance, either did Bill Bedoka. Finally Nichi Gray got out to lead a dance – turned out to be a "double header" Joanna (Jownie) dragged me out forcibly to dance. Hank Weller got on the other side of her. Everybody joined hands in a large circle facing inward. Nichi started singing – everyone (almost) responded. There were over 150 people in the circle – just slow one foot forward and then the other. When near the center (as near as possible for 150 people to get), they went back out – some women turned round and jumped with both feet to the outside. This in and out phase was performed 4 times (I believe). Then the circle broke in two at Nichi Gray. The man next to him led one half of the circle and Nichi led the other. Both sang the lead and the others responded.

Each of the two leaders of the "double header" had a coconut shell rattle which they shook while singing. [4]

This phase went on four times – the two leaders made four circles of the dance ground. The fourth circle brought Nichi back to the west side of the dance ground.

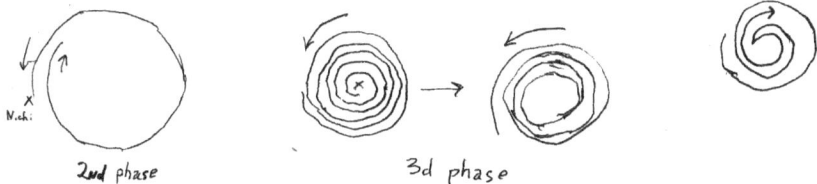

2nd phase   3d phase

Then the 3rd phase came up: – this was to wrap the dancers up into a spiral, unwind, and then wrap into another spiral – 4 spirals were made. First one in the SW quadrant of the square, then one in the SE quadrant, one in the NE quadrant, finally one in the NW quadrant. After 4 repetitions of the spiral the dance ended.

I laid down to take a nap about 3:15am. While I was on the cot they sang and danced the "4 corner dance". I didn't see it. Hank says it is a lot like the "double leader" – four spirals are wrapped up and unwound (except last one) in the 4 quadrants of the square. The coconut shell rattles were used in this dance also.

One stomp dance had the reverse movement (the spiral suddenly reverses). There was adverse comment around as that it wasn't led right. A number of stomp dances were unwound and rewrapped – a favorite trick was to rewrap the spiral around a tree in the SW corner of the square.

In the morning as it got light they were still stomp dancing. In either the last or next to last dance the man sang "boogie woogie wa•li•".

x leader

After the last dance Nichi Gray started staggering around and tilting an imaginary bottle in the air. Others, both men and women, started doing likewise. Nichi told Hank Weller, "come on, get drunk". Finally about 10 men and 6 or 8 women were staggering around with their [4a] arms on each other's shoulders. A man with a water drum with an inner tube head faced the clowns and walked backward beating the drum and leading the songs. The total effect was a counter-clockwise movement. The dancers would stagger from side to side, almost fall down, or one group would sing all the way around. One fellow played he had passed out and was dragged around during the dance by his buddies. "Carson" Tiger a teen-age boy hat a big floppy had pulled over his eyes during the whole dance. At the end of each song the dancers would let out wild yips – particularly Joanna and the other woman. While dancing imaginary bottles were tippled. The whole effect was very humerous {humorous}. "

After the drunk dance, the dancing broke up. I anticipated the "Old Dance" but was disappointed. Once thing which helped break up the dance was that Thomas Deer apprehended a bootlegger (Indian) with a 10 gallon milk can with "choc" beer in it. The culprit put up a little argument. The dancers and spectators went to see what was happening. Deer finally got a "white" "law" from town and he and Deer took the bootlegger to jail.

Everyone sat or stood around and talked – most people drove away in cars. Finally breakfast was served. This time I ate at Bennie Davis Tiger's arbor – food consisted of "skillet bread", beef, pork, cabbage, beans, potatoes, coffee, etc.

After breakfast the men got their ball sticks and the women came out – a series of ball games were played. They were playing when we left about 9:00am.

A water fight between several men and women broke out during breakfast – started in the arbor next to the chief's and spread to the chief's and to ours. It lasted longest at the chief's arbor – the whole thing was very funny to the Creeks.

Those who had taken medicine, we were told, couldn't go to sleep – they had to stay up all night. We were invited back for Green Corn Dance about the middle of July. (Ralph asking how Creeks did it?)

New Tulsa Info:

Ralph Murrow (Caddo) told me that he was curious how the Creeks could tell people to go to a certain arbor and eat. He said that with Caddos you couldn't do that – it would be up to the individual families to ask people to eat. So he asked (Willie Gray, I believe). He was told that during the year they held bingo parties (and probably box suppers) to raise money. In this manner they raised $300 or $400. When dance season comes they find out who is going to camp. Several families go together – 2 or 3 or maybe 4 and keep up an arbor. They bring whatever they have to eat. Then the money is split up among the camps to buy other food. In this way no one can complain when visitors are assigned to eat at their arbor. (This info has a disadvantage in that it went through Caddo interpretation before it came to me.)

I was talking to Willie Gray and sitting at what was left of the south arbor. It had burned down leaving only one long log seat fastened to 3 uprights. He said some one had burned it down – that they were having a hard time with that arbor since it had burned down last year also. He said that he was in charge of that arbor and that they would have to fix it again.

A large oak tree had been cut down and a huge pile of wood – logs and branches was outside the square to the east. One man kept the fire going all night.

The land on which the dance ground is belongs to a white man. We first thought it was nice that he let the Creeks use it. Then we found out that there are 14 or 15 oil wells on the place and that he charges the New Tulsa group $25/year rent to use the place. They say he sure gets mad if they are a couple of days late paying the $25.

During the stomp dancing there was someone (or people taking turns) beating time on an inner-tube water drum under the north arbor.

While we were eating dogs wandered around – even laid down under the table – the

Creeks were unconcerned. (How unlike Wichitas & Caddos). But during the stomp dances a dog wandered in front of the [5a] chief's arbor. Bennie Davis Tiger shooed him away saying "GO away! Go stomp dance!" This was very amusing to the crowd. Some of the Creeks said that he is always saying something funny – even while he is lecturing in Creek.

In summary the following formal positions were observed:

Miko (chief) – Old Man Sewell
Talker – Bennie Davis Tiger
Medecine Man – name not known
Man who picks leaders – Willy Gray {each carried a ball stick
Ass't – name not known   { " " " "
Leaders of south arbor – Willy Gray (there probably are leaders of other 3 arbors)
Deputy Marshall – Thomas Deer (do the US positions coincide with ole Creek offices?)
6 deputies – names unknown

I also noticed that Joanne (Jownie) was accorded preference among the shell-shakers. She almost always was the one behind the leader. However, if she got into the dance late, she took a position near the last of the shell-shakers. Don't know if this is formal, or just that she is the best shell-shaker. We hears a number of comments that she was so go{od}.

Willy Gray told us during the afternoon that it is hard to find leaders now – there used to be so many good singers. He also commented that good shell-shakers are rare now. [6]

Creek info:

New Tulsa Green Corn Dance: July 16, 1950

We arrived at the New Tulsa square ground about 2:00p.m Saturday afternoon. The place looked much as it did last June – with the following exceptions. The south arbor had been reerected, all the arbors had fresh oak brush on top, and there were many more people in evidence. Nichi Gray's family and others were staying in the arbor to the NW of the square ground which had been unused in June. The other unused arbor to the south was also in use – as well as one to the east of the square. A woman told us that there were 8 camps – more than they had had for some time. I talked to some of the women in JoAnne's camp for a little while and then went back to see what was happening.

The men were sitting around under the arbors – some just sitting, some talking, some playing a variety of pitch called 52. Some of the young teen-age boys were tossing a ball with sticks. Nichi Gray came to the edge of the ground and talked to me – said they were still taking medicine – had taken twice and had two more times to go.

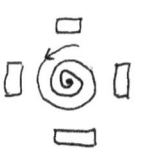 The men were actually sitting only under 3 arbors – the south, west, and north ones. Chief Sewell sat under the west arbor, as did Benny Tiger, the talker. Nichi Gray seemed to be some kind of leader in the north arbor. Under the east arbor sat the "medicine man" facing the east. Before him he had a large galvanized wash-tub. He seemed to sit and stir and 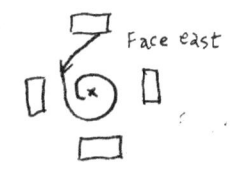 stir and stir. Robert Reed (JoAnne's husband) seemed to be some kind of assistant to the medicine man – he sat with him from time to time. There were about 10 or 12 galvanized buckets north of the medicine man's arbor. Somehow the same number of young men from the south arbor got up and went to the north (there is a creek nearby) and returned with buckets of

water. Some of these were poured into the large tub, others were left standing to the north of the arbor. Then R Reed took a grey enameled dipper full of medicine and walked c-clockwise around the fire. As he did so, he flicked water from the dipper with the palm of his hand – first to the right and then to the left – and so on as walked in a decreasing circle – his total path was a spiral. Then he returned to the medecine [6a] arbor got another dipper, walked in a spiral fashion and poured the medecine on the fire in the center of the square.

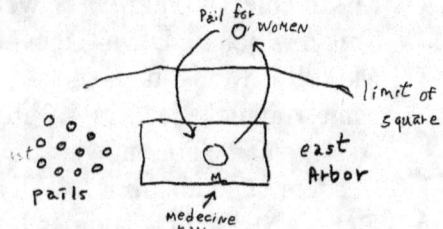

Then a pail was placed outside the square to the east of the east arbor. Carson and another teen-age boy took dippers and kept dipping medicine and going out and pouring it in the pail for the women. This was a bucket brigade effect with 2 men going in a c-clockwise fashion.

Women came from all the camps with various kinds of containers – mostly gallon lard buckets. They stood in line to get medecine – the line extending to the south. I noticed the old woman whose camp was to the east of the square went clear around the square ground to keep from going 30 or 40 steps in a clockwise fashion. The women poured medecine from the pail into their containers, took a few steps more, stopped and faced east. They took a taste of the medecine, then washed hands, feet, and face, and poured it over their hair as we saw at Arbeka last year.

Finally after the women were through, the men got to take the medecine. This was done by arbors: First the west arbor members went, when they were through the south arbor members, and then the north arbor. When their turn came, many ran and shouted. After drinking the medecine from the tub, individuals would go outside the square to the east, face east, and vomit. After taking the medecine most men seem to go down into the woods to the north – I supposed to wash at the creek. As they came back many brought pieces of wood which they threw on the wood pile to the south side of the square.

After all had taken medecine, they sat around, played cards, played ball, etc. There was a bundle of thin, limber poles with white [7] feathers tied to the tips – leaning against the front of the east arbor. after a long rest period (and probably at some kind of signal) men came from all the arbors and were handed the feathered poles – some had 2, some 3, some 4, some 5 or more

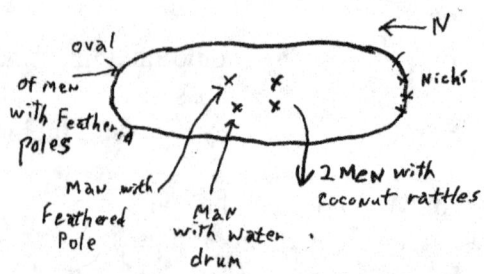

feathers tied to them – not in clusters but singly along the top of the pole, about 30 + men participated in this dance. The Feather Dance as it is popularly called started in front of the west arbor. The group formed as a long oval before the arbor – in the center were two men with coconut shell rattles, a man with a water drum made from a small stoneware crock and a piece of inner tube, and a man (Thompson Deer) with a feathered pole. As the song started all the men faced the inside of the circle. Nichi Gray led the songs. The men held the sticks up at an acute angle from their bodies and vibrated slightly. At a point in the song all turned south and danced slowly (two beats with each foot) in an arc toward the front of the south arbor. The song ends with a note held a long time – just when you think they couldn't hold it any more Thompson Deer would let out a long high pitched but descending whoop, and the song would end – the center of the oval of dancers was in front of the south arbor. Now all faced the inside of the circle and another song was started and preceded as the first (except that when they turned it was toward the east, and the song ended in front of the east arbor. In this manner, 4 circuits of the square were made in a c-clockwise fashion – 4 songs were started in front of each arbor. The 17th song took place in front of the west arbor. For this one the dancers were in a ring approximating a circle – the 4 men inside were still in the same order. At a point in the song, all danced toward the center and shook their poles violently up and down – it looked as if they were beating the 4 men inside the circle – in fact once Nichi Gray said in English something like "Let 'em have it!" At the end of this song they regrouped in the long oval of the first song. At a point in the song they turned and danced to the south arbor – as they had done for the first song. Now followed another 4 circuits (4 songs before each arbor) as had taken place in the beginning. The 16th song in this cycle brought them back to the west arbor. Now followed another song which had a dance like that which went with the 17th song. This completed the Feather Dance – there were two cycles of 16 + 1 songs.

During the Feather Dance one old woman (Chief Sewell's wife) went into the square ground and yelled derisively at the dancers – her Creek words caused laughter among the spectators. Others [7a] near me were engaging each other to get up and say something. Once Nichi Gray said something in Creek and added in English "Women, no good!" Most of the women had brought benches and chairs from the camps and sat around the limits of the square to watch the feather dance. Nichi told me later (on questioning) that today it was the women's turn to get into the men (kid them) – yesterday when the women danced (Ribbon Dance) the men could tease them while they danced.

Following the Feather Dance the men sat under their arbors – played cards, talked – or got out and threw the ball around. The medecine man sat under the east arbor and mixed another batch of medecine. Young men went and got more buckets of water for him. Finally George sprinkled medecine from a dipper and then poured a dipper full into the fire. (As he did the time before). The pail for the women was set outside the square to the east and the two teen-age boys started their dipper to bucket brigade from the medecine tub to the bucket. The women lined up with their containers – washed hands, feet, face, hair with the medecine – tasted it too. (As they had done before.)

The men sitting under the arbor had been making a number of comments – some in English. One said "Let's go, I'm hungry!" There were several other similar jabs* from time to time – all on the same theme – how hungry they were.

After the women finished the men took the medecine again – by arbors. First the west arbor, then the south, and finally the north. They drank under the east arbor and vomited outside the square to the east. After vomiting they would go in groups to the north – presumably to wash. On returning all had some kind of wood. One pair of men made a joke of it – a huge man brought a very small stick on his shoulder, while his smaller partner carried practically a whole dead tree over a foot in diameter. Many men as they threw their wood on the pile let out yips – the man clowning with the small piece gave a particularly loud one. Quite a few men coming back started to go to the east of the fire instead of around to the west in a c-counterwise manner. Men sitting under the arbors would good-naturedly yell at them to go around the fire the right

way – which they would do a little sheepishly. In general during the day I was impressed with the large amount of good-natured joking going on – they men seemed to enjoy themselves. [8]

This was the 4th and last time to take the medecine and

when they finished it was way after 6:00pm. The men sat under their arbors a while. I had been told they were going to do a Buffalo Dance and waited for this. However, Benny Tiger got up and gave a speech in Creek. Then he sang a very short song and called something in Creek (actually it was a name). At this a man would get up, go around the fire (always c-clockwise) to the west arbor and he and Benny Tiger would touch hands (actually it looked as if the man would give something to Benny – but subsequent actions seem to indicate that the reverse is true). Then the man would go back to his arbor and make a sweeping motion with his right hand from right to left (c-clockwise) in front of the arbor – while doing this he rubbed his thumb and index finger as if he were powdering and spreading some small amount of most anything. After the finishing of such a hand-pass the occupants of the arbor would sing out *Ma•do* ... This ceremony went by arbors – starting with the south one and ending with the west. Approximately 15 individuals did this – ranging in age from teen-agers to some who were about 40 years old. I heard a woman in the car next to us saying afterwards that her husband liked his name. So I asked Nichi Gray's wife who was there – she told me that the men were being given Indian names. (Remember at Arbeka last year some men were given "square names").

After giving the Indian names Benny Davis Tiger talked a short time in Creek. Then all the men took off to the various arbors and ate supper. They ate a long time and then came back and sat under the arbors again. Then two men came out of the west arbor carrying sticks about 3' long, split at the end, and with a white feather tied in the split. The leader of the two men was Willy Gray. They started at the arbor NW of the square and ran by the front of all the arbors – sometimes through them. While running they shouted in Creek. Someone told me they were telling people to get ready for the buffalo dance. Their run was a c-clockwise circuit of the camps. Then people seemed to collect from every where – many women and girls with long colorful ribbons tied on, men with braided yarn sashes over the right shoulder. Nichi Gray put on a white shirt with black, red, and yellow piping sewed around the shoulders (all patch work?*) – he also had a wide yarn belt and a feathered war-bonnet. Nichi took the small inner tube drum and stood on the buffalo (small dirt mound NE of the north arbor). Thompson and Thomas Deer were first in line and shook coconut shell rattles. People got in [8a] back of them – alternating couples – two men, two women, and so on. The women with shell and can rattles were near the front of the dancers. The dancers formed a double line (by couples) which was a long spiral c-clockwise about the buffalo mound. Nichi Gray led the songs – as he sang he turned around on the mound – also beat the small drum. The two leading men shook their rattles, the women shook their leg rattles, and many people sang along with Nichi. The dance step was two beats with each foot always forward. The effect was tremendously impressive of colorful costumes, the rattles, the singing, and Nichi and his war bonnet dancing above all (he is tall, was standing on mound, and the war bonnet was high). A number of songs were sung – and many circuits of the mound were made by the dancers. Then Nichi got down from the mound and unwound the spiral and led the long double line of dancers into the square ground and rewound the spiral around the fire – the path to the fire and the resulting spiral was c-clockwise. Here a

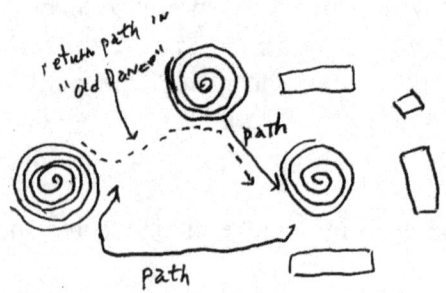

number of songs were sung and many circuits of the fire were made. Again Nichi unwound the spiral – this time he led the dancers into the ball game area and rewound the spiral around the pole with the fish on top. This time the path from the fire was clockwise (in relation to the fire), but the spiral of dancers about the pole was c-clockwise. Again a number of songs were sung and many circuits of the pole were made.

At the end of the Buffalo Dance, Willie Gray (one of the two men with feathered sticks) ran quickly away – he returned with what looked like a turtle shell rattle (one shell on the end of a stick). This was handed on to Nichi who then proceeded to lead the "Long Dance". A number of songs of this dance were sung while dancing around the ball pole. Then Nichi unwound the spiral and led the dancers into the square ground. There he rewound the spiral (c-clockwise) around the fire and finished the Long dance (about ½ was around the ball pole and ½ around the fire) – in leading them from pole to fire he just projected part of a song where he sings "*Hi Ho*" and the response is "*How*" – the dance step is two beats with each foot.

{marginal note: At the time I thought this dance was the "Old Dance" but Nichi Gray told me later it was the "Cry Dance" which has songs just a little different from the "Old Dance". Nichi said he had 3 more songs left but he quit because he was tired.}

After the Long Dance the men returned to their arbors – Benny Tiger talked in Creek. It was now almost dark. The women started feeding visitors under their arbors – men would come out and say "We can take [9] 12 over there" or "I want 8 there (pointing)". Finally after about an hour and a half everybody was fed.

While people were eating supper and afterwards, the men sat under the arbors – a few helped seat visitors at various tables. Benny Tiger gave a number of relatively short talks from time to time. The men in the north arbor sang songs every once in a while – those sounded like "Ball Game" songs and were led by Nichi Gray.

Finally about 10:00pm everyone had been fed. There was now a rather tremendous crowd. People from other square grounds had hired trucks and come in groups. I was introduced by Henry Weller to a group of 15 or 20 people (almost all men from Hanah) – the name of their square is Muddy Water. Amy and Joe Canard {Conard} were there in their pickup truck. Joe Hicks from Arbeka was there. A well known singer from Yuchi was there – some one told us that he joins the church every fall after the stomp dance season closes and then every summer goes back to stomp dancing – Rose Hunt says the Indians call them winter Christians. The Hanah group wanted a buckskin to make a drum from – that was why I was introduced to them, it was thought I might know how to get one. One of their men told me that their place had not functioned the last few years (not his words) and that they were trying to reorganize.

Benny Tiger gave another talk in Creek, Willy Gray and his ass't made their c-clockwise circuits of the fire, talking. Then the first leader came forth and the night's dancing started. This night it was just one "stomp dance" after another. There was no "4 corner dance", "Dark dance", "Double Header", etc. I slept for maybe ½ or ¾ of an hour about 3:30am, but others who were awake said nothing but stomp dancing went on. Finally around 5:15am – it was quite light but the sun wasn't yet up – Nichi Gray led the "old dance" again. Some young fellows and older women at the last ordinary stomp dance had started pretending they were drunk and cutting up a little – but drunk dance came out of it. The feathered stick carriers entered the clowning a little, but making believe they were going to rule {root ?} out the pretended drunks.

After the "old dance" people sat and stood around the edges of the square. Benny Tiger said a few words again and I heard someone say [9a] in English "Let's go shake hands". This turned out to be a mass hand-shaking ceremony. Not everyone participated – many people drove away after the Old Dance. I would estimate about 150 people were shaking hands. This ceremony looked complicated while it was going on, but I believe it was done this way: in theory there were two groups of people – the New Tulsa group and visitors – however some visitors like Grace Aikens (Caddo-Wichita) got in the home group.

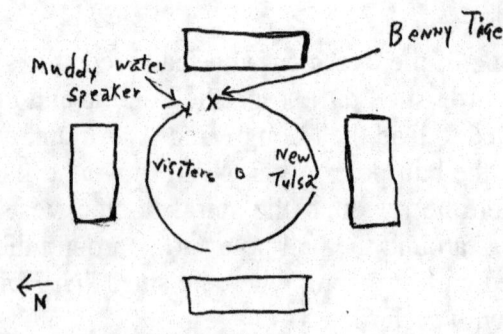

Benny Tiger first gave a long oration in Creek – must have been 8 or 10 minutes. When he finished the man from Muddy Water gave another oration in Creek – maybe 4 or 5 minutes long.

Then the two lines started shaking hands: an end person turned and shook hands with the person next to him and then went on down the line shaking hands – the person behind the leader followed, and so on. Thus at the end, everyone in one group had shaken the hand of all persons in that group.

Then the New Tulsa group went around the arc of visitors shaking their hands. Thus, at the end everyone had shaken everyone else's hand. That finished the ceremony.

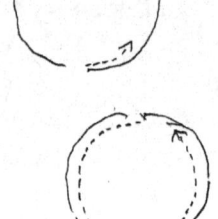

Afterwards I was talking with the man from Muddy Water and with Henry Weller. Hank said he didn't know "that you could talk so good". The man said that he had just got started – the old people were the ones who talked like that – but they needed someone in their group to do it, so {he} was trying. I asked what he had said – he said he had just said "it was nice to be together here – that all were friends – that we are all Indians – it doesn't make any difference what tribe you are, we are all friends – that it was good for everybody to come together and shake each other's hand." [10]

Now the women got breakfast and soon everyone was fed. Then the men got their ball sticks and went out by the pole and started throwing the ball around. The women and girls got out and a series of games started – like those seen last month, only more people were playing.

Mrs Sulpher and her daughter (Billy Jones) were there – the girl shook shells all night and when she talked to Iva, she couldn't hardly wait 'til the ball games started'. This was the 4th Green Corn dance of the week for her, too.

Hank Weller and Nichi Gray rounded up a group of singers and we went off to a house belonging to ____ Fixico {p204, Field ?}. There we recorded Ball Game, Duck Dance, Gar Dance, Stomp Dance, and Old Dance Songs.

Ball Game   {Leader – Nichi Gray
                {accompaniment: water drum – Nichi Gray
                        2 coconut rattles – Thomas Deer & Thompson Deer
rattles got out of time occasionally. Some singers didn't know songs at all

Duck Dance   {Leader – Nichi Gray
                {accompaniment: coconut rattle – Nichi Gray
                        can rattles – Billie Jones

Gar Dance   {Leader – Nichi Gray
                {accompaniment: coconut rattle – Nichi Gray
                        can rattles – Billie Jones

Stomp Dance

{Leaders		can rattles –
Nichi Gray	(old style)	Billie Jones
Ollie Tiger	("blues ")	
Babe Harjo	(old style)	
Thomas Harjo	("blues ")	
Nichi Gray	(old style)	
Nichi Gray	(Old Dance) (old style) Thomas Deer whooping [10a]	

Sept. 16-17, 1950 New Tulsa Stomp Dance and Ball Game

We arrived at the New Tulsa square ground at approximately 5:30. At this time the men and women were playing ball to the north of the square. This is the area with the pole with the wooden fish on top. The ball game was the same as we have seen before. After a while they stopped and the women went and cooked supper. It was dark – Bennie Tiger made an announcement in Creek. The Schmitts and Wellers were told in English that he had said that those people who hadn't eaten were to stand by the square ground. Then men from various arbors came up and told us where to go and eat.

After supper there was a very long wait for the dance – but a few things did happen from time to time. The men sat under the arbors in the square. Finally Bennie Tiger got up in front of the west arbor and made a long talk in Creek. Then various men came up to the arbor and gave money. I was sitting with Bill Lehna, chiefs of the Tullahassee Square (Seminole), and he told me a little of what was happening. It seems that only 11 members of New Tulsa took medecine this day and that there were fines for those who belonged and didn't take the medecine. The fine was 50 cents, but if they couldn't give that, they should give anything.

Then came a series of political speeches. It seems that there are 4 men running for chief of the Creek nation. Two of these are Joe Canard {Conard} (married to Amy from Arbeka) and John Davis, a preacher. After a short talk from B Tiger, a young fellow who is somewhat crippled went to the front of the west arbor and gave a <u>long</u> talk in Creek – at least a half hour. This was a speech urging people to vote for Joe Canard. Following this man Joe Canard went to the front of the west arbor and gave another very long talk in Creek. When he finished, another man went to the front of the arbor and gave another long talk – I don't know who he was urging people to vote for.

After the political speeches Nichi Gray led a number of ball game songs under the north arbor — where he customarily sits. He beat on a small inner tube drum to accompany himself.

Finally the stomp dancing started. This was the same as usual. I noticed that after every dance Bennie Tiger would say something like *hude'mo'* over several times. I asked about it and was told it was like saying "Lets have another". Tiger also gave talks from time to time – and men kept coming up to the main arbor and giving money.

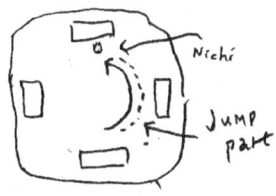

Once during a stomp dance Warren Weller got hurt in some manner. It seemed to bother the Creeks unduly to us since Warnie wasn't hurt badly. Bennie Tiger came over to where we were sitting – the Schmitts, Wellers, and other Caddos. Tiger managed to explain to us in his difficult English that he was going to give a talk about being careful while dancing. He then went in front of the west arbor and gave a talk in Creek – presumably about dancing carefully.

Once during the night they varied the regular stomp dances with a Double-Header dance. This was like we have seen before. However, we did see one new (to us) dance – the Fox Dance. For this Nichi Gray sat in the east side of the square, fading east, with the water drum. Only women danced – a couple with leg rattles. The leading women started by Nichi with the others behind her. The dance is quite slow. Each song ends up with the leader again by {near} Nichi – the last 1/3 of the circuit was a jump step — a high hopping step with feet together. [2]

Sept 16, 1950 New Tulsa [2]

There were about 8 songs during the Fox dance – one for each circuit of the square. The next morning I was talking with Nichi Gray and his wife – they said that the Fox Dance wasn't danced too good. Mrs Gray said that up at Arbeka they really knew how to do that dance.

Toward morning there was quite a bit of clowning going on. A couple of the teen age kids had rubber face masks which they put on – in the morning Bennie Tiger put one of the masks on to the delight of the crowd. Nichi Gray and Thomas Deer had taken over the duty of carrying the ball sticks and running around encouraging the dancers. Toward morning they started clowning even though they were still acting as officials – they would dance a while, sort of exaggerate the step, run around fast and yell. Joanna Tiger Reed started yelling during the next to the last dance – she can really yell, long high-pitched ones. The chief's wife also yells the same way. The last dance of the night, when it was quite light but before the sun came up, was the "Old Dance" led by Nichi Gray.

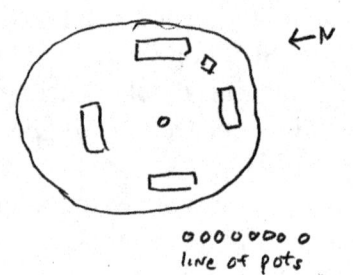

o o o o o o Do o
line of pots

When the dance ended the women went back to their arbors and got various pots and pans with food in them – cold. There was one pot of coffee. The pots were lined up in a long line extending from north to south – this was to the west of the square ground.

I was told by MacIntosh to just go down the line and help myself, which I did. I ate standing, as the rest of the men did. The women went and ate under the arbors. Bennie Davis Tiger had made an announcement in Creek at the beginning. I talked to MacIntosh while eating and asked about this new (to me) feature. He said that in the old days that {they} were strict about keeping men who had taken medecine separate from the women – now they weren't so strict, but they had decided to do this at this time. (It may have been because the ball game was to follow – KS)

After everybody had finished eating they got ready for the ball game. The men who were going to play got out on the square ground and lined up in two lines running north-south and facing each other across the fire.

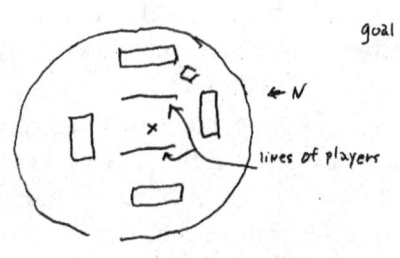

goal

←N

lines of players

The west side had more players – over twenty to about 14 for east side. The players had ball sticks over their shoulders with reddish G-strings (and some had basketball shorts) rolled up and hanging from the ends of the sticks.

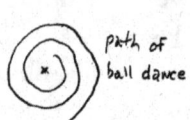

path of ball dance

Fixico counted the players [3, Sept. 16, 1950 New Tulsa] and evened up the sides by two methods. First he talked (with the help of others) some men not lined up to join the game. Then he took players from the west side and put them on the east side. Finally there were about 22 players on each side. (The Fixico is the young married man at whose house we recorded the songs.)

After the sides were paired the leader of the west team led his team off into the trees to the west of the square – actually he and his team walked to the school grounds of Spaulding where the game was to be played. Nichi Gray was leader of the east team – they stayed behind. Nichi gave a talk in Creek to his players. Nichi had two balls tied on stick – one of these was covered in grey squirrel fur and the other with red squirrel fur. Nichi held the stick with balls in his hand and led his players in a kind of stomp dance around the fire. The man just behind Nichi gave a stylized yell starting near the end of the song and continuing to the end of each song. The yell was long shrill and high pitched — held this way for some time and then near the end the pitch decreased like the fire siren. There were about 8 songs. Then Nichi led his men over to the east side of the stomp ground – they faced east and Nichi gave them another talk in Creek. Then most of his team walked to Spaulding – he got in his car. I drove my car and because several cars ahead got stuck in the mud, it was over a half hour before I got to the game ground. I missed any ceremony which the other team may have had. (Mrs Sulpher later told me that both teams were supposed to do the stomp dance in the square – and both were supposed to do it again on the ball field.)

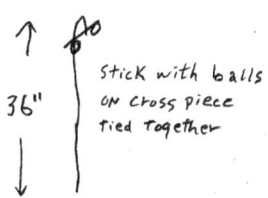

Stick with balls on cross piece tied together

36"

The players dressed in the latrines on the football and baseball field of the Spaulding school. I was told they had decided to have the game there because on their regular ball field there were some oil wells which got in the way of the game. The players had a wide variety of clothes – some played in jean overalls, some wore undershorts or basketball shorts with red G-strings — some wore just shorts. Many had their faces painted with red and blue lines — it may have been one side was red and the other blue. Quite a few had feathers in their hair — some with the horse hair whorl around the base.

After dressing each side formed in columns of twos and marched through the goals. Nichi as leader of the east team led his team through the goal which was on the south side of the field — the other team marched through the goal on the north side. The marching was timed so that the two teams met in the middle of the field. Then they formed two lines facing each other and laid their ball sticks in front of them. The goals were made of 3 pieces each of fresh wood with the bark on them — were like a football goal only smaller — about 6' wide and 7' or 8' tall.

Sept 17, 1950 New Tulsa [4]

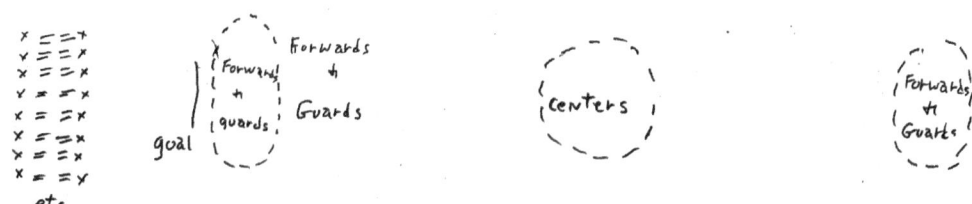

After every thing seemed to be paired off satisfactorily the players picked up their sticks. Then Bennie Tiger got in between the two lines of players and gave a talk in Creek. At the finish of the talk he gave a yell – and all the players yelled, and ran into the position for the start of the game. One group – about a third of the players stayed in the center of the field, and another group formed around the south goal and another around the north goal. This seemed to divide the players into something corresponding to centers, forwards and goal guards. Nichi Gray was a forward and was at the south goal so the teams must have marched through the goals they were to attack.

To start the game the ball was thrown up in the air in the center of the field and the forwards fought for it. The one who got it would throw it toward the goal his team was attacking – or if possible the man could run with it as far toward the goal as possible. Actually one center attacking the north goal made 6 or 7 of his team's points. A goal was scored when a player threw the ball through the goal – not over. The red and grey balls were used alternatively after goals were scored. Almost anything seemed fair – it was the roughest game I have ever seen. Many times men got hit hard accidentally with the hickory ball sticks – and hard. But at other times the hits were obviously purposeful. Sometimes a man would be running with the ball in his sticks with an opponent chasing him – if he couldn't be stopped any other way, the one chasing would hit the man with the ball with his sticks as hard as he could swing. Other times a man would be waiting poised to catch a ball with his sticks and an opponent would hit him over the head or shoulders with great force to make him miss the ball. Other times a man would be bent over to pick up a ball with his sticks and an opponent would smash him across the back. Tackling was also fair — as was shoving, tripping, pulling – in fact I didn't notice anything that was considered unfair. Several women with water buckets were out on the field – when the ball was at the opposite side of the field they would give men on their side water. Older men and other spectators wandered around the field — only getting out of the way when the ball came their way. There was no outside – anyplace the ball went there was a scramble for it. A common feature [5, Sept. 17, 1950 New Tulsa] was a sort of group stalemate where 8 or 10 players would be in a circle around the ball. They would be holding each other's sticks down on the ground to keep the other side from getting the ball. Some would be working a stick free to pry with and eventually get the ball free. At this time some would pull opponents away from the circle. At times they would be 3 or 4 minutes with the ball like this.

When hit with the ball sticks the one who was hurt would often jump up in the air and kick his feet out behind him and "gobble" — this is a noise something like a turkey gobbler makes. It is conceived of as a challenge – although it must also help psychologically to get over pain – like saying "ouch, god damn it" in English at the first pain of cutting oneself with a knife.

After the game was over I commented on the roughness of it — I was told that this was nothing like a "match game" between two towns — "this game was between friends" and it wasn't so rough. However, one young fellow told me that even in these games between "friend" "you didn't know what to expect — you never know what one of your friends might be thinking — he might think you had been looking at his wife too much and take it out on you in the game." Several of the players were cut about the face and had blood fleck over them —one man had several deep cuts over his brows and had blood literally streaming down the front of him — this was the man who scored so many goals. It is considered wrong to quit, no matter how badly you are hurt you should keep on playing. If you quit for any reason you are the equivalent of a sissy. The Creeks also believe that no matter how badly you get hurt playing ball, you will get better within 4 days. (We heard some time later that the high scorer got awfully sick after the game — and finally had to send him to the hospital — he almost died.)

There were no time outs in the game — they kept playing until the west side scored ten points — that was the number which had been decided on beforehand. I was told that the usual number for a game was 20 points, but this day it was 10 because when they got permission to use the Spaulding athletic field it was with the understanding that they would be through playing before church started — the church faces the field and the noise of the game would be distracting. Ordinarily the first team to score 20 points wins — today it was the first to score 10. There was no ceremony after the game that I saw — I did not go back to the square, however.

Misc Info.

Peyote — I talked to MacIntosh the Creek married to a Pawnee about peyote. I told him I would like to go a meeting and had wanted to go for some time — but, that I didn't want to force my way in, that I was waiting until I knew I was welcome. He told me not to wait — it's up to you to make up your mind." He was quite talkative on the subject and said things like "you might find God through peyote." [Sept 17. 1950 New Tulsa]

Macintosh talked to me about the power of fire – pointing to the fire in the center of the square. A preacher had once questioned his religion and he had told the preacher that there was some power in fire – you could take raw meat and cook it, the fire changed it, you could take flour and water and mix it and bake it – then you had bread, the fire had changed it – it proved that there was some power in the fire that was good. Through this fire you might be able to find God — God was good, he had put things on earth for men to use.

I said that I thought that Creek didn't follow peyote much. MacIntosh said that Yuchi were strong peyote followers and that also now there are many Creek you {who} follow peyote.

Gossip: While waiting for the dance to start I was talking in a group of men – Joe Canard (Creek), his political campaigner who is Hank Weller (Caddo), MacIntosh, Bill Lenha (Seminole) and perhaps one or two other Indian men. There was a lot of telling of dirty jokes and then some stories about Church people (Christians).

One of the men told a story about an Indian who gave up going to church because he had lost two wives to preachers. He got married and then started going to church – the first thing he knew the preacher had his wife. He got married again and went to church — another preacher took his wife — so he quit going to church. (Moral of story — preachers are no good.)

Macintosh told a story about an old Pawnee man that he lived with. They heard that a famous Choctaw preacher was going to be in town — that evening the old Pawnee said let's go to town and hear that man, he's supposed to be good — let's go hear what he has to say. So they went in and listened. After a while the preacher got to going on Stomp Dance — how people who did that were going straight to hell. The old Pawnee nudged Macintosh in the ribs, kidding him because he knew that MacIntosh believed in Creek religion. Then the preacher started in on the buffalo dance and how terrible that was — MacIntosh nudged the old man in the ribs because he knew he belonged to the buffalo lodge. The old man got up, disgusted, and walked out, MacIntosh too.

The young cripple fellow told a story of his experience — he was working in some town (Tulsa?) and kept going around to a church — he was the only Indian in the group. Once an Indian missionary came around to talk on the day they were electing the Sunday School superintendent. He (the young man) was nominated and didn't seem to have any opposition. Then the Indian missionary got up and gave a talk against Indians — couldn't take responsibility, etc — never said a good word for Indians — everything against them (This seems to have kept the fellow from being sup't.)

MacIntosh and Bill Lehna told stories of how they used to drink even when they went to Indian school — both went to Chilocco, I believe. Lehna was expelled for drinking — as was MacIntosh. MacIntosh was working as a printer — some fellow wanted to drink, so Mac told him to go {get} it in town — go in a back room. That fellow came home drunk (to school) and the authorities got after him — he told them MacIntosh got him the liquor. Mac said he wouldn't tell on his white friend. Then the authorities got after Mac {so he left} school and never went back. [7, Sept 16-7, 1950 New Tulsa]

Bill Lehna told me of the last dance at Tullahasse which was to come up soon – he asked me to come over. He said he was chief over there. When he got though talking to me – he went and sat under the west arbor — he was asked by Bennie Tiger – Lehna called it the "chief's arbor."

We also heard of a dance to be held at Muddy Water (Wiwogufki) on the 30th of this month. Mrs Nichi Gray said that was her town and she wanted us to come. This is a town that is reorganizing this year after a lapse of a few years.

Mrs Gray told Alice Waller and Iva (I listened) of how Mrs Sulfer had shot a woman twice at a dance at Arbeka. Alex Sulpher is the medecine man who is in great demand. It seems he has been running around with this woman. At this dance Mrs Sulpher went up to her and pulled out a gun and shot her twice – she is in critical condition, but will now pull through. Mrs Sulpher is still free. The woman has said she doesn't want to press charges. Mrs Sulpher even got her gun back. Both Alice and Mrs Gray thought that she had done wrong — Alice said she should have shot her husband — Mrs Gray agreed that would have been alright.

Sept. 15, 1951 New Tulsa Dance

This was the date for the last stomp dance of the year at New Tulsa near Spaulding. We had heard that it was to be followed by a ball game the next day and I wanted to see it. The Wellers came by and we left for New Tulsa in the afternoon.

Arrived at New Tulsa about 4:45. The men and a lot of younger women were playing ball around the pole. We were asked to eat at Joanna Reed's, Ollie Tiger's, and Nichie Gray's wife's arbor — which we did. After eating we went over to watch the ball game – it was a most spirited one. The women were pushing the men — once a couple got a man down and made believe they were going to take off his shirt and pants. This game lasted until about 6:00 p.m. The men then went and cleaned up at their arbors and ate. Then they went back to the square and Bennie Davis Tiger said something in Creek. Now all the men got up and walked to the west boundary of the square and shouted in Creek – this was the invitation to eat. One of the men told me in English they wanted us to go eat. The visitors were then directed to various arbors until all the tables were full. It took 2 or 3 sittings to feed everyone.

After everyone had eaten the men went and sat under the arbors. Bennie Tiger talked from time to time. Men were coming up to the arbor and giving Bennie money. This was in the nature of a fine for missing taking of medicine — or missing dances held throughout the year. There is not a set amount – you pay what you want to – 10 cents, 15 cents, or anything you want to give. After each person gave something Bennie would give a talk in Creek – then he would take the money over to some elderly woman of his family who sat outside the square. Even during the dance later, men came up and gave money and Bennie went through the same procedure. I realize now that many of the talks by speakers at dances are of such nature – explanation that so and so had given money and why.

Finally they got started dancing — it started with Nichi Gray leading the ball game dance. The square had another feature added this time – a rack of one forked stick and a tree with a stringer set in the fork and nailed to the tree. This was about 7' high and 12' long and was to hang ball sticks and G-strings over.

Before the ball game dance, some men hung their ball

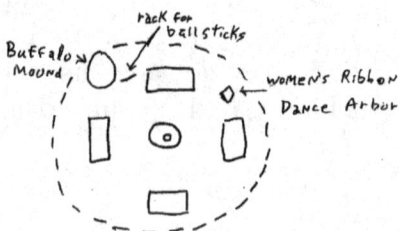

sticks – with G-string and yarn belt rolled in a little bundle hanging from the sticks – over the rack. Others carried their sticks in the ball game dance. This started with Nichie Gray standing on the buffalo mound carrying the little hooked stick with two balls attached. The men gathered around — like for a stomp dance. Nichie sang the same song as at Arbeka – the men went around in a counter-clockwise fashion. One man behind Nichie gave the siren-like yell. The others answered him — and then yipped and gobbled at the appropriate times. Those with ball sticks shook them in the air. Still singing, Nichie unwound the dance and led them out and rewound them around the fire and continued the same dance there. Finally he took them over to the rack — not in line but in a massed group where the dance ended in a big yell. Then those with sticks hung them over [2] the rack. After resting awhile under the arbors – perhaps 15 minutes – they repeated the ball game dance.

After resting a few minutes some of the men got about 3 chairs and set them before the rack with ball sticks and got Nichi Gray. Then a number of men started yelling in Creek – it was for the women to come and sing ball game songs. Finally they assembled about 15 women in a group back of Nichi Gay and the other 2 men in chairs. Nichi beat the small water drum and the others shook coconut rattles while Nichi led the singing – the women joined in at appropriate intervals tending to sing very loud and raucous compared to the men. Four or five men stood to the north and south of the group and yelled loudly from time to time at the women – especially if they let up in enthusiasm and volume. Other women came up and joined the group – until perhaps 30 in all were assembled.

Nichi Gray led perhaps 8 or 10 songs and then gave way to another man. In all there were 4 different men as leaders – 2 of the others were Jody Buck and Benny D Tiger.

A friend of Hank's who works with him at Washita told me they (the New Tulsa bunch) were doing this one up in old time style. This is the way that they ran things when they played a real match game – one between 2 different towns, while this town (say New Tulsa) was going through the ball game dance, and singing ball game songs, the other town would be doing the same thing. He said that they would sing the ball game song 4 or 5 times during the night.

Most of the ball game songs had words – Hank's friend gave me some free translations of them. Those I remember follow:

"They're fighting for the ball by a thicket."

"The ball is thrown the other way." (After fighting for it near one goal, it is thrown toward the goal this other town is attacking.)

"You can hear them yelling (challenging)." This is the one I like best.

After finishing the ball game songs, the ball game dance led by Nichie Gray was repeated again. Then they started stomp dancing. This went on until about 2:00 when a fine rain changed to a hard one and the dances stopped. Most cars left but we were boxed in and Iva and the kids {twins} slept on the floor and seats — I sat. 10 or 15 men kept the fire going in the square and stood around it all night. Finally in the morning the rain stopped and we ate breakfast at the Tiger-Reed-Gray arbor. It was a wonderful breakfast – beef, several kinds of chicken, coffee, fried pork, home canned peaches.

The ball game was postponed. There was a squirrel dinner planned for Oct. 7 and it was decided to play ball on that day.

I asked Hank's friend what the extra small arbor in the square ground was for — he said for the women to sit under when they rested from the ribbon dance.

The medicine man for New Tulsa is a man named Marks — he is also the medicine man for Tallahasee (Bill Lehna's stomp ground.)

Oct. 7, 1951 New Tulsa, Squirrel Dinner and Ball Game

We left Norman about 10:30 for New Tulsa and arrived shortly after noon. I was surprised by the large number of cars — parking was something of a difficulty. There were probably 350 people there. The Bells were with us and Bob and I walked around – met Mrs. Nichi Gray, Robert Reed – then took Bob over and introduced him to Old Man Sewell, "the chief." He actually spoke some English to us — told us that they were "going to eat, soon." I asked if Bob could take pictures and Sewell said sure.

On our arrival the men and women were playing the ball game around the pole. Benny Davis Tiger was acting as the leader, as usual – when he threw up a new ball after every point, he would give a speech. Bob took several pictures of the game.

After the game was over the women got the food ready. Thomas Deer came over to talk to Bob and myself. Told us that the men were going to eat inside the "ring" (low earth ridge around the square ground) and that the women were going to eat "there" (pointed to tables set up south of the Square.) He told us we were welcome to go to his camp and eat — I asked if it was against the rules for us to eat with the rest of the men — he said it would be perfectly all right — "there's no medicine today" (that is, it would be OK for us to eat in square since they had not taken any medicine) — any one (male) would be welcome to eat inside the ring. Deer also referred to the dinner as "dinner on the ground." I could see that the women were fixing the usual Creek style food and asked about the "squirrel dinner." Deer said that he had shot 6 squirrels and brought them — other men had done the same and that there were maybe 60 squirrels altogether. I mentioned how the Shawnee had squirrel dinners — Deer said he knew about these, he had been to a number — he is part Shawnee and part Sac and Fox. I got no hint of any ritual hunt connected with this Creek squirrel dinner.

We talked of the ball game to follow in the afternoon — Deer wasn't going to play. He said the last time he played was "the last match game" the one in which 3 or 4 fellows got killed. This game seems to have been between New Tulsa and some friendly towns on one side and Wiwogufky (Muddy Water) and their friendly towns on the other. Deer said they only threw up the ball 3 times — then they just went to it (fighting). This means they had scored 3 points in the game and then a general fight broke out — Deer said several fellows died from the fighting. We asked how long ago this was — he said about 25 years ago (1927 or so). (Later another man said the same game was about 17 years ago.) {Last huge match game was at milepost 234 on I-40.}

While we were talking to Deer, Benny Davis started talking in the square. Deer said he was telling where they were going to eat. In a few minute some men went to the camps and got containers of food and set them in a line in front of the west arbor — thus the line of food was oriented North-South. We were told just to step up and help ourselves — as all the men were doing. Several times men went out and got more food to replenish empty pots. Finally after all the men had finished, some of the men took the pots back to camp. Bones and other refuse were just thrown on the ground. While the men were standing and eating, the women sat at a long line of tables placed end to end to the south of the square. The line of tables was roughly east-west but I don't know if the direction orientation is significant. The women ate while the men were eating.

After eating the men stood around or sat under the arbors. Then Benny Davis Tiger and

Tiger h
Ball game
leaders

ball
sticks

the 2 ball game leaders started organizing their teams. Wally Fixico was leader of one side and the fellow who took such a beating in last year's game was [3] leader of the other side. I was sitting under the south arbor with Bill Lehna (chief of *Tullahassee*) while the organizing of sides took place. Bill said that when you became leader of one of the sides, you were leader for 4 years. Under the direction of Benny Tiger and the two leaders, the players were paired off. As they chose the players they laid their sticks down opposite each other.

Finally all the players were paired off — scouts went out among the people around the square and sitting under the arbors getting men to agree to play. In the end there were 30 + players on each side. Then Bennie Tiger made a talk in Creek; — Bill said he was saying they were going to have one last dance, were going to go slow. The meaning here was that this was the last dance for New Tulsa until next year and it was a going to be slow for memories sake — friends would dance together and remember the good times of the summer. Then Nichi Gray led both sides in the ball game dance around the fire in the square. It was like other ball game dances except that it was sung very slow and done at a walking pace. Nichi led them over to the rack for sticks at the end of the dance (he sung right up to the rack) and the dance ended with a big shout as the players waved their ball sticks in the air.

Following the ball game dance most of the players walked over to the field east of the square where the game was to be played. Most people drove their cars over and lined each side of the playing field. Two goals were about 120 yards apart — one to the east and the other to the west. These were narrow — made of 3 pieces of fresh blackjack oak — about 10 feet high and 4 feet wide. There were thick grass and weeds on the field and people were saying that it would be hard to find the ball.

One group of players including Nichi Gray went in a little thicket east of east goal and dressed there. The other side stayed in the woods to the west of the west goal and dressed there. Nichi Gray turned out to be on the winning side that attacked the goal to the east. After dressing the team Nichi was on followed him over toward the east goal — about 60' back of the goal he led them in the ball game dance again — as an ending he led his players up to the goal so that at the end of the song they yelled and shook their sticks toward the other goal. The other team could be heard singing the ball game {song} off in the woods west of the west goal.

Then, the two teams came to the center of the field and a long process of pairing off the players started again. Of course the placers knew which side to line up on. A few more players were recruited for the game at this time. Under the direction of Benny Tiger and the two leaders the players paired off and laid their sticks opposite each other again. This time the line of sticks went north south (as back at the square ground). After pairing off, the players listened to a talk in Creek and split up and went back to their goals. Nichi Gray led his side in the ball game dance around the east goal and at the same time one of the players of the other team led his side in the ball game dance around the west goal. As the players (dancers) came around the circle nearest the field they would yell, make faces, and shake their sticks at the other side. The two dances ended almost at the same time with the players massed in back of each goal yelling and shaking their sticks at each other. [4]

Now they went back to the center of the field and listened to another talk in Creek — this was by an old man. While he was talking the sides split up — defenders, attackers, and the group staying at the center of the field. Then while he kept up his talking he threw the ball in the air and the game started. When it is thrown up the center men don't try to catch it — they swing at it, trying to knock it toward the goal their side is attacking.

The game was like the other 2 I have seen — but much rougher than the one at Arbeka. There were several near fights that started — slugging matches with the ball sticks. These occurred in big massed groups of players trying to get a ball. I noticed that when such a fight started the other players would "gobble," raise their sticks up in the air and push together — this effectively stopped fights since the massing hampered the swinging of sticks, and the raising of so many sticks up in air blocked any swings that were taken.

The game was played until one side scored 20 points — this turned out to be the team attacking the east goal. One of the old men kept score with handfuls of little sticks. The non-playing men wandered about the field at will — often yelling stereotyped sound and phrases in Creek as their side did something or was attempting to do something. There is a definite feeling that a person belongs to either the east or west side. I would gather that among younger people the reason for being on one side or the other is obscure. Ollie Tiger's wife told me her husband and one son was on one side, and another son was on the other – she did not know why, "they" just told them to play there. One man who was drunk kept saying "$19 west side." Nobody took him up.

The ball often did get lost in the grass – the older men would often find it first and point at it – then the players would come running up and the older men would scurry to get out of the melee.

After the last goal all the players came together at the center of the field and listened to another talk in Creek by the older man who talked at the beginning. When he finished, Nichi Gray and his side went back to the east goal and did the ball game dance again. At the finish Nichi again had them massed back of the goal – Nichi was between the posts facing west – all shook their sticks and yelled. They really gloated over their victory. This dance was so noisy, and emotional, it was even exiting to watch.

Then the players went off and dressed — most people drove off — some stayed at the camps for supper. We were asked to play, but wanted to get back to Norman before {October} dark and so left.

In back of the west goal were some older women – when ever a goal was made by the side attacking this goal (the east team) they danced and waved colored handkerchiefs over their heads – very reminiscent of the war dance step the Caddo women and Plains Indians do – the waving of handkerchief, like we saw among the Arikara this summer.

Babe Hardjo was the best forward the east side had.

May 18, 1952 New Tulsa Squirrel Dinner

Hank and Alice Weller came by in the morning on their way to New Tulsa. They talked us into going. We got there shortly after noon and they were just getting ready to eat. Iva's M & F went along with us.

Thomas Deer took us around – showed us his camp. Told us that the men were going to eat in the square and the women outside. Told us (the men) we could eat at the tables if we wanted. I asked if we could eat with the men – it was OK.

Benny Davis (the talker) came over and talked to us in Creek – Thomas Deer interpreted. Benny told us that this dinner was "to feed the fire" – also that it was "for the fire". In a way he was apologizing for not having a family dinner at tables – told us to come back on May 24 – this was the day set for their medecine dance.

The women took pots of various foods to the edge of the square and the men took them into the square and lined them up N-S in front of the west arbor. We were told to go up and help ourselves – there were squirrel, beef, chicken dishes (all stewed), blue dumplings (some with beans), some with squash or sweet potato), corn bread, *sófki*, and the like. Thomas Deer told us that there was supposed to be no cake, pies, coffee (things associated with white ways) – that it was supposed to be wild foods (white chicken and beef was present.) Before we got there, they had fed the fire and square – they had taken a little of each food and sprinkled it over the fire site and around the square. This was necessary to open up the square for the summer ceremonies. After we finished eating Thomas Deer took us over to his arbor and got coffee for us.

The women ate at tables set end to end by Thomas Deer's camp – there coffee, cake, etc was served to all (Indians & visitors).

After the people finished eating the men and women played ball – some of the teen aged boys got out first – Benny Davis a little later – to yell in Creek from time to time for the women to get out there. When the women did get out there was a very spirited ball game, Ollie Tiger was in rare form.

James H. Howard
(1925 - 1982)

Born in South Dakota, Howard was trained in anthropology at the University of Nebraska (B.A., 1949; M.A., 1950) and the University of Michigan (Ph.D., 1957). In 1950-1953, he served as archeologist and preparator at the North Dakota State Historical Museum; and, in 1955-1957, he was on the staff of the Kansas City (Missouri) Museum. During the summer of 1957, he joined the staff of the Smithsonian's River Basin Surveys. Between 1957 and 1963, he taught anthropology at the University of North Dakota. Between 1963 and 1968, he served in several capacities with the University of South Dakota including assistant and associate professor, director of the Institute of Indian Studies (1963-1966), and Director of the W.H. Over Museum (1963-1968). In 1968, he joined the Department of Sociology at Oklahoma State University, where he achieved the rank of professor in 1970. In 1979, he was a consultant for exhibitions at the Western Heritage Museum in Omaha, Nebraska.

Howard's abiding interest was the people of North America, whom he studied both as an ethnologist and archeologist. Between 1949 and 1982, he worked with the Ponca, Omaha, Yankton and Yaktonai Dakota, Yamasee, Plains Ojibwa (Bungi), Delaware, Seneca-Cayuga, Prairie Potatwatomi of Kansas, Mississippi and Oklahoma Choctaw, Oklahoma Seminole, and Pawnee. His interest in these people varied from group to group. With some he carried out general culture studies; with others, special studies of such phenomena as ceremonies, art, dance, and music. For some, he was interested in environmental adaptation and land use, the latter particularly for the Pawnee, Yankton Dakota, Plains Ojibwa, Turtle Mountain Chippewa, and Ponca, for which he served as consultant and expert witness in suits brought before the United States Indian Claims Commisssion. A long-time museum man, Howard was also interested in items of Indian dress, articles associated with ceremonies, and other artifacts. He was "a thoroughgoing participant-observer, a member of the Ponca *Hethuska* Society, a sharer in ceremonial activities of many Plains tribes, and a first-rate 'powwow man'." (*American Anthropologist* 1986 (88): 692).

As an archeologist, Howard worked at Like-a-Fishhook Village in North Dakota, Spawn Mound and other sites in South Dakota, Gavin Point in Nebraska and South Dakota, Weston and Hogshooter sites in Oklahoma, and the Fortress of Louisbourg in Nova Scotia. He also conducted surveys for the Lone Star Steel Company in Haskall, Latimer, Le Flore and Pittsburg counties in Oklahoma.

While in the Army stationed in Germany he married Elfriede Heinz Howard and they later adopted a Mandan boy and a girl. The boy joined the Army and married an Ethiopian woman, but his life ended tragically when he was killed on the Crow Reservation. Jim's extensive ethnographic and native clothing collection, despite a counter offer from Japan, is now at the Milwaukee Public Museum through the efforts of Nancy Lurie. Today he is best known for his coinage of the term "pan-indien" though he was otherwise adverse to realms of theory, and often challenged native students to better grasp their own cultures, sometime giving offense in doing so.

His sudden death after a London conference was an early instance of fatal Legionnaires disease.

The 1965 Green Corn Ceremony at New Tulsa[91]

New Tulsa square ground is located about two miles south and one mile west of the little town of Spalding, near Holdenville, Oklahoma. The ground is also known as Tulsa Little River and Tulsa Little Water. Like Hickory Ground, it is of the White {now Red} division of the Upper Creek. According to our informants the ground was moved to its present location in 1922 when one of two rival factions at the old Tulsa ground, which was east of Holdenville, removed the ashes from that ground and established itself at the new site. Barney Leader, the present chief of the ground, proudly informed me that Tulsa was one of the very few grounds which has never allowed its ceremonies to lapse, even for one season, and that it has carried on the Green Corn each year, without interruption, for as long as the oldest people can remember. He stated that the people at his ground are principally Coosa, and that the name frequently appears in Busk speeches.

At present the Green Corn held at New Tulsa is one of the most popular in Oklahoma, only Arbika and Hickory Ground ranking close to it in the number of visitors. In addition to its own members the New Tulsa Busk is attended by members of several dormant or discontinued Creek and Seminole square grounds, also by a group of mixed-blood Cherokee who are organized as the Western Kituwha. The Green Corn is also visited, out of curiosity, by Kiowa, Ponca, and other Plains Indians, and by White tourists and hobbyists. Because of this, and because the leaders of the ground are men in their thirties and forties, some Creek and Cherokee sourly comment that the New Tulsa Green Corn is not really "old time." This may reflect a certain degree of jealousy, however, as we observed more traditional customs, costuming, and dances here than at Hickory Ground.

We arrived at this ground on the evening of July 8, 1965. Various members of the ground, including the chief, Barney Leader, made us welcome. He informed us that Stomp dances had been going on for the past week, working up enthusiasm for the main events to take place the 9th and 10th. There was a great deal of coming and going at the square ground, with people setting up camps, hauling water, and other tasks. A concession stand, owned by the chief and operated by his family and friends, offered ball sticks, hat roaches, peacock feathers, [103] soda pop, and candy bars for sale. Some small children were playing the single-pole ball game at the ball ground, northeast of the square ground. We were told that there would be Stomp dancing later that evening, but as we had driven several hundred miles that day we did not stay to observe the dancing.

We arrived at the ground again about 9:00 the morning of July 9th and were pleased to meet our old friend Turner Bear. He pointed out the seating of the various clans in the four beds, also the location of the sacred mound just northeast of the ground (Fig 33). We also took a closer look, in the daylight, at the ball pole. At New Tulsa the ball pole is surmounted by a painted and carved representation of a fish (Fig 26, C) done in a very Mississippian-looking style, reminiscent of the Spiro fish representations (Fig 26, D E). The fish is mounted on a pivot so that when hit squarely on either end by the ball it swings around. Many more people had arrived since the previous evening, including a number of Creeks who live in California but return each year to Oklahoma for the Green Corn.

The Ribbon dance at New Tulsa began about 10:00 a.m. There were forty women and

---

[91]   James Howard   *The Southeast Ceremonial Complex and Its Interpretation*, Missouri Archaeological Society, Memoir 6 1968.

girls taking part. Both Creek and Seminole women were represented in the group. Costume items included cloth shoulder capes with matching skirts, bead net capes, loose blouses ornamented with many hanging ribbons, silver combs with pendant ribbons, and Seminole patchwork costumes. Oklahoma Seminole patchwork has wider bands and larger design elements than that made in Florida. The first ten women all wore terrapin shell leg rattles, the next eight women and girls wore the condensed milk can variety. It was obvious that the terrapin shell variety was the more highly regarded at this ground. The first two women carried the large wooden knives which were painted with heavy native paint in a light grayish-green hue (Fig 34).

The women and girls sat in a special bower located at the southeast corner of the square. As at Hickory ground, they were ushered in and out of the square by two officials. The Ribbon dance began by the women forming a long line facing the south arbor (at this ground the singers' bed) where the two singers were seated. Each singer had a coconut-shell rattle. One of the two ushers now walked in a counter-clockwise circuit around the ground and marked certain positions before the north and west arbors by scratching the ground with his pole of office. These were the stopping points for the head woman dancer.

The singers began to sing. The head woman dancer detached herself from the other dancers and went on ahead of them to the opposite side of the square to the point marked *A* on the diagram (Fig. 33). The remainder of the dancers followed, dancing slowly (Fig. 34 and 35). Before they had reached point *A*, the head woman danced on ahead to point *B*, and before they reached this point, to point *C* (Fig 36). As they approached point *C* each woman turned 90° to the right and began to dance in place with a heavy jumping step until all formed a solid rank facing the singers once more. Each set consisted of four rounds of dancing (Fig 37). Between the sets there were speeches or sermons in the Muskogi tongue delivered by the chief's speaker. While he spoke water was carried to the women in their bower by two small boys. [105]

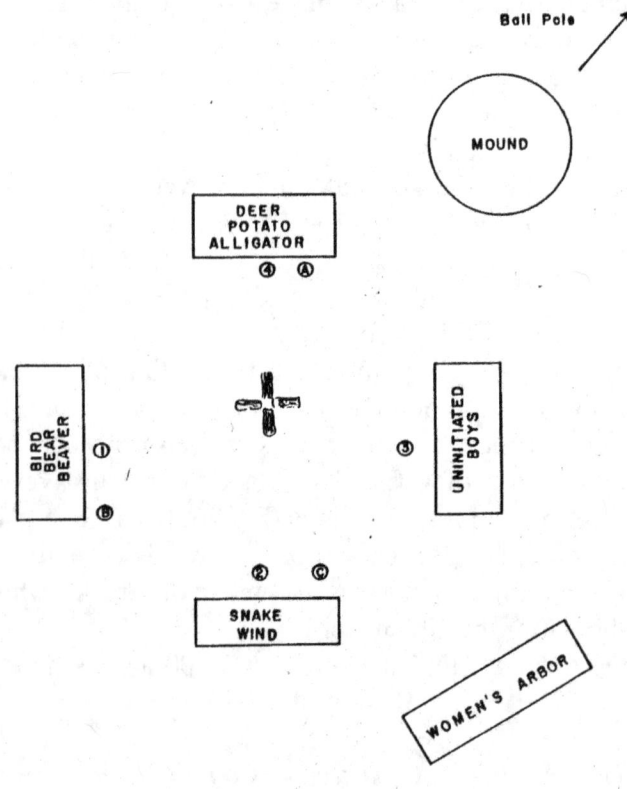

While the Ribbon dance was going on, the men and boys who belonged to the ground, if they were not already present, assembled in the arbors. Each man had brought with him his decorated *red stick* or hunting coat, and yarn sash (Fig 38). These they hung up on the rafters of the various arbors. After four sets of the Ribbon dance had been completed, two men with branches swept the {path} edge of the square ground. Now the men donned their western style hats with hat roaches hanging behind, hunting coats, and yarn sashes and went to the center of the ground, near the sacred fire. Here, assisted by the women, they danced four rounds of "old time" Stomp dance. It ended the morning dance program and the men who had been fasting were led to water by the chief and the medicine man.

All adjourned to eat lunch. In the afternoon, about 2:00pm a match of men-against-men type ball game was organised with two teams of small boys competing. The game was conducted following the old-time rules and ritual observances. Some of the small boys wore the ballplayer's costume, consisting of a hat roach tied to the hair, a triangular flap breechcloth, and a yarn sash. Most of the boys wore face paint. One small boy wore a necklace of red cloth strips imitating the red horsehair necklaces formerly worn by ball players to disguise the blood running down their bodies. Each team assembled at a separate spot in the woods where an older man lectured them, apparently in a humorous vein, as there was much laughter. The man then led the boys in a version of the Stomp dance (Fig 39). Next, each team assembled near their own goal posts, and a similar dance was performed around them. During the dance the ball, suspended from a short stick by a string, was carried in the dance by the team captain (Fig 40).

Each team divided into three groups, offense (deep in their opponents' territory), defense (near their own goal), and center (near mid-field). The center group consisted of the smaller boys, the ones in costume. The ball was put into play between the two center groups by being tossed up by an older man (Fig 41). Play was fast and furious, and provided a good idea of what the game must be when played by two groups of adults (Fig 42). As the ball neared the goal of either side a teen-age girl shook a coconut-shell rattle ominously. The score was marked with ten sticks, stuck in the ground at one side. Following the children's match ball game there were two separate men-against-women or single-pole ball games around the fish-design ball post, located about forty yards northeast of the square (Fig 43). It lasted until about 6:00p.m.

In the evening about 8:30, after everyone had dined, the evening dances were begun. There were the usual {night} deacons who picked and announced the leaders for each dance. The dancing was mostly Stomp dances (*opanka hačo*) but about 10:00 o'clock a different dance, the Doublehead dance, was introduced. It was led by an older man, who carried a coconut-shell rattle and sang. In the first figure the men and women dancers, segregated according to sex, formed two facing ranks and toe-heeled in place. This continued through several songs. Next, the singer began to lead a file of mixed dancers in a counter-clockwise direction around the sacred fire, still singing and shaking his rattle. The women then [114] joined in, pushing into the line behind the male dancers so as to alternate with them. Finally, all joined hands and the singer led the group into a tight spiral to the south edge of the square ground. The songs of this dance reminded me of those used by the Shawnee in their Cherokee dance. Claude Medford, Jr, writes (letter of October 19, 1966) that the Louisiana Tunica, Biloxi, and Choctaw all have Doublehead songs and dances. Following the performance the Stomp dances began once more. There were so many dancers on this occasion that it was often difficult for those wishing to dance to find a place close enough to the leader to hear and answer his songs above the uproar of stomping feet and women's leg rattles. Some Indian teenagers had the discourteous habit of elbowing in ahead of older persons and pushing them to the rear. The Stomp dancing continued through the night.

The next morning, about 5:00 o'clock the ashes of the old sacred fire were cleared away and a new fire was built with flint and punk. Four ears of perfect corn were laid between the four bark logs and sacrificed to the new fire after it had begun to blaze. I was told that individuals who had broken the rule and eaten new corn before this most sacred day of the Busk would have to take [117] medicine last. In former days they were required to sit in the sun rather than in the shade of the arbors.

The Feather dance at New Tulsa began about 9:00 a.m. Though generally similar to the performance at Hickory ground the songs and choreography both differed slightly. To begin the dance one man stood on the sacred mound and whooped to "call the birds." The dancers first massed at the point marked 1 on the diagram, all facing the center (Fig 33). Two men with coconut-shell rattles and one with a drum provided the accompaniment. The head singer, one of the two rattle men, began each song, then the rest took it up. The step was a simple patting of the foot in front of the body, first the left, then the right. As at Hickory Ground the poles were dipped slightly to the center in time with the music. The dance was performed at four stations, in this case all inside the square ground. They are marked 1, 2, 3, and 4 on the diagram. As the dancers marched from one station to the next there was a prolonged whoop "*Hiiiiiiiiii!*" with a diminuendo at the end, and sometimes the turkey gobble war whoop as well. On the last song of each set, as they massed before the chief's bed, the dancers clashed their feather-tipped poles together overhead.

About 10:00 a.m. after one set of the Feather dance, the scratching ceremony took place. At New Tulsa ground everyone, man, woman, and child, is scratched each year. The men were scratched more severely than the women and children, and often the scratching tool left raised welts on arms and legs. Following the scratching there was a lull in the proceedings. The women and children retired to eat lunch at the various camps while the men remained lounging in the arbors of the square.

The last three sets of the Feather dance began about 3:00 p.m. Following them were four short stomp dances, as at Hickory Ground, and a lengthy speech by the chief, Barney Leader. Next, a woman {??} circled the ground sprinkling medicine from a kettle onto the ground and over the men seated in the beds. She poured a smaller circle of the liquid around the center fire, and poured the remainder into the fire itself.

The women who had been scratched and had taken medicine previously, assembled and were given gourds of medicine from a large washtub which was placed southeast of the square. First they dipped out medicine and washed their hands and arms in it, then they drank large draughts of it. Next, the men who were fasting came, four at a time, to the east arbor to take medicine. Large pails of the brew with tin dippers were placed before the arbor and the men washed themselves in it and drank large amounts before retiring to the edge of the ground to vomit.

About 6:30p.m. the final daytime dances began. All the members of the ground attired themselves in their finest garb. For the men it was the hat and roach, a ruffled or fringed hunting coat, and a Southeastern style sash with large tassels. Most of these hunting coats were red, and one of my informants termed them "red stick" coats (Fig 44). One old man wore two red cloth baldrics or shoulder sashes under his hunting coat. The women wore their best beadwork, patchwork, or ribbonwork capes and ribbonwork or patchwork skirts. Mrs. Bowlegs [119] a member of the prominent Seminole family of that name, wore a beaded man's vest in floral designs, and bells at the ankles. All of the women who owned them wore terrapin shell or milk-can leg rattles.

The first dance, the "Buffalo dance, took place around the sacred mound outside the square (Fig 45). The drummer for the dance stood on top of the mound. Each male dancer carried one ball slick to imitate the legs of the bison. The Buffalo dance was a wild stomping in place followed by a milling about the mound as the song changed. The Buffalo dance was followed by the Old-time or Whooping dance, also called the Long dance (Fig 46). The leader led the dancers from the sacred mound into the square, around the fire (Fig 47) and then back to the mound. This was followed by four fast rounds of the Stomp dance, which ended the afternoon's activities (Fig 48). Several of the dancers paused to have their photographs taken in costume, then retired to the camps to break their day-long fast with their first taste of new corn.

About 8:00p.m. the Stomp dancing began again, and continued through the night, ending with the Drunken dance just before dawn.

On the July 6, 1968, we again attended the final day of the Green Corn at New Tulsa square ground. Fewer people were in attendance than three years previously, but there were still quite a few visitors. These included "Dode" MacIntosh, the federally appointed chief of the Creek nation and his family, also a party of Creek from the state of Alabama headed by Chief Calvin McGee.

Procedures in 1968 were identical with those recorded in 1965 with one exception. A slow dance performed by men only took place around the sacred mound just after the performance of the Buffalo dance and the Long or Whooping dance. It was led by a singer-drummer who stood atop the mound. This man intoned the first phrase of each of the dance songs which were then taken up by the dancers, singing in unison. The music was legato and quite melodic. The step was merely a rhythmic walk. The dancers following one another in a counterclockwise circuit of the mound. I was later informed by Mrs. James Cleghorn, a member of New Tulsa square ground, that this was called the "Mother" dance in English. I could not secure the Muskhogi term for it. It offers yet another example of the "mound orientation" of much Creek ceremonialism.

B.—SQUARE GROUND OF THE UPPER EUFAULA INDIANS, CREEK CONFEDERACY,
FROM THE SOUTHWEST

Creek Active Square Towns in 1912 and 1929

In Swanton's huge volume on Creeks (1928), based on fieldwork (9/1911 to 5/1912) and divided between society (23-472) and religion (473-672), diagrams of the towns are in the social section and much more extensive that his later report of 15 towns (1931). His 1912 list of towns includes 35 more than the later 15, making a total of 50 towns. The duplicated 15 are listed with their 1928 diagram's page number, followed by the other 35 with their 1928 page numbers.

Duplicated 15

Abihka 207
Alabama 263
Hilibi 258
Kasihta 265
Kealedji 251
Łałogulga Fish Pond 236
Łapłako 254
Nuyaka 218
Ochesee Seminole 283
Okchai 234
Otciapofa Hickory 211
Pakan Tallahassee 224
Tukabahchee 244
Tulsa Little River 213
Wiogufki 227

Other 35

Abihka in the West 208
Abihkutci 221
Apalachicola 270
Asilanabi 232
Atasi 249
Chiaha 279
Chiaha Seminole 292
Coosa conjectural 210
Coweta 274
Eufaula 260
Eufaula Hobayi 277
Eufaula Seminole 289
Hitchiti 272
Hitchiti Seminole 288
Kan-tcati 209
Kasihta 265
Koasati #2 243
Łikatcka Broken Arrow 276

W

Y

Entries are by titles, first names, grouped family names, subjects
page numbers ending in #0 refer to a scattered 10 page span
#f refers to a 5 page span.

Please Help Fight Typo Gnomes!